Advocacy Advertising and Large Corporations

Other Books by S. Prakash Sethi

Business Corporations and the Black Man (1970)
Up Against the Corporate Wall: Modern Corporations and Social Issues of the Seventies (1971, 1974, 1977)
Advanced Cases in Multinational Business Operations (1972)
The Corporate Dilemma (with Dow Votaw) (1973)
Management of the Multinationals (with Richard H. Holton) (1974)
The Unstable Ground: Corporate Social Policy in a Dynamic Society (1974)
Japanese Business and Social Conflict (1975)

Advocacy Advertising and Large Corporations

Social Conflict, Big Business Image, the News Media, and Public Policy

S. Prakash Sethi
University of California, Berkeley

Lexington Books
D.C. Heath and Company
Lexington, Massachusetts
Toronto

Library of Congress Cataloging in Publication Data

Sethi, S   Prakash.
  Advocacy advertising and large corporations.
  Bibliography: p.
  Includes index.
  1. Public relations—Corporations. 2. Industry—Social aspects.
ISBN 0-669-00678-5   659.2   76-6770

Copyright © 1977 by D.C. Heath and Company

Published simultaneously in Canada

Printed in the United States of America

International Standard Book Number 0-669-00678-5

Library of Congress Catalog Card Number: 76-6770

To
My wife, Donna, and sons, Amit and Ravi
A wonderful family who make it all
worthwhile

Contents

Preface

It should not come as a surprise to any informed reader that the sociopolitical environment of business in the United States has undergone a significant deterioration in the last two decades. Business institutions have suffered a marked loss in public trust and credibility. In this, business is not alone; most other social institutions, including government, church, and the academic institutions, have shared a similar fate. Moreover, the loss of credibility of business institutions, and especially large corporations, is not confined to the United States but can be found, to a greater or lesser degree, in most countries of the non-Communist world. And it is not unrealistic for American business to feel threatened. While it has suffered a loss of legitimacy along with other social institutions, the decline in the case of business has been more precipitous. Furthermore, the disclosure of widespread political bribes and payoffs at home and abroad by some of America's largest corporations has served to create skepticism about the ethics of American businesspeople and their concern for the public interest.

There is a widely held conviction among the businesspeople that although certain corporations and individuals may have been involved in wrongdoing, business as a whole has made enormous contributions to the prosperity and welfare of this country. Further, a large part of public skepticism can be traced to misunderstanding and ignorance on the part of large segments of the population; an antibusiness bias on the part of the news media and inadequate coverage of business-related topics; and an active campaign on the part of those groups who oppose business to exaggerate business's shortcomings and understate its positive contributions by inflammatory and accusatory rhetoric. The business complaint as to the reasons and sources of public discontent notwithstanding, it must strive to reduce the gap, real or alleged, between societal expectations and performance. One of the ways in which business institutions, especially large corporations, have been attempting to accomplish this is through publicity campaigns called advocacy advertising, in which they take public positions on issues in which they are involved, directly or indirectly, to explain their points of view, and often criticize those of their opponents.

This book is an attempt to take a systematic look at the whole spectrum of issues dealing with advocacy advertising. The primary focus of our inquiry is the role such advertising is expected to play in fostering the credibility of corporate behavior; the effect it is likely to have on the public's perception of corporate legitimacy; and the far-reaching societal consequences of any changes in this perception.

At present we have only limited experience with advocacy advertising in its various manifestations. The social effects of these strategies take a long time to emerge. Therefore, it is vitally important that there be vigorous public debate on the various aspects of advocacy advertising as it might affect social and economic arrangements in the society. I earnestly hope that this book will make a useful contribution to this debate by providing a framework within which the concept of advocacy advertising can be properly understood, and by identifying those underlying social values and public groups that would most likely be affected by the widespread use of advocacy advertising.

My data base has two important components. The first is a systematic study of most of the recent advocacy ad campaigns in the United States, including a detailed in-depth study of two of the more notable campaigns—i.e., American Electric Power Company, New York, and Californians Against the Pollution Initiative (CAPI), California. These studies are reported in the book. The data have been supplemented with an exhaustive survey of the literature in business, economics, and legal sources pertaining to the subject.

The American Electric Power Company case was prepared with the assistance and cooperation of Harold R. Johnson, senior vice-president, American Electric Power Service Corporation, New York, and Mr. Marlin Fitzwater, director of the News Services Division, Office of Public Affairs, United States Environmental Protection Agency, Washington, D.C. It took over a year to complete this case, and I am especially grateful to Mr. Johnson for his thoughtful comments during the many revisions of the draft.

The case study dealing with the California campaign on the Clean Environment Act Initiative of 1972 was prepared with the generous cooperation of Clem Whitaker, Jr., President, Whitaker & Baxter, a public relations firm based in San Francisco, which organized and managed the campaign for the Californians Against the Pollution Initiative (CAPI); and the late Edwin Koupal, and Joyce Koupal, co-directors of People's Lobby, the group that spearheaded the campaign in support of the initiative. Bernice F. Livingston of Diesner/Hauser/ Greenthal Company, Los Angeles, provided the media details and ad copies for the People's Lobby campaign. This case was prepared in association with William J. Tegan, a graduate student at the School of Business Administration, University of California, Berkeley. Rosainne Teegan and Trudy Garrettson carried the major burden of transcribing tapes of the various interviews.

The second component is comprised of lengthy personal interviews with responsible executives from corporations, public relations firms, the media, advertising agencies, government department and regulatory agencies, and representatives of public interest and activist groups. This book would not have been possible without the active cooperation of a large number of people who willingly gave their time and contributed their thoughts. Although space constraints make it impossible to mention all of them, I would be remiss in my obligation if I did not expressly acknowledge the notable contributions of the following persons.

Among the business executives who cooperated in this study were (in alphabetical order): Peter Allport, president, Association of National Advertisers, New York; Robert Dilenschneider, senior vice-president, Hill & Knowlton,

New York; David Finn, principal partner, David & Finn, New York; John O'Toole, president, Foote, Cone & Belding, New York; and Herbert Schmertz, vice-president, Public Affairs, Mobil Oil Company, New York. In addition, a significant number of executives from companies representing oil, electric utility, petrochemical, and other industries discussed different aspects of their companys' advertising programs but preferred to remain anonymous. I am grateful to them for their assistance. A large number of companies kindly permitted the printing of specific advertisements from their campaigns in this book. These are acknowledged separately.

Among the representatives of the news media who consented to be interviewed on record and discussed their ideas were (in alphabetical order): Richard Bausch, Advertising Department, *Newsweek;* Robert M. Bleiberg, editor, *Barron's;* John L. Cobbs, editor, *Business Week;* Osborn Elliot, editor-in-chief *Newsweek;* Garth Hite, publisher, *The Atlantic Monthly;* Marshall Loeb, senior editor, *Time;* Robert Lubar, Managing editor, *Fortune;* John E. Mandable, vice-president, Marketing and Advertising Sales, *Newsweek;* John Oakes, editorial page editor, *The New York Times;* Benjamin D. Raub, vice-president and general assistant attorney, National Broadcasting Company (NBC), New York; Kalman Seigel, letters editor, *The New York Times;* William Sheehan, president, ABC News, American Broadcasting Company (ABC), New York; William Small, senior vice-president and director of news, CBS News, CBS Inc., New York; and Lewis H. Young, editor-in-chief, *Business Week.*

My colleague Dow Votaw at the School of Business Administration, University of California, Berkeley, read the completed manuscript and offered valuable comments and criticisms. In addition, the following people reviewed one or more chapters of the manuscript and provided comments and criticisms. They are (in alphabetical order): Peter Battelle, University of Vermont; John L. Cobbs, editor, *Business Week;* Robert Dilenschneider, senior vice-president, Hill & Knowlton, New York; David M. Gardner, College of Commerce and Business Administration, University of Illinois; Garth Hite, publisher, *The Atlantic Monthly;* Charles Ludlam, attorney, Subcommittee on Separation of Power, Senate Judiciary Committee, Washington, D.C.; Jerry Mander, formerly of Freeman, Mander & Gossage, advertising agency, San Francisco; Arnold Maxwell, president, Maxwell Arnold, Inc., San Francisco; Milton Moscowitz, syndicated columnist, San Francisco; Francesco Nicosia, University of California, Berkeley; John O'Toole, president, Foote, Cone & Belding, New York; and Albert Stridsberg, editor, *Advertising World.* Their comments and criticisms have been extremely helpful in improving the manuscript and have contributed to the clarity of my thought and precision in the presentation of the subject matter. However, I must assume sole responsibility for any factual errors and bear the burden of criticism of those who may disagree with one or more aspects of the book.

Most of the work on the manuscript was completed in Boston, where I was visiting professor of management policy at Boston University during the 1975–76 academic year. I am most grateful to Dean Peter Gabriel and Associate Dean David Furer of the Graduate School of Management, Boston University, for their encouragement and for funding to cover part of the expenses required for research and secretarial assistance. Additional funding for research assistance was provided by the Committee on Research and the Institute of Business and Economic Research, University of California, Berkeley, and is acknowledged with thanks. My good friend Clark Abt, president, Abt Associates, Inc., Cambridge, Massachusetts, provided financial assistance to cover part of the travel costs. This project involved extensive traveling, and but this support, it would have been difficult to finish the book in time.

I am grateful to my research assistant, Christine Rehfuss, for carrying out most of the library research for the book. The typing of several drafts of the manuscript was a monumental job and was carried out primarily by Mary Alper, Shelley McNutt, and Jeanne Robertson at Boston University. Additional typing assistance was provided by Dena Brown, Gwen Cheeseburg, Betty Kendall, Ellen McGibbon, and Patricia Murphy at the University of California, Berkeley. They deserve my thanks for laborious and painstaking work under extremely tight schedules.

And, finally, I acknowledge with love and appreciation the contributions of my wife Donna, who not only worked long hours in transcribing the tapes of interviews, completing bibliography, and proofreading manuscript, but most important, provided a hospitable environment of encouragement and patience that made the completion of this book possible.

S. Prakash Sethi

University of California, Berkeley
July 1976

Acknowledgments for Advertisements

The advertisements in this book were reprinted with permission of the following sources:

The Advertising Council: Exhibits 1A-10, 1A-11
Allied Chemical: Exhibits 1A-1, 1A-2
American Electric Power Company: Exhibit 4-1, all exhibits in Appendix 4
American Petroleum Institute: Exhibit 1A-3
American Trucking Associations, Inc.: Exhibit 1A-4
Armco Steel Corporation: Exhibit 1A-5
Bethlehem Steel Corporation: Exhibit 1A-6
Carbonated Beverage Container Manufacturers Association: Exhibit 8A-1
Chase Manhattan Bank: Exhibits 1A-7, 1A-8
Gulf Oil Corporation: Exhibit 1A-9
Jerry Mander: Exhibit 8A-3
Knight-Ridder Newspapers: Exhibit 1A-12
Maxwell Arnold Agency: Exhibits 8A-4, 8A-6
Microdot, Inc.: Exhibit 1A-13
Mobil Oil Corporation: Exhibits 1A-14, 1A-15, 1A-16, 1A-17, 1A-18, 1A-19
National Association of Motor Bus Owners: Exhibit 1A-20
National Council of Farmer Cooperatives: Exhibit 1A-21
Pan Am Employees Awareness Committee: Exhibit 1A-21
Pennwalt Corporation: Exhibit 1A-23
People's Lobby, Inc.: Exhibit 5-1, all exhibits in Appendix 5A
Phillips Petroleum Company: Exhibit 1A-24
Public Communication Inc.: Exhibits 8A-2, 8A-5
Savings Banks Associations of New York State: Exhibit 1A-25
Warner & Swasey Company: Exhibits 1A-26, 1A-27
Whitaker & Baxter, Inc.: Exhibit 5-2, all exhibits in Appendix 5B

Part I

Dimension and Scope of Advocacy Advertising

Introduction to Part 1

Few things strengthen like the shedding of illusions

—Eric Sevareid

In the past, some businesses have occasionally resorted to the use of paid advertising space to publicize their viewpoint on controversial issues of public policy where their vital interests are at stake. However, the last three years have witnessed an upsurge in what may be called "advocacy advertising," in which the sponsoring corporations have assumed a more aggressive posture and showed a willingness to defend their activities and policies by questioning their opponents' motives, criticizing their lack of knowledge, and even casting doubt on their patriotism. Furthermore, they have taken positions on issues of wider public import in which they may or may not directly stand to gain. This has introduced a new element into institutional or public image advertising by some of the nation's largest corporations.

A recent study conducted for the federal government of public attitudes toward the American economic system showed that 56 percent of Americans want more government regulation, while only 35 percent want less. The study found that a great majority of Americans expressed negative attitudes toward the free enterprise system. Twenty-seven percent of the persons surveyed viewed inflation as the principal source of their complaints about the system, while 18 percent considered big business as the chief culprit because it created shortages, obtained political tax advantages, and tended to be monopolistic. Furthermore, 20 percent of those interviewed wanted further restrictions on business, especially large corporations, while another 20 percent sought curbs on price increases. The findings of the study have led the Advertising Council, Inc., a private nonprofit organization supported by business, to develop a three- to 5-year advertising campaign "to help create a better understanding of the American Economic System."[1]

This is not an isolated campaign. Other business groups and individual corporations have had similar campaigns for a long time; many others have launched new campaigns in the last few years. A survey by the Roper Organization conducted in December 1975 found that 37 percent of those interviewed favored "a breakup of Big Oil," up from 30 percent in May 1975. In addition, 22 percent favored a government takeover of the oil industry and 10 percent favored a government-run oil company to compete with the private companies.[2]

3

It is not surprising that the American Petroleum Institute, the oil industry's big trade organization, recently launched a campaign to counteract public hostility toward large oil companies and the mounting pressure to break them up.[3] This is in addition to the publicity campaigns that most big oil companies have going currently. The number of other blue chip corporations that have recently started similar campaigns are far too many to list individually.

This aggressive business posture reflects a feeling on the part of many corporate executives, a feeling that seems to be growing, that the traditional corporate response of either ignoring unwarranted or uninformed attacks on its activities, or a defensive stance of explaining one's position when called for, has been a failure. There is a general recognition that business credibility is low. There is also a commonly shared belief among businesspeople that the low credibility is more a consequence of exaggerated expectations on the part of the public than an indication of poor performance. Moreover, these exaggerated expectations have been fueled by groups who do not share any responsibility for their fulfillment. Business could not fulfill all these expectations, which would mean being all things to all people, and survive at the same time.

Advocacy advertising covers a broad spectrum of corporations and industries and attempts to change or sustain public opinion and social policy on specific short-term issues as well as on the values that underlie our social and political institutions. Nevertheless, all advocacy ad campaigns share certain common characteristics in terms of the corporate posture, depiction of the adversary, and claim to social legitimacy via identification with widely held social beliefs or representation of the public interest. To the extent that such advertising becomes widespread and is used by a significant number of large corporations and industry groups, there is a danger of their squeezing out alternative viewpoints from the public communication space and thereby impairing public access to information from all sources. Corporations have defended their right to advocacy advertising in similar terms, e.g., to provide the public with their position on controversial issues and also to counteract the adverse and erroneous publicity about their activities by opposing groups.

The first of the three chapters that follow is an attempt to define the nature and scope of advocacy advertising; the second is a discussion of the various rationales offered by business for the use of such advertising; and the third is devoted to the critical question of whether or not the news media are doing a satisfactory job in reporting and analyzing news related to business.

Notes

1. Timothy D. Schellhardt, "More Regulation by Government Gets 56% Backing in Poll," *The Wall Street Journal,* May 14, 1975, p. 16.

2. James Carberry, "Big Oil Besieged—Is Industry Too Strong? Its

Opponents Say Yes and Call for a Breakup," *The Wall Street Journal,* February 9, 1976, p. 1.

    3. "Oil Industry Group Plans Big Campaign to Block Legislation to Split Up Firms," *The Wall Street Journal,* November 11, 1975, p. 21. For an interesting discussion of the building public pressures against the oil industry, see Carberry, "Big Oil Besieged"; Arlen J. Large, "Big Oil Besieged—Congressional Outlook for the Breakup Plan: Wait Till Next Year," *The Wall Street Journal,* February 11, 1976, p. 1; James C. Tanner, "Big Oil Besieged—Breakup Could Bring a Gasoline Price Rise and Less Competition," *The Wall Street Journal,* February 12, 1976, p. 1.

1

The Nature and Scope of Advocacy Advertising

And the Lord said, "Behold, they are one people and they have all one language; and this is only the beginning of what they will do; and nothing that they propose to do will now be impossible for them. Come, let us go down, and there confuse their language, that they may not understand one another's speech." ... Therefore its name was called Babel, because there the Lord confused the language of all the earth....

—Genesis 11:6-9

The Concept of Advocacy Advertising

Advocacy advertising is part of that genre of advertising known as corporate image or institutional advertising. It is concerned with the propagation of ideas and elucidation of controversial social issues of public importance in a manner that supports the position and interests of the sponsor while expressly denying the accuracy of facts and downgrading the sponsor's opponents. The managerial context of advocacy advertising is that of defending the corporation's activities and modus operandi. The behavioral and social context of advocacy advertising is that of changing public perception of a corporation's actions and performance from skepticism and hostility to trust and acceptance. The political context of advocacy advertising is that of the constitutional safeguards for freedom of speech where a corporation is asserting its right to speak out on issues of public importance without any regulation or censorship on the part of other private groups or government agencies.

The term "advocacy advertising" was first used by John O'Toole, president of Foote Cone & Belding, a major advertising agency located in New York. Other terms used to describe somewhat similar phenomena are "issue-oriented advertising" (Irving Kristol); "counter advertising to counter the news" (Rance Crain, editor-in-chief of *Advertising Age*); and public interest advertising, information advertising, and adversary advertising.

Unless otherwise specifically stated, all direct quotes in this chapter are from personal interviews or written communications with the author.

Traditional corporate image advertising has as its primary emphasis building a good image for the corporation and its management or keeping the corporate name in the public eye. (Institutional advertising is another term commonly used to describe such advertising.) As contrasted with product or service advertising, it deals with the characteristics of the corporation itself rather than with those of its product or services. Such an ad campaign shows the growth and strength of the company, its various activities, and corporate programs dealing with a corporation's main constituents—e.g., shareholders, workers, suppliers, and consumers. Most important, in times of crisis or public antagonism, it attempts to build an identification between the company and those activities considered socially desirable: pollution control, conservation, minority hiring. The focus is on good public relations and the objective is to win friends. On the rare occasions when controversial issues are tackled, the emphasis is on presenting the corporate viewpoint without arguing with or criticizing the opponent's viewpoint. For these reasons, institutional advertising is expensively and beautifully produced; is generally dull, bland, and self-serving; and is seldom taken seriously by anyone. Donald Cook, former chairman and chief executive officer of American Electric Power, is not far off the mark when he states, "Most institutional advertising is dismal. It puts more people to sleep than all the somnifics sold in the nation."[1]

Unlike traditional corporate image advertising, advocacy advertising attempts to tackle controversial issues and presents facts and arguments that project the sponsor in the most positive light and opponents' arguments in the worst. It is not the job of the advocate to help the adversary, so the argument goes. The adversary is expected to demonstrate a similar behavior pattern and is considered well equipped to take care of himself. Everything is fair as long as the rules of the game are observed. The criterion for success is not how the battle was fought, but to what extent one succeeded in persuading the audience to believe in the advertiser's cause.

The analogy to the rules of the game is more apparent than real. Although in legal battles there are indeed procedural rules that must be observed, no similar rules exist for advocacy advertising. The lone exception is the "fairness doctrine" in the case of the broadcast media, which has had the effect of practically eliminating all such advertising from commercial radio and television stations. One possible constraint for print media may be the discretion exercised by a particular medium to bar certain advertisements from its pages on grounds of good taste, apparent falsehood, or a possible libel suit. The second and more potent set of restraints are self-imposed, and are based on one's perception of the likelihood, nature, direction, and intensity of the adversary's response. The fear of an adversary's escalating the war of words, both in the content and frequency of messages, acts as a more effective deterrent.

John O'Toole describes the notion of advocacy advertising in terms of us versus them—i.e., the system versus the adversary culture. The system is comprised of industries, business, and financial institutions that provide people with jobs, services, and goods and, despite some imperfections, it has served the society well. In the adversary culture are grouped those who seek basic changes in the system—political activists, consumer groups. Both sides are demanding legitimate roles in trying to influence political decisions by molding public opinion in the belief that in a pluralistic society the majority opinion will be reflected in government decisions. For various reasons, in the case of large corporations, "advertising is the only means available to provide the balance—an advocate for the system and for individual corporations within that system. It is a different kind of advertising than most of us are used to, but it is a legitimate and, for the times, a highly appropriate mutation."[2]

Another definition of advocacy advertising in terms of controversial advertising subject to the fairness doctrine has been advanced by the Federal Communications Commission (FCC).[3] The FCC states that institutional advertising designed to present a favorable public image of a particular corporation or industry is not subject to the fairness doctrine unless "the advertiser seeks to play an obvious and meaningful role in public debate."[4] The criteria of obvious and meaningful would seem to have been met "if the arguments and views expressed in the ad closely parallel the major arguments advanced by one side or the other of a public debate."[5] The commission has advocated a "conservative" test of what constitutes controversial advertising in indicating that an advertiser's participation in the public debate must be *obvious* and not based on a "subjective judgment as to the advertiser's actual intentions,"[6] or a relationship to a controversy that is tenuous, indirect, and highly inferential. FCC's stance, however, has not been popular with environmental and other public interest groups.[7] (A discussion of FCC's "fairness doctrine" and its implications for advocacy advertising is presented in Chapter 3.)

It should also be emphasized that the definition and scope of advocacy advertising, as envisaged here, is much broader than the narrow legal concept of "grassroots lobbying" with which most corporate critics generally identify all advocacy advertising. (A discussion of the legal and tax aspects of grassroots lobbying is presented in Chapter 6.) Under our concept, the focus of corporate attention, or the adversary, need not necessarily be a government body or citizens' group but could easily be another corporation or an industry whose policies are viewed as contrary to corporate interests and the general public interest as seen by this corporation. Since the actions to be effected may be greatly influenced by public opinion, the need for resorting to the public forum to discuss one's ideas becomes important. The recent sharper focus on the adversary type of advertising has been motivated largely by the campaigns conducted by oil, utility, and other energy-related industries.

American Electric Power Company (AEP), the nation's largest privately held electric utility, recently ran an ad campaign upbraiding the Environmental Protection Agency, the environmentalists, and other government and private groups for thwarting their country's efforts to increase the domestic energy supply. It accused them of imposing unnecessarily stringent environmental restrictions on the strip-mining of coal and unrealistic and expensive air pollution control standards on coal-burning power-generation plants (see Chapter 4). Mobil has also severely criticized the Federal Energy Administration, other government agencies, and environmental groups for putting unreasonable and unwise restrictions on the operation of the oil industry that have frustrated this nation's efforts toward energy self-sufficiency.[8] Mobil's campaign is purer in form than all the other campaigns analyzed here and shows more clearly the strengths and weaknesses of advocacy advertising. In addition, both campaigns have criticized government regulation in general, extolled the virtues of the free enterprise system, and identified their companies as solidly in support of the professed objectives, though not the means, of their critics—namely, self-sufficiency in energy, environmental protection, improved quality of life, and greater individual freedom and choice.

The Dimensions of Advocacy Advertising

The definitional problems related to advocacy advertising are by no means simple. One may argue that all advertising should be construed as advocating some type of action by the intended audience. Some sponsors would avoid labeling any advertising as advocacy for fear of alienating the audience and thereby frustrating the very purpose of such advertising. Thus advocacy advertising is wrapped in such euphemistic terms as "issue" advertising, "public interest" advertising, or "information" advertising. Another problem is that most such campaigns not only may use one or more types of advocacy appeals, but may also have elements of pure corporate goodwill or image advertising, and also include some product advertising. Nonetheless, an attempt has been made here to provide a classificatory framework to facilitate our understanding of advocacy advertising and also aid in the analysis of different advocacy campaigns.

Advocacy advertising can best be understood as a three-dimensional phenomenon, namely, identification of sponsor's interest, intensity of advocacy, and specificity in identifying the adversary.

Identification of Sponsor's Interest. This dimension measures the extent to which the sponsor is willing to identify his own interests with the contents of and programs advocated in the advertising message. There are five states in this dimension:

1. Disinterested sponsor. The sponsor is clearly identified. His interests are connected with the message only in a very general way. The advocacy is of a broad ideological or philosophical nature.

2. Benevolent sponsor. The sponsor's name is identified in the ad but presented only as indirectly related. The issue is presented as of broader public

concern where solutions are suggested, the sponsor's role is minimized in causal relationship with the problem, but exaggerated in solution. The advocacy appeal is of a general nature; the audience is exhorted toward some voluntary action of self-help or self-sacrifice.

3. Self-righteous sponsor. The sponsor is directly identified and openly associates his interests with those of the programs advocated in the message, e.g., utility companies and air pollution standards promulgated by the Environmental Protection Agency. The reader is asked to take action that would be of immediate help to the sponsor but would ultimately benefit the reader.

4. Participative sponsor. The sponsor's identity is apparent, but his interests are carefully disguised. Issues are presented as problems common to industry and also in the public interest.

5. Elusive sponsor. The sponsor's interests and even identity are carefully disguised to convey an image of conscious disinterest. Group names are selected to indicate a broader public constituency which the group purports to represent. Issues are tailored to reflect public benefit without any mention of the sponsor's interest.

Intensity of Advocacy. This dimension measures the intensity with which an appeal is being made and ranges from emotional to reasoned persuasion and information. Emotional appeals are often identified with ads that fall in the categories of self-righteous and elusive sponsor. Emotional appeals often involve intangible or esthetic concerns and contain few specifics as to what might be done or who should do it. Their emphasis is on building the reader's sympathy for the sponsor's actions or position on an issue. Most advocacy campaigns invariably have one or more ads with primarily emotional appeals, or individual ads contain emotional appeals along with reasoned persuasion. The ad campaigns with environment and ecology as the prime theme are generally loaded with emotional appeals. Reasoned persuasion has been used in campaigns where sponsors attempt to identify their interests with those of their readers. The theme is "We're all in this together" or "We're doing our share, but we can't accomplish much unless everybody else does his share." Some information or data to appeal to one's reasoning is always provided so that a decision can be rationalized, although the actual reasons for making a given decision may be other than rational. The campaigns are generally associated with the benevolent and elusive sponsor types. Rational and informational appeals attempt to provide information to enable the reader to decide for himself whether or not he should agree with the position taken by the sponsor. This appeal seems to have been more prevalent with disinterested sponsors, self-righteous sponsors, and elusive sponsors.

Specificity in Identifying the Adversary. The adversary can be classified in one or more of four categories: general public, government agencies, public interest or social activist groups, and competitors. It should be noted that the adversary

Table 1-1
Types of Advocacy Advertising

Recognition of Sponsor Interest	Themes of Advertising Copy	Nature of Adversary	Examples of Sponsors
1. *Disinterested Sponsor* No direct immediate benefits for the sponsor are envisaged.	General issues of public interest or with an ideological or philosophical content are presented; e.g., support of free enterprise system, association of profits with growth, opposition to foreign aid.	Government agencies and legislative bodies News media, opinion leaders, and academic institutions	Allied Chemical, Bethlehem Steel, Knight-Ridder Newspapers, Mobil Oil, Pennwalt Corporation, Phillips Petroleum Co., U.S. Steel, Warner & Swasey
2. *Benevolent Sponsor* Sponsor's interests are presented as indirectly related.	Issues of interest to sponsor are presented within the framework of overall social problem, energy shortage, role of profits, capital, technology, and cause for pollution and suggestions for their solution. Public is exhorted to make sacrifices voluntarily.	Government agencies and legislative bodies News media, opinion leaders, and academic institutions	Allied Chemical, American Can, American Electric Power, Armco Steel, Boise Cascade, Bethlehem Steel, Chase Manhattan, Dean Witter & Co., Gulf Oil, Glass Container Manufacturers Institute, Microdot, Mobil Oil, National Council of Farm Cooperatives, Inc., Southern Company, Texaco, U.S. Steel
3. *Self-righteous Sponsor* Sponsor's identity and selfish interest are directly associated with the advocated programs.	Open defense of self-interest, downgrading of opponents and their arguments. General public interests are only indirectly presented; e.g., energy shortage and oil companies, pollution controls, and utilities.	Government agencies and legislative bodies, environmental and other public interest groups, other companies and industries opposed to the sponsor's interests, news media	American Electric Power, Independent Bankers Association, Marathon Oil, Pan Am, Texaco

4. *Participative Sponsor* Sponsor's interest is carefully disguised.	Issues are presented as problems common to industry and also in the public interest; e.g., regulation of our industry.	Governmental agencies and legislative bodies, public interest groups, competing industries or firms that stand to gain from such regulation	Allied Chemical, American Trucking Association, American Petroleum Institute, Edison Electric Institute, Glass Containers Manufacturers Institute, Independent Bankers Association, Mobil Oil, National Association of Motor Bus Operators, National Council of Farm Cooperatives, Savings Bank Association of New York State
5. *Elusive Sponsor* Sponsor's identity and interest carefully disguised to convey an image of conscious disinterest. Group names are selected to indicate a broader public constituency.	Issues are tailored to public benefit and general social concern without any mention of sponsor's interest.	Sponsors of legislative programs or advocates of changes in current policies and political programs, be they government agencies or private groups	Action for Children's Television, Californians Against the Pollution Initiative, Keep America Beautiful, People's Lobby (a nonprofit activist group based in California), Public Communications, Inc. (a public interest group specializing in counteradvertising)

is invariably a different party than the group to which the ad is addressed. The objective of an ad is to change attitudes in that group of people who may be in a position, either directly or indirectly, to change the position of the adversary.

Table 1-1 provides one attempt at classifying various advertising campaigns within this framework. It should be helpful in understanding the range of activities under the advocacy advertising rubric. Some specimen ads from selected campaigns appear in Appendix 1A. Most advertisers use multiple themes and attack multiple adversaries in a specific advertisement and, certainly, in a given campaign. Consequently, sponsors appear in more than one category.

Historical Background

Notwithstanding the current upsurge in advocacy advertising, the concept has long historical roots. A brief discourse into the historical antecedents of advocacy advertising is important to put it in a proper perspective.

Corporate image advertising, of which advocacy advertising is a subset, has a long history. The Dutch East India Company, Wells Fargo, and Hudson's Bay Company engaged in advertising directed toward creating an image of the company as people-minded and as making new futures for families.[9] One of the first modern uses of corporate advertising was by AT&T, which in 1908 urged cooperation and understanding among customers. Even before World War II, companies such as Union Carbide and Warner & Swasey were running corporate advertising programs. Perhaps the greatest surge in institutional advertising came in the years immediately following World War II, when American business made a concerted effort to sell the virtues of free enterprise to America.[10]

Advocacy advertising, in some form or other, has been with us for as long as the practice of corporate institutional advertising. Not long after World War I, Textile Mills Corporation was retained by German textile interests to work toward regaining property that had been lost by the Germans during the war. The campaign, which included speeches, news items, and editorial comment, was designed to influence public and legislative sentiment and was influential in the passage of the Settlement of War Claims Act of 1928.[11] In 1936, advocacy advertising was used by California chain stores to fight a discriminatory tax.[12] In the late 1930s the National Association of Manufacturers undertook a campaign to disseminate "information by radio, motion pictures, booklets, outdoor advertising, newspapers and speakers concerning the American free enterprise system . . . and its promise for the future."[13] The stated purpose of the advertising effort was "to regain full public regard for industry," and it was conceived as a result of attacks on industry because of unemployment during the Depression.

The American Medical Association (AMA) also has for a long time used advertising to bring to public attention, and to wage a battle against, legislative proposals dealing with public health programs, specifically Medicare. By spending millions of dollars in the process, the AMA was able to forestall health legislation for forty-five years through various advertising campaigns.[14] By 1950 the AMA was involved in an elaborate campaign to prevent socialized medicine from making inroads in American society. AMA took credit for the defeat of several of its opponents in Congress. In 1961 it launched a campaign to ensure the defeat of the Medicare bill and to defend an already existing program for medical care for the elderly that the association had accepted. The AMA also involved itself extensively with the 1962 election campaign. This time, however, not one seat was lost by candidates who had campaigned for Medicare, and many anti-Medicare candidates were defeated. In 1964 the AMA turned to a newspaper and magazine ad campaign to inform the elderly of available health care and to sway public and legislative opinion. These efforts notwithstanding, the Medicare bill was signed into law late in July 1965.

One of the oldest and still continuing advocacy campaigns is that of the Warner & Swasey Company of Cleveland, Ohio, whose first corporate ads appeared in 1936 and throughout the recession of 1937-38 set the theme that "America is too great, too powerful, too dynamic to sell short; that the wise businessman should not throw in the sponge but should have complete faith that business would rise again, and that he should use the interim to modernize his equipment and so get himself in a stronger low cost position."[15] It was not until after World War II, however, that Warner & Swasey developed an advertising campaign that was aggressive and often strident in tone. Its themes included a strong defense and perpetuation of the American free enterprise system, opposition to government regulation of business, opposition to U.S. foreign aid and loans, encouragement of the public's responsibility for the continued well-being of the system, and the suggestion of actions directed at correcting weaknesses. This theme continues today, with Warner & Swasey still speaking out on issues, problems, and opportunities.

In 1954-55 the Natural Gas and Oil Resources Committee (NGO) and the General Gas Committee (GGC) carried out a nationwide information and education program about the oil and gas industry, with the avowed purpose of influencing legislation meant to exempt the natural gas industry from federal control. Individual oil and gas firms joined forces with NGO and GGC and added their own advertising and publicity efforts to those of the associations. One estimate of the amount spent by the industry and associations to influence a bill designed to remove the production of natural gas from federal regulation is between $20 and $25 million.[16] This combined effort to get natural gas free of federal price controls, however, was not successful.

The Scope of Advocacy Advertising

Total institutional image advertising by corporations has recorded significant growth in the past five years, increasing from $154 million in 1970 to $224.3 million in 1974.[17] Although 1974 registered a small decline (2 percent) in institutional advertising expenditures by corporations over 1973, the figures represented a 50 percent increase over 1970. The ten largest corporate advertisers accouned for 38.6 percent of the total institutional advertising by corporations and trade associations in 1974.[18] In 1971, of the top ten companies running institutional advertising, one was an oil firm, three were public utilities, and one was an automobile concern. By 1972, the number of oil firms engaged in corporate advertising had risen to four; utilities decreased to one, as did automobile manufacturers.[19] The ten largest corporate advertisers in 1974, in order of expenditures, were American Telephone & Telegraph, Exxon, General Motors, Shell Oil, Texaco, Phillips Petroleum, General Electric, Mobil Oil, DuPont, and International Telephone & Telegraph. Five of the top ten corporate advertisers were oil companies and accounted for $38.8 million in expenditures.

There has been a significant increase in advocacy advertising during the past few years. As Appendix 1A shows, in addition to the well-known media campaigns by Mobil Oil and American Electric Power, many other blue-chip corporations have launched similar campaigns. There is every indication that this trend is likely to continue. Some of the giants of American industry and business with current advocacy campaigns include Allied Chemical, Armco Steel, AT&T, Bethlehem Steel, Chase Manhattan, Cyprus Mines Corporation, Gulf Oil, Marathon Oil, IBM, ITT, Pan American Airways, Pennwalt Corporation, Phillips Petroleum, Potlatch Corporation, St. Regis Paper, Texaco, Union Carbide, U.S. Steel, Union Oil of California, Warner & Swasey, and Weyhauser Corporation. Among the industry trade associations with advocacy campaigns are the American Petroleum Institute, the Edison Electric Institute, the Glass Container Manufacturers Institute, and the Independent Bankers Association.

Despite the large number of advocacy campaigns, it has been difficult to estimate the dollar expenditures for advocacy advertising. The International Advertising Association (IAA) has sponsored a study of the international dimensions of the advocacy advertising. The study is being conducted by Albert Stridsberg[20] of New York University, editor of *Advertising World,* the only U.S.-based magazine about international advertising. A survey by the Association of National Advertisers of 114 large companies found 30 to 35 percent of corporate advertising to be on environmentalism, energy-related issues, or explanations of the capitalistic system.[21]

In response to an inquiry by Senator Philip A. Hart, chairman of the subcommittee on environment of the Senate Commerce Committee,[22] seven major oil companies and their trade associations indicated that in 1973 they jointly spent approximately $59.8 million on institutional/goodwill advertising. This figure represented 47.1 percent of all advertising expenditures for these companies in 1973. Only Mobil reported having spent $829,000 in political—and therefore nondeductible—advertising. Fifteen utility and utility-related companies and their trade association reported 1973 goodwill/institutional advertising expenditures of $3.54 million, representing 55.5 percent of their total reported advertising expenditures.

The problem of making better estimates for advocacy advertising is partly due to difficulties associated with definitions and reporting. The 1974 AEP campaign cost the company $3.5 million (see Chapter 4). Mobil spent an estimated $13 million in 1975 on its corporate communication program, which was sharply higher than the original investment in the program in 1970. The ad budget for newspapers and magazines, which carry all Mobil's advocacy ads, increased from $1.5 million in 1973 to approximately $5 million in 1975.[23]

Another indication of the magnitude and scope of advocacy advertising can be gauged through a new data collection and reporting service on corporate advertising by Benson & Benson of Princeton, New Jersey.[24] Named the TRACC RECORD, the service was initiated in the third quarter of 1975. TRACC RECORD provides detailed data for corporate institutional advertising by company, industry, media used, and ad content and could be a useful analytical tool for developing advertising strategy by the corporations and public policy.

According to TRACC RECORD, in the fourth quarter of 1975, energy-related topics were the main theme for more than 37 percent of total insertions in the print media for corporate institutional advertising, with oil companies and utilities accounting for more than 40 percent of all insertions in this category. Other important topics for corporate institutional advertising that could be construed as advocacy ads were economics/regulation, ecology, and corporate social responsibility. (Additional details on the TRACC RECORD and corporate advertising under different categories are provided in Appendix 1B.)

Advocacy Advertising and Issues of Public Policy

The strength of advocacy advertising for the corporate sponsor lies in two elements: (1) The content of the message is controlled and defined in a manner most favorable for the sponsor; and (2) the environment of the message is carefully controlled, thus making otherwise one-sided viewpoints appear more objective.

The sociocultural environment of the advocacy ads is that of traditional American values or widely held beliefs. By suggesting that the underlying rationale of a given advocacy message emanates from and is supported by traditional American values, the sponsor of the message expects to insulate himself from critical attack, for his adversaries must implicitly criticize these values in order to raise objections to the ad message.

Advocacy-type corporate institutional advertising has raised questions of public policy that are likely to have long-term consequences for the public's perception of the role of business in society and how that role is being performed. For example:

1. What are the long-term social and political implications of large-scale advocacy advertising, backed by multimillion-dollar budgets, by large corporations and powerful industry groups?

2. How is this type of advertising likely to affect the public's perception of business and its role in society?

3. Although the corporation's right to speak freely is recognized and must be protected, is it possible that this right may be abused because of paid access to media? Is there a need to promote the opposing viewpoint? If so, how might it be done?

4. Are any safeguards necessary to ensure an objective and balanced presentation of complex issues in these ad campaigns?

5. Who should pay for this type of advertising? Should it be considered a normal business expense and therefore tax deductible or should it be treated as an expenditure incurred primarily for the benefit of a company's stockholders and therefore charged to after-tax profits?

In a democratic society, the primary tasks of the nation are carried out by major social institutions, private and public. The society at large exercises control over these institutions and holds them accountable through an assessment of their activities. Effective control is based on three elements: (1) the quality of the information provided by the institutions; (2) the capability of the news media to manage the "public communication space" to ensure adequate access for various viewpoints; and (3) the ability of the people to sift between various ideas and select those that meet their expectations. The first two elements are thus critical to the notion of adequate public control. One of the assumptions behind advocacy advertising is that business considers its access to the public communication space limited. The conflict between the two institutions has to do with their relative perceptions of what is adequate entry. The objective is to make a better case for the legitimacy of an institution and its control over a share of society's physical and human resources.

Notes

1. "Donald Cook Takes On the Environmentalists," *Business Week,* October 26, 1974, p. 70.

2. John E. O'Toole, "Advocacy Advertising Shows the Flag," *Public Relations Journal,* November 1975, pp. 14-15.

3. Federal Communications Commission, *Fairness Doctrine and Public Interest Standards,* 39 Fed. Reg. 26372 (1974).

4. 39 Fed. Reg. 26380 (1974).

5. 39 Fed. Reg. 26381 (1974).

6. *Ibid.* See also Charles E. Ludlam, "Abatement of Corporate Image Environmental Advertising," *Ecology Law Quarterly,* 4 (1974), 247-278; 19

F.C.C. 2d 629 (1969); Wilderness Society (ESSO), 30 F.C.C. 2d 643 (1971), *reconsideration denied,* 31 F.C.C. 2d 729 (1971), *reconsideration denied,* 32 F.C.C. 2d 714 (1971).

7. Alan F. Neckritz and Lawrence B. Ordower, "Ecological Pornography and the Mass Media," *Ecology Law Quarterly* 1 (1971), 374; *Neckritz v. F.C.C.,* 502 F. 2d, 411 (D.C. Cir. 1974).

8. Michael J. Connor, "Mobil's Advocacy Ads Lead a Growing Trend, Draw Praise, Criticism," *The Wall Street Journal,* May 14, 1975, p. 1.

9. Frank Hewens and Fred Poppe, "New Imperatives for an Old Device," *Public Relations Journal,* November 1972, p. 10.

10. William Whyte, *Is Anybody Listening?* (New York: Simon and Schuster, 1952).

11. *Textile Mills Corp.* v. *Commissioner,* 314 U.S. 326 (1941).

12. John E. O'Toole, "Advocacy Advertising—Act II," *Crosscurrents in Corporate Communications: Highlights of the 1975 Fortune Corporate Communications Seminar,* No. 4 (New York, 1975).

13. *Addressograph-Multigraph Corp.,* 14 P-H TAX CT MEM 45, 058 1945).

14. Richard Harris, *A Sacred Trust* (New York: New American Library, 1966).

15. W. Wayne Talarzyk, *Contemporary Cases in Marketing* (Hinsdale, Ill.: Dryden Press, 1974), p. 49.

16. James Deakin, *The Lobbyists* (Washington, D.C.: Public Affairs Press, 1966). See also George Cooper, "The Tax Treatment of Business Grassroots Lobbying: Defining and Attaining the Public Policy Objectives," *Columbia Law Review,* 68, 5 (May 1968), 820-821

17. "1970-1971 Expenditures for Corporate and Association Advertising," *Public Relations Journal,* November 1972, p. 26; "1971-72 Expenditures for Corporate and Association Advertising," *Public Relations Journal,* November 1973, p. 30.

18. "The Price Tag on Institutional Advertising in 1974," *Public Relations Journal,* November 1975, pp. 36-37.

19. "1971-1972 Expenditures for Corporate and Association Advertising," p. 30.

20. Sylvan M. Barnet, Jr., "A Global Look at Advocacy Advertising," *Public Relations Journal,* November 1975, p. 17.

21. *Ibid.,* pp. 18-21.

22. U.S. Senate, *Energy and Environmental Objectives, Hearings Before the Subcommittee on Environment of the Committee on Commerce,* Part 2 (Washington, D.C., 93rd Congress, 2nd Session, May 6 and July 18, 1974), pp. 41, 73. The companies providing the data were Atlantic Richfield, Exxon, Gulf (estimates made by Media Access Project), Mobil, Phillips, Shell, Texaco, and American Petroleum Institute (industry trade association).

23. "Industry Feature: Corporate Advertising," *Madison Avenue Magazine,* January 1975, p. 20.

24. Information contained in this section was furnished by Benson & Benson, Inc., 33 Witherspoon Street, Princeton, N.J. 08540. The author is grateful to Mr. Kenneth A. Longman, president of Benson & Benson, for his cooperation in furnishing these data.

Appendix 1A

Specimen Ads from Selected
Advocacy Advertising Campaigns

Sponsoring Institution	*Ad Title*	*Date and Place of Appearance*
Allied Chemical	*It Takes More than Magic to Eliminate Pollution	*The New York Times,* March 2, 1976
	*Profits are for People	*Business Week,* February 23, 1976
American Petroleum Institute	From the (Detroit) *Sunday News*: Oil Industry Spokesman Answers Charges on the Energy Crisis	*The Wall Street Journal,* February 14, 1974
	*The End of the Middle East Oil Embargo . . . the End of the Energy Shortfall	*The Wall Street Journal,* Week of April 3, 1974
	You've Read the Headlines about Oil Company Profits	*The Wall Street Journal,* Week of May 7, 1974
American Trucking Associations	*What Is the Federal Highway Program Doing to the Country?	*Atlantic Monthly,* March, 1973
Armco Steel	*If You Don't Tell Them Who Will	*The Wall Street Journal,* December 11, 1975
Bethlehem Steel	*Some People Say We Must Reach "Zero" Population	*Newsweek,* August 30, 1976
Chase Manhattan Bank	*No money, no tools, No tools, no jobs. It's that simple.	*The Wall Street Journal*
	*Scream!	*The Wall Street Journal,* October 2, 1975
	Squawk!	*The Wall Street Journal,* October 7, 1975
Dean Witter	Help, One Tax Bite Is Enough	*The Wall Street Journal,* February 5, 1976
Edison Electric Institute	In Support of Nuclear Energy	*The Wall Street Journal,* April 13, 1976
Gulf Oil	*The Information Is There All Right	*The Wall Street Journal,* February 7, 1974
Independent Bankers Association	The Savings Banks Want to Compete with Us . . . Provided *We* Maintain . . . Restrictions	*The New York Times,* February 23, 1976
Keep America Beautiful under the aegis of the Advertising Council	*In the Fight Against Pollution, We Still Have So Far to Go	June 8, 1975
	*From Garbage to Garden Because Enough People Cared	June 15, 1975

Those advertisements illustrated are marked with an asterisk (*).

21

Sponsoring Institution	Ad Title	Date and Place of Appearance
Knight-Ridder Newspapers	*Which One Still Has a Free Press?	Business Week, February 23, 1976
Marathon Oil Company	The Impact of Taxes and Controls	The Wall Street Journal, November 11, 1975
Microdot, Inc.	*To: American Business. Are You Next?	The Wall Street Journal, December 17, 1975
Mobil Oil	An Open Letter to the Congress . . . And Why All Other Controls on Oil Should End Immediately	The Wall Street Journal, October 23, 1975
	*Big Oil, Little People	The New York Times, June 12, 1975
	*Energy Policy Must Be Priority Policy	The New York Times, June 19, 1975
	*Is Anybody Listening	The New York Times, January 18, 1973
	Move Over, Murphy's Law: "Bad regulation begets worse regulation"	The New York Times, February 9, 1975
	*The Soapbox Is a Lonely Place	The New York Times, May 8, 1975
	*The Unnatural Gas Shortage	The New York Times, September 21, 1972
	*Why Do Two Networks Refuse to Run This Commercial?	The New York Times, June 17, 1974
National Association of Motor Bus Owners	For what it's costing to keep Amtrak going, Uncle Sam could buy a bus ticket for every Amtrak passenger for the next two years . . . and save America's taxpayers at least $140 million	The Washington Post, September 24, 1975
	*Last year 190 million Americans paid for a train ride they never got.	The Wall Street Journal, November 18, 1975
National Council of Farmer Cooperatives	*That Rugged American Individualist Down on the Farm Needs Your Support	The Wall Street Journal, March 16, 1976
Pan American Employees Awareness Committee	An Open Letter to the American People	The Washington Post, September 19, 1974
	An Open Letter to the U.S. Congress – Equity Not Subsidy!	The Miami Herald, October 2, 1974
	*We Plead Guilty	The Miami Herald, September 22, 1974
Pennwalt Corporation	*The Competitive Enterprise System We Believe in It . . . Here's Why	The Wall Street Journal, March 31, 1976

Those advertisements illustrated are marked with an asterisk (*).

Sponsoring Institution	Ad Title	Date and Place of Appearance
Phillips Petroleum	*It's Time American Industry Took a Stand for Free Enterprise	The Wall Street Journal, February 2, 1976
Savings Bank Associations of New York State	Listen to the People	The Wall Street Journal, March 17, 1976
	*The Commercial Banks Want to Kill This Bill. If They Win, You Lose	The Wall Street Journal, April 27, 1976
United States Steel	What Makes America Work? . . . Profits. Without Them There Are No Jobs	Business Week, March 8, 1976
Warner & Swasey	*No Wonder We're Broke!	Forbes, December 1, 1975
	*Proof That There Is No Free Lunch	The Wall Street Journal, April 28, 1976

Those advertisements illustrated are marked with an asterisk (*).

It Takes More Than Magic To Eliminate Pollution...

It takes more than technology, too. It takes money—a great deal of it—to control air and water pollution, make it safer for employees to do their jobs, improve the quality and safety of products and, at the same time, conserve our nation's energy.

Since 1970, we at Allied Chemical have spent $125 million on environmental hardware alone. Nearly 500 Allied Chemical employees now work to upgrade safety, health and environmental conditions at our 150 plant locations. Over the next three years we will commit about $140 million, 12 percent of our capital spending, to environmental betterment. It's a big job and much remains to be accomplished. But our purpose and policy are to do the right thing. We are not alone in this. A survey of 130 chemical companies shows they will spend $2.4 billion between 1975 and 1977 to protect our country's environment.

Where do we and other companies get the money to pay for this work? We rely on profits. With adequate profits we can finance our environmental improvement projects. We can expand our businesses and create more jobs. We can pay a fair

dividend to stockholders. And we can pay millions in taxes that help support all kinds of governmental programs. Without adequate profits, we can do none of these things.

In a period when profits are more necessary than ever, they are far from adequate. A recent survey showed Americans think the average manufacturing corporation makes more than 30 cents profit on every sales dollar. In fact, the average in 1974 was about 5 cents.

Business can and will do the environmental job expected of it. But it's going to take more profits—not magic—to do the job.

Where Profits Are For People

Exhibit 1A-1

24

Profits Are For People...

As essential as profits are to the survival of our way of life, I know of few subjects so universally misunderstood. And a recent nationwide survey indicated that misconceptions about profits are increasing. Obviously, business is not getting the message through. The time is long overdue for some old-fashioned plain talk.

By putting profits to work, companies build new factories, modernize existing facilities, enable Americans to compete with manufacturers abroad and—most critical—create jobs for our people and opportunities for future generations. The company that doesn't make a consistent profit year in and year out withers and disappears, and so do the jobs of its employees.

Most experts agree that our economy will need at least $4 trillion in new capital during the next 10 years. Unless we plan to convert to socialism—and we certainly don't want to do that—a good part of it will have to come from corporate profits. Yet, contrary to what most Americans think, corporate profits have been shrinking. Today, the rate of profit by U.S. corporations is about 5% on sales, less than it was a decade ago. If profitability continues to shrink, we can look forward to an era of diminished economic growth and fewer jobs.

And when there is less profit to tax, our federal, state and local governments cannot obtain the revenues needed to carry out public programs, and the goals we have set for our society will be seriously threatened.

Our company—Allied Chemical—is a good example of profits at work. From 1970 to 1974, we earned net profits of $436 million and plowed back $258 million into business expansion and job-creating activities. That's about 62¢ of every dollar we earn. But this creative reinvestment of profits is only part of the story. Businesses that are profitable provide much of the support for public spending. During this same period, our company paid more than $382 million in taxes. Our employees paid taxes from their wages, and our stockholders paid taxes on their dividends. So, profits are continually recycled for everyone's benefit.

During the next few months we will be talking publicly about corporate profits because we are convinced that an understanding of this subject by our people is vital to protect America's quality of life. We invite you to read these messages and to let us know how you feel about our viewpoint.

John T. Connor
Chairman

Allied Chemical

Exhibit 1A-2

25

The end of the Arab oil embargo is good news. When the tankers now being loaded reach the U.S., Middle East oil will begin to help ease the energy shortfall.

The lifting of the embargo is not, however, a panacea for all our energy problems. That's sobering news. This nation was already in an energy bind when the embargo began five months ago. Remember...

. . . Some schools and businesses had to close for lack of fuel in the winter of 1972-73, and even some homes had trouble getting fuel.

. . . Some motorists in some areas were unable to get gasoline at times last summer.

. . . Many businesses and industries last year and for some years before tightened their belts on energy consumption.

The fact is, in recent years use of oil and natural gas has been climbing faster than the increase in supplies. Energy usage in 1973 was up 4.8% over 1972 in the U.S. in spite of conservation efforts and the embargo!

Trying to bring supply and demand back in balance again will require:

1. *Continuation of the extraordinary and commendable efforts of the American people and American industry to conserve energy.* This will slow down the growth in demand for fuel.

2. *Stepped-up activities by the American petroleum companies to develop new domestic supplies of oil and natural gas.* This will help reduce our vulnerability to interferences with foreign oil supplies in the future.

The petroleum industry is committed to both these goals. It is conserving huge volumes of energy in its own operations. And it is investing billions of dollars to find new domestic supplies of petroleum and to expand refinery capacity to process more crude oil.

Other fuels, too, must make a sizeable contribution—consistent with environmental goals that protect the health and safety of the public.

• More nuclear-powered generating plants must be built and put on stream.

• More coal must be mined and used.

• Synthetic fuels (oil and gas from coal, oil shale, tar sands) must be developed.

• Research must be pushed forward toward harnessing energy from the sun, the earth and the tides.

Meanwhile, the heaviest burden will continue to be placed on oil and natural gas—which now provide about 78% of all the energy used in this country.

America has the energy resources to meet our needs for hundreds of years.

Americans have the scientific and technical know-how to develop that energy.

The American petroleum industry has a record of more than a century of meeting the nation's energy needs.

Resources . . . know-how . . . experience. These can be joined together only through public understanding of the job to be done, and public policies that advance—not retard—the efforts to get on with this essential job.

The end of the Middle East oil embargo is not the end of the energy shortfall

American Petroleum Institute
1801 K Street, Northwest, Washington, D C 20006

Exhibit 1A-3

26

What is the federal highway program doing to the country?

Questions are being raised about the nation's highway program. Here are some of the answers —based on fact, not opinion.

Q. Whose idea was this anyway?
A. A master plan for a national highway system was proposed in 1954 by President Eisenhower. Two years later, Congress authorized the present program, with emphasis on the national system of Interstate and defense highways.

Q. Why did we need a new highway program?
A. After World War II, the nation's highway system was totally inadequate to handle the rapidly growing volume of traffic. From 1956 alone, the United States has gone from 65 million motor vehicles to 105 million today. The new system was conceived to, and *does* in fact, reduce the cost of transporting goods, make travel faster and easier for both business and pleasure drivers, save lives, and provide a vital transportation network for our national defense.

Q. Are these new modern highways safe?
A. Yes. The Interstate System saves over 6,600 lives every year, with conservative estimates projecting over 8,400 saved when the system is completed.

Q. Are highways paving over the country?
A. No. A full 80 percent of the present road system was *already there* as early as 1916. Less than 1% of land area is used for roads and streets. Much of the effort has been to improve and rebuild existing roads to modern standards, along with devising new traffic corridors.

Q. What do highways do to the ecology?
A. Ecological disruption is avoided by careful planning and careful building. Actually, more trees and shrubs and flowers have been planted than removed.

Q. Why should everybody pay for these roads?
A. Unless you drive a car, bus, or truck, you don't. But if you do, you pay your share. The Federal Government's share of the Interstate —90%—and other federal highway aid is funded entirely by special taxes on gas, oil, tires, new trucks and trailers and buses, and "use" taxes on large trucks. The user pays, nobody else.

Q. Why shouldn't some of this money be used for mass transit?
A. It already is. With the exception of a few cities, buses represent the only really practical mass transit system. And good highways make for better bus service. The bone of contention is *rail* transit. As a matter of simple justice we do not feel that car and truck owners should pay for transit systems out of monies collected in the form of special taxes and dedicated in *trust* to a highway system.

For additional facts, send for the booklet, "No Highways, No Taxes". Public Relations Dept., American Trucking Associations, Inc., 1616 P St., N.W., Washington, D.C. 20036.

American Trucking
Associations, Inc., Washington, D.C.

Exhibit 1A-4

If you don't tell them, who will?

Dear Fellow American:

After 23 months of debate and investigation — the distilling down of 2500-plus energy related bills — Congress is finally delivering to the President its answer to our real and still-growing energy problem.

It's called The House/Senate Energy Conference Report. In every respect, this bill is a "disaster." It's a patched together compromise bill that doesn't solve anything. In fact, the discouraging effects outlined below are just the "tip of the iceberg."

1) Reduces the incentive to search for domestic oil.

2) Increases our reliance on imports of foreign oil-4 million barrels a day by 1980.

3) Extends economically damaging federal regulation and control.

A November Harris public opinion poll shows that the American public is prepared to accept higher prices if that's what it takes to get more domestic supply. Your members of Congress either do not hear you or do not believe what they hear. We simply must speak up.

That's why we sent full and factual information to 45,000 Armco people, 100,000 shareholders and hundreds of customers and suppliers. And that's why we are running this ad here and in other newspapers throughout the United States.

The only real and lasting solution to our energy problem is "increased domestic supply." I urge you to join the 140,000+ Armco family in phoning, writing or wiring the President. Ask him to veto this bill. Write your Representative and Senators, urging them to sustain the veto. Then, in your best interests, encourage them to get about the task of constructing a real solution — a policy that increases domestic production and assures adequate supply.

Do it now, today. If you don't tell them, who will?

Sincerely,

C. William Verity, Jr.

C. William Verity, Jr.
Chairman of the Board
Armco Steel Corporation
Middletown, Ohio 45043

RESPONSIVE PEOPLE IN ACTION.

Exhibit 1A-5

28

Some people say we must reach "zero" pollution.

But at what cost? And how fast?

At Bethlehem Steel, we work hard—every day—to control pollution. But the cost is high. We've already spent approximately $400 million to clean up a major portion of the pollutants from the air and water we use. We consider this money well spent.

$600 million more

In an effort to meet existing pollution control laws and regulations, we have many more projects under way or anticipated in the near future. These projects are expected to cost us some $600 million over the next five years.

Where does that leave us?

Depending upon how far regulatory agencies go in stringent interpretation of the present laws and regulations, we may be faced with spending hundreds of millions more to try to

remove the last traces of pollution. We do not think that this would be money well spent.

Attempting to remove the last increment of pollution involves new and uncertain technology. The attempt will consume a considerable amount of scarce energy and natural resources. And, in many cases, it will merely transfer pollution problems to the power companies or chemical manufacturers.

Is it time for a rearrangement of priorities?

We are faced as a nation with troublesome alternatives. Do we

continue our headlong rush to implement some of the air and water clean-up standards that have yet to be proved necessary—or even sound—or shall we give equal consideration to jobs, our energy requirements, capital needs, and other demands for social priorities?

We believe the national interest now requires that we face up to the dual necessity of preserving our environment while at the same time assuring our economic progress.

Our booklet, "Steelmaking and the Environment," tells more about the problems of pollution and what we're doing to help solve them. For a free copy, write: Public Affairs Dept., Room 476-WSJ, Bethlehem Steel Corp., Bethlehem, PA 18016.

Bethlehem

Exhibit 1A–6

No money, no tools.
No tools, no jobs.

It's that simple.

Only when you've gone through it do you know how hard unemployment is.

It's being desperate and frustrated and bitter.

It's standing in line for a hand-out that won't even begin to cover the bills.

It's chasing down job leads that go nowhere.

It's dreaming up ways to hang onto the house figuring out how to say "no" to the kids — no bicycles, no new clothes, no fishing gear, no nothing. Until you connect again. If you do.

Could things be worse than they are now? Yes.

Looking ahead, our economists say one out of six American workers could be jobless in ten years. 17 million out of work. Twice as many as today. Not because you don't want to work. But because no matter how badly you want to work, you can't without tools. And tools cost money.

But American companies face a shortage of money capital.

We could fall as much as $1.5 trillion short of the money needed in the next ten years. That's $400 million a day too little. Every day. For ten years.

American business and industry just aren't going to have enough money to buy the machinery and tools needed to provide jobs for everybody who wants them.

Unless we stimulate the formation of capital. Capital the money to provide the tools, the supplies and the materials that jobs require is the best way to create real jobs.

You're the one who may be out of a job. What is each of us going to do about it? So America can have full employment. Again.

This message appears because we believe every American should be thinking about this critical problem.

THE CHASE MANHATTAN BANK, N.A.
New York 10015

Exhibit 1A–7

30

"Scream!"

It's time.

One out of six Americans could be out of work ten years from now. 17 million unemployed idle in the streets.

We're squawking. And screaming. You should be, too.

Our country must change its economic direction. Now.

Chase foresees a massive capital shortfall by 1985. With consequent high levels of unemployment. Levels double what we have now.

During the next 10 years, there are things we must do which involve significant outlays of capital: Control pollution. Provide sufficient housing. Finance our Federal budget. Become independent in energy. Improve mass transit.

And, we *must* also provide new jobs by building new plants and equipment...the materials to work on and the tools to work with. Our industrial plant today is already older than Europe's and Japan's. There's a good reason why. A Treasury Department study (covering 1963-70) clearly demonstrates that the U.S. is investing considerably less of its national output in productive capacity:

Japan	29.0%
W. Germany	20.0%
France	18.2%
Canada	17.4%
United States	13.6%

Go along as we have been, and U.S. business and industry face a capital shortfall over the next 10 years of $400 million a day *every* day.

Failure to close this capital gap could result in significantly higher unemployment and a higher inflation rate 10 years from now. Both unacceptable conditions in our opinion.

As a sensible, long-term solution, Chase proposes that thought be given to a seven-point action program:

• Encourage an ever-growing base of personal savings.

• Establish more realistic depreciation allowances.

• Give preferential tax treatment for retained corporate earnings re-invested in the business.

• Ease our harsh treatment of capital gains compared with that of most other countries.

• Stabilize fiscal and monetary policy to prevent violent swings in the economy.

• Encourage foreign investment in the U.S. economy.

• Eliminate unnecessary controls, and outmoded government regulations that restrict our free market economy.

Chase feels strongly that serious consideration of these matters is now essential. There are those who may feel differently. Even those who might think we can starve our industrial sector without starving our job opportunities.

We at Chase disagree. And will argue the point. Anytime. Anywhere.

CHASE

Exhibit 1A–8

The oil companies have been accused of withholding information on energy from your representatives in government.

This is not true.

The fact is that the major oil companies, including Gulf, have been supplying the Bureau of Mines and other Government and State Agencies with over 150 reports each month on their operations for many years.

We continue to do so.

The only generous conclusion we can draw is that those who accuse us are unaware of what facts are on hand.

The information is there, all right.

Elected officials have always had access to it.

In the future, however, Gulf suggests that it could be made more useful if all industry reports were centralized in the Federal Energy Office.

To find energy, find facts—not fault.

GULF OIL CORPORATION
P.O. Box 1403-P2 Houston, Texas 77001

Exhibit 1A-9

IN THE FIGHT AGAINST POLLUTION, WE STILL HAVE SO FAR TO GO.

The American Indian spoke a prayer over 400 years ago.

"Oh great spirit...make me walk in beauty! Make my heart respect all you have made."

In many American communities today, the spirit of that prayer is reborn.

But all around us are reminders that we still have far to go. You can help by becoming a community volunteer. Write: Keep America Beautiful, Inc., 99 Park Avenue, New York, New York 10016

**People start pollution.
People can stop it.**

Keep America Beautiful, Inc.

A Public Service of this Newspaper & The Advertising Council.

Exhibit 1A-10

FROM GARBAGE TO GARDEN BECAUSE ENOUGH PEOPLE CARED.

2000 species of plants grow at South Coast Botanic Garden in Palos Verdes Peninsula, California. Over 3 million tons of trash and garbage lie just beneath the surface.

A dump transformed into a paradise. Impossible? Not when enough people in a community get together and work.

You can help by becoming a community volunteer in your area. We'd like to send you the name of the Keep America Beautiful group nearest you.

Write: Keep America Beautiful, Inc., 99 Park Avenue, New York, New York 10016

 People start pollution. People can stop it.

Keep America Beautiful, Inc.

A Public Service of this Newspaper & The Advertising Council.

Exhibit 1A-11

34

- SPAIN
- SOUTH KOREA
- CHILE
- PERU
- BRAZIL
- PARAGUAY
- URUGUAY
- SOUTH VIETNAM
- PORTUGAL
- CUBA
- HAITI
- PANAMA
- INDIA
- CAMBODIA
- UGANDA
- PHILIPPINES

Which one still has a free press?

Is there one nation, one country in this whole list with a free press? Free to search out and print a clear and truthful account of the news as it happens?

The answer is no. Not one.

And the list is growing. More governments see a free press as a critical threat to themselves. They fear a press that is free from their indirect influence and direct control. So, the people's right to know is sacrificed. And this is only the beginning. Once the free press is lost, most other freedoms simply don't have a chance.

In this country we know a self-governing society cannot survive without a free flow of information. As citizens, we accept a free press as our right. Its protection is built into the foundation of our nation's beginning.

But with that right, comes a newspaper's obligation to the people, to give them a fair and accurate account of the news.

The 33 newspapers that make up Knight-Ridder welcome that responsibility.

We believe that no official governmental information system can be as effective as the independent, competitive reporting of individual newspapers.

Each newspaper free to serve the best interests of its community. Committed to an informed and enlightened people.

At Knight-Ridder we believe that no society can govern itself in darkness. And though the list is growing, we are dedicated to keeping this country off that list.

Philadelphia Inquirer • Philadelphia Daily News • Detroit Free Press • Miami Herald • St. Paul Dispatch • St. Paul Pioneer Press • Charlotte Observer • Charlotte News • San Jose Mercury • San Jose News • Wichita Eagle • Wichita Beacon • Akron Beacon Journal • Long Beach Press-Telegram • Long Beach Independent • Lexington Herald • Lexington Leader • Gary Post-Tribune • Duluth News-Tribune • Duluth Herald • Macon Telegraph • Macon News • Columbus Enquirer • Columbus Ledger • Pasadena Star-News • Tallahassee Democrat • Grand Forks Herald • Journal of Commerce and Commercial • Bradenton Herald • Boulder Daily Camera • Aberdeen American News • Boca Raton News • Niles Daily Star

Knight-Ridder Newspapers

Knight-Ridder Newspapers Ad No. 75-103B
4 col. x 150 lines—B&W
New York Times (all editions) (offset)—October 17, 1975
D'ARCY-MacMANUS & MASIUS
79062—WM-2—10-13-75—99831

Exhibit 1A-12

To: American Business
Are You Next?

DEAR FELLOW CHIEF EXECUTIVE OFFICER

You may be aware of the fact that the company I head is the target of a takeover attempt by General Cable. And I want to emphasize **we are going to pull out all stops, fight tooth and nail to protect our stockholders' interest** in the real value Microdot represents.

I want to let you know about the experience because you may find yourself in the same position any day.

In the abstract you may feel that in a free enterprise economy the market place is the right and only place where control of a company should be decided. But I have some observations on that point of view that I think you may want to consider.

The table below shows the performance record of Microdot since present management restructured the company in 1970—in terms of sales, earnings and dividends. Our price earnings ratio and the market price of our stock has not kept pace with our performance record. You or some of your chief executive officer friends may have had similar experiences.

MICRODOT'S RECORD

Year	Dividends	Microdot's Per Share Earnings[1]	Microdot Sales [1] (Millions)	Price Range
1970	$.40	$ .92	$114.8	$27-3/8-$ 9-3/8
1971	.40	1.08	131.2	25-7/8- 12-3/4
1972	.40	1.63	159.7	24-3/8- 15-1/8
1973	.43	2.02	207.1	17-3/8- 8-1/8
1974	.50	2.70	293.8	11-7/8- 8-1/4
1975	.60[2]	3.01–3.11 (est.)	295.0 (est.)	15-3/8- 8-3/4[3]

(1) From continuing operations. Reflects retirement of 404,298 shares in exchange for subordinated debentures in April, 1975.

(2) On December 5, 1975 Microdot declared a dividend at an annual rate of $1.00, an increase of 67%.

(3) Through December 2, 1975.

At the risk of sounding boastful, I'd like to say that **Microdot was one of only four companies of U.S. Industry which made FORTUNE 500's list of the top ten companies in sales and profit growth** over the past twenty years. Only Microdot was in the top five in sales and profit growth over the same period.

Now enter General Cable whose records show a decline in earnings of $4 million so far this year and a recent dividend cut. With $75 million from four undisclosed banks, they've applied in Ohio to make a tender offer for any or all of Microdot's stock at a price of $17 per share. The market price at the close of business on the day before their offer was $11.75 per share.

They're offering Morgan Stanley a fee of $800,000, plus expenses, to get the brokerage community to do a sales job on our stockholders and get them to tender. Even before any hearings in Ohio 305,400 shares of our outstanding total of 3.6 million shares traded in the

Exhibit 1A–13

first four trading days after the offer was announced. Obviously, a lot of fast buck artists are hoping to midwife the turnover of control.

Right now, you may be saying, "That's the risks of the game. If you can't stand the heat, stay out of the kitchen."

Or you may be saying, "There but for the grace of God go I."

But whatever you're saying, let me ask you if this is the right way to go for American business if we're going to keep the private enterprise system intact over the long term?

If no successful growth company of medium size is able to resist the raids of large outsiders, there will be no way for American stockholders to realize the potential these growth companies represent. Then there will be no future IBM, no Xerox, no Polaroid. They will be choked off and smothered as soon as they start to show their real growth potential.

Think about it. Think about it especially as affecting the outlook for your company.

Have you devoted the time necessary to set up a battle plan against such a contingency? Have you wondered if you would have any friends once the tender offer was on?

If you think this trend is dangerous, or if it just plain offends you, **let me ask you what you are going to do about it.** If you have headquarters or substantial assets in Ohio, you can write the Governor and give him your thoughts. <u>Or you can talk to Senator Williams. Or the SEC.</u> Or you can ask your bank if they're in on this raid and let them know what you think. <u>Or you can drop Morgan Stanley a line.</u> Or you can write or call General Cable's directors. I've listed their names below. Or just call me. I'd like to hear from you.

The main point I want to make is simply this—these days we are often frustrated by things that happen which seem to be beyond our control—but **here is one you can do something about. Don't wait until it happens to you—get on the phone and let those involved in this scheme know how you feel about it—remember, you don't have to do business with someone whose ethics offend you. And, if you don't tell them how strongly you feel about it—they will surely do it again—perhaps to you.**

Sincerely yours,

R. Eberstadt, Jr.
President and Chief Executive Officer

Governor James A. Rhodes
State House
Columbus, Ohio 43215

The Honorable
Harrison A. Williams, Jr.
United States Senate
Washington, D.C. 20510

Roderick Hills, Chairman
Securities and Exchange Commission
500 North Capitol Street
Washington, D.C. 20549

Morgan Stanley & Co., Inc.
1251 Avenue of the Americas
New York, N.Y. 10020

DIRECTORS OF GENERAL CABLE

A.G. Boardman, Jr. (retired)
Consultant to
Irving Trust Co.
1 Wall Street
New York, N.Y. 10015

R.P. Jensen
President: Chief Executive Officer
General Cable Corp.
500 W. Putnam Avenue
Greenwich, CT 06830

J.J. Burke
President
National Student Film Corp.
9336 W. Washington Blvd.
Culver City, CA 90230

B.D. Johnson
Consultant
United States Trust Co. of New York
45 Wall Street
New York, N.Y. 10005

F.A. Collins, Jr.
President
The Sperry & Hutchinson Company
330 Madison Avenue
New York, N.Y. 10017

D.P. Kircher
Former President and Chairman of
the Board of Singer

Exhibit 1A–13 continued

G.V. Comfort
President
George Comfort & Sons Co., Inc.
200 Madison Avenue
New York, N.Y. 10016

C.W. Nimitz, Jr.
Chairman of the Board & Chief Exec. Officer
The Perkin-Elmer Corp.
Main Avenue
Norwalk, CT 06856

F.S. Dunn
Chairman of the Finance Committee
Otis Elevator Company
245 Park Avenue
New York, N.Y. 10017

A.T. Wenzell
Executive Vice President and Director
Paine, Webber, Jackson & Curtis Inc.
140 Broadway
New York, N.Y. 10005

A.L. Fergenson
Chairman of the Board
General Cable Corp.
733 3rd Avenue
New York, N.Y. 10017

This Letter Was Sent To The Chief Executive Officers
Of America's Mid-Spectrum Corporations.

Exhibit 1A–13 continued

Big oil, little people.

Big oil. It conjures up images of expensive suits, foot-long cigars, millionaire owners.

Forget it.

There may be traces of cigar smoke hanging in the air after *any* company's board meeting. But the middle-class, middle-income man or woman is more likely to be an owner of one of the big oil companies than millionaires.

A recent survey found that nearly 14 million Americans own shares—more than two million directly and nearly 12 million indirectly—in the six largest U.S. oil companies. And nobody was counted twice.

Fourteen million people. More than the combined populations of New York, Chicago, Detroit, and Coon Rapids, Minnesota—more than six and one-half percent of the nation's total population.

With numbers like that there are bound to be a few millionaires.

But 14 million millionaires?

There goes another myth about the oil industry.

In fact, the survey showed the average shareholder in an oil company is a person who has worked hard, saved some money, and invested part of it in common stocks.

The survey estimated that there were nearly 12 million indirect shareowners who participated in "Big Oil" through purchases of mutual funds and insurance stocks, through participation in pension and profit-sharing plans, through life insurance annuities, or through trust funds.

The more than two million direct shareholders are spread throughout the 50 states. Nearly half of them—46 percent—are retired. Women outnumber men, 54 to 46 percent. Median family income is $16,400 a year (about $14,100 for retired persons).

So what?

Well, the popular misconception that "Big Oil" is run by the few for a privileged few is nonsense. There are nearly 425,000 employees in these six companies alone. And they're working for 14 million other Americans. While broad-brush attacks based on misinformation or political expediency may be aimed at large companies, they also damage millions of Americans who work for and share ownership in those firms.

There's a still more important point: A plethora of unwise bills in Congress seeking to increase government regulation while decreasing the oil industry's ability to turn a decent profit is not going to get at the root causes of our energy predicament. Only hard-nosed, unemotional action aimed at producing more energy quickly can do that.

But the oil industry will need to continue to attract the hundreds of billions of dollars that must be invested to find, produce, refine and deliver the energy this country will need by 1985. If Washington will supply the sorely needed national energy policy, we think the oil industry can help supply the energy.

Millions of little people must think so, too. They're betting their money on it.

Exhibit 1A-14

39

Energy policy must be priority policy

Looks like we've made it through another summer and fall. No major fuel shortages, no freezeouts or widespread blackouts in the United States.

Now all we have to worry about are the coming winter, spring, and next summer—and the next decade or so. The fact that the energy crisis hasn't come full-blown yet doesn't mean it has gone away. On the contrary, it only means the time of crisis is one winter nearer.

Meantime, we are losing ground.

While last winter was providentially mild in many sections, we have not used this time providently. New power plants required for urban centers have been delayed by indecision and litigation. Offshore exploration leases have been delayed; new discoveries of oil and gas have been few. New drilling has been slack. Construction of needed new refineries has been frustrated and, in fact, virtually nil.

Through still another year, we've failed to do what must be done to match our energy potential to foreseeable energy needs.

With heavy and growing reliance on imports, we've taken care of the present barely, but the future hardly at all.

So the day of reckoning still impends.

The United States cannot meet its energy requirements in the 1970s and 1980s with an energy system conceived in the 1920s and 1930s, and developed in the 1940s and 1950s.

For our society, energy is lifeblood. Unless we assure ourselves of the energy required to sustain the well-being of the American people, no arms or armament can assure the nation's security, nor can social programs assure its stability.

The Administration has said it will give the same urgent attention to energy policy that is now given to foreign policy, defense policy, fiscal policy, and social policies. The nation should hope so.

As it is, we have no overall national energy policy. Those policies we do have are fragmented, conflicting, often mutually defeating. Old rivalries between regions, old fears among competitors, old conflicts between consumers and producers have straitjacketed development of energy resources. Regulation, intended to be responsive to the public interest, has come increasingly to hinder the expansion of energy production and distribution systems.

A national energy policy fairly balancing the interests of all affected is imperative for the nation in the 1970s. Efforts to meet other priorities will be doomed to failure unless and until we fulfill this most fundamental priority.

Mobil

This ad appeared in the New York _Times_ on June 19, 1975.

Exhibit 1A–15

Is Anybody Listening?

If normally cold weather prevails this month, up to 25 percent of the workers in parts of Illinois will be laid off because plants and factories can't get enough natural gas or heating oil.

Major airlines were forced to ration their jet fuel at Kennedy airport recently.

The Federal Power Commission has proposed a long-term system for rationing natural gas.

These items all made newspaper headlines. They all mean the same thing: The U.S. is facing an energy crisis of serious and growing proportions. In a curious way, the oil industry has failed.

Oil companies knew the shortage was coming. We knew how it could be averted. For the past 20 years we have told everyone who would listen what we knew, but we failed to convince policy-makers to take the necessary steps. Some examples:

When the Federal Power Commission began regulating the wellhead price of natural gas in interstate commerce in the 1950's, oil companies told Congress that artificially low prices would increase the demand for natural gas while reducing both the incentive and the ability to search for new reserves.

When the F.P.C. said the only consideration in price controls on natural gas was low prices to the consumer in the short term, oil companies told them this objective ignored adequacy of supply in the longer term and that a shortage would result. The gas shortage is now severe and getting worse.

When federal, state, and local governments decided the environment was to be protected at all costs, we told them this would worsen the natural gas shortage. It has.

Oil companies said that unless new refineries were built in this country, a severe winter could produce critical heating oil shortages. Not a single refinery is under construction in the U.S. at this time. Law suits and regulations stemming from exaggerated environmental fears have blocked the construction of new refineries. So today U.S. refineries are producing heating oil at peak capacity—in record volumes, in fact—and still having to ration it.

Oil companies said it was a mistake to delay construction of the trans-Alaska pipeline, keeping oil from what may prove to be the largest find in U.S. history away from U.S. markets. Today many U.S. refineries are short of crude oil, and foreign supplies of it are being allocated.

Oil companies said further burdens would be placed on U.S. oil and natural gas resources if nuclear energy were not allowed to play an important role in meeting the nation's energy needs. This has happened.

Oil companies said it was a mistake to reduce exploration incentives in 1969; to suspend drilling on offshore California leases; to delay lease sales off the coast of Louisiana; and to refuse to make leases available off the U.S. East Coast. We sounded off on all these issues, but we obviously failed to persuade enough people. In 1971 fewer exploratory wells were drilled in this country than in any year since 1947.

With such a good track record for prophecy in the past, what are oil companies saying *now*?

• That while the U.S. has a strong energy resource base for the long term, in the form of coal, oil shale, uranium, and petroleum, it faces a critical oil-and-gas supply problem from now to about 1985.

• That we are not alone in this critical supply problem for the next 12 to 15 years. Europe and Japan are facing the same problem. If the U.S. does not develop greater domestic capability for producing oil and gas, we will find ourselves competing increasingly with other countries of the West for relatively scarce supplies of petroleum from exporting nations.

• That the long-term U.S. resource base can be developed, to make us almost self-sufficient in energy and thus hold our dependence on foreign sources to a reasonable level, only through the adoption of realistic national energy policies.

• That our country's fast-rising imports of oil and gas over the next 12 to 15 years—amounting to about half of our total consumption by 1985—pose balance-of-payments and security problems to which we are not giving enough attention.

• That we must rely primarily on oil and gas for energy for at least the next 12 to 15 years and accordingly must minimize our dependence on imports by finding, developing, and producing more oil and gas in this country.

• That the most promising areas for this additional petroleum lie under the waters of our outer continental shelf, and that federal leasing of this acreage for exploration should proceed apace.

• That we should be building a great deal of additional refining capacity here—particularly on the East Coast, where demand is greatest and where most of the imported oil is brought in—and stop exporting American jobs and capital on such a large scale.

• That our nation should be building superports capable of accommodating the huge tankers that reduce transportation costs.

• That atomic power plants should be built at a far faster rate.

• That we must be sensible about environmental demands and must strike a socially acceptable balance between environmental considerations and the need for additional energy supplies.

Our industry seemed finally to have made itself heard last month when the *Washington Post* said in an editorial:

"The price of gas ought to be raised…The present shortage of gas to residential consumers has risen largely because of obsolete and harmful price regulations imposed by the federal government. Despite soaring demand, the price has been held far below the cost of competing fuels. Present policy is a monument to the influence of senators and congressmen from the urban states."

Is anybody *else* listening?

This ad appeared in the New York Times on January 18, 1973.

Exhibit 1A-16

The soapbox is a lonely place

For a long time now, we've been raising our voice in ads like this one. On a variety of issues. Including the need for a sensible U.S. energy policy. Noting that without adequate return on investment, exploration for new sources of oil and gas will fall off. Making the U.S. more and more dependent on costly foreign supplies.

Sometimes, we wonder if we are talking to ourselves. Congress certainly wasn't listening when it singled out the oil industry for heavy new taxation. In addition, there are now some 500 oil-related bills before Congress, many of which would impose new regulation on the industry. Some Congressmen have even proposed a subsidized federal petroleum corporation to "compete" with private oil companies.

We don't think the companies should be expected to take such assaults lying down. So we speak out. The trouble is, not enough other businesses follow suit—and it gets pretty lonely on the soapbox.

We think there's plenty for other companies to worry about. If our Congressmen can blithely take away the depletion allowance from some oil companies, if they can tinker with the foreign tax credit to "punish" us—and if they do this even at the risk of the nation's future energy security and perhaps the whole economy—what makes anyone think they'll stop with oil?

What makes *any* industry think it's safe?

We wish there were more like the Chase Bank, which has been warning that government disincentives to investment are precipitating a critical shortage of capital. The U.S., says Chase, will need $4.1 trillion in the next ten years, just to rebuild aging industrial capacity.

And if it doesn't happen, there won't be enough jobs. Which suggests other voices should come forth. Not just business, but labor groups. Women. Minorities. Every American who has a stake in the economy. And who doesn't?

If enough voices are raised, Congress will have to listen. And it won't be so lonely out there on the soapbox.

Mobil®

This ad appeared in the New York <u>Times</u> on May 8, 1975.

Exhibit 1A–17

42

The unnatural gas shortage

The nation is drifting toward a serious—largely man-made—shortage of natural gas, the cleanest-burning major fuel and one of the most convenient.

Some parts of the country are already in a natural gas crisis. The New York State Public Service Commission has ordered all gas utilities in the state to limit sales of natural gas. New customers, both residential and commercial, have been turned away in other states.

Certain types of industry that depend on natural gas for fuel may be faced with periodic cutoffs of their supplies this winter and may have to lay off workers. Some may be kept from opening new plants, and thus from creating new jobs.

Yet the geologists and other explorationists believe there are very substantial quantities of natural gas still to be discovered in our country.

Why isn't it being discovered in sufficient volume to meet demand? How did today's shortage come about?

In 1954 the federal government began regulating wellhead prices of natural gas destined for interstate commerce. In its shortsighted efforts to protect the consumer, the government has focused on the price of gas in the short term and has ignored the consumer's stake in adequate supplies for the long term. Now the long term has arrived.

The price a producer gets for natural gas he sells into interstate commerce has been artificially depressed to uneconomically low levels. This has sent demand soaring, while at the same time reducing the incentive to risk money in the search for new supplies of gas. Inevitable result: shortage.

What can be done?

In the short term, very little. A more rational price structure would help, of course. But it generally takes from three to seven years to explore and develop production from a new field, and in certain "frontier" areas the lead time can be even longer. And some groups, well-intentioned but ill-informed, are making it impossible for oil companies to explore for new gas reserves in the most promising areas—beneath the waters of the outer continental shelf.

The irony, as far as this part of the country is concerned, is this: Any gas found beneath the waters off New England will be brought ashore by pipelines. It will burn cleanly when consumed. And it will be transported and distributed with minimal risk of environmental damage.

Meanwhile, the federal government has approved the importation of liquefied natural gas from overseas that will cost twice as much delivered to New York Harbor as domestic natural gas delivered here. This is a classic case: The government creates a man-made shortage by ill-conceived regulatory policies. Then it bails out on supply by socking the consumer with prices for imported gas that would have induced greater (and more secure) domestic gas supplies.

Our nation still has a chance to keep the gas shortage from worsening. What's most needed is broad public awareness that there is no real conflict between a clean environment and larger supplies of natural gas.

Given such awareness, the federal government can proceed with outer continental shelf lease sales and can overhaul a system of price regulation that has boomeranged spectacularly.

Exhibit 1A-18

43

Why do two networks refuse to run this commercial?

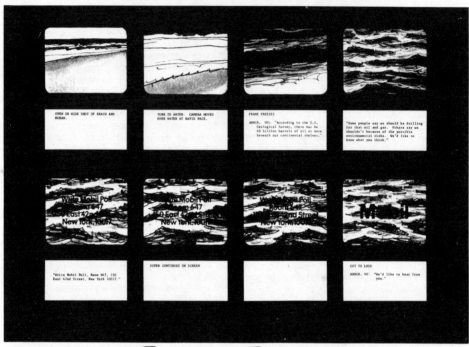

 CBS:
"We regret that the subject matter of this commercial...deals with a controversial issue of public importance and does not fall within our 'goods and services' limitation for commercial acceptance."

 ABC:
"This will advise that we have reviewed the above-captioned commercial and are unable to grant an approval for use over our facilities."

 NBC:
"Approved as submitted."

As you can see from the storyboard reproduced above, we want to ask the public how it feels about offshore drilling.

But the policies of two national television networks prevent us from asking this question.

This is dangerous, it seems to us. Any restraint on free discussion is dangerous. Any policy that restricts the flow of information or ideas is potentially harmful.

The networks say that the public's need for information is best served in news programs prepared by broadcast journalists.

Behind the networks' rejection of idea advertising may be the fear that demands for equal time will be made. We have a reasonable answer to that. We offer to pay for equal time, when the request is legitimate.

We think *more* discussion, not less, is needed of vital issues such as the issue of America's energy needs. We're willing to buy the time to say what we should be saying. We're willing to buy time so you can hear opposing views.

But two big networks aren't willing to make time available, in this case.

You know the principle at stake here. You've seen it in writing, more than once:
"Congress shall make no law... abridging the freedom of speech."

You've seen it in the First Amendment to the Constitution of the United States. So have we.

We'd like to know what you think about either of these issues. Write Room 647, 150 East 42nd Street, New York, N.Y. 10017.

Mobil®

Exhibit 1A–19

LAST YEAR 190 MILLION AMERICANS PAID FOR A TRAIN RIDE THEY NEVER GOT.

Actually, it was some 194 million Americans, since there were no more than 19 million trips taken on Amtrak trains.

The 19 million who rode paid $223 million for the trip, while the 194 million of us who did not paid $250 million just for the privilege of staying home.

We were the ones who really got taken for a ride.

The facts:

The painful truth is that Amtrak today represents more than a nickel-per-passenger-mile subsidy to support a form of transportation serving only a small percentage of America's needs. Think about it — how many times last year were you on an Amtrak train? The chances

are 9 in 10 that your answer was "never." Yet, if you pay taxes, you're paying for every mile that train travels.

By contrast, this country's intercity bus industry actually *paid* nearly $90 million in taxes last year (in addition to payroll and other miscellaneous taxes of the types also paid by Amtrak) rather than *collecting* $250 million in subsidy as Amtrak did. It costs Amtrak over 11 cents a passenger-mile to run a train in this country, more than a nickel of which is paid by the American taxpayer whether he ever boards that train or not. It only costs 5.2 cents per mile to ride the bus, approximately 10 percent of which is returned to the public via the taxes the bus pays.

Which would you say is the better way to go?

With a tax-*eating* Amtrak system which serves only 457 destinations, or a tax-*paying* bus system which serves a full 15,000 communities coast-to-coast? And don't kid yourself — the virtual nationalization of our rail system under Amtrak is a very real threat to the future existence of a free-enterprise intercity bus system.

Because not only does Amtrak not currently serve America's needs, it never can. Even if its limited routes were expanded to cover all the railroad lines in the country, still that would only total some 200,000 miles. Compare that to the bus which, because it runs on roads like

our cars, can travel *19 times* farther, or a full 3,800,000 miles of highways, local roads and streets to serve us wherever we happen to be.

Amtrak's own president says "it'll take billions of dollars, five years and billions of dollars," for him to be "totally proud" of Amtrak. Meanwhile, the finest network of roads and highways in the entire world waits right outside our door, fully operable today.

Obviously, somebody's on the wrong track.

This message paid for by America's Intercity Bus Industry, which also pays its own way in serving America's needs daily.

NATIONAL ASSOCIATION OF MOTOR BUS OWNERS
1025 Connecticut Avenue, Washington, D.C. 20036

Exhibit 1A–20

45

That rugged American individualist down on the farm needs your support.

A lot of people think the rugged individualist is a thing of the past in America. That might be true in some places, but it certainly isn't true on most of the nation's farms.

Dairy farmers like Gary and Greg Van Slyke and their families start their 14½ hour day at 4 A.M.—and those cows don't shut down for weekends or holidays, either.

Because of farmers like Gary and Greg, America has the best agricultural production in the world. But the Van Slykes, like all family farmers, need some help to compete in today's world of giant corporate buyers and sellers. That's why they belong to several cooperatives.

To help insure the future security of their families and their farms, Gary and Greg's families joined a non-profit farmer-owned milk marketing cooperative. The Van Slykes and other family farmers bargain through their cooperative to help each other get fair prices for their milk products.

But the future isn't so rosy. A law called the Capper-Volstead Act, passed in 1922 to permit the formation of modern farmer cooperatives, is under attack. Some people in government believe that Capper-Volstead permits co-ops to engage in practices that violate the nation's anti-trust laws. They want to prevent farmers like Gary and Greg Van Slyke from strengthening their cooperative effort—an effort which helps the Van Slykes stay in business and get a fair price for their milk.

What these people don't realize is that farmer cooperatives are all that stand between many family farmers and financial disaster. Co-ops give farmers like Gary and Greg Van Slyke a way to compete effectively with giant food processors and retailers. Cooperatives provide the kind of bargaining power that comes only from organized effort. Whenever farmers have joined together and formed a strong marketing cooperative, there's been more competition. And that helps consumers.

What will happen to Gary and Greg if our government alters or weakens today's farmer cooperatives? They will be forced to fend for themselves at the bargaining table, where large buyers will frequently lower the prices they will pay for their goods.

What does this mean to you? Just this: without the competition that the Van Slykes and family farmers like them provide in the food industry through cooperatives, it will be much easier for large food companies to raise prices. Very simply, the food you buy could become even more expensive.

Gary and Greg Van Slyke can't afford to lose their co-op. And neither can you. Isn't it time we all supported our farmer cooperatives?

Gary and Greg Van Slyke
Dairy Farmers

Pike, New York
Cooperative Members

Farmer Cooperatives.
They're doing the country a lot of good.

This message was brought to you by over a million farmers through their cooperative associations and organizations. For more information, contact The National Council of Farmer Cooperatives, 1129 Twentieth St., N.W., Washington, D.C. 20036. (202) 659-1525.

Exhibit 1A-21

46

WE PLEAD GUILTY

An open letter to the American people from the employees of the World's Most Experienced Airline

After a decade of dangling in a storm of outrageous discrimination both at home and abroad and writhing every time the international oil cartels raised their oil prices the 32,500 men and women of Pan American World Airways have a few confessions we would like to get off our chests.

We plead guilty first of all of having worked our tails off for nearly 50 years carrying the spirit of American private enterprise to the rest of the world. We admit also to pioneering every significant overseas air route.

We plead guilty of actively having prevented the outflow of more than four hundred million dollars a year from the American balance of payments and of kicking them directly into the nation's economy.

We plead guilty of having flown two million American servicemen out of Viet Nam on five day combat leaves on a cost plus one dollar contract. We admit also providing the defense department a fleet of perfectly maintained fully crewed airplanes that were used extensively in World War II, Berlin, Korea and Indo China.

We plead guilty of overtly supporting the American aerospace industry. Pan Am was the first to operate the flying boats, the intercontinental 707 and the Jumbo 747. We cannot say at this point in time how many billions of dollars have been generated by foreign airlines following our leadership in the purchase of these new airplanes.

We plead guilty of having once been an enormously successful private enterprise. We admit also failing to report a crime as it was taking place. The men and women of Pan Am have watched their great airline being reduced over the last decade from a healthy contributing national resource to a potentially poor paralyzed welfare patient.

Finally we've been bled white by this recent oil crisis business . . . now we're in trouble and we think that the American people can see why merely by asking a few simple questions of our own government.

Ask our own government first of all why the postal department pays the foreign airlines as much as six times what it pays Pan Am for hauling the same U.S. mail. Not receiving the same pay for the same work costs Pan Am 40 million dollars a year.

Ask our own government why nothing is ever done about overseas airports that charge Americans exorbitant landing fees. Qantas airlines for example pays under three hundred dollars to land their Jumbo 747 in San Francisco. Pan Am pays forty two hundred dollars to land in Sydney, Australia. Not paying foreign governments the same User Fees that their airlines pay in America costs Pan Am 12 million dollars a year.

Ask our own government why the U.S. export-import bank loans money to airlines of so-called underdeveloped nations like France, Japan and Saudi Arabia at six per cent interest while Pan Am pays twelve per cent. Their low interest loans are used to buy airplanes that they use to compete against Pan Am. Not allowing Pan American access to these same interest rates means that we pay seven million dollars more than the foreign airlines for the same jumbo jet.

Ask our own government why it is opposed to letting Pan Am fly passengers within our own country . . . it just doesn't make sense. The domestic airlines now have rights to the international routes that we pioneered and the foreign airlines now serve more cities in the United States than we do. The right to compete freely at home . . . the most elemental privilege of a free enterprise society . . . has always been denied Pan Am.

You see when it comes right down to it Pan Am does a lot more than compete with other airlines. We compete with whole countries. Some times even our own. The men and women of Pan Am are just not the type who enjoy asking for a handout. The only subsidy that we have ever needed was fair treatment. From our own government.

If Pan Am were allowed to have domestic routes within the United States . . . to borrow from the export/import bank . . . or to pay reasonable landing fees overseas . . . or to receive equal postal rates from our own government we wouldn't need any subsidy at all. In fact we wouldn't need to have taken up a collection to run this ad.

THE EMPLOYEES OF PAN AM

THIS MESSAGE WAS PAID FOR BY THE EMPLOYEES OF PAN AM IN FLORIDA.

Exhibit 1A–22

THE COMPETITIVE
We believe in it...

The <u>Modern</u> Little Red Hen.

Once upon a time, there was a little red hen who scratched about the barnyard until she uncovered some grains of wheat. She called her neighbors and said, "If we plant this wheat, we shall have bread to eat. Who will help me plant it?"

"Not I," said the cow.

"Not I," said the duck.

"Not I," said the pig.

"Not I," said the goose.

"Then I will," said the little red hen. And she did. The wheat grew tall and ripened into golden grain. "Who will help me reap my wheat?" asked the little red hen.

"Not I," said the duck.

"Out of my classification," said the pig.

"I'd lose my seniority," said the cow.

"I'd lose my unemployment compensation," said the goose.

"Then I will," said the little red hen, and she did.

At last it came time to bake the bread. "Who will help me bake the bread?" asked the little red hen.

"That would be overtime for me," said the cow.

"I'd lose my welfare benefits," said the duck.

"I'm a dropout and never learned how," said the pig.

"If I'm to be the only helper, that's discrimination," said the goose.

"Then I will," said the little red hen.

She baked five loaves and held them up for her neighbors to see.

They all wanted some and, in fact, demanded a share. But the little red hen said, "No, I can eat the five loaves myself."

"Excess profits!" cried the cow.

"Capitalist leech!" screamed the duck.

"I demand equal rights!" yelled the goose.

And the pig just grunted. And they painted "unfair" picket signs and marched round and round the little red hen, shouting obscenities.

When the government agent came, he said to the little red hen, "You must not be greedy."

"But I earned the bread," said the little red hen.

"Exactly," said the agent. "That is the wonderful free enterprise system. Anyone in the barnyard can earn as much as he wants. But under our modern government regulations, the productive workers must divide their product with the idle."

And they lived happily ever after, including the little red hen, who smiled and clucked, "I am grateful, I am grateful."

But her neighbors wondered why she never again baked any more bread.

In the conclusion of the required business of the 1975 Pennwalt Annual Meeting, Chairman and President William P. Drake, commenting on the state of the company's industry's economy and this in this adaptation of a modern version of the well-known fable of The Little Red Hen.

ENTERPRISE SYSTEM
...here's why:

Dedication to the simple truths implied in the story of "The Modern Little Red Hen" built this company, and has guided its successful growth.

Today, Pennwalt supplies socially useful products, including chemicals, dental products, pharmaceuticals and equipment. 80 percent of our sales are concentrated in these five major markets:

- Agriculture and food processing
- Chemical process industries
- Environmental cleanup
- Health
- Plastics

But unlike the unfortunate Modern Little Red Hen, we have been able to share our "bread" with the many who have helped produce it, while at the same time fulfilling the other obligations to society expected of a responsible, profitable corporate citizen. This sharing is in the form of equitable wages and fringe benefits, quality products fairly priced, substantial purchases, taxes, the support of charitable and cultural organizations and, from what's left, dividends to our shareholders.

That we have been successful is evidenced by the fact that we started paying a regular dividend on our common stock 114 years ago and have not missed a payment since.

We think our performance bears this out:

Net Sales.................	$405,507	$441,010	$504,034	$641,002	$713,736
Net Earnings..............	$ 13,050	$ 16,072	$ 20,113	$ 26,983	$ 31,633*
Per Share of Common Stock..	$ 1.22	$ 1.58	$ 2.13	$ 2.81	$ 3.25*

*Before special credit of $1.83 (1000) or $.19 per share.

Exhibit 1A-23

48

Exhibit 1A–24

49

The Cincotta-Conklin Bill
will make it possible
for savings banks to offer
checking accounts.

These checking accounts
will be <u>free</u>.

They will include a $1,000
overdraft privilege.

This bill, now before the
New York State Legislature, is
clearly in the public interest.

THE COMMERCIAL BANKS WANT TO KILL THIS BILL.

IF THEY WIN, YOU LOSE.

Commercial banks are opposed to this bill. They have a monopoly on checking accounts in this state and do not welcome competition. They particularly dislike the idea that savings banks will offer *free* checking accounts. To meet this competition, commercial banks will have to do the same thing or at least lower their charges.

If the commercial banks have this bill defeated or amended to death, it is the people who will lose. If you favor free checking accounts at savings banks write your State Senator or Assemblyman today.

Savings Banks
the human side of banking

SAVINGS BANKS ASSOCIATION OF NEW YORK STATE

256-10 N76 4 5A
As appearing in
Newspapers - Week of April 26, 1976
1000 Lines (5 col x 200 li)

TE PHOTO - Photo (212) 757-9292
C P Promotions   Ad No 256-10 N76 4's & 5'A   Proof One 4-22-76

TE Century Expanded/Bold 1 st
Century Expanded/Bold 1 st
17 10 Century Expanded/Ital

FOR REPRODUCTION

Exhibit 1A–25

Exhibit 1A-26

51

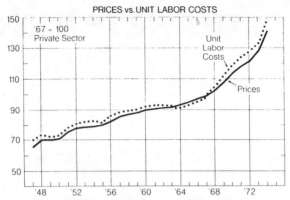

PRICES vs. UNIT LABOR COSTS

'67 = 100
Private Sector

Unit Labor Costs

Prices

Proof that there is no free lunch

All the labor contracts and threats of strikes in the world can't argue with that chart— when unearned wage increases or low productivity send unit labor costs up, *prices go up.*

And there is one way to get prices down–greater productivity.

The less you produce, the higher the cost. The higher the cost, the higher the price. The higher the price, the fewer who can buy, and therefore the fewer the jobs.

So–look at the chart, and let's get busy.

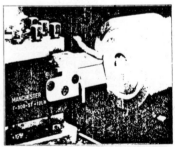

Warner & Swasey's Manchester Division offers metalworking plants lower cost per cut in cutoff, grooving and trepanning. A face grooving operation, using a Manchester carbide grooving tool, is shown here.

THE WARNER & SWASEY COMPANY
Executive Offices 11000 Cedar Avenue, Cleveland, Ohio 44106

Productivity equipment and systems in machine tools, textile and construction machinery

Exhibit 1A–27

52

Appendix 1B

The TRACC RECORD

Benson & Benson, Inc.,
Princeton, N.J.

Criteria for Defining an Institutional Advertisement

1. It is a display ad—hence all classified advertising is excluded.

2. It is placed by a manufacturer or service company—hence advertising placed by trade associations, cooperatives, political interest groups and private individuals is excluded even though these advertisements deal with topics found in corporate advertising.

3. It discusses the company, the industry, or economic and social matters.

4. It does not promote individual products or services except to illustrate another point.

5. It is not a legal notice, for which reason bank statements of conditions and notices to security holders are excluded.

Media Coverage

Coverage is based on advertisements appearing in magazines or newspapers. Currently, the data are collected from twenty magazines and newspapers. The publications included in the survey are business magazines (*Business Week, Forbes, Fortune, Harvard Business Review, Dun's Review*); daily newspapers (*The New York Times, The Washington Post, The Wall Street Journal*); weekly news magazines (*Newsweek, Sports Illustrated, Time, U.S. News & World Report, New Yorker*); and some other magazines (*Atlantic, Harper's, National Geographic, Saturday Review, Psychology Today, Scientific American, Reader's Digest*). *Dun's Review* and the *New Yorker* were added in the fourth quarter of 1975 analysis. However, the TRACC RECORD contends that the addition of these two magazines did not materially affect either quarter-to-quarter comparison or overall trends.

The intent is to show coverage in a selection representing the broadest possible spectrum, rather than an exhaustive survey, of corporate advertising. Content is classified into sixteen categories with numerous subcategories (nearly 200 in all) in each category. Each ad is classified in terms of "major topic" and

Information contained in this section was furnished by Benson & Benson, Inc., 33 Witherspoon Street, Princeton, N.J. 08540. The author is grateful to Mr. Kenneth A. Longman, president of Benson & Benson, for his cooperation in furnishing these data.

Table 1B-1
Topics Ranked by Frequency of Mention

| | 3rd Quarter 1975* | | | | 4th Quarter 1975† | | | |
| | % of Advertisers as Main Point | Mentions as | | | % of Advertisers as Main Point | Mentions as | | |
Topic		Main Point	Secondary Point	Total Mentions		Main Point	Secondary Point	Total Mentions
Energy	15.7%	13.9%	23.3%	37.2%	13.7%	13.3%	23.9%	37.2%
Economics/regulation	9.0	5.4	14.4	19.8	4.4	3.9	10.1	14.0
Ecology	7.6	4.4	10.1	14.5	6.0	3.8	6.3	10.1
Corporate social responsibility	6.6	7.5	2.1	9.6	9.1	8.7	1.1	9.8
Major capital investment	3.5	2.5	6.2	8.7	4.4	2.2	4.0	6.2
Consumerism	3.5	2.0	2.8	4.8	3.0	1.5	1.2	2.7
Recruiting/labor relations	2.0	0.8	0.9	1.7	3.6	1.5	0.8	2.3
Acquisitions/mergers	1.7	0.9	0.2	1.1	2.8	1.0	0.7	1.7

Source: Benson & Benson, Inc., Princeton, N. J., 1975.

*For all sixteen categories, *n* = 458 advertisers and 1,768 insertions.

†For all sixteen categories, *n* = 497 advertisers and 2,264 insertions.

Note: The summary code definitions for the sixteen categories are as follows: *Diversity:* Mention of various products, services, or concerns incorporated in the text of the ad or in list form. Lists of subsidiaries or mentions of multinationality are also included. *Technology:* Research, development, or application. Also includes quality control. *Productivity:* Increase in human or machine productivity. *Energy:* Technology, exploration, conservation, conversion, energy shortage, or mention of specific energy source. *Ecology:* Natural resource management, recycling, air or water pollution abatement, solid waste management. *Corporate social responsibility:* Grants to sponsor entertainment or education programs, employment or training for minority group members or women. *Consumerism:* Communication with company by the consumer, consumer protection programs (e.g., unit pricing). *Major capital investment:* Expenditures for projects, facilities, expansion, pollution controls, energy. *Financial performance:* Reference to earnings or sales, dividend announcements. *Economics and regulation:* Comments on inflation, wage and price controls, legislation, government regulation, supply and demand, or the free enterprise system. *Recruiting and labor relations:* Recruitment, working environment of company, references to strikes, employee recognition. *Acquisitions/mergers:* Merger, acquisition, and incorporation announcements, and statements for or against tender offers. *Name change or protection:* Announcement of name change or new ticker symbol, trademark protection. *Corporate activity:* Information about corporate activities or products (no attempt to sell products) not classified elsewhere. *Bicentennial:* Any reference to the Bicentennial. *Miscellaneous:* Response to rumor or legal situation, expression or appreciation, recognition received, or no ad content other than "send for information."

"secondary topics" with single ads having one major topic and one or more secondary topics. Table 1B-1 shows a comparison of ad frequency in various categories during the last two quarters of 1975.

The table shows that concern for energy-related topics was used in over 37 percent of the insertions. In terms of comparisons between the third and fourth quarters of 1975, the percentage of all advertisers decreased. For economics/ regulation, it decreased from 9 percent to 4.4 percent; for ecology, from 7.6 percent to 6 percent; but it increased for corporate social responsibility from 6.6 percent to 9.1 percent.

In the fourth quarter, there were 21 companies using energy as the main point (mentioning in five or more insertions). Of these, five were oil companies; four, utilities; and the remainder, manufacturers of oil drilling equipment, eletric power generation equipment, petrochemicals, and one bank. The oil companies and utilities accounted for over 40 percent of all insertions in this category. It is interesting to note that American Electric Power Company was at the top of the list in the category.

There were four companies using economics/regulation as the main point— Mobil Oil, American Electric Power, Bankers Trust, and ITT, in that order, with Mobil and American Electric Power accounting for 31 percent of the insertions. Ecology as the main point was used by five companies—the Bell System, Alcoa, International Paper, Potlatch Industries, and Crane. Of these, the Bell System accounted for 16 percent of the insertions, followed by Alcoa, Potlatch, and International Paper, with each accounting for 8 percent of the total insertions in this category.

There were eight companies talking about corporate social responsibility as the main point in their advertisements. Of these eight, four were oil companies (Mobil, Gulf, Exxon, and Arco) accounting for 59 percent of all insertions in this category. The other four companies were IBM (9 percent), ITT (5 percent), Hueblein (3 percent), and Xerox (3 percent).

2

The Rationale for Advocacy Advertising

The goose doesn't worry much about its reputation. It is too busy creating wealth and benefits and providing jobs, in other words, laying golden eggs. But then some dissatisfied person comes along and fires a shot at the goose ... Soon another critic takes a few shots ... finally a crowd has gathered and everyone is blasting away. The goose knows it is getting weaker ... but it still isn't worried ... The goose believes it has only to hang up there and one day the crowd will realize where the golden eggs are coming from, come to its sense and cease fire. Meantime the goose struggles to stay aloft. By now, as all of us are surely aware, the crowd shooting at the golden goose we know as business shows no signs of dispersing. Instead it has grown huge and even more hostile toward the goose. Perhaps it is time to ask: why is no one rushing to the defense of this endangered species?
—John D. Harper, retired chairman, ALCOA[1]

It may be no coincidence that advocacy advertising became significant at the time of the energy crisis and the Arab oil boycott, when the oil industry was accused of creating artificial fuel shortages, and worse, of raking in windfall profits at the expense of the general public. Furthermore, business was suffering from a lack of public confidence and the public assigned a low credibility to statements by business about its conduct.

The rationale for advocacy advertising falls into one or more of the following categories:

1. To counteract public hostility to corporate activities because of ignorance or misinformation
2. To counter the spread of misleading information by the critics of business and to fill the need for greater explication of complex issues
3. To foster the values of the free enterprise system
4. To counteract inadequate access to and bias in the news media

The first three of these four categories will be analyzed in the following pages. The fourth rationale, inadequate access to media, will be treated in a

---

Unless otherwise specifically stated, all direct quotes in this chapter are from personal interviews or written communications with the author.

57

separate chapter. This explanation has perhaps the widest currency among businessmen and therefore needs more detailed treatment. In addition, it covers a host of other issues that deserve specific attention.

To Counteract Public Hostility

This is one of the more common, prevalent, and persistent explanations given not only for advocacy advertising, but for all corporate institutional advertising. Surveys conducted by Opinion Research Corporation in 1972 show that the public's image of business and approval of its actions is now at its lowest since the early 1960s. For example, 60 percent of the people have a "low" opinion of business, one-third of the public thinks that government should limit profits, and two-thirds think that government should control prices. More than half the people think that industry is doing "very little" about air and water pollution, and more than three-fourths think that "consumer" laws are necessary. Furthermore, the public thinks that after-tax profits of corporations average 28 cents on a sales dollar, compared with slightly over 4 cents.[2] Business sees this public antipathy as a harbinger of greater public pressure for further intrusion into and increased regulation of its activities by government agencies and private groups.

It would improve our understanding of the situation if we were to analyze the logic of business actions in terms of the role of business in society. Business is a social institution and therefore must depend on a society's acceptance of its role and activities in order to survive and grow. At any given time, there is likely to be a gap between performance and societal expectations caused by certain business actions or changing expectations. A continuously widening gap would cause business to lose its legitimacy and threaten its survival.[3] Business must therefore strive to narrow this "legitimacy gap" in order to claim its share of a society's physical and human resources and to maintain maximum discretionary control over its internal decision making and external dealings. The legitimacy gap can be narrowed in one of the three ways shown in Exhibit 2-1.

BUSINESS STRATEGIES
1. Do not change performance, but change public perception of business performance through education and information.
2. If changes in public perception are not possible, change the symbols used to describe business performance, thereby making it congruent with public perception. Note that no change in actual performance is called for.
3. In case both (1) and (2) are ineffective, bring about changes in business performance, thereby closely matching it with society's expectations.

Exhibit 2-1

The strategy of public education has historically been favored by business since it is the least painful and easiest to undertake. There is a belief in large segments of the business community that the contributions of business to the American way of life have not been properly understood and appreciated. There is also the conviction that public attitudes will change once people have been informed of and educated about the virtues of American business and industry. But there is overwhelming evidence that such campaigns have been singularly unsuccessful. As early as 1952, William H. Whyte, Jr., noted the utter failure of the billion-dollar attempt of the two earlier decades to "sell business to America." According to Whyte, "The free enterprise campaign is psychologically unsound, it is abstract, it is defensive, and it is negative. Most important, in a great many of its aspects it represents a shocking lack of faith in the American people, and in some cases downright contempt."[4]

Irving Kristol suggests that one of the reasons for the failure of such campaigns may lie in the threefold confusion by business of the process of education, the procedures of advertising, and the purposes of propaganda. But he maintains that advertising is the wrong vehicle for any kind of education. The purpose of education is to foster a growth in the comprehension of abstract ideas and concepts, to raise questions about prevailing beliefs, and to encourage intellectual inquiry. Advertising, on the other hand, is intended to provide answers that are definite and specific; to persuade people to do things; and in general, to minimize inquiry and uncertainty. Kristol states:

These are two radically different modes of communication, and their admixture is corrupting to both. It also happens to be ineffectual. People just don't read advertisements in the press, or listen to them on television, in an educational frame of mind—i.e., a mind that is attentive and energetic.
Propaganda has its own unique purpose, which is to shape specific attitudes on specific issues. It can be effectual indeed—but only under special circumstances. One prerequisite for successful propaganda is that it not appear to be propaganda at all, but rather "news" or "facts" or "research." Another is that it concentrate on the vilification of one's enemy, not on the celebration of one's own virtues. . . . But the business corporation that is concerned for its integrity and self-respect is in no position to engage in this kind of unscrupulous ideological warfare—and God forbid that it should try to learn.[5]

Kristol also believes it absurd to think that institutional advertising can serve any educational purpose. Such advertising collapses into one glossy blur and only serves to pacify the anxious chief executive. Kristol's analysis is similar to the findings of a 1950 study by the Brookings Institution on the effectiveness of attempts at economic education by business. The study concluded that private efforts toward educating the public on the basis of economics, private enterprise, and competition were generally quite superficial, mostly self-serving, and largely ineffective. The study concluded that real improvements in economic education can be best achieved through improved teaching efforts in established educational institutions.[6]

In a similar vein, Whyte commented that since mass education efforts by business were geared to show "how good business has been to everyone," the so-called "facts" often provoked negative reaction. What appeared as spirited affirmation of its viewpoint to business seemed to others as unsolicited apologia or undeserved self-approbation. This was so because many of the things for which business was busily congratulating itself were in fact achieved after the strong opposition of a good part of U.S. business.[7] Marshall Loeb, a senior editor of *Time* magazine, states that "Americans understand the free enterprise system. Everyone knows what it is. Campaigns to 'educate' the people about free enterprise have tended to be loaded with cliches, which nobody listens to." There is little attention in these campaigns to the possibility that the disagreement between the corporations and the public may not be owing to lack of recognition of business's contributions to society, but instead may have resulted from the corporations' failure to appreciate and understand their own role in a society whose expectations have changed. Such an education program seldom considers the need for a change in business performance, because to do so would be to attack the status quo and thereby frustrate the purpose of the campaign. Any obvious lapses in performance are attributed to individual businesses and explained away in terms of the rotten apple theory.[a]

However, the protestations of businesspeople ring hollow when a large number of the most prestigious United States companies have been found to be bad apples. "Many of those caught undercut the rotten-apple theory by contending that most companies engage in such behavior anyway."[8] Robert M. Bleiberg, editor of *Barron's*, adds, "Current business practices might not square with the free market. Some of the worst transgressions against private enterprise come from executive suites." The quality of communication thus becomes so debased as to be ineffective.[9]

A partial answer to the problem may be found in the fact that business invariably appears to be defending the status quo rather than managing change or shaping it constructively. Consider, for example, the findings of another survey conducted by Opinion Research Corporation on behalf of the Pitney Bowes Corporation. When a cross-section of 531 U.S. corporate executives was asked whether legislation would be effective in preventing bribery of foreign government officials by U.S. nationals, 92 percent felt that it would not—that such bribery would continue despite legislation.[10] This viewpoint was further confirmed by a survey of businesspeople conducted by the Conference Board, an independent research organization financed by American companies, in

---

[a]The feeling of persecution is quite widespread among businesspeople. For example, Mr. Gabriel Hauge, Chairman of Manufacturers Hanover Trust, says that business leadership "bears a heavy burden because a few members of the fraternity knowingly broke the laws. The number of spotty apples in our barrel is doubtless no more nor less than in other barrels in society, but the obloquy falls on us." Cited in "The Embattled Businessman," *Newsweek,* February 9, 1976, p. 57.

December 1975. The survey found that "large numbers of American business-men believe that they not only have the right but even the obligation to pay bribes and kickbacks abroad to win contracts for their companies." Among the other survey findings were indications that such payoffs may be more wide-spread than had been generally believed; that businesspeople were unwilling to take the initiative in investigating unusual payments unless foreign governments first convicted the recipients of alleged bribes; and that they felt the public and the media were placing unrealistic demands on business.[11]

Notwithstanding the failure of this approach, corporate leaders continue to launch new educational campaigns—e.g., the one being planned by the oil industry group on the desirability of maintaining the present size of large oil companies because it is in the public interest.[12] Even some of business's strongest supporters have been struck by the ineptness and poor timing of some of the public relations campaigns.[13] Furthermore, the media blitz has been often so heavy that it has had the effect of overkill, leading Preston Tisch, president of Lowes Corporation, to comment that business leaders "have fallen into the habit of thinking of public opinion as something to be molded and manipulated for their own purposes. What's really needed are new higher standards of openness and accuracy."[14]

The latest effort, and one of the more ambitious of the current campaigns to promote the free enterprise system, is that recently launched by the Adver-tising Council, Inc., a nonprofit industry group based in New York. The first phase of the campaign, already completed, was made possible by a grant of $239,000 from the U.S. Department of Commerce.[15] This phase consisted of a study of the attitudes of Americans toward the United States economic system and the preparation of a booklet[17] explaining that system. The second phase of the project, comprised of production and distribution of ad campaign spots, is expected to take two years and cost $765,000.[17]

The idea for the campaign was first proposed by Howard J. Morgens, chairman of the board of Proctor & Gamble, the country's largest advertiser, in an address to the Advertising Council in December 1973 when he was given an award for public service. Entitled "The Profit Motive and Public Interest," the address laments the lack of understanding on the part of the public of "profits" and "the profit motive." Mr. Morgens argues for better education of the Ameri-can people about the free enterprise system, and suggests that businesspeople should not be defensive about their activities but should aggressively demon-strate their contributions to society. He also downgraded the role of government in economic activities by alluding to the bureaucratic inefficiencies inherent in any government operation. His address is an excellent summation of business's viewpoint about the need for promoting the free enterprise system.[18]

The Ad Council campaign has come under severe criticism from certain business and nonbusiness sources both for its sponsorship and its rationale. The Commerce Department justified the grant as falling within the scope of its basic mission to foster and promote the domestic and international commerce of the United States.[b] The subcommittee chairman, Congressman Benjamin S. Rosenthal (D, N.Y.) criticized the Commerce Department for the inappropriateness of using funds allocated for the Office of Minority Business Enterprise and Economic Development Administration for the Ad Council grant. He also pointed out that the by-laws of the Advertising Council prohibit it from accepting any government subsidy. Typical of the business criticism of the campaign were the remarks of Donald H. McGannon, chairman of Westinghouse Broadcasting and former chairman of the Ad Council: "Explaining the economic system in this country is not a simplistic thing. I don't think it can be done with spot announcements and slogans. We tried with inflation and productivity, and we were less than successful."[19]

In response to the Ad Council campaign, The People's Bicentennial Commission, a radical alternative to the official government group, has decided to launch an ad campaign to counter the "massive propaganda campaign to sell the corporate view of the American economic system." This group is threatening to seek equal time from the broadcast media if they air the council commercials under the fairness doctrine.[20]

To Counter the Spread of Misleading Information by Critics

The companies using advocacy ads rationalize their actions on the grounds that complex issues are often oversimplified, left unexplained, or given one-sided treatment in the news media, thereby creating false impressions in the minds of readers.

Hostile Critics

Business attributes a large part of the public's hostility to the rise of various groups opposed to business on intellectual grounds, opposed to economic growth, and proposing a socialist society and public control of the nation's productive resources. According to a National Association of Manufacturers' discussion paper, "One of the causes of the antibusiness bias arises from a *power struggle being played deliberately by intellectual thought leaders.*"[21] In the now-

---

[b]Robert S. Milligan, Director, Office of Policy Development, U.S. Department of Commerce states: "The average citizen today is severely challenged to understand the significance and implications of the extensive economy-related data and issues to which he or she is exposed on a continuing basis through all forms of media. This is true because of the scope of our economy, the complex interrelationships which determine its behavior, the general practice of not requiring economic course work in our secondary schools, and the technical terms traditionally used to describe economic conditions, trends and policies." *Oversight Hearings on Advertising Council,* p. 3.

famous Powell Memorandum, Justice Powell wrote: "Businessmen have not been trained or equipped to conduct guerrilla warfare with those who propagandize against the system." He goes on to state that, although businessmen have performed their traditionally assigned tasks well, "they have shown little stomach for hard-nosed contest with their critics, and little skill in effective intellectual and philosophical debate."[22]

Mobil made similar claims in responding to a petition made to the Federal Trade Commission (FTC) by six United States senators and congressmen asking the FTC to require substantiation of the various claims made by oil, utilities, and other energy-related companies in their institutional or public image advertising.[23] The company agreed with the petitioners on the need for a complete and open discussion regarding the environment and energy and contended that any restriction on this discussion would be extremely injurious to the public interest. The issue of the energy crisis was not unlike other major issues that have generated broad public concern in recent times, e.g., Vietnam and civil rights. However, it was the first time that the focus of inquiry was on the private sector of the economy—namely, the oil industry—and that there has been "a public debate on the legitimacy of the operation of particular companies such as Mobil."[24]

Mobil contended that the oil industry's critics did not have sufficient understanding of an extremely complex industry. By emphasizing the views of these critics, the news media had given undue circulation to what the company regarded as the uninformed and inaccurate view that the oil companies should be blamed for the energy shortage.

Explanation of Issues

The need for explanation of complex issues has two aspects: One is to explain more fully the corporate side of the story, which the company feels has been ignored or misrepresented by the news media or spokespersons for other interested groups. The second is the provision of better information to the public, because a poorly informed public could press for the adoption of measures that would only serve to worsen the situation.

In a sense, this is another version of "public education" strategy applied to specific issues and against specific critics. However, an analysis of the various recent advocacy ad campaigns indicates that the promise of these two objectives remains largely unfilled. (Two in-depth case studies of advocacy campaigns are presented in Chapters 4 and 5. See also Chapter 1, Appendix 1A for specimen ads of some other current advocacy campaigns.) The prime emphasis of these ads, with few important exceptions, is on getting the public's attention. Ads are just not the place for long, complicated arguments. Thus, issues are presented with catchy headlines and simple messages, with the primary emphasis on reinforcing in the minds of the readers the sponsor's position rather than explaining both sides of a controversy. In a sense, it is ironic, because an analysis of the media selection for these campaigns shows that the emphasis is on getting the attention of a particular segment of the audience—namely, the opinion makers. Yet the contents of the ads, and the simplified and somewhat superficial message, would preclude their being very effective.

Donald Cook, the former chief executive of American Electric Power (AEP) and the chief architect of its ad campaign, takes pride in the fact that the AEP ads were interesting and provocative. He maintains that the whole purpose of advertising would have been lost if the campaign had not caught audience attention. In their successful campaign against the Clean Environment Act Initiative (Proposition 9), Whitaker & Baxter, the San Francisco public relations firm, used promotional strategies that, although certainly effective from the sponsor's viewpoint, could not be considered an example of an informative, objective presentation of complex issues. Their strategy called for the campaign to be *"publicly launched by responsible conservationists, by academicians, labor spokesmen, leaders of the Democratic Party* and joined at the appropriate time in the appropriate fashion by business, industry, agriculture, and the Republican Party leadership." But these groups were used primarily to show broad support; the campaign itself would be effective "only if the utilities and the oil industry—the businesses most directly affected by the initiative—take direct control of the direction of the campaign . . ." (see Chapter 5).

The issues reduced to simple cause-effect relationships were in fact subject to a whole array of intervening variables. Furthermore, the effects on jobs, fuel supplies, and power shortages were often exaggerated to create a dramatic effect. Whitaker explained that an adequate job of discussing complex and controversial issues could not be done through half-page ads or 30-/ and 60-second commercials: "You have to be able to hold their [audience] attention, and that means it [the commercial] should be colorful . . . lively . . . something that takes it out of the ordinary."

A similar viewpoint, but from a different perspective, is echoed by the late Edwin Koupal and Joyce Koupal, co-directors of People's Lobby, a Los Angeles-based activist group and the prime architect of Proposition 9. In explaining their defeat, Joyce Koupal commented: "We did everything wrong. . . . All the . . . confrontations and the charges and countercharges were the wrong tactics for us to use." Edwin Koupal added that, in stressing the emotional aspects of the issue, "we fell into their trap and that was exactly what they wanted us to do." One of the lessons learned from this campaign and successfully employed in later campaigns was: "Keep controversy at a minimum. *Never debate.*" An analysis of the People's Lobby campaign showed it to be qualitatively no better than that of Whitaker & Baxter. It also employed scare tactics and exaggerations of truth. When asked whether, in order to accomplish ends he believed to be in the public interest he would mind using techniques similar to those of his opponents, My. Koupal responded, "I will use any of the political tools available to me as long as I don't break the law. . . . You should use all tools available to you that the political machine of the day will afford you. It is part of becoming grown up in politics, it is part of being honest with yourself in politics, it is part of being a professional." It may have been quite unintentional, but Koupal's statement epitomizes the dangers of advocacy or adversary advertising.

The idea of balanced presentation of facts does not imply that a given advocacy campaign should present all significant arguments on an issue. Businesspeople maintain that, through advocacy campaigns, they present *their* side of the issue to counterbalance the information given the public by their opponents. Thus, the information balance is achieved in the marketplace, where everyone has an opportunity to express his or her viewpoint. It is not in the nature of advocacy advertising to present a balanced picture, since one of its premises is to answer the arguments made by opponents. In an admittedly controversial issue, the sponsor is not likely to present the opposition view in a sympathetic light, because to do so would be to reduce the credibility of his own message. The same logic applies to presenting one's own side with all the qualifying or cautionary remarks needed to be objective about it.

This is borne out by an analysis of ads in the various advocacy campaigns. In the AEP and Pollution Initiative efforts, ad themes suggested that a rise in unemployment, a shortage of energy, and other calamities would befall the populace if their positions were not upheld. (It should be noted that People's Lobby, which supported the passage of the Pollution Initiative, resorted to similar tactics.) Similarly, a Mobil ad indicated that more profits for the *oil companies* would lead to more search and exploration for oil and thus to greater fuel production. If profits are not allowed to increase, the reverse will happen. These ad campaigns were criticized by analysts for containing half truths and for implying direct causal relations where none existed or could be proved.

Commenting on Mobil's ad campaign, Leo Greenland, chief executive officer of the Smith/Greenland Co. advertising agency, felt that Mobil was on a corporate ego trip and that the company was showing its concern over the nation's social problems in only a superficial way.[25] Donald M. Zuckert, executive vice-president of Ted Bates & Co., one of the nation's largest advertising agencies, was also critical of Mobil's campaign. He indicated that the company was not addressing itself to any of the issues purported to be of concern to the oil industry and the public. Instead, "What we saw was self-serving in the worst sense. They're entitled to their political beliefs as individuals but they're making their stockholders pay for an expression of a corporation view."[26]

In the area of environment, industry's advocacy ad campaign attempts to deal with pollution and other environmental problems have taken one or more of the following three forms: exaggerating the meager efforts of the industry in controlling pollution, projecting them as voluntary while in fact they may have been undertaken under threat of government prosecution; downplaying

the adverse consequences of pollution and publicizing adverse economic consequences on jobs and incomes; and implying that voluntary individual action will
largely solve the problem (thereby absolving the firm or industry of substantial
responsibility for controlling pollution). The ads generally have enticing headlines indicating serious social concern and commitment on the part of the
sponsor toward a particular environmental problem. However, the copy seldom
provides any specifics and is full of generalities and homilies like "if we all work
together, we can succeed in improving our environment."[27]

Some companies have made light of the public's concern for pollution and
the environment by treating it as a gimmick. They have thereby not only
lowered their own credibility, but have also called into question some of the real
efforts being made by a handful of companies in the areas of pollution abatement and improvement of the environment.[28]

E.B. Weiss, writing in *Advertising Age,* also chides corporations for trying to
fool people with their antipollution ads:

The current "ain't we noble" school of advertising is precisely the sort of business gambit that makes campus students uptight about business. These public
exhibitions of self-induced amazement over the advertiser's total commitment to
the public weal are indeed incredible in their bland assumption that an intelligent society can be fooled that easily.[29]

The news media have also been trying to get on the bandwagon of antipollution advertising. Several magazines have developed elaborate publicity
materials to persuade corporations to improve their image through antipollution
and environment-related institutional advertising. Most notable of these was the
attempt by *Reader's Digest* to promote an advertising supplement on the
environment that appeared in September 1971. *Reader's Digest* approached
nearly 600 companies and associations. However, despite promises of massive
promotional support by the magazine, only eight companies participated in the
program. According to a study by the Council of Economic Priorities, *Reader's
Digest* made no systematic effort to check the ad content for accuracy. CEP
analysis of four advertisements appearing in the *Digest* showed them to have
unsubstantiable and vague statements, half truths, and gross exaggerations of the
efforts made by the sponsoring companies in cleaning up the environment.[30]

Perhaps the most articulate explanation for advocacy advertising in terms of
presenting the corporation's position was offered by John O'Toole:

Advocacy advertisements do not necessarily explain complex issues any better
than other sources, but they explain the sponsor's viewpoint more thoroughly
when compared with the press reports of some of those issues. I refer specifically
to the issues that arose during the gasoline shortage and the fuel crisis. The
objection on the part of the oil companies, Mobil being the most vocal, was that
the accounts of the press tended to simplify those issues and, during the process

of simplification, put a twist on them. This is natural because it is part of the editorial functions. Mobil went into the issues in greater detail and thereby, at least, initially added to the body of information. To some extent, all information contains the bias of the person providing it, but the more sources of information that an individual has, the better judgment he can make on the issues.

It should be emphasized here that this explanation presumes away the question of the ad content and what kinds of details are being provided the reader by the corporation. In most of the antipollution ads, not only is there little balanced information about both sides of the issue, but the corporations by and large make no effort to present an accurate picture of their own role in both the creation and the abatement of pollution, and of the relationship of their activities to the overall magnitude of the problem. At least in some cases, the corporations that engaged most heavily in antipollution advertising were those found to be the biggest polluters. Although this argument is not being presented to suggest regulation or control of such advertising, it certainly raises doubts about the claims made by various corporations that this form of advertising was being employed to restore sanity and bring more rationality into the public debate.

To Foster the Values of the Free Enterprise System

Business argues that advocacy advertising is needed to foster the values of the free enterprise system, which have been eroded by the ever-expanding shadow of the welfare state, the sapping of individual initiative, freedom, and the work ethic. Thus reinforcing traditional values and beliefs will support the foundation on which free enterprise is built.[31]

The claim of American businesspeople of upholding the American values, e.g., free enterprise and individualism, runs through all of American history. This belief logically leads to the notion that no change in the system is needed and that public education is called for. Thus, Richard S. Gerstenberg, then chairman of General Motors, was being historically quite consistent when he complained in 1972: "The average American has only a hazy idea of what free enterprise means, and much less how it works." He attributed the lowering of business ratings in public opinion polls to the public's ignorance.[32]

In the long run, this argument is perhaps more dangerous and likely to be more counterproductive for the large corporations than all the other arguments combined. The modern corporation in size, scope, and operations bears no resemblance to the classical model of free and competitive markets, private enterprise, and individualism. Thus to seek legitimacy through traditional ideological values is to make corporations highly vulnerable to attack on their own grounds. Furthermore, as George Lodge argues in his book, *The New American Ideology,*

American businessmen have seldom behaved as if they believed in these traditional values.[33]

The same corporations who decry the erosion of American traditions and values and the decline of the capitalistic system are quick to espouse a different framework for the measurement of corporate legitimacy and performance when circumstances call for it. For example, during the Senate Watergate hearings examining the circumstances of ITT's acquisition of Hartford Fire Insurance Co., an ITT attorney in effect stated: "Don't visit that old idea of competition on us. The public interest requires ITT to be big and strong at home so that it can withstand the blows of Allende in Chile, Castro in Cuba, and the Japanese in general. Before you apply the antitrust laws to us, the Secretary of the Treasury, the Secretary of Commerce, and the Council of Economic Advisors should meet to decide what, in the light of our balance-of-payments problems and domestic economic difficulties, the national interest is."[34] At the same time, internal company memos showed that ITT was actively conspiring to undermine and overthrow the Allende government under the guise of protecting "liberty" and "individual freedom," which were "under attack everywhere."[35]

Nor can management legitimacy be justified on the legal model of accountability to stockholders. Melvin Eisenberg of the Boalt Law School, University of California, points out that there is a large gap between the received legal model of corporate legitimacy and the working model of corporate control. Shareholder control of the corporation is a myth perpetuated by management solely for public consumption. Management routinely uses all types of devices to minimize stockholder interference.[36]

Even if one were to assume that corporations actually do believe in capitalism and act accordingly, it is doubtful whether it will protect them from public criticism or encroachment on their prerogatives and activities. Capitalism, like any other social institution, must survive on the foundation of belief on the part of the society that it is a *just* basis for distribution of a nation's wealth. As Irving Kristol, one of the most articulate and thoughtful defenders of capitalism, points out:

There is nothing more natural about capitalist civilization than about many others that have had, or will have, their day. Capitalism represents a sum of human choices about the good life and the good society. These choices inevitably have their associated costs, and after two hundred years the conviction seems to be spreading that the costs have gone out of line.[37]

The image business and business institutions would like to have of themselves and would like the general public to have is not exactly congruent with the reality both as business sees it and as the public experiences it. Some elements of reality do correspond both with the image and the underlying ideology. But both business behavior and rhetoric abound with internal contradictions in such critical areas as government regulation, open competition, the working of the market mechanism, and the role of the individual in society and in enterprise. And yet, all such inconsistent behavior and rhetoric is justified as being within the basic framework of the American private enterprise system. Harmony between ideology and reality does not now exist, if in fact it ever did. What we have now is the creation and protection of something quite radical and different under a rubric that is more familiar, safer, and easier to live with.

An interesting example of the dichotomy between business ideology and reality appeared in a recent advocacy ad by the U.S. Steel Corporation. In this full-page ad, Walter B. Wriston, chairman of Citicorp, the parent holding company of the First National City Bank of New York, advocated a simplification of the federal income tax system, and elimination of "complex subsidies, exemptions, loopholes, deductions, tax carrybacks, and other exotic devices." His prescription: a plea for faster tax write-offs to spur capital investment.[38]

The point I am making is not that private enterprise is irrelevant or outmoded—far from it. But big business in the United States today cannot legitimize its behavior or freedom of action on ideological grounds that bear little resemblance to reality. The justification therefore must rest on criteria that are relevant, and more important, credible to large segments of society as equitable and just. Otherwise, in a free society, it is not inconceivable that people will reject these rationalizations and the institutions supporting them.

Notes

1. Cited in "The Embattled Businessman," *Newsweek,* February 16, 1976, p. 58.

2. Reported in *The Public Image of Business in a Time of Changing Values: A Discussion Paper* (New York: National Association of Manufacturers, June 1973).

3. For a further elaboration on this theme, see S. Prakash Sethi, "Dimensions of Corporate Social Performance: An Analytical Framework for Measurement and Evaluation," *California Management Review,* spring 1975, pp. 58-64.

4. William H. Whyte, Jr., *Is Anybody Listening?* (New York: Simon and Schuster, 1952), p. 8.

5. Irving Kristol, "On 'Economic Education'," *The Wall Street Journal,* February 18, 1976, p. 20.

6. "How Good Is 'Economic Education'?" *Fortune,* July 1951, pp. 84-86ff. The study was conducted by Dr. Harold Moulton and Dr. C.W. McKee.

7. Whyte, *Is Anybody Listening?* p. 14.

8. "The Embattled Businessman," p. 57. For some case histories of corporate corruption and payoffs, see S. Prakash Sethi, *Up Against the Corporate Wall,* 3rd ed. (Englewood Cliffs, N.J.: Prentice-Hall, 1977).

9. Max Ways, "Business Needs To Do a Better Job of Explaining Itself,"

Fortune, September 1972, p. 85. For a further explanation of the failure of the public relations strategy, see S. Prakash Sethi and Dow Votaw, "How Should We Develop a New Corporate Response to a Changing Social Environment," in Dow Votaw and S. Prakash Sethi (eds.), *The Corporate Dilemma: Traditional Values Versus Contemporary Problems* (Englewood Cliffs, N.J.: Prentice-Hall, 1973), pp. 191–213.

10. "Remarks on Corporate Morality," by Fred T. Allen, chairman of the board and president, Pitney Bowes, before the American Chamber of Commerce in Zurich, Switzerland, October 16, 1975.

11. Michael C. Jensen, "Many U.S. Executives Reported in Favor of Overseas Bribes," *The New York Times,* February 13, 1976, pp. 45, 49.

12. "Oil Industry Group Plans Big Campaign to Block Legislation to Split Up Firms," *The Wall Street Journal,* November 11, 1975, p. 21. See also ads by Union Oil, Texaco, and Mobil Oil that appeared in *The New York Times, The Wall Street Journal,* and *Newsweek* in May–June 1976.

13. "Oil Meets the Press: The Image Has Been Smeared and the Companies Are Largely To Be Blamed," *Dun's,* April 1974, p. 62.

14. "The Embattled Businessman," p. 56. Paradoxically, emphasis on the positive often provokes a negative reaction. If the audience is critical of corporate failures, avoidance of the issue by repeating a list of contributions tends to create further alienation. William Whyte points out: "Even with those facts for which business can rightfully claim credit, the message represents business as essentially static and defensive. It concerns what was done. That we have achieved more telephones, more bathtubs and so on per capita is fine fact, but it is not a fact that answers the aspirations and gripes of the people business is seeking to win as friends." (*In Anybody Listening?* p. 14).

15. U.S. Congress, *Oversight Hearings on Commerce Department Payment to the National Advertising Council for Promotion of the Free Enterprise System. Hearing Before the Commerce, Consumer, and Monetary Affairs Subcommittee of the Committee on Government Operations* (Washington, D.C., 94th Congress, 1st Session, July 30, 1975), p. 1. [Hereinafter referred to as *Oversight Hearings on Advertising Council.*]

16. Advertising Council, Inc., *The American Economic System . . . and Your Part in It* (New York, 1976).

17. *Oversight Hearings on Advertising Council,* p. 1. Another campaign of this type has been proposed by the Virginia State Chamber of Commerce to halt increasing criticism of the free enterprise system. See "Chamber to Study Opinion of Business," *Washington Star,* July 28, 1975.

18. Howard J. Morgens, "The Profit Motive and the Public Interest," in *Oversight Hearings on Advertising Council,* pp. 38–41.

19. Philip H. Dougherty, "Campaign on Economy Weighed," *The New York Times,* July 22, 1975.

20. Philip H. Dougherty, "2 Views of Economic System," *The New York Times,* March 15, 1976, p. 50.

21. National Association of Manufacturers, *The Public Image of Business in a Time of Changing Values* (New York: The Association, June 1973). Emphasis in original.

22. Lewis F. Powell, Jr., "Attack on American Free Enterprise System, Confidential Memorandum, August 23, 1971," reported in *Washington Report Supplement* (Washington, D.C.).

23. United States of America, Before the Federal Trade Commission. "Petition to the Federal Trade Commission. (1) For Rules to Extend the Advertising Substantiation Campaign to All Advertising, (2) To Request Substantiation for Certain Commercial Advertisements by Certain Advertisers, (3) And to Commence an Advertisement Substantiation Campaign in the Oil, Utility, and Electric Appliance Industries in Regard to Environmental or Energy-Related Claims in Commercial Advertisements." January 9, 1974. [Hereinafter referred to as "Petition Before the Federal Trade Commission."] The petitioners in this matter were Senator Birch Bayh (D, Indiana), Senator Thomas McIntyre (D, New Hampshire), Senator Frank Moss (D, Utah), Representative Les Aspin (D, Wisconsin), Representative Benjamin Rosenthal (D, New York), and Representative Andrew Young (D, Georgia).

24. United States of America, Before the Federal Trade Commission. "Memorandum of Mobil Oil Corporation in Opposition to Petition to Extend the Advertising Substantiation Resolution of the Federal Trade Commission Filed January 9, 1974," dated April 4, 1974, p. 38. [Hereinafter referred to as "Mobil's Memorandum Before the Federal Trade Commission."]

25. Industry Feature: Corporate Advertising," *Madison Avenue Magazine,* January 1976, p. 34.

26. *Ibid.,* pp. 33-34.

27. For an analysis—conducted by the admitted critics of the industry—of the various environment-related campaigns of the oil and energy-related companies, see *Hearings on Energy and Environment,* Part 2 (Washington, D.C., 93rd Cong., 2nd Sess., May 6 and July 18, 1974), pp. 39-79; "Petition Before the Federal Trade Commission," pp. 5-22; "Corporate Advertising and the Environment," *Economic Priorities Report* (New York: Council on Economic Priorities), September–October 1971, pp. 7-17, 28-35; Charles E. Ludlam, "Abatement of Corporate Image Environmental Advertising," *Ecology Law Quarterly,* 4 (1974), 247-278.

28. According to a study by the Council on Economic Priorities, the number of companies treating environment as a gimmick in an attempt to boost the sales of their products include American Tobacco, Bulova, Cott Beverage, Hask, Liggett & Meyers, Publix Shirt, Pittsburgh Plate Glass, and Texaco. "Corporate Advertising and the Environment," p. 19.

29. E.B. Weiss, "Management Don't Kid the Public With Those Noble Anti-Pollution Ads," *Advertising Age,* August 3, 1970, p. 35.

30. "Corporate Advertising and the Environment," pp. 4, 5-17.

31. Whyte, *Is Anybody Listening?* For more recent examples of this type of campaign, see advertisements by the Phillips Petroleum Company and the Warner & Swasey Company, appended to Chapter 1.

32. For an early history of the defense of business by businessmen as the guardians of American ideological values, see George C. Lodge, *The New American Ideology* (New York: Knopf, 1975). Chapter 4, Gerstenberg's statement appeared on the Op Ed page of *The New York Times,* December 29, 1972, and is cited in Lodge.

33. Lodge, *The New American Ideology.*

34. Cited in Lodge, *The New American Ideology,* p. 191.

35. Cited in Sethi, *Up Against the Corporate Wall,* 2nd ed., pp. 102-211.

36. Melvin A. Eisenberg, "Legal Models of Management Structure in the Modern Corporation: Officers, Directors, and Accountants," *California Law Review,* 63, 2 (March 1975), 375-439.

37. Irving Kristol, " 'When Virtue Loses All Her Loveliness—Some Reflections on Capitalism and the Free Society'," *The Public Interest,* fall 1970, p. 4.

38. The advertisement appeared in *The Wall Street Journal,* March 23, 1976, p. 9. "What Makes America Work—Taxes . . . But Our Federal Code Needs a Complete Change."

3

Business and the News Media
Allies or Adversaries?

We need not be theologians to see that we have shifted responsibility from making the world interesting from God to the newspaperman. We used to believe there were so many "events" in the world. If there were not many intriguing or starling occurrences, it was no fault of the reporter. He could not be expected to report what did not exist.

—Daniel Boorstin, The Image

The Media as a Target: Background of Complaint

It has now become an article of faith with businesspeople that there is a bias in the news media and among the journalists that prevents them from getting fair and objective exposure of their viewpoint. Furthermore, they contend that their access to the various media is grossly inadequate when compared with the importance, to business and society, of the issues being covered and the space and air time devoted to discussing the viewpoints of those who oppose business.

It appears that business's need to defend itself becomes more intense and its criticism of the media more acrimonious when there is increasing distrust and disapproval of the activities of business in large segments of society or when a significant number of otherwise highly reputable businesses have been charged with illegal acts or accused of socially undesirable behavior. Examples would be the oil crises of 1973–74, and issues such as industrial pollution and the environment, and bribes and political payoffs at home and abroad. Thus, the current business charges of the "economic illiteracy" of reporters and the one-sided and generally antibusiness presentation of news and events in the press should come as no surprise.

Business has lumped the news media with the adversaries it must fight. In a recent speech, Louis Banks of the Harvard Business School, a former editor of *Fortune,* suggested that although there has been significant improvement in the

---

Unless otherwise specifically stated, all direct quotes in this chapter are from personal interviews or written communications with the author.

comprehension of economic matters on the part of good news editors, in the case of everyday news coverage,

we are fed a daily diet of authoritative ignorance, most of which conveys a cheap-shot hostility to business and businessmen. Here is where the nation sees a persistently distorted image of its most productive and pervasive activity, business. . . . The reporters and the editors in the general media are woefully ignorant of the complexities and ambiguities of corporate operations, and being so, are easy targets for politicians or pressure group partisans with special axes to grind at the expense of business.[1]

In dismissing the charge of corporate millions used to propagandize the public, John Crichton, president of the American Association of Advertising Agencies (AAAA), maintains, "Anyone who reads the daily press or listens to the news should know better. Corporations are constantly under attack from every quarter. Charges by consumer groups, Congressional Committee and Subcommittee Chairmen, individual Congressmen and the various organs of federal, state and local government get front-page headlines. . . . Silence by a company in the face of attacks upon its policies and practices is interpreted as an admission of guilt. Corporate advertising provides one avenue of self-defense."[2] Neal W. O'Conner, chairman of the American Association of Advertising Agencies, claims that "when dealing with business, the news media 'more often than not' are antibusiness."[3] Similar feelings have been echoed by other business leaders and scholars.[4]

Some businesspeople also blame the universities for fostering an antibusiness bias in students. According to Frank Considine, president of National Can Corporation, higher education has been distorting the facts about the free enterprise system and business. Albert Bourland, lobbyist for General Motors, states that academic liberalism particularly affects young government staffers and turns them against business.[5]

Mr. Donald S. MacNaughton, chairman of the Prudential Insurance Company of America, feels that American journalism has been lacking in the professional tradition of self-correction:

With freedom comes responsibility, and in the opinion of many, that sense of responsibility has been lacking. Most of us are fed up with glib, shallow, inaccurate reporting and editing—tired of journalistic tastes which prefer sensationalism above the fundamentals—which allow a thespian to pose as a newsman.[6]

In justifying the need for paid advertising to present its viewpoint before the public, an executive of American Electric Power alluded to the inability of a company to compete for public attention against the pronouncement of government bureaucrats and politicians. He stated that whenever an official of the Environmental Protection Agency made a statement or put out a press release, it received widespread coverage. In the company's case, it was impossible to get a message across through the press release method. "It is unrealistic to think that we could have released 36 messages in the form of news releases and reached any significant audience" (see Chapter 4). Donald C. Cook, chairman and chief executive officer of AEP, complained that the environmentalists speak in hyperbole, "making the most exaggerated statements without facts" because "they don't have to be responsible to anybody."

In a similar vein, Rawleigh Warner, Jr., chairman of Mobil Oil, says that the purpose of the Mobil ad campaign is to defend the company against slander. "We've been willing to react because we feel we've been treated unfairly."[7] Herbert Schmertz, a Mobil vice-president and the architect of its advocacy campaign, believes there is too much accusatory journalism.[8] Frederick W. West, Jr., president of Bethlehem Steel Corporation, in a speech before the American Newspaper Publishers Association, echoed a similar complaint by saying that many reporters are out to get business and that some of them are over their heads when reporting business news. However, he believes that some of the reporting "that gets our blood up is probably more muddled than it is malicious."[9]

Other industry spokespeople and corporate executives have been equally vocal about the inability or unwillingness of the news media to give a proper balance in their news reporting or to provide corrections when they are called for:

Too often a member of Congress, a consumer advocate, an environmentalist—or any other adversary—can make sensational charges to which there are factual, sober answers that are anything but sensational. Alas, these answers rarely get much attention. It takes time to assemble facts. Once the facts are in hand, the definition of "news" today militates against their widespread exposure in the news media. . . .

Sixty seconds on the evening news tonight is all that is required to ruin a reputation, turn a politician out of office, or impair a company's profitability. The power of the press with today's methods of mass communication has become, in short, the power to destroy.[10]

It should be noted here that the criticism of media by business is not new nor is it confined to business alone. Almost every major segment of society has at one time or another criticized the media for unfair and inadequate coverage of its viewpoint when this particular segment was under social pressure for any real or alleged undesirable actions and deeds. The charges have changed somewhat since James A. Wechsler, then editor of the New York *Post,* stated in 1957 that the press had "grown comfortable, fat and self-righteous . . . and voice[d] the prejudices and preconceptions of entrenched wealth rather than those qualities of critical inquiry and rebellious spirit we associate with our noblest journalistic traditions. . . ."[11]

In 1968, the National Advisory Commission on Civil Disorder charged the media with writing and reporting the news primarily from the standpoint of a white man's world. The press by and large repeatedly, if unconsciously, reflected the biases, the paternalism, the indifferences of white America:

Our . . . fundamental criticism is that the news media have failed to analyze and report adequately on racial problems in the United States and, as a related matter, to meet the Negro's legitimate expectations in journalism. By and large, news organizations have failed to communicate to both their black and white audiences a sense of the problems America faces and the sources of potential solutions.[12]

The claims are still of bias in the presentation of issues and of inadequate access to the news media for those wishing to present their side of an issue, but now the claimants are the corporations and institutions against which Mr. Wechsler inveighed only two decades ago. Military personnel, covered extensively by the news media during the Vietnam war, are largely of the opinion that they were not given fair presentations by four news institutions: television news, television programs, newspapers, and news magazines.[13]

According to John Oakes, editorial page editor of *The New York Times*, "it is normal that business would accuse the press of bias and inadequate coverage. This is true not only in the case of business, but of political parties, and every other kind of special interest group—profit or non-profit." Garth Hite, publisher of *The Atlantic Monthly*, maintains that the complaints of media bias on the part of industry are not new although they may be a bit more aggravated now. He also feels that now there is more sophistication and that industries take media criticism much better in stride:

The oil industry has been subjected to a lot of criticism from the media. Ten or fifteeen years ago the big seven oil producers might have pulled their advertising out of censorious media. They don't do that now . . . Detroit has received criticism in the last 2 or 3 years and deservedly so . . . Years ago, if Detroit had been under this barrage of criticism, it most likely would have taken more stringent steps in withholding advertising.

The public's low esteem of business is matched by its hostility toward the news media, which is facing a legitimacy crisis of its own: the counterpart of advocacy advertising is advocacy or adversary journalism. The attempts by the news media in the late 1960s to upgrade themselves and depict the reality of the American condition often resulted in overreaction. As William Thomas, editor of the *Los Angeles Times*, comments: "We're opening up the pages to elements of society never before covered. At the same time, we run the danger of closing out what used to be the Establishment voice. The old Establishment voices aren't in the paper enough. Often we've put them in the same category that blacks occupied fifteen years ago."[14]

The Structure of the News Media and
Its Impact on News Coverage

It is analytically unsound to resort to broad generalizations in criticizing the shortcomings of the news media, for they yield neither insights as to the causes of the complaints nor help in developing alternative approaches to alleviating the problem. Instead, one must understand the internal structure of a particular medium; its technical nature, which may make reporting in a particular form more feasible and desirable; and the constituency it intends to reach and serve.

Although the overall goal of the news media may be simply stated as informing people about events relating to their lives and to their physical, socio-economic, political, and cultural environment, the operational specifics of this goal vary widely. News media are not merely vehicles of communication but have personalities of their own, and these personalities are imprinted on the news they carry, giving it a distinctive character and emphasis not inherent in the content itself. The various media:

1. Cater to different audiences—for example, local, regional, and national; and to special-interest groups—for example, business, religious, and ethnic minorities
2. Operate under different competitive conditions
3. Have different financial and personnel resources
4. Have different images in the eyes of the public and are therefore under different kinds of pressure to provide not only news but analysis and editorial comment
5. Function under different federal, state, and local statutes that regulate different aspects of their operations

In order to facilitate our analysis, we will divide the news media into two groups: mass media and special-interest media. The former group comprises those media whose purpose is to reach all audiences within certain geographical boundaries. Moreover, their coverage is of a general nature and includes a large variety of subjects. The latter group comprises those media that either aim to reach certain specified audiences (for instance, city dwellers) or cater to specialized groups (for instance, professional groups).

The general-purpose media are the more important because they have greater reach, density (they approach the same audience with more than one instrument), and frequency (they carry similar messages more than once). They also have greater financial and personnel resources. In theory, these media—which include nationally known newspapers, nationally distributed news magazines, other general-purpose periodicals that comment on issues of general interest, and network radio and television—represent all segments of the population and should therefore provide fair and adequate coverage for all "constituents." In practice, however, this ideal is nearly impossible to achieve because of two factors: One, there is less commonality of interest among various segments of the constituency of a particular news medium. Two, because of external factors a certain segment of that constituency may be the subject of critical news coverage at a given point in time, or may feel that its point of view is not being adequately represented. Technical features of the broadcast and electronic media lend them certain unique strengths but also make them subject to severe limitations on what news can be reported, how it can be reported, and the depth of treatment that can be given to a specific subject.

In the analysis of news media response that follows, I shall treat the interaction between business and the news media separately for print and electronic media.

The Print Media

The print media have generally denied the business charges of bias in news coverage, and also inadequacy of access of business groups and individual businesspeople to the media to express their viewpoints and publicly state their positions. On the question of bias, Osborn Elliot, editor in chief of *Newsweek,* says that his answer is "an absolutely flat categorical no" to the contention that "there is any antibusiness bias, conscious or unconscious, in *Newsweek.* But there certainly is an anti-crooked business bias." John Oakes of *The New York Times* also denies the existence of any systematic bias in reporting of business news. Similar opinions have been echoed by Marshal Loeb, senior editor of *Time,* and Garth Hite of the *Atlantic Monthly.* Robert M. Bleiberg, editor of the conservative business weekly *Barron's,* believes, however, that there is some validity to this complaint: "It is amply documented that corporations do not get a fair shake on television and perhaps from time to time not in the daily press throughout the country." He also feels that inadequate coverage in the past may simply have reflected a news judgment that what happens in Washington is more important to the reader than what happens on Wall Street. This is beginning to change because what happens to business is becoming all-important as far as reader interest goes; there are now more reasons to cover business and finance.

Bias in the News

A distinction should be made here between news reporting and editorials on the one hand, and coverage in general-purpose newspapers and magazines, such as *The New York Times* and *Newsweek,* and special-purpose business magazines such as *Fortune* and *Business Week,* on the other. One should also distinguish between small-town newspapers, newspapers of conservative orientation, and a few large newspapers considered liberal, such as *The New York Times,* the *Los Angeles Times,* the *Washington Post,* the *Milwaukee Journal,* and the *St. Louis Post Dispatch.*

When it comes to the news, opinions differ between the editors of general-purpose newspapers and magazines and the special-purpose business-oriented magazines. What businesspeople generally allude to as bias is discussed as lack of objectivity and superficiality in reporting. Objectivity, however, is a relative term. The very decisions about what news to cover, what prominence to give it, and what kind of followup to accord it requires a process of deliberate selectivity based on the subjective assessment of an editor as to what is relevant and important for the audience of the medium. This argument is even more germane in the case of special-interest news media, where there is a greater identity of outlook between a medium and its audience. Thus a news magazine catering to business will not only provide more coverage (compared to other news media) of news that is of interest to its audience, but more important, is likely to look at the news from the business point of view. Although the magazine might consider its news coverage to be objective reporting, such a contention might be questioned by opposing groups. It is not uncommon to see a given situation reported differently in different news media. Facts themselves are seldom in dispute, but they assume a coloration from the environment in which they are presented. The role of a medium in presenting and even creating this environment is a crucial factor in influencing audience reaction to the news.

Even if strict objectivity or neutrality were possible, it is not certain that they would help the audience or enable a medium to discharge its function properly. In an attempt to be objective, a reporter presents various sides of the issue, point-counterpoint, and the opinion omitted is the one that would mean the most to the reader—the reporter's own. Various official spokespeople who outline their positions in a manner that best serves their own purpose are quoted while the reporter is effectively barred—under the pretext of professionalism, balanced reporting, or the medium's own rules of conduct—from telling readers what he or she thinks of the credibility or motives of the various speakers quoted.

Finding objectivity difficult to achieve and to justify, the media have resorted to two approaches. Instead of being objective, they have claimed to be "fair." As David Brinkley of NBC said, "Objectivity is impossible to a normal human being. Fairness, however, is attainable, and that is what we are striving for—not objectivity [but] fairness."[15] A professor of journalism at the University of Illinois, Gene S. Graham, went even further: "Those who fancy that mass media should have no conviction at a time when conviction is a life's essential are naive at best and insulting our intelligence at worst. We can be fair minded without ignoring the obvious fact that this is not yet a land of its stated ideals.

Lincoln Steffens, in his day, did not shrink from a judgement between good and evil. But he was objective and fair and honest."[16]

What businesspeople call "bias" media people often describe as oversensitivity to adverse news. John Oakes of *The New York Times* states:

Newpapers *will* publish news that is sometimes unfavorable to the interests of a particular corporation or industry—but that's part of the function of the newspapers. The reporter in writing a news story aims at giving balanced information for the objective reader. We would not be performing our duty as newspapermen if we did not present a story in all its relevant aspects.

It is understandable that the affected businesses may not like what they read about themselves in the newspapers. They use the argument of news media bias in objecting to these stories. This alleged bias then becomes an excuse for publishing the kind of advocacy ads that we're beginning to see. The problem has developed more markedly since the oil crisis, when the oil and energy companies have become more aggressive in buying advertising space to respond to public criticism of their business.

Mr. Oakes feels that the press has the inescapable obligation to illuminate the reality behind the appearance. If in the pursuit of this course the press is cast in the role of an adversary "vis-a-vis not only government but any and all other institutions, so much the better for us and for them, and most of all for the public. The adversary position is indeed the natural position for a press that takes seriously its responsibility to uncover what is wrong or corrupt in public life, or with private institutions or individuals whose activities affect the public."[17]

Marshal Loeb, a senior editor of *Time,* also thinks the complaints of business have more to do with the type of news being covered than the manner in which it is covered:

I have little sympathy for the lament of corporate executives that the media are biased. We are in an era when all institutions are under fire—the church, government, the press, medicine, etc. Business is attacked more than many other institutions because it is highly visible. Moreover, there have been some outrageous scandals involving business, and these have fanned the criticism.

I don't think there is or should be something called "business ethics." There is just *ethics,* involving honesty, morality, etc. People properly believe that businessmen and businesswomen should not have a different level of ethics or morality than other individuals. There is no excuse for such actions as bribes and payoffs. They are causing grave political problems for the free enterprise system in many parts of the world.

Business has been criticized and is in bad repute. Some criticisms are well-founded, but some are unjustified. Businessmen should not feel overly aggrieved about the criticism.

A number of media spokespeople have ascribed the inadequate and indifferent coverage to the low priority assigned to coverage of business news and the poor quality of reporters rather than a deliberate bias on the part of the news media. Lewis H. Young, editor-in-chief of *Business Week,* feels that business coverage in most newspapers is so bad that it's not even worth talking about:

The problem is basically in the publications who like to think they are very liberal. And they think that one of the marks of being liberal is to show anti-business bias. It starts with a feeling that business is probably not good. It's an educational kind of bias: The belief that business is prepared to do anything to make a profit. This is reemphasized by a lack of understanding of how business works by newspaper reporters, since most have never worked in a business. Most *New York Times* business reporters are quite naive and unsophisticated about business. They forget that, e.g., the *New York Times* is also a business. They usually don't have the time to educate themselves. This is unlike how we function in *Business Week*.

Robert Lubar also considers the press and TV to be inadequate in their coverage of business. "They simply don't know how to do it well, and in the process of not doing it well, they distort stories. The real problem is superficialty."

David Finn of Ruder & Finn, one of the largest public relations firms in the United States, observes that a number of problems exist in this country because of the way the news media cover the news. "Even a most conscientious reporter can't spend days covering a story except in special situations. There's rarely enough time to get into it in great depth. The subject of a newspaper article is likely to feel that the whole story hasn't been told. On occasions a story may be so sparse and superficial that it gives a distorted view." Furthermore, he feels that bad news is good news for newspapers: "negative aspects of a story are more interesting to reporters than the positive aspects."

All the business magazines contacted acknowledged that despite their avowed aim of providing first-rate coverage of business news, they are not immune to receiving complaints from corporate managers and industry spokespeople who felt that a particular story portrayed them unfavorably, that they were unfairly singled out, or that the facts in the story were misstated or liable to be misunderstood.[a] The publications maintain that they cover all the news relevant to the businessperson and potential investor and that this *includes* news unfavorable to individual companies and specific industries. Truth is as each one of us sees it, says John L. Cobbs of *Business Week:* "The criticism is not that we are antibusiness but that we have a different viewpoint."

---

[a]A recent example of such a complaint was paid advertisement in the *Wall Street Journal* by the Arizona Power objecting to a news story in the *Journal* which used allegedly outdated facts and thereby derived conclusions about the future growth prospects of the company. See Ron Cooper, "How Arizona Utility Ran into Big Trouble over Costs and Rates," *The Wall Street Journal,* April 7, 1976, p. 1. The company's response in the form of paid political advertisements appeared in *The Wall Street Journal,* April 9 and 12, 1976.

Bias in Editorials

The editors and news executives of newspapers, magazines, and television (both network and independent stations) unanimously reject the bias charge as irrelevant. Editorials are by definition the position of the editors of a particular print medium or television news program. John Oakes of *The New York Times* has best expressed the general position of the various editors interviewed:

Editorially, *The New York Times* has been very critical of many business practices, not only this year, but also in earlier years. Over the years, we have been editorially critical of every special interest group that exists. Newspapers wouldn't be doing their duty if they did not express their opinion. We reserve the right to express our views in our columns. If oil companies or any other group wish to call this bias, that is their privilege.

John Loeb of *Time* says that corporations tend to interpret editorials that are critical of business to be antibusiness. "For each editorial criticizing business [in the *Times*], the reader could find a pro-business editorial. The *New York Times* is a strong defender of the capitalist system, of private enterprise. In short, business gets a pretty good shake in the national media."

Next we turn our attention to the second of the two complaints made by business against the news media, i.e., its access to the media is grossly inadequate when compared with the coverage provided opposing groups and viewpoints. The media response falls into one or more of the following categories:

1. Before a news story is reported in the press, its contents are checked for accuracy with all the interested parties, including business, and their views evaluated and reported.
2. Where businesspeople disagree with a news story or are critical of an editorial, the "letters to the editor" columns are open to them.
3. Many newspapers have special editorial space, e.g., the Op-Ed page in *The New York Times,* which is made available to outside spokespeople including top corporate executives.
4. A large part of the inadequate coverage is due to the general unwillingness on the part of top corporate executives to talk with reporters.

John Oakes of the *Times* maintains that the inadequate access complaint is poorly founded. When reporting business operations in a business story, the *Times* asks the particular firm about it. The company may not consider this to be sufficient because the headline may not be to their liking or the space allocated to their position may be deemed insufficient:

The *Times* established the Op-Ed Page about five years ago, where not only businessmen but spokesmen for an infinite variety of other groups, or just plain individuals, have an opportunity to have their say in a broad philosophical sense, and to respond to whatever criticism they have received in our editorial columns or news columns—or anywhere else. The Op-Ed Page was of course established for a much broader reason, i.e., to constitute a forum for the expression of ideas, and I think we have succeeded pretty well in that intention. In any event, we have also published the pros and cons from many groups, business and otherwise, including heads of such corporations as General Motors, IBM and Ford Motor Company.[b]

The letters to the editor column is the more traditional means for access to the media. Without exception, the media people interviewed indicated that they took special pains to publish letters critical of the positions taken by their publications. Furthermore, Kalman Seigel, letters editor of the *Times,* states that available studies indicate that the readership is high. There is an identification between the reader and the writer. It satisfies a growing desire in the people to communicate, and to break through what they feel is an unreachable establishment.

Garth Hite of the *Atlantic Monthly* reflects the views of most print media—general and special purpose—when he states:

If we do a piece that is critical of an industry (a good example is the current issue of the *Atlantic* on supermarkets), we give it an opportunity to answer. If it wants to write us letters we'll publish a whole section of letters, pro and con, about the article. . . . We have a right to control what goes into our product, but responsible publications always give the other side a chance to answer. The Supermarket Institute . . . flew a man in from Chicago to see one of our editors, the man who edited the piece. They had a good hearing here and we will publish letters and comments from interested parties, primarily supermarket people who don't like that article. We would have accommodated our critics without a visit from their lobbying group.

Newspapers and news magazines, however, must limit the number of letters they publish because of space problems. *The New York Times,* for example, receives over 60,000 letters a year, and publishes between 4 and 5 percent. Some newspapers and magazines publish a somewhat higher proportion because the

---

[b]Here are some examples of the articles written by businessmen that appeared in the Op-Ed pages of *The New York Times* during a four-month period from November 1975 through February 1976: Frank Cary, chairman, IBM, "Multinational Corporations as Development Partners," November 8, 1975, p. 27; Charles G. Bluhdorn, chairman, Gulf & Western Industries, "Uncle Santa," December 5, 1975, p. 39; William Spencer, president, First National City Bank, "Never Say Die," December 24, 1975, p. 21; Stanley Marcus, chairman of Neiman-Marcus, Dallas, "The Business Landscape," December 15, 1975, p. 30; Etcyl H. Blain, director of health and environmental research, Dow Chemical Co., "Wherein It Is Argued That Regulators Are Threatening and Inhibiting Science," January 17, 1976, p. 25; Walter E. Wriston, chairman, First National City Bank, "On Classified Loans," January 30, 1976, p. 27; Ira E. Corn Jr., chief executive officer, Michigan General Corporation, "Problem: $1 Sold Is (X) Earned," February 7, 1976, p. 21; and Nelson A. Rockefeller, "Toward Energy Independence," February 24, 1976, p. 35.

volume of letters received is not as high. However, Mr. Seigel of the *Times* points out that the space allocated every day to the letters is exactly the same as that devoted to the editorials. The attention paid to the letters column is enormous. Mr. Seigel personally reads each and every letter received at the *Times* before selecting the ones for publication. The *Times* will also offer copy-editing assistance to sharpen a letterwriter's focus or viewpoint. The paper currently imposes two rules for letters: (1) The letter must not exceed 400 words; (2) no more than two letters per writer will be accepted per year with rare and special exceptions. These rules are intended to make the space available to a larger number of people and prevent letterwriting campaigns. Other newspapers have less restrictive policies; some, like *Barron's*, have no limit on the length of the individual letters accepted for publication. But although *Barron's* has run letters longer than the original offending material, the newspaper does not have a specified space devoted to letters each day. John Oakes of the *Times* also suggested that sometimes a company felt offended by "our not publishing their letter while our refusal was based on the fact that we had already published a letter giving similar views from another company (which was not mentioned in the article)." It was considered by the newspaper that the second letter did not contribute much to the dialogue.

Most of the businesspeople interviewed are not happy with the access they receive through the letters to the editor column. They contend that often too much time elapses between the publication of the news item and the letter; the item may have been front-page headlines, while the letter is tucked away in the inside pages. The length requirements of the newspaper or magazine may impose an unreasonable burden on the letterwriter. Some companies have felt frustrated enough to resort to buying ad space to publish their letters. A vivid example of this type of frustration was a letter that Mobil wanted to publish in *The New York Times* in response to a *Times* editorial of March 25, 1975, on the question of oil import quotas. The original letter was 700 words long. The *Times* indicated a willingness to publish the letter provided Mobil reduced it to 400 words. Mobil got it down to 500 words but would not cut any further and instead published the letter as an advertisement.[c]

In another instance Mobil ran an ad (*The New York Times Book Review*,

---

[c]The advertisment appeared in the May 11, 1975, issue of *The New York Times*. The circumstances surrounding the dispute are somewhat murky and may reflect a latent antagonism between Mobil and the *Times*. According to Mr. Seigel, "Mobil said that reducing the letter to 400 words would be difficult but they would try. Then we heard nothing for a time. The next thing I heard from our advertising people to the effect that Mobil had taken advertising space to run the letter." Mr. Oakes of the *Times* commented that in his opinion Mobil was only too anxious to claim that the *Times* was unwilling to run their letter: "We have given Mobil every break. We have published other letters from them." However, Mr. Schmertz remarked that Mobil cut the letter once and when the *Times* asked the company to cut more, it refused. There was no negotiation and "on the length question there was no give on their [the *Times*] part. They knew the ad was coming and if they wanted to run it as a letter, they could have come back and said don't run the ad, we'll take the letter."

November 23, 1975) to reprint a negative review of Anthony Sampson's *The Seven Sisters,* a book critical of the large oil companies. The unfavorable review had originally appeared in Britain's *The Petroleum Economist.* The ad was Mobil's response to a front-page favorable review of the book that appeared in the *Times Book Review* of October 19, 1975. American Electric Power ran a full-page ad of the letter that Donald Cook, company president, sent to the Environmental Protection Agency because the company felt that EPA's views had received widespread publicity in the media while its response remained largely unnoticed (see Chapter 4.)

Advocacy Advertising and the Print Media

Without exception, all the print media spokespeople defended the right of the corporations to buy space and advertise their views. Oddly enough, *The New York Times,* the newspaper most criticized for its antibusiness bias and inadequate coverage of business news, has the oldest and strongest editorial policy in regard to accepting opinion ads without censorship and without regard to the extent of editorial opposition in the *Times* to the viewpoints they expressed. The first editorial on this topic appeared on December 28, 1961, in response to a complaint by the Inter-American Council that the paper permitted its advertising columns to be used to promote the sale of a book called *The Sharks and the Sardines,* by Juan Jose Arevalo, which according to the council was "false political propaganda" written by a man who was violently anti-American and produced by a publisher said to be a leader of the pro-Castro movement. According to the council spokesman, the advertisement was as much a political attack on American policy in Latin America as it was a description of the book itself. The *Times* editorial stated:

These charges go to the heart of the matter: Should the *Times* accept an advertisement containing political propaganda with which it strongly disagrees? When reduced to such fundamentals the answer is not difficult. The *Times* believes that, in furtherance of the objectives of the First Amendment of the Constitution, it should keep its advertising columns open to all points of view, no matter how strongly it disapproves of them. . . .

The guarantees of the First Amendment are not mere guarantees of the publisher's right to publish. They are, more importantly, guarantees of the public's right to know. We consider that that is what a free press truly means: the maintenance of open communication in the realm of ideas.

. . . [O]ur news policy is "to give the news impartially, without fear or favor, regardless of any party, sect or interest involved," as Adolph S. Ochs put it sixty-three years ago. Our policy with respect to political advertising is to keep our columns open to those who wish to express a particular point of view, no matter how widely divergent it may be from our own.

These policies, as we see them, comprise the essence of the freedom and the responsibility of the press.[18]

Since then the *Times* has editorially restated this position on various occasions in response to its accepting advertisements from such sponsors as the John Birch Society, the tobacco industry, fur retailers, the National Committee for Impeachment (of President Nixon), and an anti-Communist Chinese resident of the U.S. and Taiwan.[19]

Robert Lubar, managing editor of *Fortune,* believes that the use of advocacy advertising "is a perfectly legitimate extension" of the right of a company to make public its viewpoint. Osborn Elliot of *Newsweek* considers advocacy advertising to be a useful tool, although he does not feel that it is a definitive or exclusive one. Marshall Loeb of *Time* feels that these ads serve a useful purpose. They get the debate going. A company is expressing a point of view in counterpoint to another view expressed by some interest group or group of legislators:

I feel strongly that businessmen have an obligation to speak up through every possible medium. Among other things, they should take to the platforms in local neighborhood PTAs, run for elective office, speak to the press and university audiences. And they should advertise.

Similar views have been echoed by spokespeople for *Business Week* and *Barron's.*

Notwithstanding the major policy statements on behalf of national newspapers and magazines, there are variations at the implementation stage that in some cases appear to be arbitrary and even discriminatory. For example, in a survey of various news media by Robert J. Gwyn of the University of North Carolina, 13.7 percent of the newspapers responding to a questionnaire stated that they did not have any set policy for noncommercial advertising. Another 15.9 percent stated that they would accept all advertising, and over 63 percent stated that acceptance would depend on the identity of the sponsor or the nature of the copy theme. When asked whether they would agree with an open acceptance policy for noncommercial advertising on a nondiscriminatory basis, 50 percent disagreed, and 29.5 percent did not give any answer.[20] Professor Gwyn concludes that "the use of mass media as a forum for the expression of opinion by the dissenters of society is at best uncertain." Many in the media insist on closing the door to those who are considered to be acting contrary to the public interest; others refuse all opinion advertising, believing this to be in the public interest.[21]

In another study, the editors of *Business and Society Review* sent copies of a Citizens Council of America ad to about 100 newspapers and asked if they would run this ad. The ad, which had already appeared in *The New York Times* on February 16, 1972,[22] used direct quotes from Abraham Lincoln announcing his desire to maintain the separation of white and black races, and stating that he had never been in favor of bringing the social and political equality of the races. The advertisement was avowedly racist and was likely to antagonize a lot of people. Among the magazines and newspapers which said they would reject such an ad were *The Washington Post,* the *Harvard Business Review,* the *Harvard Law Review, The Fort Worth Star Telegram, The Detroit Free Press,* and the

Guy Bennett Publishing Company of Portland, Maine. Those who said they would accept the ad included *Newsday* (Long Island), *The Miami Herald/News, The Los Angeles Times,* Gannett Rochester Newspapers, the *St. Louis Post-Dispatch,* and the *Manchester Union Leader* (New Hampshire). Those sitting on the fence included the *Philadelphia Inquirer/Daily News,* and *Columbia Law Review,* the *Indianapolis Star/News, The Dallas Morning News,* the *Louisville Times/ Courier-Journal,* and *The Christian Science Monitor.*[23]

The Broadcast Media

The nature of business complaints against the broadcast media are similar to those made against the print media, but sharper. Herbert Schmertz, vice-president of public affairs for Mobil, contends that the structure of television news coverage prevents adequate coverage of a complex issue. The demand for a large audience makes any news coverage, in part, a type of entertainment: "Put the two of them together and you've inadequate coverage and inadequate information." Moreover, he contends that there is nothing sacred about the way television covers the news: "There is no law that says it has to be that way. This is their approach to the problem. There is nothing to prevent their giving in-depth coverage to a particular topic." Some representatives of the print media concur with the charge of poor and inadequate coverage of news on television, but they maintain that the charge applies to all types of news and is perhaps inherent in the technical nature of the medium itself. On one end of the spectrum is Robert Bleiberg of *Barron's,* who says:

There is no doubt in my mind that there is antibusiness bias in a good deal of reporting. Television, notably the network news programs and documentaries, goes out of its way to exaggerate the flaws of business and minimize the achievements. Television bias has been amply documented by such groups as Accuracy in Media and the National News Council.

According to Marshall Loeb of *Time,* TV does an abominable job of any news that is not a visual story; the medium concentrates on stock market bulletins and scandals.

Representatives of the broadcast media disagree with most, if not all, of these complaints. William Sheehan, president of ABC news, says that given the time constraints within which they have to work and the selection of stories they have to make, they handle things with fairness and balance. Therefore, any group that has a special interest will feel their particular subject is not handled very well:

We make a very concerted effort in talking to people on all sides. Most of the time it is not just two sides in a controversy—it is very hard to find an issue where there is a yes or no—but three or four or five different positions, which makes it difficult. We try to give expression to all points of view.

However, Mr. Sheehan admits that on rare occasions mistakes do happen, particularly in daily news reporting where things are being done in a hurry. Under these circumstances, the news media have an obligation to acknowledge their mistakes, and ABC does that.

William Small, senior vice-president and director of news at CBS, concurs with Mr. Sheehan's viewpoint by saying "We hear this from people who are unhappy with the flow of news when it doesn't go the way they want it to go." Although he does admit that past coverage of business and economic news has been inadequate, the situation has been remedied in the past two years by adding economic consultants to the staff to assist CBS reporters in analyzing economic and business-related issues in their reporting. In addition, CBS has added reporters with strong backgrounds in economic news. But Mr. Small says this is not what business is talking about. The kind of coverage business would like is friendly coverage: "The great flaw in their complaint and what is galling to us is that they always want it on their own terms." He went on to say that record would show that business has had sufficient access to the networks; CBS, in fact, has had a great many businesspeople and economists on the air in the recent past.

ABC and NBC dismiss the complaints of inadequate coverage and lack of expertise on the part of their reporters and commentators. Business is not a monolithic entity, it is argued. The oil business is not like the broadcasting business or the garment business. One can no more be an expert in business than he or she can be an expert on such diverse industries as automobiles, steel, electronics, banking and insurance, retail trading, and transportation. By the same logic, a news medium should have experts on such topics as monetary policies, international trade, foreign exchange, and economic development. A news reporter does not have to be an expert in the activity he or she is covering for a story. The reporter should know or find out who the experts are and then ask intelligent questions to dig out facts and stories that are newsworthy. What is more, good reporters do just that.

Furthermore, broadcast media people have been almost unanimous in their complaint that top business executives have been generally unavailable to reporters to give their viewpoints. "Sometimes people on the business side of the fence don't want to be interviewed" says Benjamin D. Raub, vice-president and assistant general attorney for NBC. It is not unlike the days of the civil rights issue, when networks were charged with having a pro-civil rights bias. In those days it was hard to get anyone on TV who favored states' rights. Another spokesperson argues that when a corporation is in trouble and reporters want to interview the president of the company, they are given some junior public relations person instead. If that happens, business cannot claim lack of access or bias. William Small of CBS says that businesspeople want their views to be filtered through very highly paid, very clever public relations people:

Take the case of Red Dye No. 2. We went to the company for an interview.

They wouldn't give an interview but would give a 90-second statement if we promised not to edit one word of it. The whole function of journalism relates to proper editing of raw material. You don't just turn over a glob of time to an advocate and say that's yours.

Herbert Schmertz of Mobil Oil concedes that there may be some truth to the statement that a lot of companies just will not make their top people available for interviewing by news reporters. But he also feels that reporters have always been able to find ways to get at the news if they are persistent. Mobil, on its part, has been making "diligent efforts to make our top people available to the press." The company organizes a weekly luncheon at which top management people meet with two or three reporters for on-the-record discussion. "I don't see a great interest on the part of top TV reporters to come to us over here," Mr. Schmertz comments, "I have written Dan Rather three or four letters. He has never even answered." Mr. Small of CBS retorts that reporters must pick their own stories and interview people of their choice: "We don't compel our people to sit down with a corporation president. I have difficulty with it ideologically. They want to brainwash people." If Mr. Schmertz considers that it is such a successful technique, then "every corporation in America would be inviting our people to lunch. We would be getting very fat and not getting much news."

The Regulated Nature of the Broadcast Media and the Fairness Doctrine

Unlike the print media, the broadcast media do not allow any advocacy advertising on the air. This is so because of the regulated nature of the media and also its physical characteristics in terms of limited air time. However, in order to discuss and properly analyze the media response to advocacy advertising, it is necessary to understand the nature of regulation and the application of what is known as the fairness doctrine, a brief discussion of which is presented below.

Since the amendment of the Communications Act in 1949, radio and television broadcasters have been required to present a fair and balanced coverage of controversial topics. The concept is known as the fairness doctrine. Increasingly, it has been argued that commercial advertising in the broadcast media raises important environmental, consumer, and health issues and therefore should be subject to the equal-time provisions of the fairness doctrine, by which broadcasters are required to provide free air time to those who oppose the views expressed in the original commercials but cannot afford to buy the air time.

The application of the fairness doctrine to commercials has a long and tortuous history of court cases in which the FCC has tried to limit its application to narrowly defined areas while other groups, feeling they have been denied reasonable access to air channels, have constantly tried to broaden its scope. A brief history of the development of the fairness doctrine and its application is presented in Appendix 3.

The 1974 FCC Fairness Report. The current status of the fairness doctrine as it has evolved over the years is given in the 1974 FCC policy statement in which the commission presented a major change in its fairness doctrine policy.[24] The FCC developed guidelines emphasizing the fostering of open debate on public issues and addressing the question of whether the fairness doctrine had been consistent with that goal while also recognizing the commercial base of the broadcast system and the importance of avoiding the erosion of this base. In its statement of standards the FCC divided advertisements into those that could be classified as editorial in nature and those for commercial products or services.

Commericals that consist of "direct and substantial commentary on important public issues . . . should be recognized for what they are—editorials paid for by the sponsor." The FCC also addressed the problem of institutional advertisements that "appeared to have discussed public issues, but which did not explicitly address the ultimate matter in controversy."[25] When considering the fairness doctrine in relation to these ads, the FCC expect(s)

. . . licensees to do nothing more than to make a reasonable, common sense judgement as to whether the "advertisement" presents a meaningful statement which obviously addresses, and advocates a point of view on, a controversial issue of public importance. This determination cannot be made in a vacuum: . . . the licensee must take into account his general knowledge of the issues and arguments in the ongoing public debate . . . [this] relationship of the ad to the debate . . . is critical. If the ad bears only a tenuous relationship to that debate, or one drawn by unnecessary inference, the fairness doctrine would clearly not be applicable.[26]

The FCC also stated it would review licensees' judgments in such cases only to determine their reasonableness and good faith and would not reverse a decision unless the facts are clear that the "advertisement" is a presentation of one side of a specific public issue.

The FCC moved to restrict the application of the Banzhaf decision (Appendix 3A), which pertained to cigarette advertising on radio and televison, to other product advertisements by stating: "While such an approach may have represented good policy from the standpoint of the public health, the precedent is not at all in keeping with the basic purposes of the fairness doctrine . . . , we believe that standard product commercials, such as the old cigarette ads, make no meaningful contribution toward informing the public on any side of any issue."[27] In addition, the FCC asserted that applying the fairness doctrine to product ads would at best provide the public with only one side of a public controversy, since the original product ads would not address a controversy as such but would extol the virtues of a certain type of product. The balancing ads would therefore have to be focused on promoting an alternative view of the product. This, the FCC claimed, "would engage both broadcasters and the commission in the trivial task of 'balancing' two set of commercials which contributed nothing to public understanding of the underlying issue." Thus, the commission concluded that the fairness doctrine should be applied "only to those 'commercials' which are devoted in an obvious and meaningful way to the discussion of public issues."[28]

Right of Access. Aside from the issue of fairness is the question of access to the broadcast media for those wishing to express a viewpoint on a controversial public issue. The right of access by commercial advertisers was severely limited by the FCC and later the Supreme Court when it was decided that neither the Communications Act of 1934 nor the First Amendment requires broadcasters to accept paid editorial advertisements. In its decision in *Columbia Broadcasting Systems, Inc.* v. *Democratic National Committee* and *Business Executives Move for Vietnam Peace* v. *FCC,* the Supreme Court affirmed an FCC decision that broadcasters were not required to air ads submitted by the Democratic National Committee soliciting funds and commenting on public issues or BEM ads calling for an immediate end to the Vietnam war.[29] The Court, in Chief Justice Burger's majority opinion, concluded that the intent of Congress in the 1934 Communications Act was "to permit private broadcasting to develop with the widest journalistic freedom consistent with its public obligations . . . [only] when the interests of the public are found to outweigh private journalistic interests of the broadcasters . . . [will] government power be asserted. . . ."[30] He further stated that the right to exercise editorial judgment was granted to the broadcaster.

In addition, the Court did not find any reason to require broadcasters to accept paid editorial ads and cited a number of "undesirable effects" of doing so, among them that the right of access would favor the wealthy or those with access to wealth; that the application of the fairness doctrine to editorial advertising would place a financial hardship on broadcasters; that the granting of a right to access could disseminate journalistic responsibility among many advertisers rather than leaving it with the licensee; that the right to access could involve the FCC and the government in exercising far greater control over broadcasters; and that the FCC was "entitled to take into account the reality that . . . viewers constitute a 'captive audience'" for ads that appear; "it is no answer to say that because we tolerate pervasive commercial advertisements we can also live with its political counterparts."[31]

The Court, however, did note that Congress had given the commission the flexibility to experiment with new ideas as changing conditions require and stated that "at some future date Congress or the Commission—or the broadcasters—may devise some kind of limited right of access that is both practicable and desirable."[32] In its *Fairness Report,* the FCC rejected the idea of a system of mandated access, either free or paid, and stated that the public's interest in free expression through broadcasting would be best served through continued reliance on the fairness doctrine, which left questions of access and the specific handling of public issues to the licensee's journalistic discretion. Requiring broadcasters to accept paid "advertorials"would heavily weight the system in favor of the wealthy and would "draw [the] Commission into deciding a broadcaster's good faith . . . the sort of government intrusion which . . . [the FCC has] sought to avoid in developing and administering the fairness doctrine."[33]

This stance of maintaining broadcast discretion in the hands of the licensee was reaffirmed in *NBC* v. *FCC*[34] when the D.C. circuit court, reversing an FCC decision, held that fairness balancing was not required for an NBC News documentary entitled "Pensions: The Broken Promise" in which NBC examined some private pension plans and the problems associated with them. Using the words of Chief Justice Burger, the court stated:

For better or worse, editing is what editors are for; and editing is selection and choice of material. That editors—newspaper or broadcast—can and do abuse this power is beyond doubt, but that is no reason to deny the discretion Congress provided. Calculated risks of abuse are taken in order to preserve higher values. The presence of these rights is nothing new; the authors of the Bill of Rights accepted the reality that these risks were evils for which there was no acceptable remedy other than a spirit of moderation and a sense of responsibility—and civility—on the part of those who exercise the guaranteed freedom of expression.[35]

Unless the licensee has violated the assumption of good faith and reasonable discretion, the court continued, "the principle of deference to licensee judgements . . . is an integral part of the fairness doctrine and a fixture that has been reiterated and applied with fidelity by the courts."[36]

Advocacy Advertising and the Broadcast Media

The broadcast media, with the concurrence and support of both the Supreme Court and the Federal Communication Commission, have instituted a ban on accepting commercials of a controversial nature. This has not, however, stopped the controversy. The environmental groups feel that some of the supposedly noncontroversial corporate image advertising on the air is indeed editorial advertising. Corporations feel that this policy has blocked them from correcting biased and erroneous programming on business-related issues, especially by network television. In this connection, Mobil's efforts to get access to the media offer a good illustration of how the television networks and the corporations view each others' activities in providing information to the public concerning business and economic issues. In the winter of 1972-73, Mobil's chairman, Raleigh Warner, spent three hours with Walter Cronkite. The edited version of the discussion that later appeared on the air led Mr. Warner to complain that to those who edited the raw material, "fairness did not seem an overriding preoccupation." In another instance, Mobil responded with a 22-page complaint with the National News Council charging ABC's closeup documentary series of March 20, 1974, which took a look at the energy crisis, with factual errors and unwarranted and unfair interpretations.

The latest incidence in this running confrontation is a full-page Mobil ad entitled "Whatever Happened to Fair Play?" which appeared in *The Wall Street Journal, The New York Times,* and the *New York Daily News* in early March 1976. This ad was a response to a five-part series on oil prices that appeared on NBC's New York station between February 23 and 27, 1976. The ad copy made 17 points decorated with 17 hatchets to indicate that facts were emasculated by the program's reporter, Liz Trotta. Although there were indeed certain inaccuracies in Ms. Trotta's reporting, some of Mobil's complaints pertained not to the facts but to Ms. Trotta's interpretations of the crisis and also the solutions suggested by some of the oil industry critics.

The events leading to the publication of the ad and since then offer an idea of how Mobil would like network reporting to take place. Mobil was asked for an interview but declined to participate. According to the ad, "Experience has shown us how what we say on pre-recorded TV, as contrasted to live, is edited out or watered down. And the treatment accorded to the oil people who did appear makes us doubly glad we weren't there."[37]

Benjamin D. Raub of NBC's law department reviewed the program and concluded that Mobil's charges could not be sustained on the basis of what was said and shown. However, NBC realized that the program had generated a furor and therefore scheduled a 90-minute repeat program with time devoted to discussion with oil industry representatives. (As of this writing, the program had not yet been aired.) Although Mr. Schmertz has agreed to go on the program, he is not happy with the arrangement:

They are controlling the format, length, time, the number of people on it, and will tolerate no long statements from me. If you're going to have a debate then participants should have the right to discuss format. NBC has taken 40 minutes to present its views on the oil issue. They are now taking 90 minutes where they are going to rerun their views in the first 40 minutes. They have given themselves 80 minutes. It leaves 50 minutes for 8 participants to have a discussion on all the issues: ourselves and our critics. That leaves about 6 minutes per person. Where do we get a chance to present our views in some reasonable and fair format? NBC is not giving us any opportunity to do that. They have an obligation to let the debaters sit down and develop a rational structure. They are a party participant in this debate as much as they say they're not. As party participant on one side of the debate, they have an obligation to discuss the format with the other side and they won't.

Mobil has repeatedly tried to buy time on TV to express its views and also to respond to its critics. In opposing this, William Sheehan, president of ABC News, says:

I don't think that advocacy commercials should be for sale. An advocacy ad dealing with an issue like energy conservation contributes a lot of imagery and heat, but not very much light, or intelligent discussion. I wouldn't like to see these things decided in just 30-second or 60-second commercials on TV or radio. It would be a bad kind of debate where the one with the most money would get the most time on the air. Either that, or the one with the slickest presentation would have the compelling argument in the minds of the public. I think it's better to handle these things in the way that we are currently handling them.

Mr. Raub of NBC concurs with this notion, and adds that broadcasters should determine agenda: "Sale of time for that purpose would permit those with money to determine agenda." If the issue is important enough to be covered from the public's point of view, it should and would be covered through regular news programs. Mobil's Schmertz responds that neither he nor his company is interested in setting agenda but instead would limit the discussion to answering criticisms previously made in NBC programs. Moreover, in case there is a problem with the fairness doctrine, Mobil would pay twice as much in order that its opponents could answer, provided the networks would take the ads without censorship. The networks would also select the critics. Mr. Schmertz also commented on network concern about protecting those without money: "Are they protecting the corner grocery store against A&P?" Moreover, "there's no shortage of time to buy." Mr. Schmertz says:

There are salesmen around trying to sell time all the time. How do they know how much they are going to get until they try it. Maybe they won't get very much. Maybe very few companies are interested. Maybe we're the only company that is interested. If there is a huge demand then some system of rationing will have to be devised. But they have never tested it.

William Small of CBS is not persuaded by these arguments.

Networks have to be the judge of what they want to put on the air. If Mr. Schmertz wants a network he can form one. A network is not a licensed entity. Anyone can form one. Mobil has a lot of money and Mr. Schmertz can go out and get a hundred or two hundred stations and he will have a network.

He feels that by allowing commercial time for advocacy advertising, networks would be allowing people with money to buy air time and exposure: "The large corporations would be buying the networks—I don't think that actually would happen, but that is the basic danger."

Analysis

The preceding discussion leads me to conclude that, despite the all-inclusive nature of the criticism leveled at the news media by corporate executives, their complaints are primarily directed at the three or four major newspapers, notably *The New York Times,* and the news programs and documentaries on network television. The efforts of the news media notwithstanding, there are indeed some limits to how much access can be accorded to business or other groups that wish to express their opinion of a particular news story or editorial. There is some element of truth in business complaints. The need for dramatic visual impact in television news has made it a prey to "contrived events":[d] News is created to attract television cameras, whose very presence becomes an integral part of the event or the news being covered. Various studies have shown that radical groups or disgruntled minorities have resorted to carefully staged events in order to get on network news because this was the only way for them to get national attention.[38]

But the picture is far from bleak. First, a distinction should be made between special-purpose print media (business and trade magazines) and general (mass) print media (newspapers and magazines). Second, a distinction should be made between the local and the national press. It would seem that business news media will provide fair coverage for the business viewpoint. As Mr. Bleiberg of *Barron's* points out, no one would argue that *The Wall Street Journal* or *Business Week* are biased. Nor should there be too much concern for the vast majority of newspapers with primarily local orientation. Constrained by funds from hiring a sufficient number of reporters and heavily dependent on advertising, they are only too happy to accept press releases from the public relations department of various companies and print them as news stories. According to Otis Chandler, publisher of the *Los Angeles Times,* although businesspeople complain about the dull and poor reporting of economic issues by local newspapers, they also resent aggressive and investigative coverage. Moreover, the hostility of small-town newspapers to "radical" and "left wing" groups is not a secret. It is therefore unlikely that the business viewpoint will not get fair exposure. For example, in California an industry-controlled lobbying group, Californians Against the Pollution Initiative (CAPI), fighting the enactment of Proposition 9, the Clean Environment Act of 1972, was successful in getting a

---

[d]Daniel Boorstin in his now classic book *The Image* refers to the notion of "pseudo events" and implies that the whole of American society is caught up in a desire to have constant "occurrences" or "happenings" and when they do not take place nationally, there is a demand for creating pseudo events. "By harboring, nourishing, and ever-enlarging our extravagant expectations we create the demand for the illusions with which we deceive ourselves. And which we pay others to make to deceive us." (p. 5) For an absorbing discussion of how pseudo events envelop various facets of our lives, see pp. 7–44.

large majority of local newspapers to write stories against Proposition 9 in which the analysis of its adverse economic impact was based almost exclusively on arguments developed by CAPI. CAPI even managed to enlist the aid of then Lieutenant-Governor Ed Reinecke, who sent a memo on official stationery to editors, publishers, and station managers throughout California. The memo was virtually a verbatim reproduction of a CAPI pamphlet criticizing Proposition 9 (see Chapter 5).

Another instance of pro-business bias by local and regional newspapers was reported in *Media & Consumer*. During the summer of 1972, the Federal Trade Commission charged A&P with deceptive advertising. To get maximum news coverage, the announcement was made at a Washington press conference on a Thursday afternoon at 2 P.M. The conference was attended by 27 reporters and both UPI and AP carried long wire stories giving details of the FTC charge and the A&P response. The FTC investigation was based on intensive price surveys conducted in six cities: Atlanta, Georgia; Chapel Hill, North Carolina; Chicago, Illinois; Durham, New Hampshire; and Raleigh, South Carolina. The *Media & Consumer* investigation revealed that eight out of twelve dailies in these cities did not run the story the day of the news conference or ever. Of the remaining four, only one carried the full UPI dispatch the following day, while the other three ran abbreviated versions of varying sizes.[39]

Print media have also helped corporations to improve the credibility of their advertising messages. Thus one finds that the annual awards for distinguished advertising in the public interest given by the *Saturday Review* routinely go to companies in oil, extraction, and energy production. The trouble here is that the awards are given for the ad copy and campaign without any regard to the company's record in performing the deeds it promotes in the ads. According to the Council on Economic Priorities, six out of seven paper makers who did environmental advertising, the sole exception being the Container Corporation, were those found to have distinctly unimpressive environmental records. Of the seven, four firms (Potlatch Forests, St. Regis, Hammermill, and International Paper) were cited for having the worst histories of neglect in controlling pulp mill pollution.[40] St. Regis was one of the two top award winners in the category of public relations or image advertising.[41]

Similarly, a distinction should be made between the network news in television broadcasting and the news programs of local independent stations. The station programs generally concentrate on local news and seldom venture into national controversies on economic issues. Furthermore, these stations have been known to yield to pressure by business. It was reported that TV stations in some localities had either fired their consumer affairs reporters or changed their assignments when advertisers threatened to withdraw their advertising from those stations.[42] Recent reports indicate that when New York's nonprofit public television station WNET (Channel 13) sought industry support for its programming, it was forced to drop its investigative and muckraking programs as the price of funding for other programs.[43]

Nevertheless, business is in a dilemma. In its attempt to reach opinion leaders, it must use the media of their choice. However, the environment in these media is hostile to business because the media are being inundated with revelations of activities that business would like to describe as necessary evils but that other groups consider illegal, unprofessional, and unethical. Thus we find that while Phillips Petroleum is extolling the virtues of free enterprise in paid advertising, the news stories tell us of a court case in which the company admitted to making illegal political campaign payments in the United States.[44] Or as the Council on Economic Priorities reported in 1970 in a study of the pulp and paper industry in the United States, the companies with the best track records on pollution control kept the lowest profile, while the worst polluters did the most advertising.[45] Thus the strength of a company's statements is considerably weakened when its integrity and social performance are under question.

The issue of alleged news media bias and inadequate access has three important dimensions that need attention.

1. A major problem lies in the general unwillingness of corporate executives to talk to journalists. Corporate executives find it disconcerting to be asked questions that appear to them to be hostile, insensitive, or lacking in proper understanding of the complexity of the issues involved. Moreover, they fear their views will be distorted or presented out of context. Thus, devoid of strong support from the corporation, journalists are forced to seek information from whatever sources they can find—and some of the most accessible may have an antibusiness bias. Businesspeople also lose their credibility by insisting that the press blandly swallow some of their pronouncements as gospel when "just about nobody believes those smarmy formulations about your friendly corporation existing only to serve you, to scale new heights of progress, to defend the American System."[46] A "statement of truth" written primarily by the person involved in events inevitably reflects his or her view of the world. Thus, insisting that reporters accept only the businessperson's view to be more "objective" and his or her values to be more "relevant" has probably made reporters more determined to be independent—and in this context, more critical. Self-isolation by businesspeople in the belief that it is better to have less of a bad press than more of a good press runs the risk of having more of the former and none of the latter—and in the long run is counterproductive.

My own experience while doing research for this book bears out this point. Most of the people I approached in the news media—including newspaper, magazine, and television network news executives—government agencies, and public interest groups, were forthcoming in their comments to me. Talking with business executives, however, yielded only mixed results. A large number of corporate executives and industry association officials were fully cooperative and provided thoughtful insights into the business position on various issues. But a significant number wished to remain anonymous and were unwilling to have their comments attributed for quotation. Quite a few senior executives declined to discuss the issues, saying that it was against company policy; a few companies would not even allow copies of their advertisements to be included in this book for illustrative purposes.

2. The suggestion that television and radio stations should accept opinion ads without restriction and denying the station right to edit is likely to raise more problems than it would solve. As we have seen earlier, the Supreme Court declared in the case of *Columbia Broadcasting Company* v. *The National Democratic Committee* that the right to exercise editorial judgment belonged to the broadcasters and that any other alternative would dissipate journalistic responsibility from the broadcaster among many advertisers, a not wholly desirable alternative.

At face value, Mr. Schmertz's suggestion would be tantamount to reducing the broadcast media to the status of a common carrier; air time would be sold on a nondiscriminatory basis subject to the constraint of ability to pay. And his contention notwithstanding, there would be no logical basis for limiting such sale of air time to those wishing to respond to the "inadequacies" of news programs previously aired by the media. It would still be the company that would decide what parts of a news program need responding to, regardless of the relative importance of these parts in the overall makeup of the original program. Thus a company would be able to channel the direction of debate and also focus public attention on those points it wishes to discuss. The fact that a company is willing to pay for the air time for its opponents would not alter this situation. Moreover, some companies argue that there is nothing to stop the broadcast media from criticizing a company's advocacy commercials. However, it should be apparent that this would also result in forcing a particular type of agenda on the broadcasters, a situation that could become unmanageable if only a few large corporations were to allocate multimillion-dollar advertising budgets to advocacy commercials on TV.

This corporate contention also assumes that every other segment of society, especially those opposing business, is treated differently by the media. Mr. Small of CBS asks why business should have the right to have its views presented on the air unedited; why should not business "undergo the same process that others [government, consumer groups] have gone through, which is a critical examination by the journalists?" He goes on to say that if businesspeople

want to have a favorable image and report on their activities they must get in the public arena. You can't hire stalking horses to do it for you. If I were a head of a corporation . . . I would much rather have the opportunity to talk with the "reporters" and persuade them of our position than to ignore them and let them go away with hostility. American business as a whole would gain a lot

more from constant attempts to tell their story than from hiding in a shell
expecting public relations men to handle it all for them.

Irving Kristol offers another approach to businesses in their dealings with the
news media. He maintains that although journalists may be biased in a "liberal"
direction, they are by and large intellectually honest, committed to telling the
truth, and anxious for acceptance by their peers as professionals. Thus, if a corporation were to find a journalist guilty of a flagrant error, it should expose him
or her through relentless publicity via paid advertisement rather than through
indignant letters to the editor. Kristol cautions, however, that such an approach
will not work in extolling the virtues of free enterprise; it should be used only
to defend a specific corporation against slander. The objective is not to change
public opinion directly, but to influence journalistic performance in the longer
run.[47]
    Simple and straightforward as this idea may seem, it has limited relevance
to business's general gripe against the news media or the specific objectives it
seeks to accomplish through advocacy advertising. If we accept the notion of
most journalists being intellectually honest and having high professional
standards, one would think that cases of flagrant error would be few and far
between. A reputable journalist would not find it difficult to admit to a mistake
and make amends. But what the businessperson is complaining of is not the
occasional error of omission or commission, but the general coverage of news,
which he or she feels tends to overemphasize the wrongs of business and understate its many good deeds. The issue is concerned not so much with factual
reporting as with perspective. The latter is a normative decision and therefore
subject to different interpretations depending on one's sociopolitical philosophy
and economic interests. To the extent that business needs to make its position
better understood, there are a variety of ways of accomplishing it (see Chapters
8 and 9).
    3. One can argue that a part of the conflict and misunderstanding between
business and the news media arises because business does not fully realize the
necessity for the news media to cater to a diverse and heterogeneous audience.
Therefore, *a large part of what business might consider unfair presentation might
simply be a fair presentation of news seen from another person's viewpoint.* Consider the possibility that the failure of the corporation to communicate with the
people and inform and educate them may be not so much a factor of ignorance
or bias on the part of the journalists and the news media, but of the unwillingness of the corporation to tell the truth and the *whole* truth about its activities.
The corporation has been found wanting in this regard. Corporate executives
seem "unwilling to admit publicly that the corporation is anything short of
perfect."[48] For example, when the vice-chairman of General Motors complains
that "business is somehow losing credibility with the public," there is a note of

puzzlement in his statement, as if he cannot believe anything could be wrong with GM's own behavior. He goes on to say that "business is doing its share of the job and we in the business community have to communicate this to the public. We have to teach, for example, that profits and progress go hand in hand."[49] There are no specifics as to what GM has been doing or what is meant by progress.

Reaching media may be a matter of corporations' having to learn how to get coverage. Robert Dilenschneider, a senior vice-president in the public relations firm of Hill & Knowlton, feels that news media would give corporations more coverage if the companies talked in terms of what is in the public's interest, e.g., consumers, senior citizens, minority groups, unemployed, or people in general. Companies should not talk about problems but about solutions. News media look for solutions, and if there are no solutions they are likely to come up with a negative story. One doesn't have to have paid advertising to reach people. Nonpaid communication can be more effective if done properly: "One has only to look at how the business image has declined. Nobody is taking ads against business, but it is because of non-paid communication."

Self-improvement by the New Media

The preceeding discussion is not intended to convey the impression that the news media are perfect and that there is no scope for improvement. Even the most respected journalists and ardent supporters of the news media concede to the need for developing better standards of reporting and the exercise of greater self-restraint on the part of journalists.[e]

One measure by which the news media can contribute to improved reporting of various viewpoints is to set up additional internal standards for checking into the type of news coverage provided. As John Oakes of *The New York Times* states: "Newspapermen have a special obligation to retain public confidence through conscious and deliberate effort to open ourselves to the public, to pay particular attention to complaints of unfairness, inaccuracy, bias, vindictiveness—that is, to make ourselves *voluntarily* accountable. Some newspapers have already gone a considerable distance in doing just this—but not many and certainly not enough."[50] An approach to attaining the objective would be through the installation of an in-house critic who would question the relevance and direction of various news stories covered in that particular newspaper or

---

[e]There have been numerous press reports on the past Watergate zeal of investigative reporters where in their attempts at discovering wrongdoing by corporate and public officials, journalists have done sloppy investigative work and developed some stories that were either inaccurate or blown out of proportion. See for example, "Jugular Journalism," *Newsweek*, May 10, 1976, p. 79; and "Discretion Urged in Press Power," *The New York Times*, May 4, 1976, p. 14.

magazine, or on the programs of that radio or television station. Unfortunately, most of the news media people I interviewed were reluctant to discuss this topic or concede that there may be a need for such a critic. To date, only one major newspaper (the *Washington Post*) has installed such a critic, Charles Seib, and the system appears to be working well.

More recently, CBS rejected a proposal that it hire an in-house critic with the "responsibility of receiving and investigating complaints from the public about unfair and inaccurate programs." The proposal was made by Accuracy in Media, Inc., a Washington-based organization. In rejecting the proposal CBS Chairman William S. Paley alluded to the high degree of independence and integrity achieved by the journalists employed by CBS News and indicated that it would be "way off base" to give one person "such control and high degree of authority over a worldwide news organization."[51] My proposal, however, is quite different. I do not belive that the in-house critic should have authority to investigate reports of inaccuracy or bias in specific news stories. These should be handled through normal channels. Moreover, I have faith in the diversity of viewpoints and integrity of individual newspeople. My perception of the in-house critic's job is to question any systemwide tendencies in covering certain types of news and the manner in which they are covered. The emphasis is on the long-term trends rather than specific items; such a person is not an ombudsman for readers investigating individual complaints.

Notes

1. Louis Banks, "Media Responsibility for Economic Literacy," speech given at the Annual John Hancock Awards for Excellence in Business and Financial Journalism. "A Bicentennial Examination of the Free Market System," John Hancock Mutual Life Insurance Co., Boston, October 28, 1975. See also "People in Business: Executives vs. the Newsmen," *The New York Times*, October 22, 1975, p. 59.

2. Letter to Senator Philip A. Hart (D, Mich.), dated July 16, 1974.

3. A speech before the Syracuse Press Club as reported in "Advertising" in *The New York Times*, November 24, 1975, p. 57.

4. "The Embattled Businessman, " *Newsweek*, February 16, 1976, p. 58; Irving Kristol, "On 'Economic Eduction,'" *The Wall Street Journal*, February 18, 1976, p. 20.

5. Cited in "The Embattled Businessman," pp. 57-58.

6. Donald S. MacNaughton, "The Businessman Versus the Journalist," *The New York Times*, March 7, 1976, section 3, p. 14.

7. Michael J. Connor, "Arguing Back: Mobil's Advocacy Ads Lead a Growing Trend, Draw Praise, Criticism," *The Wall Street Journal*, May 14, 1975, p. 1.

8. "The New Concerns About the Press," *Fortune,* April 1975, p. 130.

9. Deridre Carmody, "Reporters Chided on Business News," *The New York Times,* May 5, 1976, p. 38.

10. MacNaughton, "The Businessman Versus the Journalist," p. 13.

11. James A. Wechsler, in *Bulletin of the American Society of Newspaper Editors,* February 1, 1957, p. 5, quoted from J. Edward Gerald, *The Social Responsibility of the Press* (Minneapolis: The University of Minnesota Press, 1963), p. 108.

12. *Report of the National Commission on Civil Disorders* (New York: Dutton, 1968), p. 366.

13. James Clotfelter and B. Guy Peters, "Mass Media and the Military: Selected Ratings of Fairness," *Journalism Quarterly,* 52 (summer 1974), 332-334.

14. "The New Concerns About the Press," p. 130.

15. "TV's Credibility Gap," *Newsweek,* January 6, 1969, pp. 42-43.

16. Gene S. Graham, "The Responsibilities of the Doubly Damned," *Quill,* February 1968, p. 8.

17. John B. Oakes, "Confidence in the Press," *The New York Times,* May 5, 1976, p. 37.

18. "The Freedom of Advertising," Editorial, *The New York Times,* December 28, 1961.

19. These editorials appeared in the *Times* under the titles "The Birch Advertisement," December 20, 1963; "Fur Christmas," December 14, 1967; "Cigarettes and Advertising," August 29, 1969; "Freedom to Advertise," June 16, 1972; and "The Chinese Protest," May 17, 1973.

20. Robert J. Gwyn, "Opinion Advertising and the Free Market of Ideas," *Public Opinion Quarterly,* summer 1970, pp. 246-255.

21. *Ibid.,* p. 255.

22. The advertisement, entitled "Lincoln's Hopes for the Negro: In His Own Words," appeared in *The New York Times,* February 16, 1972.

23. Nat Hentoff, "Would You Run This Ad? A Survey of Publishers," *Business and Society Review,* 14 (summer 1975), 8-13.

24. Federal Communications Commission, *Fairness Doctrine and Public Interest Standards, Fairness Report Regarding Handling of Public Issues,* 39 Fed. Reg. 26372 (July 18, 1974).

25. *Ibid.,* p. 60.

26. *Ibid.,* p. 64.

27. *Ibid.,* pp. 67-68.

28. *Ibid.,* p. 70.

29. 412 U.S. 94 (1973); 450 F. 2d 642 (D.C. Cir. 1971) rev'd sub nom. *Columbia Broadcasting System, Inc.* v. *Democratic National Committee,* 412 U.S. 94 (1973). For a discussion and criticism of the FCC and Supreme Court decisions, see Nicholas Johnson and Tracy A. Westen, "A Twentieth-Century

Soapbox: The Right to Purchase Radio and Television Time," *Virginia Law Review,* 57 (1971), 547, and Gary William Maeder, "A Right of Access to the Broadcast Media for Paid Editorial Advertising—A Plea to Congress," *UCLA Law Review,* 22 (1974), 258.

30. *CBS* v. *DNC,* 412 U.S. 94 (1973) at 110.

31. *Ibid.,* 123, 124, 125, 127-128.

32. *Ibid.,* 122, 131.

33. FCC, *Fairness Report,* p. 80.

34. *NBC* v. *FCC,* 516 F. 2d 1101 (1974).

35. *Ibid.,* p. 1113, quoted from *CBS* v. *DNC,* 412 U.S. 94 (1971), 124-25.

36. *Ibid.,* p. 1115.

37. "Whatever Happened to Fair Play," advertisement by Mobil Oil Company in *The New York Times,* March 5, 1976, p. 56. For a somewhat critical discussion of Mobil's complaints against the broadcast media, see Gerald Astor, "The Gospel According to Mobil, *More,* 6, 4 (April 1976), 12-15.

38. S. Prakash Sethi, "Kodak-FIGHT Controversy," in *Up Against the Corporate Wall* 2nd ed. (Englewood Cliffs, N.J.: Prentice-Hall, 1974), pp. 279-300; see also J. Edward Gerald, *The Social Responsibility of the Press* (Minneapolis: University of Minnesota Press, 1963); Gene S. Graham, "History in the (Deliberate) Making: A Challenge of Modern Journalism," *Niemen Reports,* September 1966; Leslie R. Collit, "The Mask of Objectivity," *Nation,* June 17, 1968; Alan Wells (ed.), *Mass Media and Society* (Palo Alto, Calif.: National Press Books, 1972); John D. Stevens and William E. Porter, *The Rest of the Elephant: Perspectives on the Mass Media* (Englewood Cliffs, N.J.: Prentice-Hall, 1973); John B. Donovan, "Mass Communication and the Adversary Establishment," *Intellect,* May-June 1975, p. 256.

39. Jean Snyder, "Even Though Own Readers Are Victims, Papers Ignore FTC Complaint Against A&P," *Media & Consumer,* December 1972, p. 13.

40. Council on Economic Priorities, *Corporate Advertising and the Environment, Economic Priorities Report, September-October 1971,* 2, 3 (New York, October 1971), p. 28.

41. "A Sense of Advocacy in Advertising," *Saturday Review,* June 15, 1974 p. 50.

42. Liz Roman Gallese, "Boston's Sharon King Becomes Local TV Star by Knocking Products," *The Wall Street Journal,* October 20, 1975, p. 1.

43. "Riding Out the Storm at Channel 13 with Jay Iselin," *The New York Times,* November 9, 1975, section 2, pp. 1, 29.

44. William E. Blundell, "Phillips Petroleum to Turn Over Control to Outside Directors in Settlement Suit," *The Wall Street Journal,* February 19, 1976, p. 7.

45. "Corporate Advertising and the Environment," p. 28.

46. Thomas Griffith, "Must Business Fight the Press," *Fortune,* June 1974, p. 214. See also Enno Hobbing, "Business Must Explain Itself," *Business and*

Society Review, fall 1972; Adler Norman, "The Sounds of Executive Silence," *Harvard Business Review,* July–August 1971 p. 100; R.W. Armstrong, "Why Management Won't Talk," *Public Relations Journal,* November 1970, p. 6; and Max Ways, "Business Needs To Do a Better Job of Explaining Itself," *Fortune,* September 1972, p. 85.

47. Kristol, "On 'Economic Education,'" p. 20.

48. E.B.Weiss, "Management: Don't Kid the Public with Those Noble Anti-Pollution Ads," *Advertising Age,* August 3, 1970, p. 36.

49. Cited in *Ibid.*

50. John B. Oakes, "Confidence in the Press," *The New York Times,* May 5, 1976, p. 37.

51. "CBS Lists Record Profits, Rejects an In-House Critic," *The New York Times,* April 22, 1976, p. 49.

Appendix 3
FCC and the Fairness Doctrine:
Historical Developments

The Communications Act of 1934, as originally enacted, provided:

If any license shall permit any person who is a legally qualified candidate for any public office to use a broadcasting station, he shall afford equal opportunities to all other such candidates for that office in the use of such broadcasting station. . . . [1]

In 1949 the FCC added to the "equal opportunities" requirement of section 315 an "affirmative responsibility on the part of broadcast licensees to provide a reasonable amount of time for the presentation over their facilities of programs devoted to the discussion and considerations of public issues . . . [the] duty includes the making of reasonable provision for the discussion of controversial issues of public importance in the community served, and to make sufficient time available for full discussion thereof."[2]

In its amendment of section 315, Congress approved the fairness doctrine by recognizing "the obligation imposed upon [broadcasters] . . . to operate in the public interest and to afford reasonable opportunity for the discussion of conflicting views on issues of public importance."[3]

Thus, broadcast licensees are required, after broadcasting a controversial issue, to seek out opposing viewpoints from the community, and, if the spokesperson is unable to pay for the time, to provide access free of charge. The penalties for noncompliance with the fairness doctrine range from a notice of violation issued by the FCC to nonrenewal of the license. Enforcement of the doctrine is largely dependent on public complaints submitted to the FCC.[4]

In determining the applicability of the fairness doctrine to commercial advertisements, the FCC and the courts have considered product and institutional ads separately. For both types, the decisions have produced a confusion of standards for fairness.

Product Commercials

The FCC first considered the applicability of the fairness doctrine to commercial product advertising in 1946. The case, *In re Sam Morris,*[5] involved a radio station's refusal to broadcast advertising messages advocating abstinence from alcohol. Recognizing the possibility that product advertising could include controversial public issues, the commission warned broadcasters that, as part of their public service duty, they might be required to broadcast messages that conflicted with paid commercial ads by stating:

Differences concerning the relative statements of one product over another do not usually divide the community by raising basic and important . . . issues. But . . . it may well do so . . . [the] controversy . . . may assume the proportions of a controverted issue of public importance. The fact that the occasion for the controversy happens to be the advertising of a product cannot serve to diminish the duty of the broadcaster to treat it as such an issue.[6]

Again in 1963, the FCC, in its notice to licensees concerning their fairness doctrine responsibilities, emphasized its concern with "substance rather than . . . label or form" and restated that it is "immaterial whether a . . . program or viewpoint is . . . a paid announcement."[7] But it was not until 1967 that the FCC handed down its first ruling on advertising and the fairness doctrine. The case involved a fairness doctrine complaint by John Banzhaf claiming that a television station airing cigarette commercials had refused to allow opposing spokespeople air time to speak on the advisability of cigarette smoking and therefore had violated the fairness doctrine. The FCC decision in the Banzhaf case,[8] affirmed by the court of appeals for the District of Columbia circuit,[9] held that a "controversial issue of public importance was inherent in the advertising of cigarettes and thus required the broadcasters to present programs with the anti-smoking viewpoint."[10] This requirement stemmed from the broadcaster's duty to operate in the public interest, which included the responsibility to inform the public of health hazards associated with smoking.

In its decision the FCC "defined the controversial issue of public importance to be the desirability of smoking portrayed in the commercials, despite the fact that the commercials made no affirmative health claims"[11] and emphasized the government's concern with cigarette smoking and related health hazards as a situation that made cigarette commercials unique. Thus, the FCC attempted to prevent extension of the Banzhaf ruling to other advertised products.[12] In addition, the FCC recognized advertising's unique position with respect to whether a broadcaster had provided balanced coverage of the issues. Because the cigarette ads were numerous, repetitive, and continuous, the FCC asserted that a balanced presentation required more than "an occasional program a few times a year or . . . some appropriate announcements once or twice a week."[13]

Adhering to its ruling that cigarette ads constitute a unique situation, the FCC refused to hold a hearing on a radio station's license renewal despite a fairness complaint against the station. The complaint involved the station's discontinuance of union ads that supported the boycott of a store while continuing to air the store's regular product advertising. The courts, however, in *Retail Store Employees Union, Local 880, R.C.I.A.* v. *FCC,*[14] reversed the FCC decision, stating that the product ad inherently raised on one side of the boycott issue and interpreted the Banzhaf decision to mean some advertisements "could carry an implicit as well as an explicit message."[15] In this case the D.C. circuit court expanded the potential application of the fairness doctrine to product commercials that did not deal with health hazards by suggesting that the FCC "question whether licensee refusal of the labor union's advertisements was consistent with national policy favoring equalization of labor-management bargaining powers."[16]

Again, in *In re Neckritz* (Chevron),[17] the FCC refused to apply the fairness doctrine to advertisements for an additive to Chevron gasoline and claims that "gasoline with F-310 turns dirty smoke into good, clean mileage,"[18] asserting that the ads did not deal with a public controversy since Chevron had not raised the issue of air pollution but rather had advanced a claim for product efficiency.

Despite the FCC's continued attempts to prevent the extension of the Banzhaf decision to other product commercials, the courts again reversed an FCC decision and extended fairness scrutiny to advertisements promoting cars with large engines and high-test leaded gasoline. In *Friends of the Earth* v. *FCC*[19] they found it impossible to distinguish between the health hazards of cigarette smoking and those of car-generated air pollution and therefore stated: "When there is evidence, as there is here, that the hazards to health implicit in air pollution are enlarged and aggravated by such products, then the parallel with cigarette advertising is exact and the relevance of *Banzhaf* inescapable."

The court's reversal of the FCC decision in *Friends of the Earth* prompted the FCC to reconsider the Chevron case, *In re Neckritz*,[20] but once again the commission refused to extend the Banzhaf decision, stating there was no evidence indicating that F-310 was a public health hazard and, even if some hazard were involved, the expert opinion was much more divided than in the cigarette smoking issue.[21]

Institutional Advertising

Institutional advertising may raise the issue of fairness doctrine applicability when the ad "tracks arguments being made in the community on one side of an issue."[22] The FCC decided in favor of applying the fairness doctrine in the National Broadcasting (Esso)[23] and Media Access Project[24] cases. In the National Broadcasting case, two environmental groups filed a complaint against NBC for running Esso ads concerning oil development in Alaska. The ads, they claimed, raised the issue of the need for rapid development of Alaskan oil reserves and the capability of transporting the oil across the tundra without causing environmental damage. The issue of the Alaskan pipeline and oil development on the North Slope was, at the time the ads were broadcast, before the courts and being debated by the public. In *Media Access Project*, the ads of Georgia Power Company raised the issue of the company's rate increase request.

In *National Broadcasting,* the FCC found the arguments in the Esso ads to have a "cognizable bearing on the controversy, and in *Media Access* to 'clearly' present one side of the rate increase issue. In both cases, therefore, the institutional ads were found to be subject to fairness doctrine requirements." However, in a series of military advertising cases that included *San Francisco Women for Peace,*[25] *David C. Green,*[26] and *Alan F. Neckritz,*[27] the FCC refused to find any controversial issues that required the application of the fairness doctrine. In each of the cases the complainant sought an FCC ruling that the broadcast licensees were not fulfilling fairness responsibilities since they had refused to broadcast messages that opposed military service after accepting military recruitment advertising. In a decision affirmed by the District of Columbia circuit court, the FCC reasoned that although "the war and the draft were controversial . . . these issues were not raised by the advertisements, and . . . no evidence had been produced indicating that the stations had failed in their general obligation to serve community needs by presenting contrasting sides of the issues."[28] The decisions in the military advertising cases might be explained, however, in terms of the "traditional deference to national security needs, the intensely political nature of the war issue, the huge administrative problems potentially connected with monitoring complaints based on the advertisements, and the fact that a public sponsor was involved,"[29] rather than in terms of tightening of fairness doctrine applicability. In *In re Neckritz,* although the commercials in addition to product advertising exhibited some of the characteristics of institutional ads, the FCC ruled the fairness doctrine did not apply.[30]

In all these cases one predominant problem is the confusion of standards for judging the relationship between a controversial public issue and the advertisement in question and thus the applicability of the fairness doctrine. The standards used include those employed in *Neckritz,* which states that the advertisement must deal "directly" with the issue; that of *National Broadcasting,* which speaks of advertisements "inherently" raising and having "a cognizable bearing on" the issue; and that of *Media Access,* which focuses on an advertisement that "clearly presents" the issue.[31] Spurred by the confusion in dealing with the fairness doctrine and by the increasing demands for access to the broadcast media, the FCC developed its 1974 statement on the application of the fairness doctrine to product and image commercials. Details of this policy statement are discussed in the text.

Notes

1. Communications Act of 1934 Ch. 652, S 315(a), 48 Stat. 1088 (1934), as amended, 47 U.S.C. S 315(a) (1970), amended (Supp. II, 1972).

2. *The Report on Editorializing by Broadcast Licensees,* 13 FCC 1246, 1249 (1949).

3. 47 U.S.C. 315 (a) (1970).

4. Steven J. Simmons, "Commercial Advertising and the Fairness Doctrine: The New FCC Policy in Perspective," *Columbia Law Review,* 75 (1975), 1087.

5. 11 FCC 197 (1946).

6. 11 FCC at 198, 199 (1946). As quoted in Simmons, "Commercial Advertising," p. 1095.

7. Controversial Issue Programming, 40 FCC 571, 572 (1963). As quoted in Simmons, "Commercial Advertising," p. 1088.

8. WCBS-TV, Applicability of the Fairness Doctrine to Cigarette Advertising, 9 FCC 2d 921 (1967).

9. *Banzhaf* v. *FCC,* 405 F. 2d 1082 (D.C. Cir. 1968), *cert. denied,* 396 U.S. 842 (1969).

10. John C. Moore, "Notes: Advertising and Recent Developments in the Fairness Doctrine," *Washington and Lee Law Review,* 29 (1972), 87.

11. WCBS-TV, 9 FCC 2d 921, 938, 939 (1967). Quoted from Simmons, "Commercial Advertising," p. 1088.

12. Simmons, "Commercial Advertising," p. 1088.

13. 9 FCC 2d at 942.

14. 436 F. 2d 248 (D.C. Cir. 1970).

15. Id at 258, quoted from Simmons, "Commercial Advertising," p. 1098.

16. Id at 259, quoted from Simmons, "Commercial Advertising," p. 1098.

17. 29 FCC 2d 807 (1971), reconsidered 37 FCC 2d 528 (1972).

18. 29 FCC 2d at 807.

19. 449 F. 2d 1164 (D.C. Cir. 1971).

20. *Ibid.,* p. 1169, quoted from Simmons, "Commercial Advertising," p. 1097.

21. *Ibid.,* p. 531.

22. Simmons, "Commercial Advertising," p. 1089.

23. 30 FCC 2d 643 (1971).

24. 44 FCC 2d 755 (1973).

25. 24 FCC 2d 156 (1970), *aff'd sub nom. Green* v. *FCC,* 447 F. 2d 323 (D.C. Cir. 1971).

26. 24 FCC 2d 171 (1970), *aff'd sub nom. Green* v. *FCC,* 447 F. 2d 323 (D.C. Cir. 1971).

27. 24 FCC 2d at 175 (1970), *aff'd,* 446 F. 2d 501 (9th Cir. 1971).

28. 24 FCC 2d at 172, 173 quoted from Simmons, "Commercial Advertising," p. 1092.

29. Simmons, "Commercial Advertising," p. 1012.

30. 29 FCC 2d 807 (1971) *reconsidered,* 37 FCC 2d 528 (1972).

31. Simmons, "Commercial Advertising," p. 1094.

Part II
Advocacy Advertising in Action

Introduction to Part II

All of us get our thoughts entangled in metaphors, and act fatally on the strength of them.

—George Elliot, Middle March

The metamorphosis of ideas into actions is rarely totally or completely faithful. What appears logical and rational as an abstract thought becomes distorted when applied to specific situations. This may happen because those who preach advocacy of a particular idea do not have total commitment to it and are unwilling to sacrifice their own interest to pursue the adoption of the idea to its fullest extent; it may be desirable to modify the idea in practice in order to persuade others to adopt it; the process of communication through which the advocates of an idea attempt to persuade others to follow imposes certain constraints on the manner in which the ideas are put into practice.

This section contains two in-depth case studies of advocacy advertising. They demonstrate the gap between the rhetoric and the rationale of advocacy advertising on the one hand, and the reality and the practice of advocacy advertising on the other hand. They are a microcosm that amplifies both the strengths and the weaknesses of advocacy advertising as it is currently practiced in the United States. And, finally, they serve as the background against which one can begin to assess the substance of the public policy arguments raised by the supporters and critics of current advocacy advertising practices and how they might be changed or controlled, if indeed such a course of action is desirable or necessary.

4

America Has More Coal Than the Middle East Has Oil: Let's Dig It

The American Electric Power Company Advocacy Campaign

The spirit of liberty is the spirit that is not sure it is right.

—Learned Hand

In February 1974,[a] a full-page ad appeared in the nation's major daily newspapers and weeklies with the headline, "We Have More Coal Than They Have Oil—Let's Use It." The top half of the ad page carried a caricature of two Arab sheikhs standing in front of a Rolls Royce. The "We" in the caption referred to the United States; "They" were the Middle Eastern countries. The text suggested that the United States has abundant resources of coal—enough to meet our needs for 500 years—and that it could be the major solution to our energy problems provided we use it immediately and fully. The ad recognized the environmental and pollution problems related to using this coal, but claimed "They are nothing that American ingenuity cannot lick" (Exhibit 4A-1; all campaign advertisements appear in the appendix to this chapter).

With this advertisement, American Electric Power Company, Inc. (AEP), and its then chairman, Donald C. Cook, launched a media campaign that has made the two cartoon sheikhs the most well known in the United States. It also brought to public attention the complex battle that the nation's utilities had hitherto fought in Congress, the White House, state legislatures, and the courts against major environmental groups, government regulators, conservationists, and just about everyone else who was considered unsympathetic to their problems and who differed with their views of how these problems might be solved. The campaign, which lasted until December 1974, eventually included 36 ads that cost the company over $3.6 million. After a pause of nine months, the ads have started appearing again.

Unless otherwise specifically stated, all direct quotes in this chapter are from personal interviews or written communications with the author.

[a]The first ad appeared on February 5, 1974, in *The New York Times, The Wall Street Journal, Washington Post,* and 69 dailies and 192 weeklies in the area served by American Electric Power System's group of companies. It appeared in the February 9, 1974, issue of *Business Week;* the February 11, 1974, issues of *Times, Newsweek,* and *U.S. News;* and the March 1975 issue of *Fortune.*

American Electric Power Company (AEP)

No examination of AEP and its campaign would be complete without looking at its chairman and chief executive officer, Donald C. Cook, whose personal beliefs are closely intertwined with the interests of the company.

AEP is the largest producer of electric power in the United States and is one of the most profitable. AEP is an investor-owned public utility holding company that owns the stock of seven electric company subsidiaries in addition to other subsidiaries engaged in businesses directly related to electric energy, such as coal mining and power generation. Although based in New York, AEP's service area encompasses parts of Virginia (Appalachian Power Company); Indiana (Indiana Michigan Electric Company); Ohio (Ohio Power Company); Kentucky (Kentucky Power Company); Tennessee (Kingsport Power Company); Michigan (I & M and Michigan Power Company); and West Virginia (Appalachian Power and Wheeling Electric Company). Collectively they are known as the American Electric Power System. Servicing 41,260 square miles, 2,964 communities, and a population of 5,901,000, the AEP System has a total power supply capability of about 18,000 megawatts, third only to the Tennessee Valley Authority and the Southern Company. Ninety percent of AEP's capacity is coal-fired.

Relying heavily on economies of scale, AEP operates the largest cooling towers, among the tallest smokestacks, the largest strip-mining machine, and one of the largest generating stations in the nation. AEP has been, for a number of years, the country's most efficient electric generating utility. The growth and strength of AEP have been based on coal since its founding in 1906, which was significant during the time the electric utility industry was moving toward the use of oil and nuclear power. But this was before the Arab oil embargo and resultant increase in oil prices and the nuclear power industry's failure to meet expectations. Today, AEP and its coal-burning capacities occupy an enviable position in the power industry.[1]

Donald C. Cook—who until his retirement in December 1975 was the chairman and chief executive officer—came to AEP in 1953 after serving for two years as chairman of the SEC, where he started his government service in 1935. His career with the government included work in the Department of Justice and for committees of the Senate and House of Representatives. Describing himself as a "New Dealer" and "imbued with remaking America," Cook is deeply concerned with the country's power crisis and with the financial difficulties besetting utilities. In addition, he strongly believes in the use of domestic coal to help solve these problems.[2] Cook's stand on the scrubber issue and the Department of Interior's reluctance to permit the mining of large deposits of federally owned low-sulfur coal in the West is characterized by his allegation that "our government prevents us from burning the coal we can mine and prevents us from mining the coal we can burn!"[3] Cook, despite his long experience with the government, is willing to state his criticisms of it. He explains, "I saw first hand the awesome powers of the government, and I saw enough of the government operation to know that justice does not always prevail and righteousness does not always triumph."[4]

The AEP advertising campaign promoting American energy independence and criticizing the "extreme" environmentalists is widely attributed to the leadership of Donald Cook. Because he is "a strong-willed and scrappy man, Cook's style is to come out fighting rather than work quietly behind the scenes, as other utility executives are doing. As a result, AEP, which generates more electricity than any other private utility, is increasingly identified in the public eye as the leading critic of environmental rules."[5] Cook counters this view with the statement that "the government, and assuredly the EPA, think they're the only people to love their country. I don't need some EPA bureaucrat to tell me about the woods, or the land, or the water."[6]

The very basis for AEP's generating capability, a system based on the burning of coal, places it in the forefront of the environmental debate. The company has shown foresight and responsibility in dealing with some environmental issues. Because some of its plants are located on small rivers, in 1958 AEP voluntarily built its first mechanical cooling tower, and the western hemisphere's first natural-draft cooling tower in 1963, to prevent thermal pollution. Nine additional towers are now in operation, with more planned. A 56-station network of monitoring stations set up by AEP measures particulate matter and gases such as sulfure oxide in the area surrounding 12 coal-burning plants. For the past thirty years AEP has conducted a land reclamation program in strip-mined areas of southeastern Ohio. The company has planted 35 million trees on a 35,000 acre recreation area that attracts 25,000 visitors annually. "Hell," says Cook, "I don't think Quarles (of EPA) could spell reclamation 30 years ago."[7]

In other areas, however, AEP has been forced into taking action only by law. The burning of coal produces tons of fly ash that are dispersed through tall smokestacks. "Some of its plants employed inefficient equipment, while others were long uncontrolled, although fly ash collectors were developed decades ago."[8] In most cases these plants were located in rural areas, and AEP was content, despite complaints of excessive dust, to disperse the sooty particles through tall smokestacks. AEP has now started upgrading its plants with highly efficient electrostatic precipitators that will bring all its plants into compliance with particulate standards by 1978. The cost of this refitting is estimated to be over $500 million. As of 1974, AEP has invested $374 million in environmental control, a figure that is expected to grow to $1 billion within the next three years.

AEP's Ad Campaign

The Background

The AEP campaign originated in December 1973, two months before the appearance of the first ad. At that time, in response to President Nixon's energy message, the company published a double-page advertisement in the country's leading newspapers and news magazines (Exhibit 4-1) in which AEP pointed out that two imperative steps in resolving the crisis, particularly the assurance of an adequate supply of electric power, had been omitted. The ad generated a flurry of news stories and editorial comment that led the company to believe there would be some response from the administration. However, according to a company spokesman:

Nearly two months passed and still little or nothing was being done other than talk. There seemed to be little inclination to face and deal with some of the fundamental issues involved in the energy crisis. For example, nothing was being done about making possible the greater utilization or availability of coal—our most abundant raw energy. It was quite clear to many knowledgeable people in the field of energy that coal had to assume a key role in any solution to the energy crisis both short-term and for many years into the future. In addition, the coal supply/demand problem was worsening daily with the result that coal prices were skyrocketing.

At the time the ads were appearing, it was unclear what specific objectives AEP was trying to accomplish, as the ads covered a variety of subjects and themes. The company's 1974 annual report made the following statement with regard to the objectives of the campaign (the statement claimed that it was the first time an electric utility had run a continuing ad campaign in the national press):

We did it because we had something important to say to the widest possible audience. . . .
Our main objective was to point out the vital importance of utilizing coal—our most abundant and most available fuel—to the maximum. In so doing we criticized those government policies that were restricting the burning of some coal and the mining of other coal, even while not restricting the export of this fuel so essential to America.
On the other hand, we supported the Clean Air Act, applauding its aims while asking only that utilities be given some choice in how to meet them. We also supported land reclamation after surface mining, asking only that any law not be so severe as to totally ban such mining.
We believe the series was in the public interest, contributing to better understanding of some of the reasons for the nation's energy dilemma. . . .[9]

With a six-month perspective, after the termination of the campaign, a company official summarized the objectives of the campaign as to bring to the attention of the public the following major points:

1. The energy crisis was more accurately a crisis in oil and gas supply.
2. We must place greater reliance on our domestic energy resources.
3. The only domestic fuel reserve in very large supply is coal. Therefore, all unnecessary restrictions on its digging and use should be removed forthwith.

MR. PRESIDENT,

We Agree With Your Messages On the Energy Crisis

You ordered a number of measures to conserve energy and to make more energy sources available. You called upon the Congress and the entire nation to take other steps to solve the energy crisis. We applaud your directive banning the conversion of power plants from coal to oil. We endorse your efforts to speed up nuclear power plant construction and licensing. In fact, we agree wholeheartedly with what you said.

But, Mr. President, You Omitted Two Imperative Steps

Immediate action on these two steps, by both you and the Congress, will go a long way toward resolving our energy crisis—particularly in the assurance of an adequate electric power supply.

I Action: Modify the Environmental Protection Agency requirements which would measure power plant sulfur dioxide emissions at the top of the chimneys. The emissions are not going to stay there. They will be dissipated. Instead, measure them realistically, at ground level, where people, animals and plants live and grow!

Result: Power plants could then burn the billions of tons of mineable, higher-sulfur Eastern coal now available. This coal—when used in conjunction with extra-high chimneys ("tall stacks") and air monitoring devices, and burned at reduced levels during periods of poor atmospheric conditions—represents the most workable and satisfactory answer to the sulfur problem at this time. With these controls it can be burned without violating air-quality standards.

II Action: Make available for leasing for mining the large reserves of Government owned low-sulfur coal in the Far West. At the same time seek and establish attainable standards for reclamation of the land after mining.

Result: These coal reserves, withheld from use several years ago by the Department of the Interior, would provide billions of tons of critically needed low-sulfur coal for the nation's power supply. And the land would be restored for as good a use as at present. Possibly better.

These two steps will benefit the nation immediately in several ways:

- Consumers will continue to receive the electric power they need.
- The use of dwindling oil and gas supplies by electric power plants will be sharply reduced, making these fuels available for other critical needs.
- A reasonable balance between the need for energy and the need for a wholesome environment will be maintained.
- The economy of the nation will be safeguarded.
- And a long step forward will have been taken toward your goal of making our nation self-sufficient in energy by 1980.

Mr. President, Here's What We're Already Doing

As a major producer of electricity, we're taking positive action to serve our 1,700,000 customers in the states of Ohio, Indiana, Michigan, Virginia, West Virginia, Kentucky and Tennessee.

Capacity: We now have under construction 4,800,000 kilowatts of additional generating capacity, both coal-fired and nuclear, and have plans to start construction of another 2,600,000 kw in the near future.

Fuel: We are mining, or contracting for, the additional tons of coal required to fuel these plants. And we are arranging the means to assure its delivery.

Environment: we are spending $300,000,000 in the next two years alone to protect the environment by:
1. Building giant cooling towers.
2. Building plant chimneys over 1,000 feet high.
3. Installing highly efficient dust collecting equipment.
4. Installing elaborate systems to monitor the air at ground level near our power plants.
5. Pursuing our exploration of other clean-air systems.

Conservation: We are urging our customers not to waste electricity and to use only what they need. We are also cutting back our own thermostats, reducing vehicle speeds, and turning off our outdoor decorative lighting.

Our Efforts Have Produced Results

No electric power shortage exists anywhere on the seven-state American Electric Power System. No shortage will ever exist as long as we are permitted to build, without unreasonable delay, the new facilities required for the generation and delivery of electric power.

And as long as we are permitted to use, without unreasonable restriction, the nation's most abundant, most available fuel . . . coal.

To Do Our Job All We Need Is Half A Chance

An electric power shortage exists in some areas of the country now. It can be prevented from spreading across the entire country—and, indeed, can be solved where it now exists—if the electric utility industry is given a reasonable chance to do its job.

In short, let us burn coal, the available fuel. Let us burn it without unnecessary restrictions, such as unreasonable EPA emission standards and the unrealistic proposal for short-term variances. A short-term variance which permits a power plant to use available coal, instead of unavailable oil, on a temporary basis is no answer at all. No coal supplier could possibly develop the necessary mining facilities under such an uncertain short-term proposition. Unless coal can be used as more than an interim fuel, this abundant resource cannot solve our present or future energy problems.

Mr. President, we do have an energy crisis of the greatest seriousness on our hands. Fortunately, the Federal government itself has the means immediately at hand to largely deal with it. *Won't you please take the necessary steps by modifying the EPA regulations and making government-owned, low-sulfur, Western coal available?*

"We need new rules if we are to meet this challenge." In your second energy message you said. We could not agree more.

Immediate action toward new rules is action in the national interest!

(signature)

Donald C. Cook
Chairman

American Electric Power System

Appalachian Power Co., Indiana & Michigan Electric Co., Kentucky Power Co., Kingsport Power Co., Michigan Power Co., Ohio Power Co., Wheeling Electric Co.

Advertised in U.S.News & World Report

Exhibit 4-1

Table 4-1

American Electric Power Advertising Program Schedule, 1974

Publication	Arabs	Children's	Veins	Galloping Unemployment	Generate More	Open Letter	Happen Again	Baloney	We Must	Blind	Rejected	Have You Heard	Government Has	Innocent Plant	Critical	Unmask	Hot Air	Export
Time	2/11	3/4	3/18	4/1	4/8		4/15	4/22	4/29	5/7	5/14	5/21	5/28	6/4	6/11	6/18	6/24	7/1
Newsweek	2/11	3/4	3/18	4/1	4/8		4/15	4/22	4/29	5/7	5/14	5/21	5/28	6/4	6/11	6/18	6/24	7/8
U.S. News	2/11	3/4	3/18	4/1	4/8		4/15	4/22	4/29	5/7	5/14	5/21	5/28	6/4	6/11	6/18	6/24	7/8
Business Week	2/9	3/2	3/16	3/30	4/6		4/13	4/20	4/27	5/5	5/12	5/19	5/26	6/2	6/9	6/16	6/22	6/29
Fortune	Mar.	Apr.	May	June														
Science					4/19													
Spectrum (IEEE)														June				
Forbes																		
The New York Times	2/5	2/26	3/12	3/26	4/3		4/9	4/16	4/23	4/30	5/7	5/15	5/21	5/28	6/4	6/11	6/18	6/25
The Wall Street Journal	2/5	2/26	3/13	3/26	4/3	4/9		4/18	4/23	5/1	5/7	5/16	5/21	5/28	6/4	6/11	6/18	7/2
Washington Post	2/5	2/26	3/12	3/26	4/2		4/9	4/16	4/23	4/30	5/7	5/14	5/21	5/28	6/4	6/11	6/18	6/25
Financial World																		
The Miner			Nov.															
Service area*	2/5	2/26	Nov.	3/26	4/2	4/9	4/9	4/16	4/23	4/30	5/7	5/14	5/21	5/28	6/4	6/11	6/18	7/2
Western papers†	2/13																	

Source: American Electric Power Company, Inc.

*Service area papers: 69 dailies, 192 weeklies.

†Western papers: Denver Post, Great Falls Tribune, Casper Tribune, Billings Gazette.

4. Electric power fueled by coal can make a major contribution, currently and in the future, to resolving the nation's energy problems and at the same time, provide for protection and enhancement of the environment.

However, neither the statement in the annual report nor subsequent statements ever explicitly dealt with one of the major focuses of the campaign that generated the most heated controversy and was the subject of intense debate; that is, EPA was advocating the installation of scrubbers on smokestacks to remove pollutants in order to meet the Clean Air Act requirements. A large segment of the utility industry, with AEP in the lead, was strongly opposed to gas stack scrubbers.[10]

Media Strategy

Table 4-1 provides details of ad placement in various media. The emphasis was on placing ads in the three major news weekly magazines plus *Business Week* and also three of the nationally prominent newspapers—*The New York Times, The Wall Street Journal,* and the *Washington Post.* In addition, widespread coverage was achieved in AEP's seven-state service area through placements in local newspapers from February through October.

What Time	Environ- mentalists	We Burn	Speak Out	We've Won	Computerized	UHV	They're Trying	Requiem	Rich	Requiem	Letter	Amen	Philadelphia	Scrubber Stories	Maybe	Yesterday	We Repeat	What's Wrong
7/15	8/5	8/19	9/2	9/9				10/14	10/7	10/21		10/28	11/4	11/11	11/18	11/25	12/2	12/9
7/22	8/12			9/9				10/14		10/21				11/11				
7/22	8/12			9/9				10/14		10/28								
7/13	8/3		8/31					10/12		10/19								
								10/15		11/1								
7/9	7/31	8/13	8/27	9/4	9/11	9/17	9/24	10/2	10/9	10/15	10/22	10/24	10/25	11/7	11/14	11/18	11/25	12/3
7/16	8/6		8/27	9/4		9/17		10/1		10/15			10/29					
7/9	7/30	8/13	8/27	9/4	9/10	9/17	9/24	10/1	10/8	10/15	10/22	10/25	10/29	11/7	11/12	11/20	11/25	12/4
				10/30														
	7/30	8/13	8/27															

The number of insertions totaled 5,690 in 277 publications, of which 69 daily newspapers and 192 weekly newspapers were located in the AEP service area. Circulation of the 277 publications totaled 17,949,966. At no time were all the publications used for a single ad. Reader exposures based upon circulation, including pass-along readership, can be assumed to have been substantially greater than circulation of the publications. Estimates of pass-along readership vary from 2.5 to 6.4 times circulation. Advertisements were not planned as a program in advance, but were developed in response to specific events. The emphasis was on being "current" and keyed to what the company believed to be major energy issues. Thus it was not unusual for the company to withdraw an ad only days before it was scheduled to appear and substitute a more timely ad.

The campaign included a total of 36 advertisements (see appendix, Exhibits 4A-1 to 4A-36). A large part of the ad campaign was devoted to criticism, often acrimonious, of the EPA and its insistence that utilities install gas stack scrubbers on coal-burning power plants. Thus to critics it appeared that AEP's campaign was motivated more by self-interest than by consumer and public interest. Cook strongly denies this charge. He states, "The environmentalists have an advantage because they don't have to be responsible to anybody. They can speak in terms of hyperbole, making the most exaggerated statements without facts. And, what's more, they regularly do so."[11] He went on to say that while he believed in protecting the environment, the cost of doing so should bear some reasonable relationship to the benefits obtained. Otherwise the excessive environmental requirements would impose an unreasonable burden on all our citizens, make an unwarranted contribution to inflation, and constitute an unwise and wasteful misallocation of the nation's limited and precious resources.[12]

A general classification of the advertisements by the author (Table 4-2) shows that 21 of the 36 ads were devoted to criticism of scrubbers and defense of AEP supported measures; and criticism of Environmental Protection Agency, Clean Air Act, and pollution control standards and time tables. Thus, it lends some credence to this charge. Of course, it is possible that AEP may have found its interests similar to those of the public—an identity with which the critics found it difficult to agree.

Ad Copy

The copy was generally direct and to the point. However, Mr. Harold Johnson of AEP insists:

The ad copy was completely factual and we stand by every statement made in our ads. Each ad was checked and rechecked by our people in engineering, legal, environment, and top management to ensure its accuracy. Furthermore, Mr. Cook personally examined and approved each ad before it was released for running in the news media.

Table 4-2
Copy Themes and Sequencing of Ads

Ad Copy Themes	No. of Ads*	Sequence in which Ads Appeared†
1. Encourage and allow greater usage of coal	6	1, 2, 3, 5, 8, 15
2. Less energy = less employment	2	4, 7
3. Imported oil and gas make U.S. more vulnerable to foreign pressure	3	6, 26, 28
4. Criticism of EPA, Clean Air Act, and pollution control standards and time tables	8	9, 10, 16, 19, 21, 22, 29, 33
5. Criticism of scrubbers and defense of AEP-supported measures	13	11, 12, 14–18, 21, 27, 29–32
6. Urging federal government to release more federal land for coal mining	2	13, 35
7. Defending AEP record in conservation and pollution control	6	20, 22–25, 34
8. Criticism of coal exports	2	18, 36

*Some copy themes are included in more than one category.
†Note: Ad sequence also corresponds to the exhibit numbers identifying various ads reproduced in the appendix.

The headlines used were quite provocative (Table 4-3) and were designed to draw readers' attention to the copy themes. The pictures used in the ads were well coordinated with the headlines and seemed to suggest certain conclusions to be drawn from those ads.

Reaction to the Campaign

The reaction to the ad campaign ranged from highly favorable to quite critical. While the sources of most of the favorable and adverse comments were predictable, the intensity of the criticism from some quarters was unexpected. Critics charged the campaign was misguided and overly simplistic and likely to do more harm than good to the cause of greater public understanding of the complex issues of energy growth, pollution, and environment. Critics also accused AEP of publishing inaccurate and incomplete information in specific ads and of using clichés that bordered on playing on emotions instead of reasoning.

General Public Reaction

AEP did not do any before-and-after public opinion survey to indicate any changes in the general public's attitude toward the company, and more important, the understanding of the various issues raised in the campaign. However, if news reports and editorial comments are any indications, the campaign was successful in heightening public awareness of AEP as a public utility and also of some of the issues raised in various ads. Harold R. Johnson of AEP states:

While it has not been possible to tabulate all of the responses to the advertising program (they came by mail, telephone, personal conversations with employees throughout our company, and media), our overall reports show that we received more favorable than unfavorable reactions. The change that took place in public reaction should be of interest. The response during the first few weeks was largely critical. As the advertising continued, the responses changed to approximately 50–50. During the last two months, the response was largely favorable and has continued to be predominately favorable once the advertising ended.

The Environmental Protection Agency, on the other hand, received more than 200 letters criticizing the ads. Mr. Cook also admits having received critical letters from college students. However, he is not concerned about the adverse criticism because it implies a higher degree of public interest. He comments:

They [college students] are good, earnest young people and shouldn't be discouraged. It's wonderful for them to have ideals and stand up for themselves.... But there's a big difference between the right to speak out and the formulation of national policy on the basis of ignorance. They know as much about this subject as the hot dog vendor here in front of 2 Broadway.[13]

Table 4-3

Classification of Ad Headlines Under Various Themes

Copy Theme 1. Encourage and Allow Greater Usage of Coal

  1 We have more coal than they have oil. Let's use it!
  2 We have enough coal to fill the energy needs of our children's children's children's children's children's children's children's children's children's children's children's children's children's children's children's children. Let's dig it.
  3 America has energy to burn . . . in its veins.
  5 The most sensible way to help solve the energy shortage is to generate more electricity. More, not less. And from coal.
  8 Baloney.
 15 Coal. It is critical to nuclear energy!

Copy Theme 2. Less Energy = Less Employment

  4 Generate Less Energy Sure. And generate galloping unemployment!
  7 An open letter on energy to those who are still employed.

Copy Theme 3. Imported Oil and Gas Make U.S. More Vulnerable to Foreign Pressure

  6 It happened to us once. It can happen again. And again.
 26 They're trying to tell us something. We're foolish not to listen.
 28 The rich get richer while we struggle with inflation!

Copy Theme 4. Criticism of EPA, Clean Air Act, and Pollution Standards and Timetables

  9 In America we're still not conserving the energy we should. We must. We absolutely must!
 10 Are we blind to the real energy crisis?
 16 Let's unmask the old bugaboo. The fact is: coal-burning power plants are not hopeless polluters.
 19 Just about this time next year lots of people may be asking, "What time is the electricity on today?"
 21 We burn at those who block the burning of vast amounts of America's coal. And would like to claim they don't.
 22 To speak out, clearly and fairly Not only is it a constitutional right . . . it is a moral duty.
 29 Half a story is worse than none.
 33 "Maybe we should buy American coal fields."

Copy Theme 5. Criticism of Scrubbers and Defense of AEP Supported Measures

 11 Scrubbers described, examined and rejected.
 12 Have you heard the one about the scrubbers?
 14 Announcing the INNOCENT plant A gigantic coal-burner to gladden the hearts of the most avid environmentalists.
 15 Coal. It is critical to nuclear energy!
 16 Let's unmask the old bugaboo. The fact is: coal-burning power plants are not hopeless polluters.
 17 Hot Air vs. Clean Air
 18 Although America is critically short, we are exporting energy!
 21 We burn at those who block the burning of vast amounts of America's coal. And would like to claim they don't.
 27 Requiem for scrubbers.
 29 Half a story is worse than none.
 30 Amen!
 31 The Philadelphia, Pa. Story – or – It's time some people learned you can't fool all of the people.
 32 Have you heard any good scrubber stories lately?

Copy Theme 6. Urging Federal Government to Release More Federal Land for Coal Mining

 13 The government has something the people need but won't release it. Why?
 35 We repeat a suggestion we abhor.

124

Table 4–3 continued

Copy Theme 7. Defending AEP Record in Conservation and Pollution Control

20 We were environmentalists long before it was popular.
   We've got nearly a billion in investments to prove it.
22 To speak out, clearly and fairly Not only is it a constitutional right . . . it is a moral duty.
23 We've won it again! And no wonder.
24 Now. Clean air, computerized.
25 Canada Italy France Russia and others are all probing UHV where do we stand?
34 Our yesterday is the world's tomorrow!

Copy Theme 8. Criticism of Coal Exports

18 Although America is critically short, we are exporting energy!
36 What's wrong with this picture? It's inflation by the carload.

Furthermore, he maintains that the whole purpose of the advertising was to attract audience attention. "Most institutional advertising is dismal," says Mr. Cook; "It puts more people to sleep than all the somnifics sold in the nation. If we were to accomplish anything, we had to put together advertisements that would provoke interest."[14]

But it is this emphasis on "provoking interest" that critics claim is likely to be harmful in the long run because it is achieved at the cost of objective and fair presentation of the issues. Even the supporters of the campaign were somewhat uncomfortable with its overall approach. One utility executive stated, "The ad campaign may have been overdone, but I'm not sure you get it done unless you overdo it in this day and age. And you can't let an important issue be decided by default."[15] John O'Toole, president of Foote Cone & Belding, advertising agency, also agreed with the basic premise of the ad campaign by stating, "The best way to present any ad is to make it in terms of the reader's selfish interest, and that's the way [AEP's ads] were presented."[16] Mr. O'Toole, however, had some qualms about singling out an identifiable ethnic group.

It appears both commentators were measuring the ad campaign's effectiveness in narrow terms; i.e., increased awareness and recall on the part of the audience about the contents and sponsor of various ads. What is more important from AEP's as well as society's viewpoint is whether it improved public understanding of the issues and open discussion thereof and whether AEP was perceived by the public as an interested party in the broader societal sense, one whose pronouncements should receive greater credibility as objective, fair, and balanced. An analysis of the ad contents in terms of other available information does not give a clear-cut decision in favor of the company. The judgment on the second proposition must await the passage of time.

AEP was criticized for the use of Arab caricatures by one of its stockholders at the company's annual meeting. Claiming that he was an American of Arab descent, the stockholder characterized the ad campaign as "offensive" and "potentially dangerous." Mr. Cook brushed aside the comments as coming from a distinct minority, saying that he had received a lot of letters praising the campaign.[17]

Industry Reaction

The electric utility industry was overwhelmingly in favor of the positions taken by Cook concerning the use of scrubbers, clean air standards, the Environmental Protection Agency, and open pit mining. Relatively few objected to the simplified explanations of various problems dealt with in the ads. One suggested that the battle with EPA, which he considered to be moderate and sympathetic, should have been fought in the courts rather than in the press. However, none of the executives wanted to be identified.[18] It is not clear whether these executives were afraid of EPA and government pressure, as Mr. Cook implies, or whether they had private doubts about AEP's strategy and tactics and the contents of various ads.

Reaction of EPA and Environmentalists—Criticism of the Contents of Various Advertisements

The Environmental Protection Agency and its top administrators objected vehemently to the entire tenor of the ad campaign and also accused Cook of distorting the truth and making false claims in various ads. In this, they were joined by various environmentalists.

In one of its ads, AEP implied that generating less energy is sure to generate "galloping unemployment" (Exhibit 4A-4), the implication being that those who "obstruct" the growth of energy sources are contributing to a direct increase in unemployment. This ad so irked John Sawhill, head of the Federal Energy Administration, that he wrote AEP urging the company "to cease this kind of advertising. It masks the total energy problem and gives the incorrect impression that conservation implies strongly negative impacts."[19]

There is indeed some truth to Sawhill's contention. Most analysts agree that current rate of electricity growth (5 percent) can easily be halved without any major impact on employment. Strong conservation methods like manufacturing lighter cars, better insulation, shifting more freight to railroads, and designing more efficient buildings and appliances can help achieve significant fuel economies. Indeed, it is argued that without strong conservation measures, the United States can never achieve self-sufficiency in energy.[20] Mr. Johnson of AEP disagrees with this contention. He states:

The direct correlation between energy use and GNP, including standard of living, is an established fact. . . . Without adequate electric power, industry production must be curtailed and this impacts jobs. Environmental protection, the shortage of gas and oil, the formation of homes for new families are creating new demands for electric power. There is a lot of surface thinking about the future demands for electric power and the available supply to meet those demands, which, if not changed, can only result in tragic consequences for our economy and the people of our country.

EPA took a strong stand against one ad captioned, "We Burn at Those Who Block the Burning of Vast Amounts of America's Coal (Exhibit 4A-21). This ad charged EPA with blocking "the burning of millions of tons of good American coal" by "promulgating unnecessarily restrictive regulations." In a letter to Donald Cook, which was also released to the press, Russell Train charged AEP with completely distorting the agency's position on the burning of coal. The press release pointed out EPA's flexible policies and also its support of various legislative measures to ease the burning of larger quantities of coal, its support of "intermittent control systems" as interim measures, and its willingness to try alternative methods of pollution control. Train's letter drew an indignant reply from Cook that later became the subject of another ad in the series (Exhibit 4A-29).

A letter to AEP from Russell Peterson, chairman of the White House Council on Environmental Quality, criticizing one ad as "irresponsible" and "subversive of the public interest" drew an equally strong response from Cook, who accused Peterson of "vituperative and oppressive conduct." And Peterson's release of his letter to the press before Cook could reply led the AEP Chairman to write to President Nixon asking for an investigation into Peterson's "official and clandestine activities."[21]

Other AEP claims have also been attacked by EPA and the environmentalists. For example, AEP has stated unequivocally that gas scrubbers do not work, will not work at reasonable cost, and that EPA's official hearings proved that point conclusively. EPA points out that the conclusions of the hearings and the recommendations of the panel were quite different than what AEP stated in the ads. The hearings concluded that gas stack scrubber technology (flue gas desulfurization [FGD] system) was available and, when operating properly, could reduce SO_2 emissions by 85 to 90 percent; that few utilities have developed specific plans to install FGD systems; and that strong efforts be made to encourage utilities to launch adequate programs for the installation of FGD systems. EPA further stated that AEP's contentions to the contrary, between November 1973, the time of original hearings, and September 1974, the total number of FGD units committed, under construction, or operational had increased from 51 to 93, and the number of on-line units had increased to 19 with 3 additional systems scheduled to start up by December 1974. The EPA hearings also pointed out that two of the alternatives proposed by AEP for meeting clean air requirements, low-sulfur fuel and coal gasification and liquification, were not practical for the foreseeable future.

While the "Conclusions and Recommendations" of the EPA SO_2 Hearing

128

Panel were to the effect the scrubbers are a proven technology, evidence in a court case in Pennsylvania against Pennsylvania Power Company and hearings held in Ohio before the Ohio Environmental Protection Agency would lead one to a different conclusion. In the Pennsylvania case, the Commonwealth of Pennsylvania attempted to require Pennsylvania Power Company to install an FGD system on its New Castle Plant, a system which the company believed to be undemonstrated and unworkable. The court held that "the use of devices or processes for removal of sulfur dioxide emissions remains theoretical. No device is commercially available today with an adequate degree of reliability to solve the problems of sulfur dioxide control, as would permit Penn Power to comply with the Commonwealth regulations." In dismissing the action against the company, the court also stated:

Without in any way reflecting on the Department of Environmental Resources field enforcement or legal enforcement officers, and considering only those persons within the hierarchy of the department who were responsible for the enactment of the sulfur dioxide control regulations, we apparently have a classic example of the validity of the Peter Principle.

The decision of the lower court was upheld on appeal both by the Commonwealth Court of Pennsylvania and by the Pennsylvania Supreme Court.

In 1974 the Ohio electric utilities litigated the issue as to whether FGD systems were technically and economically feasible before a hearing examiner panel of the Ohio Environmental Protection Agency. All testimony in this hearing was under oath and included that of numerous U.S. EPA officials. The hearing panel found, among other things, that:

Epidemiological and toxicological studies demonstrate that sulfur dioxide and particulate matter can produce adverse health effects over a wide range of concentrations.

Ground level ambient SO_2 concentrations are affected more by emission sources having short stacks than by sources emitting through chimneys having large effective stack height.

Reliable flue gas desulfurization technology which can be applied by the Ohio electric utilities to achieve compliance with pertinent regulations has not been demonstrated to a degree which would justify its installation.

Tall stacks, by enhancing the dispersion of pollutants, can be used as a means of controlling ambient air concentrations of sulfur dioxide in most cases. They have futher shown that in those cases where topography or meteorological conditions make tall stacks alone a questionable device, they can be combined with a program for limiting emissions through the use of load reduction or the burning of low sulfur fuels, or both, and that such a program can be enforced through the use of adequate monitoring and meteorological prediction.

While tall stacks generally can be effectively designed to account for adverse topographical and meteorological conditions, tall stacks, in themselves, are not adequate as a control device for particulate emissions.

Tall stacks, either alone, or in combination with other control devices, are an effective means of controlling ambient concentrations.

Flue gas desulfurization is not a presently available, technologically feasible method of SO_2 control which may be employed by the Ohio electric utilities.

AEP ads also claimed that scrubbers would cause horrendous problems of waste disposal. For example, one ad (Exhibit 4A-12) reads:

On a major installation, [gas stack scrubbers] would emit tons of wet-waste sludge that would confront an ecologist with a disposal nightmare. Applied to a 12,000 megawatt coal fired system, lime scrubbers would in only five years produce enough of this oozy gook to cover, for instance, 10 square miles of Washington, D.C. five feet deep.

Critics have accused AEP of grandstanding and of using scare tactics. In the first place, some FGD systems either produce no sludge or produce salable by-products. Second, sludge can be dried into inert salable landfill and used to fill gravel pits and abandoned strip mines (Philadelphia Electric, Boston Edison, Louisville Gas & Electric, Kansas City Power and Light Company, Commonwealth Edison, and Duquesne Light Co.). But Mr. Johnson of AEP states:

Let's not disillusion ourselves that the sludge problem has been resolved. It is a gargantuan problem and one which has yet to be licked. While regenerative scrubbers should reduce the waste disposal problem, they are technologically far down the road. All you have to do is look at the vast amount of sludge that is produced and the new major environmental problems being created, not to mention the tremendous land use involved.

Another controversy was caused by an AEP ad entitled "The Philadelphia, Pa. Story" (Exhibit 4A-31). In this ad, AEP accused EPA of exaggerating the facts about Philadelphia electric by stating that the company was investing $68 million in scrubbers, while in truth the utility had agreed to spend only $20.3 million. Soon after the publication of this ad, EPA issued a press release charging AEP with fact distortion, if not falsehood.[22]

The Ad Campaign—A Cost Benefit Analysis

To what extent was the campaign effective in achieving AEP's objectives? We know that it created a high degree of public awareness, but beyond this point the answers are not so clear cut.

Postponement of Clean Air Act Requirements

An executive of AEP stated that the campaign brought to the attention of a vast number of people the collision course on which the utility industry and the environmentalists and regulators were embarked and made it clear that something had to be done or there would be an economic crisis. He gives the campaign credit for "persuading the White House, the EPA, and important Senators and Congressmen to postpone the enforcement of Clean Air Act standards from 1975 to 1985."

Ability to Attract Public Attention

The more fundamental issue, according to Mr. Johnson of AEP, is the inability of a company to compete with government bureaucrats and politicians for the public attention.

Whenever Mr. Train or Mr. Quarles [of EPA] wish to make a statement or put out a press release, they get widespread coverage. When a high official of government makes a public statement, it is automatically considered news and widely publicized. This is not true of industry and results in a significant communications advantage people in government have over industry.

We couldn't get our message across by the press release method. It is unrealistic to think that we could have released 36 messages in the form of news releases and reached any significant audience. A worthwhile study in communications would be to compare the total column inches of space EPA releases and public statements pertaining to FGD systems received, and the column inches devoted to this subject in paid advertising by AEP. I feel certain public exposure to the EPA viewpoint substantially exceeded the AEP viewpoint.

Industry Support

The campaign was not successful in getting other utilities to join with AEP in openly supporting the latter's position on scrubbers, EPA, open-pit mining, or relaxation of the pollution control requirements under the Clean Air Act. As we have noted earlier, there was no question that various industry executives were in agreement with Cook's viewpoint and also sympathetic to his approach.

None of them, however, was willing to be publicly identified with AEP or the ad campaign. This position rattled Mr. Cook, who felt that the industry had let him down.[23]

Benefits to the Company and the Consumers

The AEP spokesman agreed that the ad campaign dealt with some controversial issues which could be construed as political in nature, but he also contended that all the themes were in the company interest and in the public interest. He strongly rejected the notion that the ads should be subjected to some type of "ad substantiation" or proof of accuracy, or that they should not be considered a legitimate business expense and therefore tax deductible:

Our company will have no problem substantiating each and every statement contained in our ads. However, I do not feel that some outside body should control the contents of our ads. This would amount to censorship and abridgement of our rights under the First Amendment.

Corporate interests cannot be narrowly defined as strictly related to product promotion. Traditionally, institutional advertising has been treated as a legitimate business expense. What happens to the economy and how government regulates business can and does affect corporate profits in a major way, and therefore impacts company operations and its survival. An ad campaign designed to correct serious wrongs is of major importance to a company's performance and consequently to the public it serves.

The AEP ad campaign had a direct consumer interest. The company's coal consumption in 1974 amounted to 32.4 million tons and was more in 1975. A major objective of the advertising program was to encourage increased coal production and therefore reduce the price of coal.

Coal price savings go directly to the company's customers via the fuel cost included in their electric bills. A saving of $1 per ton would result in a benefit in excess of $30 million to customers. This is a fundamental economic consideration that, in our view, must be taken into account in any economic and social evaluation of the expenditures made by AEP for its communications effort through advertising.

In the 1974 Hearings before Senator Philip Hart (D., Michigan) of the Subcommittee on Environment, Harvey Shulman of Media Access Project argued that most of the recent image/goodwill advertising by energy-related companies and utilities (AEP included) was political in nature, falls within the category of grassroots lobbying, and should be a nondeductible expense for tax purposes under the Internal Revenue Service and Federal Power Commission regulations for the treatment of advertising expenditures.[24] However, spokespeople for various companies contended that the new liberalized definition of lobbying under the 1962 Revenue Code allows deductibility of institutional ads which aim to present views on economic, financial, social, or other subjects of a general nature (see Chapter 6.) In the case of AEP, Mr. Joseph Dowd, vice-president and counsel, stated:

In the case of our current advertising program, tax and rate-making factors applicable to this advertising were *not* a consideration. Presumably, these questions will be decided at the appropriate time by the tax and regulatory authorities. However, . . . in order to bring home the point that these factors really were not a consideration in our ad program—and in order to prevent this very peripheral issue from detracting from the very important message that we are trying to convey—we propose, for accounting purposes, to charge the costs of our current advertising program to FPC Account No. 426.4—a below the line account—even though . . . we believe that they could properly be accounted for above the line. Our objective has been to lay the facts regarding energy supply problems before our customers and the American public generally just as effectively as possible. This, we believe, we are doing—and, in the context of our current energy problems, this we believe we have an obligation to do.[25]

Effect—EPA's Viewpoint

In retrospect, the EPA considered the effect of the ad campaign to be a positive one that strengthened the position of the agency with the general public, the Congress, and the administration. In terms of the general public, Marlin Fitzwater of the EPA commented:

The campaign has been of great advantage to us in educating the public on the issue of scrubbers. People focused on the issue who otherwise wouldn't have. The ads gave us a chance to make our case before an audience we otherwise did not have. It also provided us with a platform to combat AEP's arguments. But for the ad campaign, we probably could have talked till we were blue in the face about how great scrubbers are and why they should be installed, and the chances are that nobody would have listened because the scrubber issue often seems so complicated and esoteric.

The polls tend to confirm that public support for the environment is pretty strong. The last election tends to confirm this viewpoint as the electorate supported those congressmen who were considered in favor of conservation and pollution control. The high exposure to the issue provided by the AEP campaign helped us by giving further visibility to EPA and its position.

Another important factor in the opinion of the EPA was the total environment of the ad campaign, the reaction of the press, and the generally low credibility of business. The general public viewed the ad campaign as another attempt at brainwashing through large-scale advertising. This view was further strengthened by an interesting backlash in major East Coast newspapers on specific ads.

The Washington Post and *The New York Times* ran editorials critical of AEP's campaign and techniques. The editorial comments and news analysis of the ads in *The Wall Street Journal, Newsweek, Business Week,* and *Time* were not totally complimentary to AEP either. Mr. Fitzwater comments:

At the same time the media was carrying the advertising message, it was also carrying an editorial message. The people who saw those ads and then read the editorials probably thought that big business was trying to shaft the public interest.

EPA believed that the "misleading and inaccurate" statements provided the agency an opportunity to state its case to the public. The agency pointed out that it was indeed quite flexible in its position and has supported a compromise that would allow more time (until 1985 as opposed to 1975) for some of the plants in the less populated areas to meet the Clean Air Act requirements. And it was a realistic position. Due to unavailability of equipment and other associated constraints, all the coal-burning plants could not have installed the scrubbers even if they had wanted to.

If one were to assume that the ads were aimed at generating public pressure on Congress and the administration to alter their positions, according to EPA the campaign had the opposite effect: "We have benefited very specifically in the internal policy debate by virtue of the press backlash to these advertisements. The strong public and press support reinforced the Administration's position to require the installation of FGD systems on coal-burning power plants to control sulfur oxide."

Postscript

It appears that the controversy on the use of scrubbers and acrimony between the U.S. Environmental Protection Agency and the nation's utilities are far from over.

On February 29, 1976, *Los Angeles Times* published a news story stating that "reports from a major Environmental Protection Agency program were systematically distorted by a former agency scientist (Dr. John F. Finklea) in an effort to prove that pollution from sulfur-bearing fuels had an adverse effect on human health." The story was put together through interviews with government and nongovernment scientists, most of them unidentified, and suggested that this distortion "has resulted in a mounting controversy over the need to spend billions in controlling sulfur pollution from electric power plants and raised questions about the credibility of EPA research."[26]

The EPA reports were published in 1974 and were prepared as part of the Agency's Community Health and Environmental Surveillance System (CHESS).

The newspaper said that extensive interviews with scientists and others had shown that Dr. John F. Finklea rewrote the work of agency scientists, often deleting what the researchers felt were important qualifiers on experimental results. In congressional hearings later held to investigate these charges, a variety of scientists denied the allegations made in the *Los Angeles Times* article and also defended John F. Finklea's conduct.[27] Russell E. Train, EPA administrator, testified that the CHESS study represented a reasonable approach to understanding the relationships between ambient pollutant concentrations and adverse health effects. He also stated that contrary to the allegations in the *Los Angeles Times* article, EPA did not use the CHESS studies as the basis for imposing a multibillion-dollar emissions control strategy on the nation's utility industry. "The truth is that the direction of this program was determined by scientific information in existence before the CHESS studies were initiated. Thus even if one were to assume the worst about CHESS, which I do not, this would in no way call into question the Agency's sulfur oxide regulatory program."[28]

The only negative testimony was given by Dr. Robert W. Buenchley, an epidemiologist at the University of New Mexico's Cancer Research and Treatment Center and formerly a public health analyst with the EPA's Health Effects Program. Dr. Buenchley, however, acknowledged that he had not been assigned to write on the CHESS study reports, but said he shared office space with those who were and had read many of the original drafts.[29]

Dr. David P. Rall, Director of the National Institute of Environmental Health Sciences, Department of Health, Education, and Welfare, testified that in 1973 he was asked by the HEW secretary and also by the director of the Office of Management and Budget to organize a cooperative study to examine existing scientific information, including the CHESS data, on the health effects of sulfur oxides. He stated:

Our independent review of the available scientific literature and extensive discussions with expert scientists from the United States and abroad led us to conclude . . . that there was no basis for relaxing existing sulfur oxide primary ambient air quality standards.

He went on to say that he agreed with the conclusions of the NAS–NRC report on Air Quality and Stationary Source Emission Control dated March, 1975, which stated:

Tall stacks and/or intermittent control systems make it possible to meet ambient sulfur dioxide standards in carefully defined situations. [However] the Committee does not recommend their use unless it is for carefully defined situations for an interim period until other strategies (e.g., flue gas desulfurization, low-sulfur fuel) can be implemented. . . . The application of tall stacks and/or intermittent control will not reduce total emissions of sulfur oxides to any significant degree; . . .[30]

Commenting on the news report, Marlin Fitzwater, director of New Services, EPA, said:

Much of the basis for these stories appears to have come from sources related to the electric power industry. Certainly, the industry has utilized the stories to every public relations advantage in an apparent attempt to discredit EPA's regulatory program. We are gratified that the charges have been so completely refuted. . . .

Notes

1. "Donald C. Cook of American Electric Power," *Nation's Business.* September 1974, pp. 46–48.

2. "Donald Cook Takes On the Environmentalists," *Business Week*, October 26, 1974, pp. 66-73.

3. "Donald C. Cook of American Electric Power," p. 52.

4. Sanford L. Jacobs, "Firm's Ad Campaign 'Isn't Very Bright' Arab Holder Asserts, *The Wall Street Journal*, April 25, 1975, p. 18.

5. "Donald Cook . . . Environmentalists," p. 67.

6. *Ibid.*, p. 70.

7. "Donald Cook . . . Environmentalists," p. 70.

8. *Ibid.*, p. 68.

9. Annual Report, 1974, American Electric Power Company, New York, p. 16.

10. For a discussion of the arguments, pro and con, on scrubbers, see: U.S. Environmental Protection Agency, *National Public Hearings on Power Plant Compliance With Sulfur Oxide Air Pollution Regulations, Report of the Hearing Panel* (Washington, D.C., January 1974). Kurt E. Yeager, "Stacks vs. Scrubbers," Research Progress Report F-F-3, Electric Power Research Institute, July 1975. U.S. Environmental Protection Agency, *Flue Gas Desulfurization: Installations and Operations* (Washington, D.C., September 1974). *Commonwealth of Pennsylvania vs. Pennsylvania Power Company,* in the Court of Common Pleas of Lawrence County, PA, No. 2 of 1972, April 19, 1973. "Consolidated Electric Utility Hearing Examiner's Report and Recommendation," Before the Ohio Environmental Protection Agency, in the Matter of Consolidated Electric Utility Cases, Case No. 73-A-P-120 *et al.,* Columbus, Ohio, September 6, 1974. Gladwin Hall, "Power Plant in Kansas 'Scrubs' Pollutants from Dirty Coal," *The New York Times,* September 8, 1975, p. 21. "A Utility Defends a Scrubbing Plant," *Business Week,* August 31, 1974, p. 80. "Donald Cook Takes on the Environmentalists," *Business Week,* October 26, 1974, p. 69. Edwin McDowell, "The Big Battle Over 'Scrubbers'," *The Wall Street Journal,* February 7, 1975, p. 10. Raymond E. Kary, "Scrubbers: Are They the Answer—Or the Problem?" Speech before the National Governors' Conference, Annapolis, Maryland,

November 17–19, 1975. Edwin McDowell, "Donald Cook and Those Funny Ads," *The Wall Street Journal*, February 7, 1975, p. 10; February 10, 1975, p. 20.

11. "Donald C. Cook of American Electric Power," p. 52.

12. AEP Annual Report 1974, p. 4

13. "Donald Cook . . . Environmentalists," p. 70.

14. *Ibid.*, p. 68.

15. McDowell, "Donald Cook and Those Funny Ads," p. 20.

16. *Ibid.*

17. Jacobs, "Firm's Ad Campaign 'Isn't Very Bright,'" p. 18.

18. "Donald Cook and Those Funny Ads," p. 20.

19. "Donald Cook . . . Environmentalists," p. 68.

20. *Ibid.*

21. "Donald Cook . . . Environmentalists," pp. 66–67.

22. U.S. Environmental Protection Agency press release dated October 25, 1974.

23. "Donald Cook and Those Funny Ads," p. 20.

24. U.S. Senate, *Energy and Environmental Objectives, Hearings Before the Subcommittee on Environment of the Committee on Commerce,* Part 2 (Washington, D.C., 93rd Congress, 2nd Session, pp. 39–68.

25. *Ibid.*, p. 113.

26. W.B. Rood, "EPA Study—The Findings Got Distorted," *Los Angeles Times,* February 29, 1976. See also Michael Loescher, "EPA Restudies Pollution Data in 14 States," *The Tampa Tribune,* March 4, 1976.

27. U.S. Congress, *Hearings Before the Subcommittee on Health and the Environment of the Committee on Interstate and Foreign Commerce, and the Subcommittee on Environment and the Atmosphere of the Committee on Science and Technology,* April 9, 1976.

28. *Ibid.*, statement of Russell E. Train.

29. W.B. Rood, "Scientist Denies Bias on Reports," *Los Angeles Times,* April 11, 1976, part I, p. 16.

30. *Ibid.*, pp. 5–6.

Appendix 4
The American Electric Power
Advocacy Ads

We have more coal than they have oil. Let's use it!

America *is* self-sufficient in one fossil fuel source of energy: COAL. We're sitting on about half of the world's known supply — enough for over 500 years!

It can be the major solution to our present energy problems.

Coal *can* be used instead of oil or gas for the production of electricity.

Electricity, in turn, can be used for virtually all energy needs, except some forms of transportation.

And when electricity is fully put to use, the staggering amounts of oil and gas saved can be diverted to other more critical uses. Such as transportation.

To be sure, burning the coal at hand as well as extracting new coal as quickly as possible, is not without its problems.

And when you start to tick off such things as labor stability, price controls, hopper cars, environmental resistance, new mine de-

velopment and land reclamation, the problems seem formidable.

But they are nothing that American ingenuity cannot lick.

Coal — good old reliable coal — can help solve the energy crisis if America is determined to do so, and we have never known timidity to be our national characteristic.

Let's start using that coal. Fully.

Now.

American Electric Power Company, Inc.

Exhibit 4A-1

138

We have
enough coal
to fill
the energy needs
of our
children's children's children's
children's children's children's
children's children's children's
children's children's children's
children's children's children's
children.

Let's dig it.

That's 16 generations, or nearly 500 years.

We have underground over four times more energy in coal than the Middle East has in oil. We're sitting on about one half the world's known supply of coal.

But that's the trouble. We're sitting on it. This country isn't mining any more coal today than it did in 1920.

We must raise our coal output, dramatically, now.

Like any major accomplishment, it won't be easy. Success will require full cooperation from industry, from labor, from government and from the people.

It will require reasonable modification of restraints, faster leasing of Federal coal lands, and reliable incentives for capital investments.

And many an unselfish decision.

But the effort will be worth it. Because this reliable resource, coal, can be burned to produce electricity — which can heat and light and cook and manufacture and move masses of people and goods by rail.

And set free enormous amounts of oil and gas for uses where there's no suitable substitute.

Why wait?

For the sake of our nation, and that of our children's, children's, children's, children's, children's, children's, children's, children's, children's, children's, children's, children's, children's, children:

Let's dig it!

American Electric Power Company, Inc.

Exhibit 4A-2

139

America has underground one half the world's known supply of coal

enough coal to satisfy our energy needs for about 500 years

four times more energy available in coal than the Middle East has in oil.

America has energy to burn ...in its veins.

It is now strikingly obvious that a nation's strength and status are directly proportionate to its independent supplies of energy.

And America's are not so independent.

Chances are our gas and oil will be completely depleted by the turn of the century while, by 1979, we may be importing half our petroleum needs.

And there we are, more than ever at the mercy of others.

Thank heaven for coal.

America is blessed with a super-abundance of this reliable fuel. We are, in fact, the Saudi Arabia of coal with about half the world's known supply under our feet.

Coal: 90% of our fossil resources presently being used for only 17% of our needs.

Coal that can be brought to the surface and burned right now to generate electricity—itself a great and versatile power which can perform so many of the functions now the unnecessary burden of precious oil and gas.

If America is determined to get out from under the thumb of oil-rich nations, the shift to electricity generated by coal is not only necessary, it is inevitable.

We have the power in our veins.

What are we waiting for.

America has more coal than the Middle East has oil. Let's dig it!

American Electric Power Company, Inc.

Exhibit 4A–3

140

Sure. And generate galloping unemployment!

There's no more nonsensical a concept than "generate less" as a solution to our energy crisis.

The nonsense is revealed by this evidence: it took energy to produce everything we have in this country.

Everything.

Since we produce more than any other nation, America uses 35% of the world's energy and enjoys the highest standard of living.

Just start listening to the critics of our society, start generating less energy, and the plummet begins.

Less production, fewer jobs, lower demand for products, followed by still further diminished production and galloping unemployment until America is eventually reduced to the hard life.

That is what no - growth critics advocate — whether they realize it or not.

America's population is growing and it is going to take more — not less — energy merely to maintain our present standard of living.

And the poor are still with us. What of them? Reduced energy will hurt them the most.

With oil and gas in short supply where will that energy come from?

It can come from electricity, generated by coal—which won't come near short supply for over 500 years.

And once we've dug it we can begin to put electricity to work in all the places where it can be used, and assign to oil and gas those tasks where nothing else can be.

Coal—reliable coal—is the solution.

But coal can't be used unless our representatives begin to act:

1. To reasonably modify the Clean Air Act so that more of our coals may be burned.

2. To release the vast reserves of U.S. Government owned low-sulfur coal in the West.

If America didn't own about half the world's known supply, every working man would really have something to worry about.

And that's not nonsense.

America has more coal than the Middle East has oil. Let's dig it!

American Electric Power Company, Inc.

Exhibit 4A–4

The most sensible way to help solve the energy shortage is to generate more electricity.

More, not less. And from coal.

Ridiculous? Hardly.

It is, rather, a logical conclusion after cold analysis of America's plight, and energy resources.

And it's based on these truths:

1. We do have an energy crisis. More specifically, we have an oil and natural gas crisis.

2. We need to take a hard look at all the fuels we have, then make it possible to use each wisely for its most critical use.

3. America has a vast amount of coal—about half the world's known supply, or enough to meet our energy needs for 500 years.

4. Coal should be used instead of oil to generate electricity wherever practical, thereby saving a staggering amount of oil.

5. Electricity generated by coal can be used instead of oil and gas for countless energy needs, with a few exceptions —such as some forms of transportation.

6. The result will be still more savings of oil and gas, which can then be diverted to more critical uses where there is no suitable substitute.

One of the most crucial applications for electricity is in heating.

We must heat our homes and offices and there's no more efficient way than with the electric "Heat Pump" system—for it is an energy multiplier that actually delivers up to two times* more energy than it takes to power the device.

So you see, the most sensible way to help solve the energy shortage is to generate more—not less —electricity. And from coal.

You can quote us on that.

America has more coal than the Middle East has oil. Let's dig it!

American Electric Power Company, Inc.

How the remarkable Heat Pump works. All air contains a measure of heat, even in temperatures well below freezing. The heat pump doesn't produce heat, it transfers heat. It absorbs heat from the outside air and discharges it inside the house at the temperature desired. Simple, efficient and a real contribution to energy conservation. That's the heat pump—the energy multiplier.

*The precise amount depends on the climate in which it is used.

Exhibit 4A–5

142

It happened to us once.
It can happen again.
And again.

As long as we remain so dependent upon oil imports, a crippling embargo can happen again.

But not if we reassess our fuel assets and take the actions necessary to make us more self-sufficient.

What is the best and fastest way?

Not the exotic paths of geothermal, tidal or solar energy. As intriguing as they may seem they're probably decades away from being our answer.

Coal . . . and electricity generated by coal . . . is the answer.

America owns half the world's known supply. And coal composes nearly 90% of our fossil fuel resources.

We must begin a crash program to dig it and put it to work as quickly, cleanly and efficiently as possible.

We must make it practical for companies to invest in mine development and for people to work in mines.

We must make the necessary modifications in the Clean Air Act so that more of our coals may be burned.

We must release the vast resources of U.S. Government-owned low sulfur coal in the west.

Unless we do these things we will remain vulnerable to an oil embargo that can happen again.

And again.

But worse, we will create a shortage of electric power that will touch the life of every American and plunge our country into economic chaos.

That's not fiction — that's fact.

American Electric Power System

Appalachian Power Co., Indiana & Michigan Electric Co., Kentucky Power Co., Kingsport Power Co., Michigan Power Co., Ohio Power Co., Wheeling Electric Co.

Exhibit 4A–6

An open letter on energy to those who are still employed.

Look around you at the slowdown.

Look at the new business burdens, at the exploding costs, at the shelved plans, at the lowered budgets, at the friend out of work — and the impact of reduced energy becomes slightly visible.

Yet, today, there are those who shrill for less energy and no growth.

Either they know not what they say or they callously elect to ignore this fact: jobs and a comfortable standard of living are possible only with the availability of great quantities of energy.

That's exactly how America, which uses 35% of the world's energy, achieved the level most of its citizens enjoy.

America is, in fact, obligated to produce a growing supply of energy because of its increasing population and its remaining poor.

Those millions have every right to hope for all the things that give decency to life.

Reduced energy would reduce them, and many more with them, to a life of despair.

With oil and gas in short supply where will all that energy come from?

It can come from electricity, generated by coal — which won't come near short supply for over 500 years.

And once we've dug it we can begin to put electricity to work in all the places where it can be used, and assign to precious oil and gas those tasks where nothing else can be.

Coal — reliable coal — is the solution.

Fortunately, the United States Government is the world's largest owner of coal. The people's coal. The solution to the people's energy problem!

If it can only be dug and burned we won't have to worry about the job-shaking effects of an oil embargo, or an energy shortage — on our friends or on ourselves.

So, look around you and do something.

If it seems to you that some in government are more absorbed in managing the problem than in solving it — send this ad to your Congressman.

He is your friend — your ultimate protection against a bureaucracy. He's interested in helping you, but needs to know how you feel about it.

Tell him.

It will cost you 10¢ but it might save your job.

America has more coal than the Middle East has oil. Let's dig it!

American Electric Power System

Appalachian Power Co., Indiana & Michigan Electric Co., Kentucky Power Co., Kingsport Power Co., Michigan Power Co., Ohio Power Co., Wheeling Electric Co.

Exhibit 4A-7

144

Baloney.

The oil embargo is ended . . . for now. But the fuel crisis is as grave as ever.

With or without an embargo the world has a fuel crisis.

Because the world supply of oil and gas—which we depend on today for so much of our energy—is limited.

We can't go blithely along thinking that we can use oil and gas the way we have.

Or that the world has an endless supply of oil and gas. They must be conserved to do the jobs only they can do.

We are depending upon oil and gas to do too many things.

Together they represent only 5% of our nation's energy sources. Yet we're making that 5% fulfill over 75% of our needs.

How do we get out of this box? We dig our way out. Literally.

America is lucky. We own half the world's known supply of coal. All we have to do is dig it and put it to work.

With it we can generate electricity that can take the place of precious oil and gas in so many ways.

But all that coal can't be used properly and fully unless our representatives begin to act:

1. To amend the Clean Air Act so that more of our coals can be burned.

2. Release the vast reserves of U.S. government-owned low sulfur coal in the west.

With coal representing nearly 90% of our fossil fuel resources and abundant enough to fill our energy needs for about 500 years, aren't we foolish if we don't put it to work?

Coal and electricity generated by coal—used wisely, not wasted—is the most sensible answer to the fuel and energy crisis.

And that's no baloney!

America has more coal than the Middle East has oil. Let's dig it!

American Electric Power System

Appalachian Power Co., Indiana & Michigan Electric Co., Kentucky Power Co., Kingsport Power Co., Michigan Power Co., Ohio Power Co., Wheeling Electric Co.

Exhibit 4A-8

145

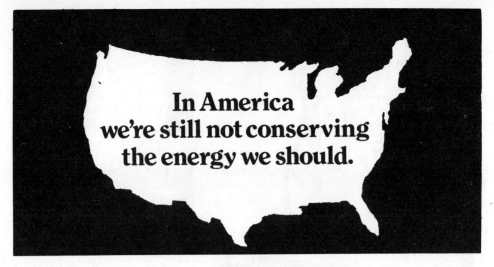

In America
we're still not conserving
the energy we should.

we
must.

we absolutely must!

Conservation of energy is critical to our country's future. Waste cannot be tolerated.

Americans responded brilliantly to the President's call to conserve energy. And the response must continue. For the energy crisis is far from over.

The Government, industry and energy producers must conserve and use wisely the energy fuels we possess.

Here, and worldwide, oil and natural gas reserves are dwindling. They must be conserved. We must turn from the abusive use of these limited fuels and commit to the use of our most abundant fuel—coal.

The most wasteful thing we're doing is not using coal. We have all the coal we need for nearly 500 years of energy needs...and we're sitting on it.

Why?

Because the Clean Air Act establishes unreasonable standards for today's technology, that prohibit the burning of much of our coal. Reasonable modifications would allow the burning of coal while still protecting the environment.

Because the U.S. Government hasn't released the vast reserves of low-sulfur coal it owns in the West. They must be freed.

For a country pledged to energy conservation and dedicated to energy independence, it is total folly to waste vital oil and gas, of which we have relatively little, and neglect the full use of coal, of which we have half the world's known supply.

Until we change our course we will not be conserving energy the way we should.

And we must . . . we absolutely must!

America has more coal than the Middle East has oil. Let's dig it!

American Electric Power System

Appalachian Power Co., Indiana & Michigan Electric Co., Kentucky Power Co., Kingsport Power Co., Michigan Power Co., Ohio Power Co., Wheeling Electric Co.

Exhibit 4A-9

Are we blind to the real energy crisis?

The sad answer to that question could be yes. Unless we are aware of these facts:

By mid 1975 all industry in America, including electric utilities, must comply with the standards of the Clean Air Act. There is a possibility of a permissable extension to mid '76.

But whether it be '75 or '76, for many utilities there is no way on God's green earth that the present sulfur-dioxide emission standards can be met.

The "stack gas scrubber" that some say is the answer to remov-

ing sulfur-dioxide, doesn't exist in a practical working sense.

If such scrubbers did exist they couldn't be installed in time.

If they did exist and could be installed, the resulting ground pollution would be worse than any potential air pollution.

It is absolutely imperative that the Clean Air Act be amended. There is no other way.

The courts have already made it impossible for any government agency — including the Environmental Protection Agency — to grant a last minute reprieve.

Unless the Clean Air Act is amended we will have a *real* energy crisis.

And unless some responsible corporation brings these facts to light, this country of ours could be headed into chaos.

And shedding light is the sole purpose of this advertisement.

America has more coal than the Middle East has oil. Let's dig it!

American Electric Power System

Appalachian Power Co., Indiana & Michigan Electric Co., Kentucky Power Co., Kingsport Power Co., Michigan Power Co., Ohio Power Co., Wheeling Electric Co.

Exhibit 4A–10

147

Scrubbers described, examined and rejected.

The Environmental Protection Agency recommends that electric utilities install "stack gas scrubbers" to control sulfur-oxide emissions and meet the standards that have been set.

WHAT IS A "STACK GAS SCRUBBER?"

There are many "stack gas scrubber" systems. All have been tested. Some — the most promising — more than others.

Simply stated, the scrubber is designed to eliminate most of the sulfur-oxide emissions by creating, in a chamber, a violent rainstorm of water laced with huge quantities of a chemical, limestone or lime for instance.

WHAT DOES CAREFUL EXAMINATION REVEAL?

Problems. Horrendous problems. Scrubber systems do remove sulfur-oxides. But in the process all of them are plagued with one or more problems that make them unreliable and impractical for a major electric utility.

Many scrubber systems produce a by-product that clogs the operation or erodes or corrodes the mechanism. Faults that cause shut downs. An impossible situation for an electric utility that must have a reliable power supply operation that will work all day, every day.

If the system doesn't clog and shut down it creates massive amounts of sludge. Some — like the most popular and most studied system, the wet lime or limestone scrubber — do both.

To understand the vastness of the amount of ground-polluting sludge produced, consider this. If limestone scrubbers were applied to a 12,000 megawatt coal-fired system they would in only five years produce enough of this "oozy gook" to destroy and cover 10 square miles of America to a depth of 5 feet. How's that for a system that's supposed to solve pollution problems!

If it doesn't have either of these major faults chances are it will have some of

several less dramatic problems. And chances are it hasn't been tested at a coal-burning plant.

WHAT MAKES AMERICAN ELECTRIC POWER REJECT SCRUBBERS?

The problems revealed. The score card on scrubber tests. Time and time again proven too unreliable, too impractical for electric utility use.

But a greater overriding reason is the sincere belief that there are better ways to solve the sulfur-oxide emission problem.

One way is to release the enormous reserves of U.S. Government-owned low sulfur coal in the West. And at the same time continue the investment of time, energy and money in the development of the technology to clean high-sulfur coal before it is burned.

Such a positive program, we think, is in the best interest of the people we serve and the country we live in.

American Electric Power System

Appalachian Power Co., Indiana & Michigan Electric Co., Kentucky Power Co., Kingsport Power Co., Michigan Power Co., Ohio Power Co., Wheeling Electric Co.

Exhibit 4A–11

148

Have you heard the one about the scrubbers?

You'll appreciate this more if you bear in mind that "stack gas scrubbers" are monstrous contraptions designed to absorb most of the sulfur-oxide emissions from manufacturing plants, electric power plants, and the like.

They require huge amounts of chemicals, usually lime or limestone, which then become saturated with the residue.

There are many kinds of scrubbers. They do remove sulfur-oxides, when they work.

But those suitable for a sizeable coal-fired utility clog the works, and cause prolonged shut downs.

But our story isn't about clogs, repairs, or reliability.

It's about environmental protection.

We are all concerned about the cleanliness of the air, the water and the land. They belong to us all.

And that's reason enough for *us* to shrink from the most promising, the wet limestone scrubber.

On a major installation, it would emit tons of wet-waste sludge that would confront an ecologist with a disposal nightmare.

Applied to a 12,000 megawatt coal-fired system, limestone scrubbers would in only five years produce enough of this oozy gook to cover, for instance, 10 square miles of Washington D.C., five feet deep.

Saturated gook.

Which could leach polluting chemicals into the ground and its water.

Which would have to be fenced

or patrolled for the safety of those under 5'6"

The irony of it is that "stack gas scrubbers" are strongly recommended by the Environmental Protection Agency—even though not required by the Federal Clean Air Act.

There are better, safer ways to protect the public health and welfare.

One is to release the vast reserves of Government owned low-sulfur coal in the West.

Another is to up-date the Clean Air Act to allow time for the development of the technology to clean high-sulfur coal before it is burned.

To sit and do neither would be a tragic comedy; a comedy of errors whose consequences would be tragic.

American Electric Power System

Exhibit 4A-12

The government has something the people need but won't release it.

Why?

Out in the West, the U.S. Government owns vast reserves of clean low-sulfur coal. It is desperately needed to solve America's energy problem.

Yet it's not released.

Why?

Some say mining will scar the land. They're suspicious of private enterprise; they do not believe industry will act responsibly, and restore the land.

And their voices block the release of this non-polluting coal.

We can't speak for others—but long before environmental groups were formed or reclamation laws framed, American Electric Power was restoring mined land to a con-

dition more productive, enjoyable and valuable than before the coal was mined.

What we did and are still doing to 125,000 acres of famished farmland in Ohio is a national model for beautification of mined terrain.

Any responsible corporation experienced in land reclamation can develop and carry out a plan to mine the Western coal and return the land to a condition as good as or better than it was before.

But.

If private corporations aren't trusted to do the job, let the U.S. Government, itself, mine the coal.

The U.S. Government can restore the land exactly the way the U.S. people want it to.

The U.S. Government can fix the price of coal to include reclamation costs.

The U.S. Government can guarantee that no company will profit from the mining.

The U.S. Government can control allocation to users who need low-sulfur coal.

It's the people's coal, and the people need it.

Now.

America has more coal than the Middle East has oil. Let's dig it!

American Electric Power System

Appalachian Power Co., Indiana & Michigan Electric Co., Kentucky Power Co., Kingsport Power Co., Michigan Power Co., Ohio Power Co., Wheeling Electric Co.

Exhibit 4A–13

150

Announcing the INNOCENT plant

A gigantic coal-burner to gladden the hearts of the most avid environmentalists.

As soon as you mention "coal-burning power plant" many people respond "guilty of pollution".

The automatic response is often without awareness that such a plant can be innocent.

We're about to build a giant of a one in West Virginia that will meet all environmental standards in a state that maintains some pretty impressive standards.

1,300,000 kilowatts big, it will burn locally produced low-sulfur coal. And will be fitted with multi-millions of dollars worth of modern pollution controls that make it a virtual environmental dream house.

Its precipitators will remove 99.7% of the fly ash.

The remainder (three-tenths-of-one-percent) will rush up a stack about as high as the Empire State building to be dissipated at a point 200 times taller than you are.

Every minute its 500 ft. cooling tower will change 600,000 gallons of hot water back to cool water. Result: the river is protected against harmful thermal change.

Clean water-vapor plumes are the only evidence to anyone driving by that this Gargantuan servant of man is working.

To make a coal-burning power plant so innocent of pollution it would elicit ovations from the most avid environmentalist, only two things are needed.

First, a willingness to invest millions in controls to protect the environment.

Second, the availability of low-sulfur coal—which is in cornucopian abundance in the West, but so limited in the East for use in boilers we doubt if many plants "Innocent" could be built without those Western reserves.

There's a third thing, of course: the dedication to being a good neighbor in the first place.

America has more coal than the Middle East has oil. Let's dig it!

American Electric Power System

Appalachian Power Co., Indiana & Michigan Electric Co., Kentucky Power Co., Kingsport Power Co., Michigan Power Co., Ohio Power Co., Wheeling Electric Co.

Exhibit 4A-14

151

Coal.
It is critical to nuclear energy!

America's nuclear reactors can't use natural uranium ore. It must be refined, purified, enriched. That's done in a diffusion plant. There are just three diffusion plants in the United States, all under the control of the Atomic Energy Commission.

The operation of the diffusion plants requires huge quantities of electricity. And nearly all of that electricity is generated by burning middle western and border states coal.

So ... coal is needed ...
to generate the electricity
to run the diffusion plant
to enrich the uranium
to use in the reactor
to generate nuclear energy.

It's that simple and that critical.

The role of nuclear energy is important to many sections of our country. Take the New England area for example.

There are six nuclear energy plants in operation in Maine, Vermont, Connecticut and Massachusetts. They have a capacity of more than 4 million kilowatts. That's 20% of New England's generating capability. They need enriched uranium from diffusion plants.

Block the burning of coal by unrealistic environmental standards flowing from the Clean Air Act and you deliver a devastating blow to the capacity of this country's diffusion plants.

There is no desire or need to cripple, destroy or kill the Clean Air Act. There is, however, a need

to up-date the Act to reflect the practical levels dictated by today's technology.

There is one other need. The need to release the enormous reserves of low-sulfur coal the U.S. Government owns in the West.

Release it and you eliminate coal-burning pollution control problems and assure sufficient generation of electricity ...
to run the diffusion plant
to enrich the uranium
to use in the reactor
to generate nuclear energy.

America has more coal than the Middle East has oil. Let's dig it!

American Electric Power System

Appalachian Power Co., Indiana & Michigan Electric Co., Kentucky Power Co., Kingsport Power Co., Michigan Power Co., Ohio Power Co., Wheeling Electric Co.

Exhibit 4A–15

152

Let's unmask the old bugaboo.

The fact is: coal-burning power plants are not hopeless polluters.

The damaging misconception that a coal-burning power plant can't be a good neighbor — can't be compatible with the environment— has caused many to write off coal, our most abundant most available fuel.

The fact is that only two things are necessary. First, a willingness to invest millions of dollars in pollution controls. Such as high efficiency electrostatic precipitators to eliminate fly ash emissions.

And cooling towers where needed to safeguard water quality. To eliminate the discharge of heat into adjacent waterways.

The second is the availability of low-sulfur coal. Like the gigantic reserves the U.S. Government owns in the West.

Release this clean low-sulfur coal — the people's coal — and power plants equipped with available controls can meet today's stringent environmental standards.

More electricity can then be generated by coal instead of precious oil and gas.

And electricity can be used to perform many tasks currently the unnecessary burden of short supply oil and gas.

Coal is an important key to the solution of our energy problems. The low-sulfur coal in the West is an important key to scotching the mind-closing misconception that coal-burning power plants always pollute.

Because they don't!

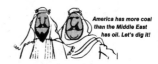

America has more coal than the Middle East has oil. Let's dig it!

American Electric Power System

Appalachian Power Co., Indiana & Michigan Electric Co., Kentucky Power Co., Kingsport Power Co., Michigan Power Co., Ohio Power Co., Wheeling Electric Co.

Exhibit 4A–16

153

HOT AIR VS. CLEAN AIR

To get clean air, it's a lot of hot air to suggest that today's stack gas scrubbers are the answer for major electric utilities.

Wet limestone scrubbers produce a by-product that clogs or corrodes the mechanism, causing shut downs. Insufficient reliability for a power plant.

They also produce a sludge of oozy gook ten times, by weight, greater than the sulfur they remove.

Applied to a 12,000 megawatt electric system they would, in just five years, spew so much of this almost-everlasting sludge it would cover 10 square miles to a depth of 5 feet.

To require the mass installation of this primitive, monstrously expensive, unproven technology on the nation's power plants would, in our view, create a national environmental tragedy and further feed the fires of inflation.

It is regrettable that workable technology doesn't exist.

Until it does, there is an alternate system that should be approved. It combines:

1. Tall chimney stacks to disperse emissions high in the atmosphere.

2. A sophisticated ground-level air monitoring system to assure constant air quality control.

It works.

We're using it.

It is the recommended plan of the Federal Power Commission, and the U. S. Government's own electric power system, the T.V.A.

There's still another solution.

Release the vast western reserves of low-sulfur coal being held by the Government.

With low-sulfur coal and workable, efficient, pollution-control devices America can have power plants clean enough to gladden the hearts of the most avid environmentalists.

And that's not hot air.

America has more coal than the Middle East has oil. Let's dig it!

American Electric Power System

Appalachian Power Co., Indiana & Michigan Electric Co., Kentucky Power Co., Kingsport Power Co., Michigan Power Co., Ohio Power Co., Wheeling Electric Co.

Exhibit 4A–17

154

Although America is critically short, we are exporting energy!

There is a law in this country which says export restrictions can be placed on items in short supply.

If energy isn't in short supply, what is?

Yet we will export over 53,000,000 tons of coal this year. That's a staggering 1.1 *quadrillion* units of energy Americans will be without.

Only a small portion of that coal is what you might call poor-quality. About 42 million tons of it is America's best.

42 million tons of environmentally compatible coal is enough to operate twelve of the very largest generating units in the nation for a full year!

Enough to satisfy the electric needs of the entire states of New York and New Jersey. Combined. Winter, spring, summer and fall.

Remember.

This is coal being mined by American labor at a time when there is a shortage of miners.

This is coal being hauled across the land when there is a shortage of hopper cars and engines.

Engines and hopper cars and miners who could be working for an energy-short U.S.A.

Remember, too, that this is coal made more prized by the fact that the U.S. Government continues to sit on huge 50 ft. seams of low-sulfur coal in the West.

There is no way that the exported coal can miss contributing to our inflation.

All of which leads to but one conclusion: restrict coal exports.

Surely, if the Arabs could restrict the export of oil for which they had no critical national need, we shouldn't hesitate to restrict mined coal—which America needs so badly.

America has more coal than the Middle East has oil. Let's dig it!

American Electric Power System

Appalachian Power Co., Indiana & Michigan Electric Co., Kentucky Power Co., Kingsport Power Co., Michigan Power Co., Ohio Power Co., Wheeling Electric Co.

Exhibit 4A-18

155

Just about this time next year lots of people may be asking,

"What time is the electricity on today?"

The gloomy prospect that significant areas of this country could reach the point of part time electricity usage seems unbelievable.

But, it could happen as early as the middle of next year.

This is not the doomsday prediction of an electric utility. It is the studied conclusion of the Federal Power Commission.

An FPC news release of a staff study declared that by 1975 "many steam electric power plants could be ordered to shut down because they do not conform to air quality standards".

Strict adherence to unreasonable regulations that are not necessary to protect health, would only jeopardize the nation's electric power supply.

The FPC is not talking about the ambient air standards of the Clean Air Act. They refer to the unrealistic requirement that emissions be measured at the top of the stack, instead of at the ground level where people live and breathe.

We completely support the mandate of the Clean Air Act to protect human health. But, like the Federal Power Commission, we question the wisdom of regulations that assume the existence of a workable, reliable and non-polluting commercial technology which doesn't even exist.

Unless action is taken now even the most diligent conservation of energy, which is so necessary, will fail to avert the forced curtailment of power.

Requirements must be adjusted to allow the use of alternate methods of meeting the standards of the Act. It's not the *method* that counts,

it's the *result*. And we can deliver the *result*.

One method that does exist . . . and does work . . . electronically measures air quality at ground level, and sets in motion constant air quality controls to meet the standards. Automatically.

The Federal Power Commission recommends it. The government's own electric power system, the Tennessee Valley Authority recommends it. So do we.

Additionally, the vast resources of clean, low-sulfur coal the government owns in the West must be released. This coal is the peoples' coal and the people need it. It takes time to open mines and time is running out. Soon even this solution will come too late.

But if action is taken today, no one need ask, "What time is the electricity on?" tomorrow.

American Electric Power System

Appalachian Power Co., Indiana & Michigan Electric Co., Kentucky Power Co., Kingsport Power Co., Michigan Power Co., Ohio Power Co., Wheeling Electric Co.

Exhibit 4A-19

156

Once this was famished farmland, then our stripmine. We reclaimed it into lovely woodland and lakes — a tiny part of our investment in environment.

We were environmentalists long before it was popular.

We've got nearly a billion in investments to prove it.

We've never been reluctant to invest in projects or workable controls to enhance and protect the environment.

Like electrostatic precipitators that today remove 99.7% of the fly ash. We began with mechanical dust collectors as early as 1918. Installed and tested our first electrostatic precipitator in 1941. That's 26 years before the Clean Air Act.

Today we're in the midst of a massive five year program of new installations and backfitting of existing precipitators. The cost? Over five hundred million dollars.

Or cooling towers, where they are needed to safeguard water quality. We were the first in the Western Hemisphere to build a natural draft cooling tower. We

have more power generation cooled by towers than any electric utility in the country.

Today we are operating, building or designing 13 cooling towers to eliminate the discharge of heat into adjacent waterways. The cost? Over one hundred million dollars.

Or tall chimney stacks that disperse sulfur-oxides over a wide area in the upper atmosphere.

We couple these tall stacks (as high as 1200 feet — that's slightly less than the Empire State Building) with an extensive, computerized, system of ground-level monitoring to assure that the quality of air is not harmful to human health, animals or plants.

We've invested tens of millions

of dollars in these tall stacks and ground-level monitoring because it's a system that works. A system that permits full compliance with ambient air standards of the Clean Air Act.

These major investments, plus many less dramatic ones are proof of our nearly one billion dollar commitment to enhance and protect the environment.

Proof too, of our historic concern for the environment. Even before it was popular.

America has more coal than the Middle East has oil. Let's dig it!

American Electric Power System

Appalachian Power Co., Indiana & Michigan Electric Co., Kentucky Power Co., Kingsport Power Co., Michigan Power Co., Ohio Power Co., Wheeling Electric Co.

Exhibit 4A-20

157

We burn at those who block the burning of vast amounts of America's coal.

And would like to claim they don't.

The Environmental Protection Agency by promulgating—or causing to be promulgated—unnecessarily restrictive regulations, will block the burning of millions of tons of good American coal.

Coal that is critical to America's energy needs.

They have decided that, in implementing the Clean Air Act, the only way to protect human health from stack gas emissions is to measure the sulfur-oxides at the top of the stack—instead of at ground level where people live and breathe.

That's nonsense.

There is a workable, practical, alternate way to meet the ambient air standards of the Clean Air Act.

It is endorsed by the Federal Power Commission, the Government's own Tennessee Valley Authority and the Federal Energy Administration. But E.P.A. won't accept it.

Will E.P.A. accept the responsibility for the economic effect their restrictive decision will have on the country?

Oh no! They'll try to wriggle off the hook by saying you can burn all the coal in America if you'll just install stack gas scrubbers.

That's more nonsense.

The naked truth is that there does not exist today a reliable non-polluting stack gas scrubber for electric utility use to eliminate sulfur-oxide emissions. A conclusion shared by the Federal Power

Commission, T.V.A., and other respected authorities.

At a time when America needs all the coal it can get, it is absolutely senseless for the E.P.A. to stubbornly insist on a particular method for meeting the ambient air standards of the Clean Air Act. It is the results that are important—not the method. And we can deliver the results.

It would be a crime if a significant portion of this vast American asset went unused because the Environmental Protection Agency could see only one way . . . their way . . . to meet the mandate of the Clean Air Act.

We know their way won't work. That's what burns.

American Electric Power System

Appalachian Power Co., Indiana & Michigan Electric Co., Kentucky Power Co., Kingsport Power Co., Michigan Power Co., Ohio Power Co., Wheeling Electric Co.

Exhibit 4A–21

158

To speak out, clearly and fairly

Not only is it a constitutional right...it is a moral duty.

We believe that the inalienable right to free speech carries with it many obligations, among which is the duty to speak clearly and fairly of impending danger.

We believe that to remain silent, especially when knowledge and experience in depth cry to be aired, is a moral dereliction of that duty.

We believe that to many our national energy crisis began and ended with the oil embargo — an unfortunate misconception. That was an oil crisis, mislabeled an energy crisis.

We believe that the danger of a real, a severe and lasting energy crisis wherein great sections of our nation will be faced with part time electrical usage, is too close. That belief is shared in essence by the Federal Power Commission.

We believe we must reassess our natural fuel resources—recognize that we and the world have a limited supply of oil and gas—that

we cannot depend upon foreign imports—that we have a super abundance of coal—that we as a nation must make a commitment to coal.

We believe there is a need for environmental controls to protect the land, the air, the water.

We endorse the mandate of the Clean Air Act to protect public health and we endorse the goals of rational environmentalists.

We believe, regrettably, that a limited number of fanatical environmentalists have succeeded in misleading the public and many of our elected representatives about environmental needs. All too often they have plumped for standards that result in environmental overkill—that have little if any scientific proof of demonstrable need.

We believe that too little is being done too slowly—that too many have no real understanding of the time lag between approval to act and full operational capacity. Mines

can't be opened overnight, equipment can't be procured overnight.

We believe it is folly to pressure for the purchase and installation of pollution control equipment that has been proven time and time again unreliable for major utility use.

We believe that a great contribution to solving our energy problems and eliminating air pollution would result from the release of the vast reserves of Government-owned clean fuel—the low sulfur coal in the West.

We believe we must conserve energy at every level. To waste energy is as wrong as inaction on the vital energy needs of our country.

We believe we must express our sincere beliefs about our energy problems and the solutions to those problems. To do less would allow expertise to go unused, misconceptions to go unchallenged and, possibly, economic chaos to strike our country.

American Electric Power System

Appalachian Power Co., Indiana & Michigan Electric Co., Kentucky Power Co., Kingsport Power Co., Michigan Power Co., Ohio Power Co., Wheeling Electric Co.

Exhibit 4A-22

159

We've won it again!

And no wonder.

Our efficiency is by design not chance.

It results from the practical application of the most advanced technology available today. Much of it created by our own engineers or in concert with leading manufacturers of electric utility equipment throughout the world.

In the last 10 years we have won the coveted "MOST EFFICIENT" title no less than seven times. And we've never been out of the top three.

You should know that "most efficient" means we are able to squeeze more electricity out of the fuel burned than any other electric power company in America.

That's conservation.

In fact, if it were possible for the next 99 utilities to have operated as efficiently as we did during 1973, America would have saved 65,000,000 tons of coal or over 243,000,000 barrels of oil.

If we know enough about advanced technology to make possible our being rated number one, isn't it reasonable to believe we know enough to judge stack gas scrubbers for what they are — monstrous, theoretical, unreliable, so called "anti-pollution" contraptions that contribute nothing to power generation except problems and pollution.

We do know enough . . . and we do so judge.

America has more coal than the Middle East has oil. Let's dig it!

American Electric Power System

Appalachian Power Co., Indiana & Michigan Electric Co., Kentucky Power Co., Kingsport Power Co., Michigan Power Co., Ohio Power Co., Wheeling Electric Co.

Exhibit 4A–23

160

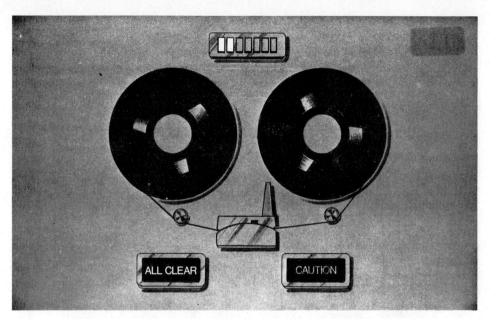

Now. Clean air, computerized.

The American Electric Power System has installed and is operating a sophisticated minute by minute computerized monitoring system to measure and control ambient air quality around its major generating areas.

Sixty one monitoring stations are located around 12 plants. Sensing instruments in each station measure not only sulfur and nitrogen oxide concentrations in the ambient air but also suspended particulate matter, wind direction and velocity, air temperature and in some areas fog density, humidity and rainfall.

These air quality measurements are continuously transmitted over A.E.P.'s microwave communications network to a computer center which in turn transmits data back to both our Power Production and Control Center in Canton, Ohio and the 12 generating plants in the network.

When the system reveals poor atmospheric conditions we can adjust electrical loads or temporarily shift to scarce lower sulfur fuels.

This efficient electronic system in concert with our tall chimney stacks that disperse and dissipate gases high in the upper atmosphere will allow us even when burning relatively high sulfur coal to meet the ambient air standards of the Clean Air Act.

The Federal Power Commission, the government's own electric power system the Tennessee Valley Authority and the Federal Energy Administration endorse this practical alternative to the impos-

sible requirement of meeting air standards by emission measurements taken at the top of the stack.

But this workable system is not acceptable to the Environmental Protection Agency.

Nevertheless we have taken this positive step because it is a system that allows us to meet the air quality standards of the Clean Air Act, whose mandate to protect human health we endorse.

For controlled air quality there is nothing better . . . today.

America has more coal than the Middle East has oil. Let's dig it!

American Electric Power System

Appalachian Power Co., Indiana & Michigan Electric Co., Kentucky Power Co., Kingsport Power Co., Michigan Power Co., Ohio Power Co., Wheeling Electric Co.

Exhibit 4A–24

161

Exhibit 4A–25

162

They're trying to tell us something.

We're foolish not to listen.

The Arab nations have indicated their intention to control oil production in order to keep prices up.

They're just not going to let the world use their limited resource as a cheap fuel.

For them it may be the right thing to do. For us it's a chilling signal and we should take warning.

What they're trying to tell us is we'd better

stop depending on oil for so many uses. Oil should be used only when there is no practical alternative.

Unlike many nations, we're fortunate. We have a superabundance of coal that can be used instead of precious oil for many of our energy needs.

We're sitting on half the world's known supply of coal — enough for over 500 years.

It may well be impossible for us to become totally independent. But certainly we can

reduce our dependence on foreign fuel.

We as a nation must make a commitment to coal. Face and solve any problems that exist.

And ask not if coal has a place in America's future, for coal is America's future. But ask only what needs to be done, by reasonable men, to use this vast and valuable asset.

Let's end this senseless delay. Let's pull our foot off the brake and get America going.   Now!

American Electric Power System

Appalachian Power Co., Indiana & Michigan Electric Co., Kentucky Power Co., Kingsport Power Co., Michigan Power Co., Ohio Power Co., Wheeling Electric Co.

Exhibit 4A–26

163

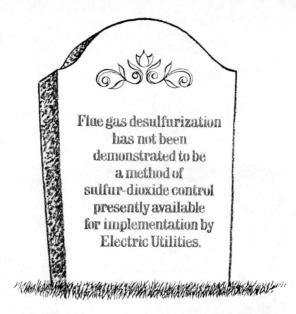

Flue gas desulfurization has not been demonstrated to be a method of sulfur-dioxide control presently available for implementation by Electric Utilities.

Requiem for scrubbers

That epitaph is taken from a 417 page report just released by the hearing examiners for the Environmental Protection Agency of Ohio.

And in case you don't recognize it from the language they're talking about "stack gas scrubbers" — as undeveloped, unreliable and unacceptable for electric utility use.

The hearing took 12 long weeks. Grueling testimony, with thorough cross examination, by experts, engineers, lawyers, scientists, businessmen—even manufacturers of scrubbers themselves.

If ever there was a grilling this was it.

Undoubtedly the most comprehensive and up to date presentation on the control of power plant sulfur-dioxide emissions ever held in any forum, anywhere in this country.

The findings of this exhaustive report—which parallel our published

position—cannot be seriously challenged by anyone wishing to avoid ridicule.

It covered every major scrubber test the Environmental Protection Agency has ever bragged about.

- Commonwealth Edison
- Illinois Power Co.
- Boston Edison
- Louisville Gas & Electric
- Mitsui Aluminum Plant
- Kansas City Power & Light
- Union Electric of St. Louis

One after the other the record shows they failed to meet the criteria established by the National Academy of Engineering.

They simply failed to demonstrate the degree of reliability necessary for electric utility use.

And yet, to this day, EPA insists these monstrous contraptions are available, work, are reliable . . . and electric utilities should invest many

billions of dollars in them.

If that isn't fanning the fires of inflation, wasting precious assets and wrongfully burdening the electric costs of the American people, then we shouldn't be allowed to generate another kilowatt.

Are these examiners alone? They are not! Many respected authorities share their conclusion: The Tennessee Valley Authority. The Federal Energy Administration. The Atomic Energy Commission. The Federal Power Commission and others.

E.P.A.'s stubborn, continued plumping for stack gas scrubbers is an energy-paralyzing activity that is stalling vital legislation and severely inhibiting by uncertainty, investment in the development of new coal mines.

Isn't it about time someone redirected E.P.A.'s energies into more constructive channels?

American Electric Power System

Appalachian Power Co . Indiana & Michigan Electric Co . Kentucky Power Co . Kingsport Power Co . Michigan Power Co . Ohio Power Co . Wheeling Electric Co.

Exhibit 4A–27

164

The rich get richer
while we struggle with inflation!

The oil countries of the Middle East are getting richer and richer. Their problem is they don't know what to do with all the money they have.

What they have done to the price of oil has had an unbelievable effect upon our economy.

True, there are other forces at play. But few, if any, products you buy have not been affected by their skyrocketing oil prices.

Result? Inflation at every turn. And Americans and America poorer for it.

What can we do?
Reduce our dependence on foreign fuel.

How?
By using to the fullest our own natural resources. Coal for instance. We're sitting on half the world's known supply . . . enough to take care of our energy needs for 500 years.

Coal is a viable alternative to oil for many of our energy needs. The problem is we've been frightened by stories about what a "bad" fuel coal is.

Nonsense!

America has vast supplies of low-sulfur coal that won't pollute the air. Much of it is in the West, under Government control, and they won't release it. Why? Why?

Additionally, millions upon millions of tons of higher sulfur coal can be burned and still meet the ambient air standards of the Clean Air Act by using tall stacks and the intermittent control system.

This system is a practical alternative to the impractical, unproven, unreliable stack gas scrubber system recommended by the Environmental Protection Agency.

It really is no longer a question of whether coal has a place in America's future. Coal is America's future.

And since we have more coal than the Middle East has oil, we must start using it.

Fully. Now.

If we don't we'll be the poorer for it.

American Electric Power System

Appalachian Power Co . Indiana & Michigan Electric Co . Kentucky Power Co . Kingsport Power Co . Michigan Power Co . Ohio Power Co . Wheeling Electric Co

Exhibit 4A-28

165

Exhibit 4A-29. The Whole Story: American Electric Power Company's Reply to Mr. Russell E. Train, Administrator, Environmental Protection Agency.

Dear Mr. Train:

This is in response to your letter to me of August 23, 1974, copies of which you apparently forwarded for publication in the September 2 issue of The New York Times and the September 5 issue of The Washington Post.

Your letter refers to our advertisement which first appeared on August 13 and which carried the headline "We burn at those who block the burning of vast amounts of America's coal—and would like to claim they don't".

Your letter attempts to disprove the statements contained in our advertisement and to defend those actions of your Agency which must inevitably have the effect of prohibiting the burning of vast amounts of our Nation's coal—while at the same time denying that you are doing so.

Your letter further confirms the accuracy of our advertisement and, in fact, provides another concrete example of what we are objecting to.

In responding to your letter, let me first delineate the areas of agreement. We certainly agree that ". . . it is vital that we find ways to use effectively this Nation's abundant coal resources." This, of course, has been the basic theme and purpose of AEP's current ad program (to which you and your Deputy, Mr. Quarles, object so strenuously). We also agree that it is ". . . vital that the methods adopted provide real protection to the public health."

That is precisely why we advocate a policy of tall stacks and sophisticated and detailed monitoring, with supplementary controls where necessary, as the only presently effective method of assuring the continuous maintenance of the health-related primary SO_2 ambient standards in a manner that will permit the continued burning of America's readily available and abundant coal resources.

Therefore, we too ". . . believe that the Nation can protect public health while also assuring an adequate supply of energy" although, unlike EPA, we have proposed a *feasible* way to achieve that objective.

While we and EPA appear to be in agreement on the basic goals, we part company at that point. As we see it, three basic areas of disagreement exist between us:

1. EPA contends that SO_2 scrubber technology has been sufficiently demonstrated for widespread application to large power plants. We believe this to be pernicious nonsense from which most of our other problems stem.

2. EPA continues to press for the installation of scrubbers, in lieu of tall stacks, monitoring, and supplementary controls, as the sole method of achieving the ambient standards in cases where sufficient quantities of low sulfur fuel do not exist. AEP advocates the use of tall stacks, sophisticated and detailed monitoring, and supplemental controls wherever they will do the job of protecting the public health.

3. EPA contends that the Clean Air Act *requires* constant and rigid emission limitations. AEP believes that the Clean Air Act, properly construed, permits the use of any method which effectively achieves and maintains the national ambient standards.

However, before elaborating further upon these basic areas of disagreement, I will deal with a number of specific contentions contained in your letter.

a. You state that EPA " . . . has adopted policies and supported a number of legislative amendments that would allow the use of greater amounts of coal . . .".

In our view these policies to the extent that they prove effective, would merely reduce, to a very limited extent, the effects of other much broader and more fundamental EPA policies, i.e., support for constant and rigid emission controls and opposition to tall stacks, which, in effect, prohibit the burning of our Nation's vast supply of high sulfur eastern coal.

For example, you point to EPA's December 1972 "clean fuels policy" as permitting the burning of 90 million tons per year of . . . coal . . ." that ". . . could not have been used beyond mid-1975".

You do not tell us why this 90 million annual tons of coal could not be burned after mid-1975 nor do you mention that an additional 160 million annual tons, which your "clean fuels policy" does not reach, cannot be burned after mid-1975. The reason is clear: EPA's insistence upon the inclusion in state implementation plans of constant and rigid emission limitations as the *only* method of meeting the ambient SO_2 standards.

166

For example, within the past few weeks you disapproved portions of the New York and Kentucky implementation plans because they might have been construed as permitting the use of supplemental controls in lieu of constant and rigid emission limitations. I suggest that it is more than slightly disingenuous for you to persist in a policy which prohibits the burning of 250 million annual tons of coal—more than enough to supply the electric power requirements of *twelve* New York City Metropolitan Areas for one year—and then to suggest that you are actually promoting the greater use of coal simply because you are urging the States to extend the application of the secondary standards beyond mid-1975, thereby deferring the prohibition against 90 millions tons of the 250 million annual tons you are rendering unusable.

b. Next in this vein you cite EPA's support of those amendments to the Clean Air Act which, under certain circumstances, mandate the conversion of power plants from oil to coal.

But anyone knowledgeable in this area knows that this legislation was little more than an effort by its supporters to create the impression that they were acting in a positive and meaningful way in the midst of last winter's fuel crisis—while, in fact, it did little or nothing to improve the energy situation and worsened the coal supply situation.

The July 11th issue of The New York Times reported Mr. Quarles as indicating that, under EPA's interpretation of this legislation, it appeared that only two power plants in the entire nation would be eligible for mandatory conversion. Furthermore—and of controlling importance in our view—the amendments, while purporting to require an increase in the usage of coal, did not have the effect of increasing the supply of coal by even one lump. The only effect has been to increase the potential demand without increasing the supply. For EPA to cite its support of this legislation as an example of its efforts to increase the availability of coal is another example of inaccurate and unsupportable "double-talk".

c. As a third example, you cite EPA's support of proposed amendments to the Clean Air Act which are sponsored by the Administration and which are presently pending in the Congress. There are ten such amendments.

You failed to note that EPA opposed and, in fact, sabotaged two of these amendments which are by far of the greatest importance to ensure the continuation of an adequate energy and fuel supply.

First, your Agency vigorously opposed the clarifying amendment proposed by the Administration which would explicitly recognize tall stacks, sophisticated monitoring, and supplemental controls as a valid and effective method of meeting the ambient SO_2 standards and which would thereby permit the continued burning of the Nation's high sulfur eastern coals in a manner compatible with the protection of the public health and welfare.

Secondly, you also opposed a clarifying amendment which would eliminate the very serious problems created by the courts in the "no significant deterioration" litigation instituted by the Sierra Club. While I understand your recently reproposed regulations on this matter (39 F.R. 31000) to be a distinct improvement over those originally proposed in July of 1973, the fact of the matter is that no matter how intelligently the anti-deterioration concept is administered by EPA, it must inevitably involve a further and perhaps very major restriction upon our Nation's energy supply and the use of coal.

EPA opposed this concept all the way to the United States Supreme Court in the *Sierra Club* litigation. I am, therefore particularly puzzled by your refusal to support the Administration's amendment which reflects the exact substantive position which your Agency supported in the courts.

d. You specifically refer to your support of one particular amendment which you state " . . . would allow the Agency to continue, until 1979 if necessary, to tailor-make its air quality compliance dates for power plants—based on the availability of low sulfur coal, emission control systems, etc." Our understanding of this provision is that it would be carried out through the use of § 113 enforcement orders and that such enforcement orders would require plants to meet constant and rigid emission limitations by or before 1979. This, in turn, would involve a commitment by the plants, either to burn conforming fuel—which EPA admits does not exist in sufficient quantities—or to install scrubbers—which virtually everyone, with the notable exception of EPA, believes not to have been sufficiently demonstrated for widespread application to large power plants. In the meantime, these plants would be permitted to operate on a supplementary control basis.

Furthermore, the issuance of enforcement orders under the amendment would involve a determination by EPA as to whether the plants' failure to meet the mid-1975 compliance

167

date was due in any degree to "bad faith". Where "bad faith" is found, the civil and criminal penalties of the Act would be invoked.

Recent utterances by EPA officials lead us to suspect that a company's position on scrubber technology and its willingness to express or publicize that position may be a major and perhaps a controlling consideration in EPA's determination of whether or not to couple civil or criminal penalties with its enforcement orders.

A program that would tie the continued burning of existing coal supplies to a commitment to install a presently unproven technology and to refrain from any criticism of such technology is not, in our view, a responsible, helpful or constructive program.

e. One last but important point with respect to your contention that EPA is pursuing policies " . . . that would allow the use of greater amounts of coal to meet the Nation's energy needs"—i.e., your position on the pending surface mining legislation. You declined to support H.R. 12898 which imposed stringent reclamation requirements in a manner compatible with the mining of sufficient quantities of coal to meet the Nation's future energy requirements.

Instead, your Agency threw its support behind a bill (H.R. 11500) which would have the effect of prohibiting the mining of billions of tons of the Nation's coal reserves which are minable under existing law.

We would hardly characterize this as an EPA policy designed to promote the greater use of coal.

In view of all of the foregoing, we stand by the statement in our August 13 advertisement that EPA's policies "will block the burning of millions of tons of good American coal". That statement is neither inaccurate nor untrue as you contend—rather, its truth is obvious and is compelled by the facts set forth above. If anything, the ad *understates* rather than *"misstates"* EPA's role in blocking the burning of American coal.

I will now elaborate upon those basic areas of disagreement which I briefly referred to earlier in this letter:

SCRUBBER TECHNOLOGY

We do not believe that scrubber technology has advanced to the stage where its widespread application to large-scale power plants would be prudent. We are a major and sophisticated engineering organization and believe that our engineering judgment is entitled to considerable weight.

Likewise, we believe that the engineering judgment of comparable organizations, such as the Southern System and the federal government's own Tennessee Valley Authority, also should be accorded considerable weight. Our views on scrubbers are shared by the Federal Power Commission and the Federal Energy Administration.

The fact of the matter is that EPA stands virtually alone on this issue. Only EPA is advocating scrubbers.

Only EPA is attempting to tie the continued burning of the Nation's high sulfur coals to their installation at power plants throughout the country. The fact that a number of scrubbers are operating sporadically or that a number of companies have agreed to install scrubbers does not go to the question of how well they work. In major part, that merely reflects EPA pressure on the industry to install unproven and highly expensive technology.

Today your Agency stands even more alone on this issue than it did early last week, for on September 6, 1974 the 417 page Report and Recommendations of a three-member Ohio EPA panel of hearing examiners was issued *In the Matter of Consolidated Electric Utility Cases* (Case No. 73 A-P-120, *et al*). At page 6 of that Report the following statement appears:

> The Hearing Panel believes this to be the most comprehensive and up-to-date presentation of factual issues relating to the control of sulfur dioxide emissions from electric generating plants yet presented in any forum anywhere in this country. Extensive briefs and reply briefs exhaustively treated the legal and factual issues involved in these cases.

The Report and Recommendations were based upon the record complied during the course of an evidentiary hearing which commenced on March 4, 1974 and concluded on May 23, 1974.

The transcript consisted of more than 6,800 pages of testimony which was subject to cross-examination.

168

Witnesses were selected from among the Nation's most outstanding experts in their respective fields. Ohio Power Company, an AEP subsidiary, was involved in this proceeding, as was your Agency which provided a number of expert witnesses.

With respect to the issue of scrubber technology "[v]ery extensive evidence was presented on both sides of this question" and the burden of proving that scrubber technology has not been adequately demonstrated rested with the electric companies.

Testimony was presented with respect to all significant demonstration projects and processes here and abroad.

The *unanimous* verdict of the Hearing Panel was that—

"... RELIABLE FLUE GAS DESULFURIZATION TECHNOLOGY WHICH CAN BE APPLIED BY THE OHIO ELECTRIC UTILITIES TO ACHIEVE COMPLIANCE WITH PERTINENT REGULATIONS HAS NOT BEEN DEMONSTRATED TO A DEGREE WHICH WOULD JUSTIFY ITS INSTALLATION."

We hope that this Ohio decision will lead to a reconsideration of EPA's position on scrubber technology, for we believe that it is from this position that many of our problems stem.

If your Agency would recognize that scrubber technology has not been adequately demonstrated, we believe it would inevitably follow that—at least for an interim period until we can develop some more feasible technology, e.g., coal liquefaction or gasification—tall stacks, sophisticated and detailed monitoring and supplementary controls would also be recognized for what they are—a currently available, feasible and effective method of protecting the public health and welfare.

Before concluding on the matter of scrubber technology. I must take issue with two additional statements contained in your letter.

First, you appear to suggest that the technical problems with scrubbers have been in the nature of "start-up problems". But this is clearly not the fact.

Many of these problems inhere in or are fundamental to the process. In this connection, I suggest that you review pages 103–171 of the Ohio EPA Report and Recommendations on this matter.

Second, at page 1 of your letter you state that achieving the goals of the Clean Air Act "is a complex and difficult task" and that AEP's and program "contributes little to its reasoned resolution . . .".

On our part, we can think of no greater over-simplification of a complex issue than the oft repeated statements by you and Mr. Quarles on national TV and in press conferences to the effect that scrubber technology is here and all that the electric utility industry need do is to "stop dragging its feet" and install it.

In this connection, we suggest that you consider the exhaustive records made, and the carefully thought out opinions based on such records, in the Ohio EPA Report and the decisions of the Pennsylvania Courts in the *Pennsylvania Power Company* litigation.

TALL STACKS AND SUPPLEMENTARY CONTROLS

The effectiveness of tall stacks, sophisticated and detailed monitoring, and supplementary controls as a method of complying with the ambient standards was also exhaustively explored in the Ohio EPA proceeding. The electric utilities had the burden of proving their workability and they carried that burden.

The Hearing Panel *unanimously* concluded that the electric utilities have shown that—

"TALL STACKS, BY ENHANCING THE DISPERSION OF POLLUTANTS, CAN BE USED AS A MEANS OF CONTROLLING AMBIENT AIR CONCENTRATIONS OF SULFUR DIOXIDE IN MOST CASES. THEY HAVE FURTHER SHOWN THAT IN THOSE CASES WHERE TOPOGRAPHY OR METEOROLOGICAL CONDITIONS MAKE TALL STACKS ALONE A QUESTIONABLE DEVICE, THEY CAN BE COMBINED WITH A PROGRAM FOR LIMITING EMISSIONS THROUGH THE USE OF LOAD REDUCTION OR THE BURNING OF LOW SULFUR FUELS, OR BOTH, AND THAT SUCH A PROGRAM CAN BE ENFORCED THROUGH THE USE OF ADEQUATE MONITORING AND METEOROLOGICAL PREDICTION." The Hearing Panel went on to find that "TALL STACKS, EITHER ALONE OR IN COMBINATION WITH SUPPLEMENTARY CONTROL PROGRAMS ARE AN EFFECTIVE MEANS OF MEETING AMBIENT AIR QUALITY STANDARDS."

In arriving at these findings, the Hearing Panel had before it the testimony of EPA's

Dr. Finklea on the "sulfate issue" (which appears to have replaced "difficulty of enforcement" which was previously asserted as EPA's principal objection to tall stacks).

On the sulfate issue, the Hearing Panel unanimously concluded that ". . . more research needs to be done in order to establish the threat posed."

While dealing with the subject of health effects, I would also note that we take major exception to the statement in the first paragraph of your letter which says that our August 13 advertisement "disregards the very real health problems associated with coal burning."

The fact is that we advocate tall stacks, sophisticated and detailed monitoring and supplementary controls as the *only* presently available method for assuring the maintenance of the national ambient standards—including the primary standards which were designed to protect the public health and which are required by law to "contain an adequate margin of safety".

If your Agency has done its job properly in promulgating the primary standards, I do not understand how you can possibly accuse us of disregarding health effects when the goal of our program is to comply fully with the health-related primary standards.

CONSTANT EMISSION LIMITATIONS

In your letter you contend that AEP has argued that "emission limitations themselves are not required by the Clean Air Act, but this assertion has been rejected in a decision by the 5th U.S. Circuit Court of Appeals."

By approving the Georgia implementation plan which was the subject of the Fifth Circuit litigation and which contained emission limitations which varied depending upon stack height, and then by defending your action in the courts until your voluntary capitulation just prior to oral argument in that case, EPA apparently agreed with AEP up until May 7, 1973 at which time your Agency reversed its position. This reversal of position undoubtedly had an effect on the court's decision. However, unlike EPA, AEP has not reversed its position.

We continue to believe that the Clean Air Act does not *require* constant and rigid emission limitations as the *sole* method of achieving and maintaining the ambient standards. We continue to believe that the Fifth Circuit—which is but one of eleven Circuits—was wrong and that its holding will not be followed by other Circuits. In this connection, on September 6th, Kentucky Power Company, an AEP subsidiary, together with other Kentucky electric suppliers petitioned the Sixth Circuit for review of EPA's recent action in reapproving Kentucky's implementation plan while disapproving a portion of that plan because EPA construed the disapproved portion as possibly permitting the use of tall stacks and supplementary controls.

We believe that the Sixth Circuit will not follow the Fifth Circuit and we are most disappointed that EPA did not "stick to its guns" on this issue.

It is also relevant here to note again that, on this most important issue, not only has EPA reversed its position on the question of statutory interpretation but it has also vigorously opposed the Administration's proposal on the substantive question—i.e., to clarify any ambiguity in the existing legislation by explicitly authorizing the use of the tall stack, sophisticated and detailed monitoring, and supplementary controls.

Finally, I think it is appropriate and important to emphasize that, as we have stated in a subsequent ad, first published August 27, we have both a constitutional right and an obligation to speak out on issues which are vital to the welfare of our Company, our customers and our Nation.

We are convinced that our position on scrubber technology is sound. It is forthright and it is receiving ever-increasing support from those who have been able to view the issue with any degree of objectivity.

We believe Mr. Quarles' ad hominem harangue against AEP's position on scrubber technology which I endured at an EPA meeting of utility executives on March 7 was unbecoming and not helpful. This was followed two business days later by a call from your Region V office to AEP's General Counsel advising him that we would soon be in receipt of §114 letters requiring detailed information on all of our plants in Region V.

Nor do we regard Mr. Quarles' outburst against our advertising program during the July 23, 1974 conference of the Atomic Industrial Forum as being justified or helpful.

Despite the fact that the AIF Conference was convened to discuss effluent standards under the Water Pollution Control Act Amendments of 1972, Mr. Quarles devoted about one-third of his address to an attack on our advertising program and carried to the rostrum with him copies of several of our ads.

Not only were Mr. Quarles' remarks totally out of place at a Conference of this type, but they were inaccurate and appeared to carry with them veiled threats of regulatory controls over AEP and utility industry advertising and a veiled warning to the rest of the industry against airing any views similar to ours.

Another aspect of what appears to be a pattern of intimidation involves the proposed Blue Ridge Hydroelectric and Pumped Storage Project of Appalachian Power Company, an AEP subsidiary.

On July 15, 1974, in a letter to Congressman Mizell, you indicated your support of H.R. 11120, which has as its purpose the killing of the Blue Ridge Project.

Your Agency was a party to the Federal Power Commission proceeding involving Blue Ridge and was fully aware that Blue Ridge is badly needed for power purposes and will involve a minimal adverse impact upon the environment.

Your Agency was fully aware of the flood control, recreational and low flow augmentation benefits to be provided by the project. Your Agency was also fully aware that, due to natural streamflow generation and the provision of the pumping energy by the most efficient thermal plants on the AEP System, less coal would be burned by the AEP System with Blue Ridge than with the next best alternative to Blue Ridge—resulting in conservation of our Nation's natural resources and a cleaner environment.

Despite these overwhelming factors in favor of Blue Ridge, you nevertheless chose to throw the weight of your Agency behind a back-door bill to kill the project.

Our air pollution goals appear to be the same as EPA's—the protection of the public health. But AEP has the additional responsibility of providing an adequate and reliable supply of electric energy to almost six million people in seven States who are totally dependent on us for power supply in their homes and in their jobs. We will continue to do our level best to meet both of these responsibilities—but we can do so only if those regulating our operations, including EPA, adopt realistic, sensible and feasible policies.

One of the primary purposes of our advertising program is to do what we can to ensure that such policies will be realistic, sensible and feasible.

Very truly yours,
Donald C. Cook, Chairman

This letter appeared in ad 29 of the series, entitled "Half a Story Is Worse Than None."

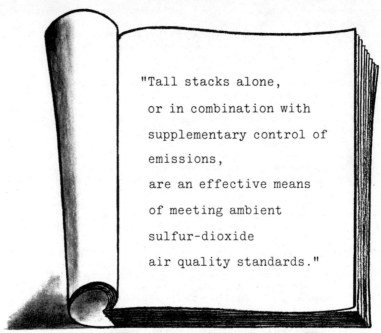

"Tall stacks alone,
or in combination with
supplementary control of
emissions,
are an effective means
of meeting ambient
sulfur-dioxide
air quality standards."

Amen!

That hallelujah quote is in the newly released 417 page report by the Hearing Examiners for the Environmental Protection Agency of Ohio.

It was an exhaustive 12-week hearing—with 6,830 pages of testimony by experts from both E.P.A. and the utilities. Testimony subjected to thorough cross examination.

Without question, the most current and comprehensive investigation of the facts about sulfur-dioxide emissions ever conducted in any forum, anywhere in the country.

The report concluded that the use of tall stacks and an intermittent control system had met the burden of proof. It is an effective method for meeting the clean air standards.

Little wonder it is endorsed by the Federal Power Commission,

TVA, and the Federal Energy Administration, as a practical alternative to the Environmental Protection Agency's impossible requirement of meeting air standards by measuring emission at the top of the stack.

Despite the evidence E.P.A., blinded by a distorted vision of righteousness, refuses acceptance. An energy paralyzing attitude.

Refuses, knowing that they will block the burning of millions upon millions of tons of precious coal. Coal that needn't violate the clean air standards.

Refuses, knowing the economic impact on states where coal is a vital industry. Thousands unemployed. Millions lost in state tax revenues. More millions lost by businesses that supply the coal industry.

In one state alone, Ohio, it is

estimated that the economic loss would be $114 million a year!

That's pennies compared to the economic devastation of a power shortage in Ohio—the heart of the American Ruhr, with its industries intertwined with others in our nation. Hardly a family would go untouched.

At a time when America needs all the coal it can get, when we are all struggling with inflation, we refuse to be silent.

We will speak out and hope that the people will join us in telling E.P.A. that we all want clear air . . . not through E.P.A.'s inflationary unreliable, billion dollar stack gas scrubber, but through the proven, effective tall stack and intermittent control system.

When E.P.A. sees the wisdom of this direction, we'll say AMEN.

American Electric Power System

Appalachian Power Co., Indiana & Michigan Electric Co., Kentucky Power Co., Kingsport Power Co., Michigan Power Co., Ohio Power Co., Wheeling Electric Co.

Exhibit 4A–30

The Philadelphia, Pa. Story

-or-
It's time some people learned you can't fool all of the people.

As you know by now, E.P.A. is headstrong for scrubbers.

It would dearly love people to believe that those monstrous contraptions, designed to capture sulfur-oxide emissions, are reliable.

They're not.

In fact, after hearing exhaustive testimony from many experts, the *state* E.P.A. examiners in Ohio issued a 417-page report stating categorically that scrubbers are unreliable for major utility use.

That was on September 6.

Nevertheless—19 days later—E.P.A., Washington, D.C., charged right ahead with a news release that Philadelphia Electric had agreed to invest $68 million in scrubbers.

And was thereby hoisted on its own lance.

Here's how. The utility agreed, in truth, to spend $20.3 million . . . not $68 million...to install four devices.

Three are related to the removal of particulate matter . . . not sulfur oxides.

Most all utilities have "particulate" removal devices—the most popular being electrostatic precipitators—so there's nothing newsworthy about them.

The fourth device (E.P.A.'s beloved sulfur-oxide scrubber) is only an experiment.

It is to be tested on one third of one generating unit at one plant.

And if the experiment fails—as so many before it have—Philadelphia Electric is under no obligation to invest further. It can abandon the whole mess.

Which leads to a few embarrassing questions:

1. If sulfur-oxide scrubbers work, as E.P.A. has been publicly claiming, why did it agree to yet another test?

2. Why did the news release shamelessly assume success of the test and headline a $68 million investment, while trying to bury the $20.3 million

figure ($18.7 million of which had already been spent)?

3. Why was the word "test" hidden 381 words into the release?

And, lastly—is E.P.A. ready to resort to any artifice to create an impression of widespread acceptance of scrubbers?

Even a good end, as most everyone knows, never justifies mischievous means.

The goal America is most interested in is escape from oppression —escape from the inflationary vise of the oil-rich nations.

The good means is to be able to burn all the coal America can get, including the clean low-sulfur coal in the West.

Fully.

Using tall stacks and the intermittent control system to assure clean air.

That's the story which would have rung the bell in Philadelphia.

American Electric Power System

Appalachian Power Co. , Indiana & Michigan Electric Co , Kentucky Power Co , Kingsport Power Co , Michigan Power Co , Ohio Power Co , Wheeling Electric Co.

Exhibit 4A–31

173

Have you heard any good scrubber stories lately?

"Stack gas scrubbers," you'll recall, are those unreliable monstrous contraptions calculated to capture sulfur-oxide emissions.

Using lime or limestone, they produce tons of oozy, polluting, gook far worse than the condition they're intended to cure.

Stories about them abound.

Most center around scrubber supporters who refuse to be deterred by the facts.

Here's one in three parts:

On Sept. 6 — after conducting the most thorough review and assessment of scrubbers ever made, anywhere — the Ohio E.P.A. panel of hearing examiners released a 417-page report concluding that scrubbers weren't reliable enough to be installed.

On Sept. 23, the national head of

E.P.A. testified before a House Committee to the effect that scrubber technology is here, and is reliable.

Worse, two days later a subordinate official said in a news release that scrubbers could be installed and could operate reliably 90% of the time.

Comical — except that the subject is so serious.

Here's one on sludge:

The United States Department of the Interior has said that, if limestone scrubbers became widely used they would, by 1980, be producing 71,400,000 tons of gook a year.

By our calculations that would cover about 10 square miles, 10 feet deep . . . every year.

Nonchalantly, E.P.A. waves away sludge disposal as not "insur-

mountable." Which led one wag to write:

There once was a man from Rhode I., Who didn't quite see eye to eye With the experts on scrubbers. So he donned only rubbers, Then waded through gook to his tie.

If in place of limestone you used a chemical like magnesium-oxide that might produce a usable by-product, there would not be sludge. But . . . before long there would be enough elemental sulfur to wreck the industry and enough sulfuric acid to fill tank cars coast to coast.

Another insurmountable mess.

E.P.A.'s dedication to a technology that doesn't work, meanwhile, blocks the burning of millions of tons of precious American coal — coal, our ace against Middle East oil.

In the midst of inflation, that's no joke.

American Electric Power System

Appalachian Power Co., Indiana & Michigan Electric Co., Kentucky Power Co., Kingsport Power Co., Michigan Power Co., Ohio Power Co., Wheeling Electric Co.

Exhibit 4A–32

"Maybe we should buy American coal fields."

The Middle East oil countries are fast capturing the world's money. There isn't much they're incapable of buying. So it could happen.

They *are* looking for ways to invest their money. And they do recognize an asset when they see one. Which is something we seem to have trouble doing.

America owns half of the world's known supply of one of mankind's great energy assets: Coal.

In fact, we have underground nearly four times more energy in coal than the Middle East has in oil.

And what are we doing with it? Regrettably, too little.

We're still making only a lip service commitment to the full use of coal despite the fact that coal represents 90% of our fossil resources.

Why aren't we using this great asset?

Two reasons.

The Environmental Protection Agency won't let us burn much of the Eastern coal we can mine.

And the U.S. Interior Department won't let us mine the vast amounts of Western coal we could burn.

If—until a practical and reliable process is developed for cleaning coal before or after it is burned— E.P.A. would recognize and approve the tall stack and intermittent control system, America could burn nearly all of the Eastern coal.

And in case you think the tall stack system won't protect the environment, you should know it has been proven that—coupled with sophisticated monitoring devices— it assures meeting the standards of the Clean Air Act.

You should also know that tall stacks have been found to be efficient and are endorsed by the Federal Power Commission, TVA, the Federal Energy Administration and the governments of England, Russia and Israel.

If E.P.A. would agree to the use of tall stacks to control air quality, and if the government would release the tremendous resources of clean low-sulfur coal in the West, great steps would be made in fighting inflation and freeing us from the economic grip of the oil rich Arab nations.

Let's begin a crash program to dig and put all our coal to work as quickly, cleanly and efficiently as possible.

The Arabs know how to use their natural asset to help themselves. Let's use ours—coal—to help ourselves.

American Electric Power System

Appalachian Power Co., Indiana & Michigan Electric Co., Kentucky Power Co., Kingsport Power Co., Michigan Power Co., Ohio Power Co., Wheeling Electric Co.

Exhibit 4A–33

175

In electric
power generation...

Our yesterday is the world's tomorrow!

In the early 1950's it became evident, to us at A.E.P., that if the electric utility industry was to maintain its remarkable record of keeping up with the needs of the country, new power generation technology was necessary.

The limiting world of sub-critical pressures of 2000 to 2400 pounds per square inch had to be challenged.

And so, in 1953, we announced such a project. It was to become known as Philo 6.

In concert with Babcock & Wilcox and General Electric we explored the unknown...boilers and turbines that could withstand super-critical pressures as high as 4500 pounds per square inch... steam temperatures of 1150 degrees Fahrenheit.

Pressure so high that the whole mass of water never bubbles, but turns to steam—instantly.

By '55 a steam generator of chromium and nickel alloy steel had been designed to cope with super-critical high temperature generation.

And new chemical controls for ultra-pure water developed that were so exacting it was necessary to shift the decimal point three places for laboratory analytical work.

By mid '57 Philo 6 was operating commercially. A whole new world for bigger, more economical, more efficient generation was born.

Philo 6, with a generating capacity of 125,000 kilowatts, was the prototype for our massive 1,300,000 kilowatt units.

Today A.E.P. alone has more super-critical power generation than any country in the rest of the world.

And in our country A.E.P. has more,efficient super-critical generation than any other power utility.

Certainly, if we had the vision and ability to develop such advanced technology, isn't it reasonable to believe that we know enough to judge "stack gas scrubbers" for what they are—unreliable so-called "anti-pollution" contraptions that contribute nothing to power generation but pollution and problems.

For all the world to know: that is our position . . . yesterday and tomorrow . . . on today's stack gas scrubbers.

American Electric Power System

Appalachian Power Co . Indiana & Michigan Electric Co . Kentucky Power Co . Kingsport Power Co . Michigan Power Co . Ohio Power Co . Wheeling Electric Co

Exhibit 4A–34

176

We repeat
a suggestion we abhor.

The shock of the oil embargo hit us more than a year ago.

Since then the volume of rhetoric on the energy crisis has far outweighed this country's action.

Time... precious time is wasting.

Out in the West, the U.S. Government owns vast reserves of clean low-sulfur coal. It is desperately needed to solve America's energy problem.

Yet it's not released.

Why?

Some say mining will scar the land.

They're suspicious of private enterprise; they do not believe industry will act responsibly, and restore the land.

And their voices block the release of this non-polluting coal.

We can't speak for others—but long before environmental groups were formed or reclamation laws

framed, American Electric Power was restoring mined land to a condition more productive, enjoyable and valuable than before the coal was mined.

What we did and are still doing to 125,000 acres of famished farmland in Ohio is a national model for beautification of mined terrain.

Any responsible corporation experienced in land reclamation can develop and carry out a plan to mine the Western coal and return the land to a condition as good as or better than it was before.

But.

If private corporations aren't trusted to do the job, let the U.S. Government, itself, mine the coal.

The U.S. Government can restore the land the way the U.S. people want it to.

The U.S. Government can fix the price of coal to include reclamation costs.

The U.S. Government can guarantee that no company will profit from the mining.

The U.S. Government can control allocation to users who need low-sulfur coal.

We have great pride in American industry. Despite over-chronicled abuses industry has made magnificent contributions to the greatness of America.

We abhor the thought of the government mining Western coal. There is no doubt that responsible industry can do it better.

But, if it has to be ... so be it.

The clean Western coal is the people's coal. And the people need it ... now.

LET'S GET GOING!

America has more coal than the Middle East has oil. Let's dig it!

American Electric Power System

Appalachian Power Co., Indiana & Michigan Electric Co., Kentucky Power Co., Kingsport Power Co., Michigan Power Co., Ohio Power Co., Wheeling Electric Co.

Exhibit 4A–35

177

What's wrong with this picture?
It's inflation by the carload.

The price of oil imports from the Middle East is exorbitant.

So, now, is the price of our domestic coal.

In fact, the increase in the open-market price of domestic coal has been greater than the increase in the price of imported oil.

Both are among the major causes of our inflation. Both are caused by demand far exceeding supply.

In the case of oil, the Arab cartel fixed extortionate prices. In the case of coal, the U.S. Government has both limited the burning of Eastern coal and prohibited the expanded mining of Western coal.

Yet America is actually *decreasing* its supply of above-ground coal. The evidence is in the recent photo, above.

The panorama shows just part of the hundreds upon hundreds of hopper cars loaded with coal awaiting export to other countries.

Export!

At a time of record demand here in America.

At a time when stocks of mined coal are declining drastically.

At a time when American utilities and industry are in dire need of this precious fuel.

At a time when Environmental Protection Agency regulations will block the burning of millions of tons of Eastern coal.

At a time when the U.S. Department of the Interior won't release millions of tons of clean Western coal that could be burned.

At a time of inflation.

Despite these overwhelming reasons not to export, America in '74 will ship out about 55,000,000 tons— 42,000,000 of which is among America's best coal. And 80% of that is suitable for utility boilers.

Even the most conscientious conservation of energy—which we all recognize as necessary—will be hard pressed to make up for this loss.

We urge Federal Executive action to restrict exports to no more than 50% of existing levels.

Such action will help dwindling coal piles, reduce demand for Middle East oil, ease the coal-car shortage, further the goal of Project Independence . . . and help whip inflation now.

It will even improve America's balance of payments—for, the more lower-priced coal we have available to burn the less higher-priced oil we will have to import.

The Middle East restricts the export of oil, Canada restricts natural gas, and Australia restricts uranium.

It's time we controlled the export of resources for which America, itself, has a critical need.

America has more coal than the Middle East has oil. Let's dig it!

American Electric Power System

Appalachian Power Co., Indiana & Michigan Electric Co., Kentucky Power Co., Kingsport Power Co., Michigan Power Co., Ohio Power Co., Wheeling Electric Co.

Exhibit 4A–36

178

5

The Selling of an Idea—In the Public Interest
The California Campaign to Enact Proposition 9,
The Clean Environment Act of 1972

> *"The rule is, jam tomorrow, and jam yesterday—*
> *but never jam today."*
> *"It must come sometime to 'jam today,"* Alice objected.
> *"No, it can't," said the queen. "It's jam every other*
> *day, you know."*
>
> *—Lewis Carrol, Through the*
> *Looking Glass and What Alice Found There*

On June 6, 1972, the California voters rejected Proposition 9, The Clean Environment Act of 1972, by a margin of almost 2 to 1. The proposition had received widespread local and national publicity and was projected as a fight between David and Goliath, between big business and little people, between vested interests backed by powerful political and financial resources and citizen groups spontaneously created to fight for a cause they believed in against heavy odds. It was an excellent example of the interplay between various interest groups—business, the social activists, the conservationists—all clamoring to protect the public interest. It was the first major test of the strength and political savvy of a non-profit, politically activist group called People's Lobby, the prime mover behind the initiative.

Apart from the interests of the various parties involved and the legitimacy of their cause, the case provides an excellent study in the art of public persuasion in a pluralistic society and in the process of public policy formulation by the citizenry at-large when publicly elected officials have been unable or unwilling to enact programs and legislation in a given direction. The fascination of the case and its major importance as an analytical tool lies in the fact that it is an attempt to sell an idea or a promise. In this sense, it falls into a distinctly separate category from those of selling products and services, and political campaigns. In the case of products and services, the seller offers a tangible product and fulfilment of certain needs and desires the buyer wants satisfied. The advertisement or communication message has an aura of authenticity and

---

Unless otherwise specifically stated, all direct quotations attributed to various spokespeople are from personal interviews and written communications with the author.

179

relevance around it to which the receiver of the message can relate. Thus without in any way underrating the complexity of product advertising, one could say that the tangible nature of the product or service provides a link between the seller and the buyer, thereby making the job of communication simpler and more straightforward.

The political campaign offers a higher level of complexity in that it is selling a promise of performance in the future. However, even here the public can relate to the candidate—a tangible thing—and if he or she has previously run for a public office, evaluate promises and appeals in terms of past performance.[1] The selling of a mere idea is a still higher level of abstraction and presents a more difficult and complex problem in persuasion. It has the following general characteristics:

1. In most cases, the recipient of the message is only vaguely aware of a need for what the communicator of the idea is selling and is not sure whether he wants it, to what extent, in what form, and at what cost.
2. The promise of delivery is almost always in the future. The nature of rewards are generally esthetic or intangible in nature, e.g., clean air, better quality of life, preservation of life.
3. The rewards are also likely to be in the nature of public goods and lie in the public domain. Thus the communicatee may not enjoy any special privileges as a result of his buying (voting for) this service. He has only the commonly shared rights with the rest of the community. Nor is he deprived of the enjoyment of public goods thus created if he declines to vote for community purchase of such services.
4. Although the promised benefits lie in the uncertain future, the costs in terms of taxes, high prices, and restrictions on personal consumption and life styles may be immediate and real. Furthermore, although the benefits may be shared equally by all members of a community, the costs may fall disproportionately on various buyers depending on income, home ownership, or some other similar criterion.
5. The promisers of rewards are generally unknown groups with no prior track record who purport to act in the public interest, including the interest of the communicatee. The potential buyer has little information or resources to evaluate the credibility or credentials of these groups.
6. The groups that oppose the sale of these ideas also present themselves as acting in the interest of the communicatee. In this case, however, the groups are all too real, with apparent vested interest in seeing that the idea does not succeed. Thus, although their credibility may be suspect, the projected costs to the communicatee, if he buys the idea, appear more realistic and therefore frightening.

The Initiative

The initiative is a device that empowers the people of California to directly initiate laws. This right was obtained through a special election held on October 10, 1911, which amended Article IV, Sections 22-25 of the California constitution. It is identical to laws enacted by the legislature, with one exception: "An initiative statute may not be amended, except by another initiative statute or by a statute passed by the legislature and approved by the people, unless the original initiative statute provides to the contrary."[2]

In November 1970, an initiative petition sponsored by the People's Lobby was filed with the California attorney general and the secretary of state, its title being "The Clean Environment Act." In May 1971, the secretary of state certified that the clean environment initiative would appear on the June 6, 1972, election ballot; People's Lobby had obtained the required number of signatures. The official ballot summary read as follows:

Primary Election, June 6, 1972. Proposition 9. Environment. Initiative. Specifies permissible composition and quality of gasoline and other fuels for internal combustion engines. Authorizes shutting down of businesses and factories violating air pollution standards. Imposes restrictions on leasing and extraction of oil and gas from tidelands or submerged lands, or onshore areas within one mile of mean high tide line. Prohibits construction of atomic powered electric generating plants for five years. Establishes restrictions on manufacture, sale, and use of pesticides. Prohibits enforcement officials from having conflicting interests. Provides for relief by injunction and mandate to prevent violations. Imposes penal action and civil penalties.[3]

Proposition 9, the environment initiative, nee the Clean Environment Act of 1972, contained twenty-three sections aimed at rewriting a good portion of the California pollution control laws. The affected issue areas were these:

1. Air pollution—stationary and vehicular sources (sections 3, 4, 5, 6, 8, and sections 2 and 11)
2. Energy development—oil drilling and nuclear facility construction (sections 12, 13, 16, and 17)
3. Pesticides—chlorinated hydrocarbons (section 18)
4. Government procedure—public information access, conflict of interest, class actions, repeal, and amendment (sections 7, 9, 10, 14, 15, 19, 20, 21, 22, and 23)

The Proponents

The chief architects of Proposition 9 were the husband and wife team of the late Edwin Koupal and Joyce Koupal, and the nonprofit organization they launched in 1969 and called People's Lobby, Inc. In 1967 and 1968, the Koupals had attempted to recall Governor Ronald Reagan, who Mrs. Koupal refers to as "a fascist who should be recalled; he was hurting people." When this attempt failed, they decided to try to do something about the smog that shrouded Los Angeles. They moved from Sacramento to Los Angeles and formed the People's Lobby.

People's Lobby, Inc.

A nonprofit organization, People's Lobby operates from a headquarters near Los Angeles. People's Lobby owns the headquarters. The Koupals have no financial interest in any of the equipment, buildings, etc. They live in the building and provide security and volunteer staff time for the rent. It functions with a staff that varies in size but according to Joyce Koupal averages around 50 members. Most of the staff members, however, are volunteers and only four employees are salaried. The size of the organization in terms of the number of members, is not easily discernible. Assemblyman Brown asserts "they have almost no members" and Leo McCarthy, also an assemblyman from San Francisco, claims People's Lobby is "a paper membership, the whole thing is run by four or five people."[4] Mrs. Koupal, however, explains that the claimed membership of 20,000 stems from the fact that 20,000 people have donated money to the Lobby. That was during the CEA campaign and anyone who had donated money was considered a member. The mailing list was prepared from the financial statements filed with the secretary of state.

The organization itself, according to Joyce Koupal, is different from other similar organizations:

We are not structured bureaucratically. The people who are in the Lobby are people who are adverse to that kind of structure and yet they want to have a piece of the action or be involved in the decision making. In the beginning the People's Lobby was really a dictatorship run by Ed and me. After the Clean Environment Campaign, we started the Steering Board and got them involved in the decision-making roles. We found out that in an initiative group like we are, you have a democracy in the off years while you are deciding policy and initiatives, but during an initiative campaign you have a benign dictatorship, all controlled by one person. And it just has to be done that way. It is kind of a dual-type organization.

Ed Koupal believed that legislators had been staying about three issues behind people and there was no way to make them catch up or get ahead because three issues behind was a safe place to be. The initiative process grabs the leadership role and forces the issue so legally in front of them that they cannot escape it. It automatically makes government responsive to the people. By running initiatives and educating people concerning its side of the controversy, People's Lobby claims to provide voters with opposing information concerning an issue.

In Joyce Koupal's opinion, "if people have all the facts and they want to vote something in, that's fine. . . . People get a one-sided view of the facts. They are stampeded into making decisions which are probably not in their best interest and they don't even know it. And so what we have been trying to do is equalize what is happening."

Launching the Initiative

The Koupals, with the aid of volunteer attorney Roger Jon Diamond and other interested persons, drafted the Clean Environment Act, as it was called by its proponents. It was originally named the "Pollution Initiative" by the California attorney general. Its proponents argued this name in court, and on March 31, 1972, Judge Lawrence J. Rittenband ruled in their favor. The initiative was referred to as the "Environment Initiative" on the official ballot.[5]

To qualify the initiative for the ballot, 325,000 valid signatures were required. The People's Lobby volunteers were able to obtain 339,000 signatures—220,000 in Los Angeles County and 180,000 in the twenty-seven other counties. To obtain a signature, a volunteer would ask, "Are you a registered voter?" If the answer was affirmative, he or she would be asked to "sign against smog." According to Mr. Koupal, "Fewer than 5 percent would refuse to sign. After all, people pretty well knew that they can't breathe the air or drink the water. The response rate rose to 99 percent when those who refused at first read what was at the top of the petition form or talked to us about it."[6] The next step was to translate the voter's address into a precinct number, a cumbersome and time-consuming task, so that it could be checked by a county registrar.

By May of 1971 the proponents of the initiative had secured the required number of signatures and had qualified the initiative for the June 6, 1972, primary election ballot. Collecting them had cost the People's Lobby only $8,000 because it was done with volunteers. Had they used a professional firm, People's Lobby believed, it would have cost between 25¢ and 50¢ per signature, or between $81,250 and $162,500.

Financing the Campaign

People's Lobby did not have any major contributors and therefore resorted to innovative ways of generating small donations whose cost of collection was minimal. One of these was by using bicycle riders in a campaign called "Bike for Life." Using its then only paid employee, People's Lobby went throughout the state getting people—usually school children—to ride a bicycle over a 30- to 40-mile route. The riders would obtain their own sponsors.[7] The program raised $174,032 in the 1972 fiscal year. The entire initiative campaign was largely supported through small individual contributions, with the exception of two large contributions of $1,000 each from actor Paul Newman and Congressman Fortney H. Stark (D, California). A significant amount of support also came through membership dues—$10 for adults and $2 for students. The total resources available to run the campaign eventually amounted to $233,421.05, of which $82,348, or 35 percent, was donated in amounts of $25 or less. In contrast, the opponents of the initiative received a total of $586 in contributions of less than $25. The campaign expenditures of the People's Lobby in supporting Proposition 9 amounted to approximately 12.56 percent of the $1,483,971 spent by the opposition (see the section on the opponents). Although the difference in spending is quite substantial, it does not convey the whole story. People's Lobby was able to get the necessary signatures for the initiative petition by using volunteers, thereby saving between $73,000 and $146,000. Similarly, in the conduct of actual campaign, People's Lobby used ingenious methods to garner as much free publicity as possible and thereby reduce the need for cash. Thus, the tremendous difference in campaign expenditures by the two sides notwithstanding, People's Lobby's campaign activities were greater than their expenditures would indicate.

The Campaign Strategy

People's Lobby's campaign strategy had three main components:

1. Secure the support of influential opinion leaders, especially among such established conservation and environmental groups as the Sierra Club; of congressmen and legislators; of the League of Women Voters; and of activist groups and students.

2. Develop an effective means of refuting the charges of the opposition— Californians Against the Pollution Initiative (CAPI), large corporations and industry groups, and individual opinion leaders who advocated the defeat of Proposition 9.

3. Create public awareness and understanding of the position of People's Lobby and generate support for Proposition 9 through mass media campaigns.

Community Support

People's Lobby realized from the start that it must have broad-based community support in order to succeed. To achieve this end, the initiative was drafted in terms that would encompass the concerns of all environmental and conservation groups. This also opened the initiative to the charge of being vague and of requiring much legislation. The People's Lobby answer:

The initiative was written in sweeping terms to cover all situations. The draftsmen of the initiative could have anticipated problem areas and accordingly drafted a more conservative document. However, it was felt that it would be better to err on the side of strong environmental protection measures than on the side of weakness. That is, it was felt that it would be better to exceed the constitutional limit in certain areas. If a court were so to rule, the initiative in effect would be cut down and returned to constitutional limitation. If the initiative were drafted too conservatively, there would have been a gap between what it accomplished and what it could have constitutionally accomplished.

In a recent interview, Mrs. Koupal reasserted this position, stating that "the Clean Environment Act was drafted precisely like it was for a reason. We over-drafted because we didn't want to give up one inch."

People's Lobby was able to put together a group of attorneys, business-people, associated student unions, educators, environmental organizations and individuals, labor organizations, physicians, and politicians. On the list of politicians were two U.S. congressmen (Ronald Dellums and Jerome Waldie), one U.S. senator (Mike Gravel of Alaska), and two state senators (David Roberti of California and Nicholas Coleman of Minnesota). The supporting labor organizations were teachers unions or individual union members, rather than the union itself.

Unfortunately, this was not enough when compared with the support generated by the opponents of the Proposition 9. Inadequate support was particularly critical in the case of People's Lobby because of its lack of financial resources and the need for volunteers. Among the environmental organizations, the Sierra Club chose to remain neutral and did not support Proposition 9. The loss of Sierra Club support was a serious disadvantage to the People's Lobby because of the former's credentials as a reputable and well-established group concerned with environmental issues at the local and national levels.

Another major element in the drive for community support was door-to-door canvassing with volunteers and holding small group discussions and seminars. This was in sharp contrast to the Whitaker & Baxter approach, which aimed at "hammering home its message ('Too many Bugs in Proposition 9') in a deluge of media-oriented messages."

The proponents of the initiative made use of their supporters whenever they could. For example, the "Voter's Argument for the Clean Environment Act," as it appeared in the official argument on the ballot, was signed by William M. Bennett, member of the California State Board of Equalization and attorney; Congressman Fortney H. Stark; and Hifinio Romo, United Rubber Workers Union 131, AFL-CIO. Inside the cover of this reprint of both official arguments and rebuttals was a copy of the letter from the United Rubber, Cork, Linoleum, and Plastic Workers of America, signed by Mr. Romo, the union treasurer. The letter calls the Clean Environment Act "the greatest public service yet."[8]

Strategy for Counteracting the Opposition's Charges

People's Lobby felt that one of the ways to undermine the credibility of the opponents and also bring to public attention "the inaccuracies and falsehoods on which their campaign was based" was to expose the underlying motives of those who sought to defeat Proposition 9. People's Lobby was relentless on this point because it felt that the opposition was dominated by big business and big money and was using its resources to undermine the efforts of People's Lobby and sell the public short. When asked whether these tactics did not amount to a smear campaign and a strategy of coercion, the late Mr. Koupal replied:

I will use any of the political tools available to me as long as I don't break the law. Too many times we find the people who call themselves environmentalists, civil rightists, etc., idealistically say "we are not going to do the same thing our opposition does." "Even if we lose, we know we lose with the highest morals." Well, I don't agree with that at all. It is your idea and your law, and if you feel honest enough to have written it in the first place to bring it to the voters, then you should use all tools available to you that the political machine of the day will afford you.

It is part of becoming grown up in politics. It is a part of being honest with yourself in politics. It is part of being a professional.

The sympathizers of People's Lobby assisted them by anonymously providing evidence that was embarrassing and potentially incriminating to the opposition. One of the more important pieces of this type, and the one People's Lobby tried to publicize the most, was the Miller Memorandum (Exhibit 5-1). This memorandum, dated June 4, 1971, was addressed to Mr. Otto N. Miller, chairman of the board, Standard Oil of California, San Francisco (SOCAL) by his lobbyist, Mr. James L. Wanvig.[9] In this memo, Mr. Wanvig recommends that SOCAL urgently take steps to launch a counterattack against "the so-called Clean Environment Initiative." It suggested among other things the setting up a "front" organization "to organize and manage the campaign . . . that organization should be a citizens committee instead of a chamber of commerce of California Manufacturer's Association effort, both of which are 'too identified in the public mind with business interests'"; and cautioned against asking Governor Reagan to spearhead the campaign because "Governor Reagan would be no great asset with respect to 18, 19, and 20 year olds who may be voting by June 1972."

The memo enclosed copy of a "Preliminary Plan Against the People's Lobby Initiative" (see the section on the opponents), prepared by Whitaker & Baxter, a San Francisco-based public relations firm, and recommended that this firm be retained to organize and conduct the campaign against Proposition 9. The original memo, a copy of which was reproduced by the People's Lobby, contains handwritten notes by Mr. Miller indicating his complete agreement with all the points made by Mr. Wanvig.

It is debatable whether the disclosure of this memorandum and other related documents helped the cause of the pollution initiative. In one of its publications, People's Lobby lamented:

In 1972 People's Lobby reprinted hundreds of thousands of these copies [Miller

Exhibit 5-1. Memorandum.

June 4, 1971

People's Lobby Initiative

Mr. O.N. Miller
18th Floor
Building

As you requested, this memorandum outlines the most urgent questions that must be faced in connection with the so-called "clean environment" initiative, which the People's Lobby has qualified for the primary election in June, 1972. A copy of CMA's summary of the proposal is attached.

Selection of "Front" Organization

From discussions with people who are more or less my counterparts in other oil, gas and electric companies, I have learned that some companies are proposing that the California Chamber of Commerce should be the "front" to organize and manage the campaign against this measure. There are also some indications that the staff of the California Manufacturers Association might like to be the focal point of the campaign.

While the support of both of these organizations will be valuable, the choice of either to front the campaign would, in my judgment, be a serious mistake. Both are much too identified in the public mind with business interests, and either would evoke a certain amount of unnecessary negative public reaction.

I believe it would be far better to organize a citizens committee with a very broad base, including well-known conservationists, Democrats, labor leaders, and minority group leaders. I am confident that this can be done if skillful campaign managers are employed to do it.

The Role of Governor Reagan

I have also learned that there is a fair amount of sentiment within the business community to ask Governor Reagan to spearhead the organization of a campaign effort against the measure. I think that too would be a mistake. The people behind this measure are the same ones who circulated petitions to recall Governor Reagan some time back, and they would delight in having him as a target. I think too, that Governor Reagan would be no great asset with respect to the 18, 19 and 20 year-olds who may be voting by June, 1972. Certainly, the Governor's support along with that of responsible Democrats, should be sought in due course, but I do not think he should be asked to take the lead.

Selection of Campaign Managers

Both Spencer, Roberts and Whitaker & Baxter have let it be known that they would like to be chosen to manage the campaign against this measure. As I have told you before, I think these are the two best campaign organizations in California, and I strongly urge that one or both of them be retained. I believe this step not only is important in winning the campaign, but also in avoiding the extraneous difficulties that often result when less experienced people manage a campaign.

As between these two firms, my recommendation for this particular job would be Whitaker & Baxter. I think the record is clear that Whitaker & Baxter has more experience and more success in running campaigns on measures than has Spencer, Roberts. I believe Whitaker & Baxter also has broader and better contacts with Democrats, labor leaders, agriculture, conservationists, and other elements of the community who have perhaps as great, if less direct, a stake in this measure as the energy companies. Spencer, Roberts is almost entirely Republican oriented and has specialized in elections of candidates rather than ballot issues.

Exhibit 5-1. continued

Urgency

While I think it is important that the citizens most directly concerned choose a campaign manager who can start organizing a citizens committee at an early date, I believe it is even more urgent to head-off the efforts I mentioned above to put the Chamber of Commerce and the Governor into positions of leadership in organizing the campaign. If you agree, you might wish to make your views known to Mr. Burnham Enersen and others before leaving the city for any extended period.

James L. Wanvig [initialed]

Enc.
cc Messrs. James E. O'Brien
George T. Ballou

Memorandum and Whitaker & Baxter Plan] throughout the campaign. In spite of the fact that people had the actual facts about these activities in their hands, from the people who intended to carry them out, they [Whitaker & Baxter] conducted this campaign exactly as outlined and beat us by more than 2 to 1 vote.[10]

In another case, People's Lobby obtained copies of letters written by executives of Gulf Energy and Environmental Systems to employees and supervisors of the corporation. The letters pointed out the sections of the initiative that directly affected Gulf operations and urged a no vote. One letter spelled out the following requirement:

Any employee who is invited or who volunteers to make a speech, prepare an abstract, or present a paper before any group or organization; prepare an article for any publication; or be interviewed by any publication editor or reporter must obtain in advance of any commitment the approval of the appropriate division vice president, division director, or other officer to whom he is accountable.[11]

People's Lobby also obtained a copy of a letter dated July 15, 1971, by R. Frederick Fischer, co-chairman, Sierra Club Legal Committee, to Mrs. Kent Dedrick of Palo Alto, in which Mr. Fischer found fault with most of the provisions of the Clean Environment Act Initiative as rigid, unrealistic, and in many cases hard to enforce and implement, and indicated that he "would strongly oppose this measure as a Sierra Club legislative proposal. Whether the Club may wish to enlist itself as an endorser of the legislation for reasons of its own is, of course, a decision for the Club to make."[12]

Roger Diamond, the public interest attorney who had the prime responsibility for drafting the initiative, responded to Mr. Fischer's letter. Although he painstakingly refuted individual charges made by Mr. Fischer, the tenor of his comments was quite sarcastic, a fact conceded by Mr. Diamond in his letter.[13] How the People's Lobby secured a copy of the letter less than thirty days after it was written is not known. Mr. Diamond's letter also attacked Mr. Fischer's competence. After reading Mr. Diamond's letter, it is difficult to imagine that the Sierra Club would endorse the measure. Perhaps People's Lobby had already written off the possibility of any support from the Sierra Club.

People's Lobby also publicly attacked prominent members of the Californians Against the Pollution Initiative (CAPI) for selling out to big money. The following exchange between the author and Mr. and Mrs. Koupal explains their rationale for such tactics:

Sethi: It seems to me that by attacking the integrity of various prominent citizens and also exaggerating the environmental dangers if the initiative is not enacted into the law, you were using the same smear and scare tactics you accused the opposition of.

Edwin Koupal: I do not like the words "smear tactics." Whitaker & Baxter filled their citizens committee with people who had some ax to grind or something they had to protect. They put up Dr. Emil Mrak [chancellor emeritus, University of California, Davis] as a great white father. They have the power to give money and grants to professors who then go out and bastardize the grant system and their Ph.D.'s. Another element is the financial involvement of these people in the industry itself. How can a professor like Emil Mrak stand up in front of the students and teach them about pesticides when he has a financial interest in the selling of pesticides and it makes him a fortune? These types of people in our society have to be eliminated from positions of power.

When you take Tom Lantos [another CAPI supporter], who has actually taken state funds, and expose him to the public, that is not a smear campaign, that is truth and fact and something that should be made public knowledge.

Joyce Koupal: We did not use scare tactics in our advertising either. It was CAPI that ran ads saying since we are trying to get rid of the DDT that kills mosquitoes, we must therefore love mosquitoes, that we are a religious cult that worships the mosquito and I am the head religious leader.

We tried to give quality information. Whitaker & Baxter want to work in gray areas so as to propagandize the public and stampede them into an emotional state. A confused voter will vote either "no" or not at all in such a situation—thus the result is status quo.

Whitaker & Baxter's strategies for running national campaigns have not changed over the years. They emphasize the development of opinion leaders, finding them, keeping in touch with them and convincing them with one-to-one communication and burying them in tons of material.

They have also developed a free news service to the small independent newspapers that are fed liberally in off years so that there will be certain "editorial support" for W & B managed activities during the election years.

The buying of every kind of news media and "types of personalities" that we all have—is hit from every angle, i.e., you may be a husband, a father, a hunter, a businessman, etc. Ads are bought and articles run favoring W & B's perspective in every special-interest newspaper, magazine, and newsletter. You get hit with the short, hard message everywhere you look, and from every aspect of your personality. Over and over—you are buried in the message—and it works.

The Media Campaign

The media campaign of People's Lobby for the Clean Environment Act initiative suffered from lack of funds. However, when one considers the factor of unpredictability of receipts to the anemic size of funds, any planning for an organized campaign becomes all but impossible. Of the total campaign expenditures of $186,511 for Proposition 9, People's Lobby spent 25 percent on radio air time and recording expenditures, 13 percent on magazines and newspapers, 15 percent on printing and other media, and less than 3 percent on television and videotape. The remaining funds were allocated to postage and shipping (4.5 percent) and miscellaneous expenditures (39.5 percent).

In the beginning, People's Lobby was quite successful in generating news stories about its campaign as it put out a stream of press releases setting forth its viewpoint and challenging the veracity of the claims made by CAPI. The exposure did not, however, last very long. According to Joyce Koupal, "The newspapers ran pretty good articles very early in the campaign when nobody was watching. Then the editors and the owners came down on their reporters heads and there was no way we could even get a news story."

Another method to counteract the opposition's media barrage was to write the editors and publishers of newspapers and magazines and the managers of TV and radio stations in California pointing out to them the alleged inaccuracies in the press kits sent to them by Whitaker & Baxter and urging them to seek corrections and clarifications from People's Lobby. In another letter, People's Lobby asked the newspapers and TV and radio stations to provide substantiation and proof of accuracy of the statements contained in CAPI's commercials.

Lack of financing did not affect the professional quality of the ad message or the production of commercials. People's Lobby was able to attract professional people who donated their time and resources to produce first-rate magazine and newspaper advertisements and radio and television commercials.

The largest part of the media campaign was devoted to airing 60-second and 30-second radio commercials concentrated between May 23 and June 5, 1972, i.e., the last two weeks of the campaign period. In all, a total of 2,567 spots were used with about 50 percent going to the Los Angeles area and the remaining distributed in the rest of California. In addition, newspaper ads of varying sizes were used at the rate of one insertion per newspaper in 20 local and regional newspapers and magazines. A considerable amount of People's Lobby resources was devoted to a direct mail campaign in an effort to reach potential contributors and voters. TV advertising was almost nonexistent: three commercials were produced and occasionally aired. According to Bernice F. Livingston of Diener/ Hauser/Greenthal, a Los Angeles-based advertising agency, "We developed a careful plan to buy time in order to achieve maximum audience reach and frequency. However, unpredictability of finances made the plan implementation quite difficult. Despite these handicaps, we were able to reach most of our targeted audience by concentrating on the densely populated areas and also putting most of our resources in radio during the final weeks of the campaign."

Exhibit 5A-1 gives the text of nine specimen radio commercials used by People's Lobby.[a] The commercials contain multimessages generally of the negative type, namely, warning of health hazards, big business manipulation of government and people, and what pollution can do to the quality of life for present and future generations if the measures proposed in Proposition 9 are not enacted. There is one case of a positive appeal in which the passage of Proposition 9 is associated with more jobs and improved economy.

The newspaper and magazine ads are reproduced in Exhibits 5A-2 to 5A-6. Three of the five advertisements have long messages. One presents pro and con arguments for Proposition 9; it is a good example of an attempt to present a balanced argument (Exhibit 5A-3). Another presents arguments in favor of the initiative (Exhibit 5A-5), while a third (Exhibit 5A-4) provides a long list of people who have endorsed Proposition 9. Against this list, the ad carries a big headline and four categories of people who are against the proposition. The names mentioned are oil companies, power companies, big industrial polluters, and the chemical industry. The nonendorsers occupy less than 5 percent of the ad space. The remaining two ads (Exhibits 5A-2 and 5A-6) are primarily of the reminder type, urging people to vote for the Clean Environment Act initiative. Television commercials are presented in Exhibits 5A-7 to 5A-9. Exhibit 5A-7 is a 5-minute commercial that discusses substantive issues involved in Proposition 9. Exhibit 5A-8 is a 60-second spot discussing refinery-related air pollution and how Proposition 9 would prevent it. Exhibit 5A-9 is a 30-second spot and through cartoon format associates clean air with the passage of Proposition 9.

It was earlier noted that People's Lobby mailed hundreds of thousands of copies of the Miller Memorandum. In addition, the Lobby published an economic analysis of the effect of the passage of Clean Environment Act initiative and distributed it among concerned citizens. Entitled "Economics of a Clean Environment,"[14] the document detailed the losses to property, agriculture, and human health due to pollution; the costs of cleaning the environment through controlling emissions; the savings made in agriculture, fuel, motor vehicle operations, and better health with a cleaner environment; and additional jobs that would be created through increased activity in pollution control areas.

The Opposition

The formation of the opposition group came about primarily as a consequence of Whitaker & Baxter's apprising various corporations and industry groups about

---

[a]The People's Lobby media campaign exhibits (5A-1 through 5A-9) all appear in Appendix 5A.

the potential dangers to the industry and the economy of California if Proposition 9 were enacted. An example of the corporate initiative and activity in the formation of the opposition can be found in a memo dated June 4, 1971, by James L. Wanvig, the lobbyist for Standard Oil, and addressed to Otto Miller, then president of Standard Oil of California. The memo, which was developed at Mr. Miller's request, outlined a series of steps to be followed to defeat the "People's Lobby Initiative" (Exhibit 5-1). Included in this memorandum was a "Preliminary Plan of Campaign Against the People's Lobby Initiative Submitted by Whitaker & Baxter," dated June 1, 1971 (Exhibit 5-2).

Whitaker & Baxter

Whitaker & Baxter, long established in San Francisco, is a public relations and campaign management firm that provides services for groups and candidates both in California and throughout the nation. The firm has managed election campaigns of Republicans and Democrats and conducted public referendum campaigns on issues ranging from increased salaries for California teachers to the Clean Environment Act. Comparing his profession with that of an attorney, Whitaker explained that an attorney could be an advocate for anyone, and properly so, because he was not dealing with philosophy. A firm like Whitaker & Baxter could not do so because it had to have a philosophy.

In addition to conducting an actual issue or election campaign, Whitaker & Baxter serves as a type of monitoring agency for its clients: "We alert our clients to any issue that we think may be of consequence to them. We have monitored for all types of clients and maybe one in one hundred times something will come of an issue we notice, but at least our clients are aware of the issues that are developing and won't be surprised in mid-stream." Furthermore, Whitaker & Baxter pays detailed attention to the specifics of any campaign they manage. "We do our own writing, all our own production for all media types, our own news writing. We oversee our own organization department, our own press department, our own mail department. This is a little unusual. Most firms don't do this, but we feel that if we do it here, we are doing it as we want it done. We feel that we are more competent as a result of our experience in getting this done right," Whitaker explained. Consequently, the firm usually limits itself to two or three undertakings at any one time.

The actual operation of a campaign involves an extensive publicity effort aimed at reaching every segment of the public. While mass media advertising is an important part of any campaign, Whitaker & Baxter also relies on a personal contact to reach its intended audience.

We run a total publicity campaign to overly simplify it. We do not deal with paid media alone but try to take our issue to the public through every existing

Exhibit 5-2. Preliminary Plan of Campaign
Against the People's Lobby Initiative
Submitted by Whitaker & Baxter, June 1, 1971

The People's Lobby initiative constitutes one of the gravest threats to the well being of the people of California yet devised.

The measure synthesizes into legislative form one of the most acute issues of this era— the balancing of the environment in which we live with the fuel, food, fibre and energy essential to life itself.

The People's Lobby initiative proposes to resolve the issue by:

1. severely restricting the fuels and sources of energy available to the people in their homes and businesses; and

2. eliminating and limiting the chemicals which can be introduced into the ecocycle in the production of food and fibre.

This truly is an issue the people must decide and it must truly be a people's campaign to determine how much people are willing to endure in loss of jobs, higher prices, and less of the niceties of life to enhance the environment.

Obviously, there must be a balance between need and nicety—between a pastoral society and industrial-service society.

The question the people of California must decide at the June 6, 1972 ballot—or at any statewide special election called in the interim—is whether the People's Lobby initiative provides that balance.

The measure does not provide the balance if viewed rationally and, in our opinion, will not be accepted by the electorate if the issues are properly and effectively posed.

The considerable danger is that the measure will not be dealt with effectively but will be cast in the light its promoters intend as a great environmental test between the people and the business and industrial "despoilers" of our land, a crusade which could be joined with near religious fervor and which would have but one outcome.

In short, the campaign against the People's Lobby initiative must not be spearheaded *publicly* by business and industry. *It should be publicly launched by responsible conservationists, by academicians, labor spokesmen, leaders of the Democratic Party* and joined at the appropriate time in the appropriate fashion by business, industry, agriculture, and the Republican Party leadership.

This strategy insures greater credibility to the thesis the People's Lobby initiative is so extreme, so destructive of people's lives, that responsible environmentalists are embarrassed by it and urge its defeat.

Time is of the essence if the strategy is to be employed successfully.

A public citizens committee must be formed and announced quickly under the leadership of men known to be Democratic-conservationists, highly respected scientists and academicians, and key labor leaders of the state to create the people against the People's Lobby posture essential to this campaign.

Then membership should be quickly built throughout all spectrums of society—through the hundreds of responsible and powerful statewide organizations of every type.

The committee should take its detailed, thoughtful, well prepared case to the media— broadcast and print. It should seek out every forum, every potential ally, every potential resource, to be brought to bear in reaching the public generally.

A public committee of this type, a campaign based on the strategy proposed, can be most effective only if the utilities and the oil industry—the businesses most directly affected by the initiative—take direct control of the direction of the campaign, rather than have a dozen or more well-meaning groups take the lead and in the doing create a big business versus people's issue which can only be self-defeating.

The involvement of the principal oil companies and the principal utilities—and the other affected businesses and industries which should be added to the support base—*is not a public involvement.* Rather, in a non-publicized sense, it is a means of directing the campaign under the aegis of a *public* citizens committee as outlined. In the doing, total control of the public campaign strategy and direction is maintained.

Exhibit 5-2 continued

In the weeks immediately ahead, while the citizens committee is being formed there are several critical research projects which should be launched:

1. The initiative itself must be analyzed fully by each company affected so that the limitations it would impose are susceptible to lay interpretation. What plants would be affected? What fuels would be restricted or eliminated? What would happen to cost of operation? What truly happens to the availability of energy for domestic, industrial and business use? What about steel plants? Borax plants? Etc., and infinitum?

2. What existing federal and state regulations are presently in play and what conflicts are posed between existing federal and state law and regulation with the strictures of the People's Lobby initiative?

3. Intensive opinion research must be undertaken to test public attitudes on all relevant matters and to test the public validity of arguments to be set forth in the course of the campaign.

This data must of necessity be funneled to a central point for effective usage and working with assigned industry personnel, the campaign managers—whose responsibility it will be to translate the myriad data to clearly understandable public terms—should provide that service.

The campaign managers also should contract for the required analysis of existing federal and state regulation and law as it applies to the initiative. They also should devise and be responsible for the intensive public opinion research and testing.

In a framework of time the campaign should be viewed as follows:

1. Announcement of the public citizens committee by the week of June 21, 1971. The committee will be expanded obviously right up to election day.

2. An immediate start on industry research, to be completed preliminarily within 30 days.

3. An immediate start on matching federal and state regulation to the initiative to be completed within 30 days.

4. Structure of the public opinion survey to test voter attitudes and campaign arguments for placement into the field within 30–45 days, conclusion to be within 60 days of placement in the field.

5. Compilation of an initial fact sheet for early use with media and state and local organizations. All media and all principal organizations should be contacted both by mail and in person with emphasis on securing the endorsement of every possible endorsing entity by March 1, 1972.

Assuming a special statewide election is not called prior to June, 1972—in which event timing and effort would have to be revised drastically—the goal of the campaign between the present and March 1, 1972 should be to try to win the campaign, insofar as that is possible, before advertising media must be committed.

The reason for this, of course, is that the greater the degree of success prior to the use of paid media, the greater the prospect for conducting the campaign at a cost far below the sums required for intensive 90-day, all-out media-supported campaigns.

In summary, so long as qualification of the People's Lobby initiative is an unfortunate fact—its existence should be viewed as an opportunity.

The opportunity is to join one of the most important issues confronting the country in an affirmative, not defensive, stance.

Stated in simplest terms, there is an opportunity here to secure a public expression of support for the desire of people to have the light go on when they throw the switch or to buy an apple free of worms—all in keeping with the acknowledged desire for the cleanest environment possible consistent with life on earth.

That expression of support at the polls, an expression directly achievable in legislative bodies at any level, should provide a true measure of what people want in life. It is a catalyst around which responsible alternatives can be sought and achieved in legislative halls on the many similar issues existent and on which decisions must be reached.

Based on the above, we recommend:

1. Creation of a small steering committee which would not become public composed of the delegated spokesmen for the principal utilities and oil companies.

Exhibit 5-2 continued

2. Approval of campaign underwriting by this committee.
3. Creation of a broadened, non-public finance committee to raise the requisite campaign budget.
4. Retention of campaign management which will bring forth the effort subject to steering committee approval.
5. Approval of a preliminary campaign budget to finance all phases of the campaign until March 1, 1972, in an estimated amount of $600,000.
6. Submission of and approval of a paid media budget for the period of time from March 1, 1972 to June 6, 1972 to be submitted by January 1, 1972 at which time the effectiveness of the preliminary campaign can be judged and an intelligent media budget devised to fit existing circumstances.

forum. That might be a panel show, a talk show, a rotary club meeting, wherever we can go. If we have something of sufficient consequence we call a press conference. If we have people who are sufficiently newsworthy, we move them around the state for a number of press conferences. This is a whole other campaign within a campaign that runs continuously from beginning to end. We seek out every existing forum and try to get on that forum with someone who is competent, newsworthy, and interesting. If we get there, we make news. If we are good, we make effective news. In a local campaign this personal contact frequently is carried to the extreme of block by block campaigning where theoretically we cover every house in every neighborhood in a series of face-to-face encounters.

Planning and Organizing the Campaign

Whitaker & Baxter based its plan on the premise that business and industry must not publicly lead the campaign. It saw "considerable danger" in letting the campaign become a "test between the people and the business and industrial 'despoilers' of our land" as "its promoters intend." The proposed strategy was to be as follows:

1. Organize a citizens' committee led by Democratic conservationists, scientists, academicians, and labor leaders
2. Through a steering committee, maintain "nonpublic" direct control of the campaign by the "affected businessess and industries," particularly the utilities and principal oil companies
3. Use the steering committee to raise the required campaign budget
4. Generate the research and data necessary to launch an effective campaign

The plan was accepted. The opposition group was called Californians Against the Pollution Initiative (CAPI). Its address was 870 Market Street, San Francisco—which is also the address of Whitaker & Baxter. There were four co-chairmen of CAPI: Dr. Emil M. Mrak, chancellor emeritus, University of California, Davis; Joseph J. Diviny, first vice-president, International Brotherhood of Teamsters; Dr. J.E. McKee, professor of environmental engineering; former member of the Advisory Committee on Reactor Safeguards, Atomic Energy Commission; and Myron W. Doornbos, president, Southern Council of Conservation Clubs.

These were the men who were to be visible to the public. They were chosen to lend credibility to the opposition argument and because they could bring supporters into the fold. For example, Dr. Mrak had headed the Mrak Commission, which had reported on the carcinogenic threat of DDT. Mr. Diviny headed the Teamsters Union, upon which section 2, particularly with regard to the sulfur content in diesel fuel, would have had the most profound effect. Mr. Dornbos headed the Southern Council of Conservation Clubs and later "admitted under oath that the membership is largely hunters, motorcyclists, dune buggy enthusiasts, and the like."[15]

Financing the Campaign

The position of chief fund raiser for CAPI was held by J. Simon Fluor, honorary chairman of Fluor Corporation. Mr. Fluor and other fund raisers managed to raise $1.5 million. The petroleum and chemical industry accounted for 40.5 percent of the total contributions, followed by utilities, with 10.5 percent; automotive, 7.9 percent; and transportation, 4.9 percent. These amounted to a total of 63.8 percent of contributions, and reflected the goal of Whitaker & Baxter in their preliminary plan—to maintain "direct control." Noticeably absent are the major electronics manufacturers—IBM, Hewlett-Packard, Xerox, Fairchild Camera, National Semi-conductor—members of the "clean" electronics industry.

These figures somewhat understate the total amounts raised for the campaign to defeat Proposition 9. For example, Gulf Oil Corporation contributed $25,000 to CAPI, but also spent an additional $27,181 conducting its own campaign. Bechtel Corporation is another example: it contributed $25,000 to CAPI, yet records of the California secretary of state show a total expenditure of $65,391.04. Bechtel reported that of this additional $40,366.04, $25,000 was paid to Stanford Research Institute, and $14,541.04 was paid to Kaiser Industries Corporation for Bechtel's portion of newspaper advertising costs.

The Campaign Strategy

Clem Whitaker, Jr., president of Whitaker & Baxter, dismisses the People's Lobby contention that the CAPI campaign was based on the Preliminary Plan and that there was some kind of conspiracy. In an interview with the author, he stated:

That plan was six months or a year after the fact by the time they [People's Lobby] got hold of it. It has certain elements of broad strategy which we kept but most of it was changed when we developed specific plans for the campaign.

This was not a secret plan. We had been following the activities of People's Lobby as well as many other groups to the extent they affect the operations of our clients. At that time we had a small retainer from Standard Oil of California (SOCAL). When we felt we had enough information, we developed the general outline of a plan, which was circulated throughout the business community on the basis that if there was an interest in developing a campaign against Proposition 9, we would be interested in managing it.

The first step in the development of a campaign strategy was to hire the firm of Kahl Associates, research consultants in government and public affairs from Washington, D.C., to do a thorough analysis of the technical, legal, and political aspects of the Clean Environment Act initiative as it was drawn.[16] Among other things, the analysis concluded that the initiative had some serious flaws in its content and construction "which could have the unfortunate effect of retarding some environmental programs." Based on their analysis, Kahl Associates suggested that a successful campaign strategy should have the following elements:

1. It should emphasize the broad character of the opposition to Proposition 9 by seeking and publishing the endorsement of influential people from all segments of the California population. This would also mean that business would keep a low profile, and People's Lobby would be projected as an extremist group with little serious public support.
2. It should hammer home the point that the initiative was poorly drafted and, if enacted, would not only do the cause of "environmental improvement" irreparable harm but would also be highly damaging to the economy of California and would result in unemployment and economic stagnation.
3. Campaign leaders should communicate with opinion leaders and the news media to enlist their support for further disseminating the CAPI viewpoint and opposition to the initiative.
4. It should launch an effective media campaign to persuade the people to vote against the passage of Proposition 9.

Generating Broad Public Support

The preliminary plan called for the creation of a citizens committee to run the campaign while its "control" remained with business and industry. Although the Citizens Committee was so organized, Mr. Whitaker rejects the charge that it was a "front" organization:

It is a rational plan to take an issue to the public where there is a public interest in it that overrides the individual interests of elements of the business community and it is simpler to communicate with people in terms of public interest with spokesmen who are not identified with self-interest groups, to wit, the head of an oil company, the head of a utility, the head of something else.

They have a bona fide interest and it is publicly stated. But you have to override their interest, and the whole theme of this campaign was what the pollution initiative means to the people—you or me—not to somebody in between. And at that point, if indeed you are right that there is an effect that commands the interest of academicians, labor people, environmentalists and the rest, they should be the spokesmen.

As to the role of large corporations, Mr. Whitaker stated:

They were the financial contributors, not the contributors to the campaign. The campaign could not have been won with them, it had to be won with the other people who were involved. *Contributors are not just money.* [Emphasis added.]

One of the reasons for this strategy was that in the minds of the public, the contributors were identified not only as contributors but also as major beneficiaries of the campaign. We were indeed making a distinction that in this case the contributors were doing it for a selfless reason—not only were their interests to be protected, but it was in the larger public interest.

People's Lobby may think this distinction is arbitrary. However, this depends on what side of the issue you stand. The opposition is invariably perceived as evil, devious, overfinanced, undersexed or something. It would be true regardless of whether the argument is coming from the left or from the right.

CAPI was able to enlist the support of a large number of conservationists, labor leaders, and politicians. One of their primary efforts was launched in the direction of the Sierra Club, the most prestigious conservation organization in the United States. On July 15, 1971, R. Frederick Fischer, co-chairman of the Sierra Club Legal Committee, sent a letter (cited in the preceding section) to Mrs. Kent Dedrick, the Sierra Club secretary, stating, "I do not believe the Club should endorse it." This letter later turned up on CAPI letterheads calling for a no vote on Proposition No. 9. Another letter written to Judge Raymond Sherwin, president of the Sierra Club, by Norman B. Livermore, secretary of the State Resources Agency, called on the Sierra Club "not to go on record supporting the People's Lobby Initiative." This letter appeared on the same CAPI letterhead, calling for a no vote.

In the political arena, CAPI was instrumental in getting Lieutenant Governor Ed Reinecke to send a memo dated March 28, 1972, on state stationery, to editors, publishers, and station managers throughout California. The memo follows exactly a pamphlet printed by CAPI entitled "How the Pollution Initiative Affects You" and calls the initiative "an irrational doomsdayer's approach." Labor also turned out to be a staunch ally of the opposition. The second largest single contributor to the campaign was the Construction Industry Advancement Fund, which contributed $50,000. The California Labor Federation, AFL–CIO, adopted a statement on March 9, 1972, calling for a "no" vote on Proposition 9. They called Proposition 9 "a destructive proposal that would create unemployment and ignore the basic economic needs of California."[17] Altogether, according to Mr. Whitaker, CAPI received some 2,300 "no" endorsements on Proposition 9.

Communicating with Opinion Leaders and Reaching
Various Groups

CAPI set up a speaker's bureau to provide speakers to fraternal organizations, college and university groups, women's organizations, and local chambers of commerce to explain the defects in the initiative and how it would affect them. They also prepared an elaborate kit for members of the news media and made regular followups. The cornerstone of this direct mail campaign was a beautifully produced 16-page black, red, and yellow pamphlet entitled "How the Pollution Initiative Affects You." The pamphlet stated that if Proposition 9 were enacted:

1. You will not be able to provide yourself and your families with necessities of life.
2. You can be turned in by a neighbor—and arrested—if you fail to throw away a can of ant or other insect poison.
3. You may be forced to junk your relatively new car.
4. You may have to go back to the scrub board and laundry tub for washing clothes.
5. Your very life will be endangered. Epidemic diseases such as typhoid fever, malaria, yellow fever, and encephalitis . . . will no longer be subject to effective control.
6. When hundreds of thousands of people lose their jobs because plants are shut down, . . . it is the working people—white collar, blue collar, small owners, minorities—who are directly affected. The odd combination of wealthy "ecology" extremists and commune-living drop-outs who find the Pollution Initiative groovy are relatively unaffected.
7. The people of California can distinguish between motherhood and suicide.

This was a major piece in the CAPI program. Over 825,000 copies of it were mailed. The philosophy of emphasizing the adverse effects of the passage of Proposition 9 was best summarized by Mr. Whitaker:

The major thrust of the entire effort was to deal with the issue in terms of what it meant to individual people and then trying to take them through it in terms of personal consequences to them. It meant the Initiative should be postured not as a proposal but as a fact and what the consequences would be under those circumstances.

CAPI received widespread support—both solicited and unsolicited—in terms of public and media criticism of the initiative as a poorly written law that on balance would do more harm than good. In addition to the neutral position taken by the Sierra Club, the western regional office of the Audubon Society also came out in opposition to Proposition 9. Most major newspapers in California opposed the passage of Proposition 9 on the grounds that it would be a bad law, thereby lending credibility to CAPI's arguments. Among the newspapers who opposed the passage of Proposition 9 were *The Los Angeles Times, San Francisco Chronicle, San Francisco Examiner, Long Beach Independent, San Diego Union-Tribune, The Sacramento Bee,* and *Oakland Tribune.*

CAPI realized that People's Lobby had made great progress with the students on the various campuses in the state and had presumably gotten endorsements from student groups up and down the state but felt it would be inadvisable to abandon that segment of the electorate. To counter the influence of People's Lobby, CAPI picked three students, one from UCLA, one from UC, and one from Stanford, all recent graduates. They were brought in and exposed to the CAPI viewpoint, material, and arguments, and asked to go home with the material and develop an approach to argue the CAPI position with students.

We sent them to every campus in the state, to every student newspaper, and they did truly a superb job. People's Lobby had claimed to have the endorsement of a whole series of universities and colleges. These kids found out that wasn't true. As a consequence, we felt that there was greater understanding about our position on the college campuses.

Mrs. Koupal offers the following explanation:

We made the ballot over one year prior to the election. We immediately went out and organized on all the campuses in the state and got endorsements of many of the student body groups and various officers. CAPI explains that they discovered we didn't really have those endorsements.

Demonstrating how very naive and inexperienced we were, we did not realize that these student body groups change office and elect every semester. Our endorsements (which were real and in writing) were moot by election time.

The Media Campaign

Prior to March 1, 1972, the bulk of the campaign was aimed at enlisting supporters for a no vote. In addition to the basic pamphlet, "How the Pollution Initiative Affects You," CAPI distributed "Voters Arguments Against Proposition 9" (Exhibit 5B-1)[b] CAPI distributed over 1.6 million copies of the two promo-

---

[b]The CAPI media campaign exhibits (5B-1 through 5B-9) all appear in Appendix 5B.

tional pieces, i.e., basic pamphlet and Voters Arguments. There were about 50 other promotional pieces of which over 800,000 copies were distributed. In addition, thousands of leaflets were produced and mailed by supporting organizations.

In the two months immediately prior to the election, heavy use was made of outdoor advertising, particularly transit posters and 7-sheets. First, transit posters were mounted on the sides of 605 buses and streetcars in nine metropolitan areas. This form of advertising was used to obtain widespread and repeated exposure. Second, two painted billboards (Exhibit 5B-2) were positioned for maximum visibility by the heavy traffic crossing the San Francisco-Oakland Bay Bridge. The final form of outdoor advertising used was "7 Sheets," or compact sidewalk posters (Exhibit 5B-3).

TV and Radio. During the three-week period before the election, both radio and television were used extensively to reach the voters (Exhibit 5B-4). A series of five filmed TV spots dramatizing the main arguments against Proposition 9 were produced and aired. There were one 60-second spot, one 30-second, two 20-second, and one 10-second (ID) spots. In all, 1,788 were run by twenty-nine television stations in the San Francisco-San Jose, Sacramento-Stockton, San Diego, and Los Angeles markets during the three weeks, and in both the Fresno and Bakersfield markets during the final week. Three radio spots, 60 seconds, 30 seconds, and 10 seconds, were taped and placed with 215 stations during the final two weeks. The total of spots run was 8,099.

Newspapers. As the election drew near, the long-planned climactic push of the advertising campaign was launched. During the last two weeks before election day, outdoor advertising was augmented by a statewide newspaper advertising program. Five 3-column by 14-inch ads were placed in 111 dailies on the following schedule:

YOU AND YOUR CAR (Exhibit 5B-5)   May 22

FRAUDULENT WAY (Exhibit 5B-6)   May 24

THE SACRED MOSQUITOES (Exhibit 5B-7)   May 26

TRUCKS AND TRAINS (Exhibit 5B-8)   May 30

RATIONING ELECTRIC POWER (Exhibit 5B-9)   June 1

Two of these ads, Trucks and Trains" and "The Sacred Mosquitoes," were placed in 465 weekly papers on the publication date nearest May 24 and May 31, respectively. On the final weekend prior to election day, a 5-column, 17-inch ad displaying a sampling of the individuals and organizations endorsing the No-on-9 campaign was run throughout the state.

The effectiveness of this massive media effort was measured at the ballot box on June 6, 1972. Proposition 9 lost by a 2 to 1 margin. CAPI was criticized by People's Lobby and some other groups for using scare tactics in their advertising campaigns and for projecting the opposition as weird and irrational people. (See, for example, the ad entitled "The Sacred Mosquitoes of California".)

A spokesman for Whitaker & Baxter, the public relations and advertising firm that prepared the advertisement, concedes the advertisement "is in error." He says his firm used as its source material a 1970 publication issued by a fruit and vegetable growers association, and he says the ad isn't scheduled to appear again. The Whitaker & Baxter spokesman says the ad shouldn't have included "typhoid," which is caused by bacteria transmitted in contaminated water, but should have said "typhus" instead. Typhus, however, is caused primarily by insanitary living conditions and is transmitted by body lice, according to medical sources.[18]

When asked whether such scare tactics were not in fact debasing the process of public communication and creating more public misinformation, Mr. Whitaker commented:

It may have been a function of the need to simplify issues in a 30-second or 60-second time constraint. When you go to a play, if it is dull, you are going to fall asleep and you won't pay any attention to it. The same is true when you are trying to command people's attention in any other way. You have to be able to hold their attention, and that means it should be colorful, it should be lively, it should be sad, it should be something that takes it out of the ordinary.

Sethi: Isn't there then a danger that by resorting to that sort of effect, exaggeration and overdramatization, there might be a tendency to degenerate the issues into very simplified notions and miseducate people? It seems to me this is especially important in the case of "idea" advertising where one of the perennial complaints by business has been a lack of understanding on the part of the news media of complex economic and technological issues. The result has been that business's position and viewpoint on these issues is either misrepresented or completely ignored.

Whitaker: You have to go back to the structure of an issue campaign and how it comes about. You cannot launch a campaign of this type three weeks before the election with a series of catchy, colorful spots. You couldn't hope to win. You launch this by doing the massive kind of research and in-depth studies of the issue that it requires to isolate the elements—good and bad—within it so that you can discuss them. You take that documentation to people and organizations who will sit and take the time to go through the whole problem and they will make decisions that this is good or this is bad or you are right or you are wrong on the basis of considerable analysis. Once you have established, and we term this an organizational base, once you have established that, then you can go out and begin to do your job publicly, issue by issue by issue, in publicity, in news conferences, in mailings of materials. By the time you get down to the last two or three weeks, of course you are down to the refined, last extract of issue with which you can deal in thirty to sixty seconds.

The Outcome: Evaluation by the Participants

In discussing the outcome of the campaign Mr. Whitaker said "They [People's Lobby] had a bad issue. That's the major thing. It's fatal if you have an organized opposition." Mr. Whitaker further observed: "If they [PL] had drafted it better, it would have meant a better initiative from their point of view. However, if they really were serious about all these specific standards for pollution abatement, they would have lost anyway. It just would have been more difficult."

The specificity and complexity of the initiative as drafted by People's Lobby and the exploitation of this issue by CAPI have been discussed in the earlier sections and need not be repeated here. The remainder of the arguments in terms of why People's Lobby lost and CAPI won could be summarized in terms of money, emotionalism, and inexperience in organization and campaigning on the part of People's Lobby, and the political muscle of big business employed by CAPI.

Money

According to the late Mr. Koupal, money was *the* reason PL lost the campaign. Other contributory factors were their lack of understanding of the process of politics and the process of advertising. "Now that I understand these, I will never lose another issue to Whitaker and Baxter." Koupal maintains that because of the lack of money, they could not do sufficient audience research or buy enough advertising to gain effective audience reach or frequency in their ad campaign:

We bought our ads wrong. We had a volunteer person buying our ads. Being a volunteer, he was more into movie advertising, rather than day to day commercial advertising. We didn't have the money to have Mervin Fields run a poll to see what we were doing. We couldn't make any test runs in the media to see how our message applied to the political public at that moment. We did the best we could. We operated on a day to day basis. That's why we feel that you have to limit money in campaigns to let the issue speak instead of the emotion.

The author suggested to Mr. Koupal an alternative way of looking at equalizing resources between the two opposing groups would be to look not at campaign expenditures but the total efforts expended by each group regardless of whether they were purchased or received in kind through volunteer help. The following dialog is illustrative of PL's viewpoint:

Sethi: It seems to me that by limiting campaign expenditures in monetary terms, you would be putting at a competitive disadvantage, those groups or causes which may be unpopular at a given point in time and therefore may not be able to attract volunteer help. For example, you seek to limit expenditures on advertising and put restrictions on total spending because you cannot attract big contributors to your cause. Yet you do not see anything wrong in using 10,000 volunteers because they are available to you. Why shouldn't the opposition charge you with taking unfair advantage because you would not limit the use of volunteers, and also would not let them *buy* help for their cause which your 10,000 volunteers provide to you?

Joyce and Edwin Koupal: Volunteer help cannot be equated with money because people are taking part in the political process. Money, on the other hand, is used to manipulate people against their self-interest.

Moreover, the idea that people going door to door wins campaigns is absolutely outrageous and absurd, particularly in the case of initiatives. The real way initiative campaigns are won or lost is by turning the minds of opinion leaders. You don't need a whole lot of people to go to opinion leaders.

Emotionalism

Joyce Koupal stated that emotionalism and inexperience could also be attributed some of the responsibility for the failure of the PL campaign. To generate support for the initiative, it was necessary that people have a chance to consider the proposition rationally and feel safe about it. Therefore, a quiet campaign was desirable from the viewpoint of People's Lobby. According to Joyce Koupal:

Anybody who is trying to kill an initiative or stop it would create a controversy and make outrageous claims so that there is a huge battle going on. Psychologically, when people get involved in controversy and are faced with uncertainty, they take to status quo—and will stay with what they have. We did everything wrong in the campaign for the Clean Environment Act. All the things, the confrontations and the charges and countercharges, were the wrong tactics for us to use. They [CAPI] were absolutely delighted that we were doing these things.

Edwin Koupal added that PL advertised emotionally instead of institutionally. Instead of carrying out a campaign, they concentrated on answering CAPI's charges. Thus PL got on the negative side instead of getting on a positive thrust. "We fell into their trap and that was exactly what they wanted us to do. We would never do that again. There are certain ways you learn from campaigns. We are a little better at it now." Mr. Whitaker of CAPI also agrees to the introduction of emotionalism on the part of the Koupals in the campaign. He states:

Their [People's Lobby] campaign was very simplistic and often bordered on being hysterical. At one time they reached a point where they wanted to campaign against Standard Oil [of California] and nothing else. Well the people could not care less about a campaign like that. We ignored that totally. But he [Koupal] campaigns the same way today as he did 10 years ago. That's his nature. He is an emotional type campaigner.

To this Mrs. Koupal retorts: "This was the first campaign Ed was involved in so Whitaker had an enlarged view of Ed's participation in such politics."

Based on their experience with the Clean Environment Act initiative, People's Lobby developed a campaign strategy which led to their success in a later campaign to pass the Political Reform Act Initiative in 1974. This strategy was outlined in a PL publication as follows:

1. A well drafted document is hard to fight. Draw in people who know the field. Seek advice from expert attorneys.
2. Timing is important from both practical and political standpoints.
3. Secure a broad base of support at the very beginning. Get all endorsements in writing. Get to opinion leaders.
4. Carefully evaluate potential opposition.
5. Dry up the money sources of the opposition. Never let them get off the ground.
6. Keep the opposition "off balance."
7. Keep controversy at a minimum—NEVER DEBATE.
8. If a legal dispute arises—settle in court.
9. Set up your own opinion polls. They clearly define the strong and weak areas in your campaign.
10. Distribute literature wisely. Look for opportunities to piggyback your material with candidates and get on state mailers. People's Lobby used this method to send over 5 million pieces of 'YES ON 9' literature.[19]

Mr. Whitaker, however, does not see the success of People's lobby in the Political Reform Act Initiative in quite those terms. Instead he attributes PL's success to the failure of the opposition. "The [People's Lobby] would have lost on the Political Reform Act if there had been any intelligent campaign against it." There was public concern over some of the excesses that had occurred in the past in the political process. There was no effective opposition against it. Mr. Whitaker comments, "I think people, good people, who were just as disgusted with the whole Watergate mess as the supporters of the Political Reform Initiative, did not want to get involved in opposing an issue where in the public mind they could be accused of defending excesses—and they walked away from it. That was a mistake, in my opinion, but that is the reason they weren't there."

Political Power

Another reason for the failure of their campaign was attributed to arm-twisting by the politicians in power who were opposed to Proposition 9. According to Mr. Koupal:

With us it was a one-to-one form of persuasion for the votes. With them it was arm-twising every inch of the way all over the state. They even applied pressure from the labor unions on the candidates so they would withdraw their endorsements.

We could not buy ads to battle them, and we couldn't get newspaper stories to battle them. I don't know anybody who would have had the power or the strength to win against such pressure and under those conditions with the laws as they existed in those days and with the way the courts acted. There was no place to stop it.

People's Lobby contended that all the facilities of the state of California were pitted against them. Whenever they made a statement on pesticides or some other aspect of agriculture, the Agriculture Department would come up with a big promotional program indicating either that the state was already working on it, had thought of it in the first place, or the PL's program was unworkable and PL's statements had no scientific proof.

It should be stated to the credit of the Koupals and People's Lobby that many of the sections contained in the Clean Environment Act have subsequently passed into law. DDT was banned shortly after the CEA was defeated. Persistent chlorinated hydrocarbons have also been banned. EPA is phasing lead out of gasoline and the California Air Resources Board is now working up to mandatory in-stack monitors in industrial stacks. The conflict of interest sections were enlarged upon and passed into law by Proposition 9, the Political Reform Act of 1974, which People's Lobby drafted and qualified and helped to pass. On the debit side, the initiative to control and regulate the construction of nuclear power plants was defeated by a 2 to 1 margin by the voters of California in June 1975.

Notes

1. For an excellent and thoroughly absorbing discussion of a political campaign, see Joe McGinnis, *The Selling of the President* (New York: Trident Press, 1969).

2. Portfolio of documents prepared by People's Lobby. [Hereinafter referred to as People's Lobby, Portfolio No. 1, 1971.]

3. "Initiative Measure to be Submitted Directly to the Electors," as

reprinted in Kahl Associates, *Policy Analysis of the California Pollution Initiative* (Washington, D.C., February 1972), p. 411.

4. Jerry Carrol, "People's Lobby—A Thorn for Politicians," *San Francisco Chronicle,* April 7, 1975, p. 9.

5. *People's Lobby* v. *Reinecke,* Los Angeles Superior Court, Decision No. WEC 25264, 1972.

6. Lynn Lilliston, "One Man's Family in Pollution War," *The Los Angeles Times,* July 30, 1971, p. 4.

7. Richard R. Leger, "Sweeping 'Clean Environment' Referendum in California Looks Too Close to Call Now," *The Wall Street Journal,* June 1, 1972, p. 25.

8. People's Lobby, *Pro and Con* (1971), p. 2.

9. "Memorandum dated June 4, 1971, from James L. Wanvig to O.N. Miller," reprinted in People's Lobby, *Proposition 9, The Political Reform Act—A Fact for California, A Proposal for America* (Los Angeles, July 1974), pp. 58–59. [Hereinafter referred to as *The Political Reform Act.*]

10. People's Lobby, *The Political Reform Act,* p. 57.

11. Gulf Energy and Environmental Systems letters in the California State Archives.

12. "Letter dated July 15, 1971, from Mr. R. Frederick Fischer to Mrs. Kent Dedrick," reprinted in People's Lobby, Portfolio No. 1.

13. "Letter dated September 30, 1971, from Mr. Roger Diamond, attorney for People's Lobby, to R. Frederick Fischer of Sierra Club," reprinted in People's Lobby, Portfolio No. 1.

14. People's Lobby, *Economics of a Clean Environment* (Los Angeles: People's Lobby Press, 1971).

15. William Ristow, "The Old Coalition," *San Francisco Bay Guardian,* April 27, 1972.

16. Kahl Associates, *Policy Analysis of the California Pollution Initiative,* p. 2.

17. "News," California Labor Federation, AFL–CIO, March 9, 1972, p. 1.

18. *Ibid.*

19. *The Political Reform Act,* p. 7.

Appendix 5A

The People's Lobby Media Campaign

Exhibit 5A-1. Text of Radio Commercials
in Support of Proposition 9
Sponsored by
People's Lobby, Inc.

No. 1   What happens if something goes wrong with a nuclear power plant?

(Sound effect:—very long sustained blast)

An accident could cause Hiroshima-like destruction. The Atomic Energy Commission found out last year that the fail safe devices on nuclear power plants don't necessarily work. . . . Proposition nine calls for a little sanity in terms of nuclear power plants. . . . Let's check into them a little more before we start stringing them the length and breadth of earthquake-prone California. . . .

Vote Yes on Proposition Nine . . . The Clean Environment Act . . . You'll be voting for better health, more jobs, a stronger economy . . . and a safe place to live. . . .

Vote Yes on Proposition Nine. . . .

No. 2   Why should you vote *Yes* on Proposition Nine?

It seems that the little guy always pays the way for big industry. . . .

Right now we've got economic controls . . . wages are controlled . . . But prices are rising . . . and industrial profits get bigger every day . . . they make the money . . . you pay the taxes. . . . Industry makes a mess . . . *your* tax money pays to clean it up. . . .

It's time to tell the big guys that you're tired of paying for their profits . . . tell them you're tired of living in a filthy environment that they've created. . . .

Tell them that you're voting for your health . . . and the health of your children . . . tell them by voting *Yes* on Proposition Nine . . . the Clean Environment Act.

No. 3   My uncle is dying of emphysema and the oil companies are telling me that I need lead in my gasoline. . . .

I'm not buying that . . . and I'm not buying their lead. . . .

I'm voting *Yes* on Proposition Nine . . . that's the Clean Environment Act.

Vote *Yes* on Proposition Nine . . . The Clean Environment Act.

No. 4   Proposition Nine is a battle of big business profits against a clean environment for people to live in. . . .

Vote *No* on the Clean Environment Act if you want worse smog, dirtier water, and more dangerous chemicals in your food. . . .

Vote *No* if you want the oil companies and big business to keep raking in the dollars . . . while you lay out your hard-earned tax money to clean up the mess. . . .

But I'm voting *Yes* on Proposition Nine . . . that's the Clean Environment Act.

No. 5   Proposition nine says that gasoline and diesel fuel should be cleaner . . . and the big gasoline companies say that it's impossible . . . they just can't do it. . . . Here are the facts:
Right now the Union Oil Company is producing, advertising and selling a diesel fuel that's three times better than what proposition nine asks. . . . Why do they keep telling us they can't make cleaner fuels when they already have them. . . .

210

You have a choice in this election. . . . You can vote for a clean environment or you can vote for bigger profits for industry. . . .

Vote *Yes* on proposition nine . . . The Clean Environment Act.

No. 6   You've probably been hearing a lot about how much money it'll cost to clean up pollution . . . and it's always tax money they're talking about . . . your money and my money. . . .

Proposition nine changes all that. . . . It requires the industries that create pollution to pay for cleaning it up. . . .

Let's put the responsibility back where it belongs. . . . They made the mess . . . they should clean it up. . . .

Vote *yes* on proposition nine . . . The Clean Environment Act . . . Vote *yes* for a better place to live. . . .

No. 7   Yes we all drive cars . . . Yes we all need fuel to run the cars . . . But no we don't have to ruin our cities and countrysides by polluting ourselves beyond salvation. . . . Concerned citizens created proposition nine . . . The Clean Environment Act . . . Concerned citizens *must* vote yes on proposition nine on June 6th. . . .

You won't lose your car . . . You won't lose your job . . . You may save your life. . . . Clean days shouldn't be a once in a while special treat . . . Clean days *can be* an everyday. . . . You owe it to the birds and trees and the fish *and* yourself to vote yes June 6th on proposition nine.

No. 8   It takes thousands and thousands and thousands of years for radioactive material to stop being radioactive. . . .
And just a few months ago the Atomic Energy Commission discovered that the safety devices on nuclear power plants *don't work*. . . .

You can't clean up a nuclear power spill the way you can clean up an oil spill. . . . There are a lot of ways to generate electricity cleanly . . . natural steam . . . MHD . . . even nuclear power. . . . But let's make sure it's safe before we use it. . . . Proposition Nine . . . The Clean Environment Act . . . gives us five years to invent a safe power plant. . . . What's the hurry. . . .

No. 9   Our children's future is up for election on June 6th. . . . We'll decide whether our children live in a world of poisonous gases and dangerous chemicals or if they'll live in a healthy world with clean air and clean water. . . . The big oil companies don't want the Clean Environment Act . . . Because it means they'll have to spend some of their excess profits cleaning up their mess. . . . We *can't* let them get away with it again. . . . Vote *yes* on Proposition Nine . . . The Clean Environment Act. . . . Vote *yes* for our children's future. . . .

Exhibit 5A-2

It's time for us to let the special interests know that we the people are running California. California belongs to us and we will not allow them to despoil and pollute her any longer. The legislature has known for more than a year and a half that Proposition 9 was going to be on the ballot June 6, 1972, but in all that time they have not been able to enact one pollution control measure, let alone one which might be better than Proposition 9. The special interests do not want to clean up. We the people must act. We must vote for Proposition 9, the Clean Environment Act.

TOGETHER WE CAN BUILD A STRONGER ECONOMY

We can make California the center of a whole new industry—the pollution control industry. Many economists think pollution control will be a bigger industry in the next thirty years than aerospace has been in the past thirty years. When we pass Proposition 9, we will create a market for pollution control devices. This means more jobs. As we build such equipment, the rest of the nation will demand that their air and water be cleaned up too, and California will become the supplier to the nation and ultimately the world. California led the way in demanding auto emission controls. Now we will lead the way in demanding a truly healthy and clean environment.

WE CAN'T BE FOOLED AGAIN

We won't accept the old either/or argument—"either you and your children breathe dirty air, or you will lose your job." It's far cheaper to clean up a dirty smokestack or filthy sewer than it is to move a whole factory to another location. (Another location which doesn't want their pollution anyway and where they would have to build the same pollution control devices we are demanding here.) However, the cheapest thing of all is to scare us, to keep us from writing and enforcing anti-pollution laws, then the special interests, the polluters, don't have to do anything at all. We have to pay the costs of their pollution—in health care costs, mentally retarded children, property damage and lowered property values. It's time for the polluters to pay the costs—the costs of cleaning up their own filth.

Let's Answer Some of their Arguments with Some Facts

POWER FAILURES

We are more likely to have power failures if Proposition 9 does NOT pass than if it does succeed. Our power companies have tried to rush us into nuclear fission power plant construction before all the dangers and problems have been adequately solved. Most people do not want a nuclear power plant built near them, and the delays in construction of these plants have been and will continue to be very great.

When Proposition 9 passes, the power companies will be forced to consider other sources of power, at least for the next five years. Some immediate expansion of present fossil fuel (oil and gas) plants is possible and can be accomplished much more quickly to take care of our immediate needs. Proposition 9 assures that these fossil fuel plants will be clean and not pollute the atmosphere. In the Los Angeles basin today, where anti-pollution laws are tougher, electrical plants contribute 1.1 percent to our pollution problem.

In the long run, better, cheaper, safer, and completely clean power supplies can be developed. Geothermal power (power created by using the steam from beneath the earth's surface), is already being used in some parts of California, Italy, Japan and Israel. The largest geothermal fields in the world are beneath California, and Proposition 9 with its five year moratorium on the construction of nuclear fission power plants will encourage their development.

Other possibilities include the use of fuel cells like the ones which powered the men on the moon. Solar power, magnetohydrodynamic generators (MHD), nuclear fusion power, and even using power of the wind or the tides are being suggested by scientists who are concerned about pollution.

In the past thirty years, 84 percent of our research into energy sources has gone into nuclear fission energy, while truly clean sources have been neglected. Proposition 9 will help to bring a rethinking of our energy goals, research and sources.

NUCLEAR POWER

Nuclear fission power is Not Clean. Radiation pollution is a serious problem. Last November a nuclear power plant in Minnesota poured 50,000 gallons of radioactive wastes into the Mississippi River just above the water intakes for Minneapolis-St. Paul. Before these intakes could be closed, some of the cities' water supply was contaminated, to say nothing of the River itself. Accidents have occurred at many nuclear facilities, but so far only the lives of workers in these plants have been sacrificed. Since nothing which involves people is infallible, how soon before an entire city or region of the country is contaminated with radiation?

According to the Atomic Energy Commission, the safety devices on nuclear power plants have not been properly tested. When one type of fail-safe device was tested last year, it failed. The result was that out of a total of eight nuclear power plants now in operation, three were asked to shut down until they modified their safety equipment while the other five were asked to operate at 30 to 40 percent of total capacity. Thus nuclear fission power is not even a reliable source of electricity, since new emergencies may cause new shutdowns. Also nuclear fission is a temporary expedient, since we have only enough fuel to power these plants for about thirty years, and then even more dangerous breeder plants must be used to increase our supply of nuclear fuel.

The products of nuclear fission are highly dangerous, and if they escape into our air or water, they will last MANY THOUSANDS of years. Plutonium 239 has a half-life of 24,000 YEARS. This means that if you put one pound of plutonium into the atmosphere today, one-half pound will still be there in 24,000 years! So far we still do not have an adequate means of disposing of nuclear power plant wastes which will add up to tons of lethal material in a very few years. The whole of written human history has only lasted for 10,000 years, so how can we guarantee that we can guard these nuclear wastes for thousands of years to make sure they do not contaminate the earth, its air and its water?

What happens if a truck or train carrying nuclear wastes or fuels has an accident?

What happens if an earthquake damages a plant in California? At present, the San Onofre plant is built to withstand an earthquake force of 1/2 G (1/2 the force of gravity). The February 1971 earthquake in Los Angeles was measured at a force of 1 G—twice the capacity of the San Onofre plant. What would happen if a nuclear power plant were near the epicenter of a major quake?

We believe a five year moratorium on nuclear fission power plant construction is only a minimum requirement when we are talking about earthquakes and 24,000 years of radiation pollution.

The opposition claims that removing the lead from gasoline in four years will make it impossible for you to drive your cars which are presently in use. THIS IS NOT TRUE.

The standards proposed by Proposition 9 are identical to the standards proposed by the Environmental Protection Agency. The State of California has also proposed the same standards, but they would allow five years to phase them in instead of four.

What will this do to your car? You will need a tuneup of your engine in which the mechanic will retard the spark and possibly change the spark plugs on your car. In some cases, you will have to put in a thicker head gasket to reduce the compression ratio slightly. (The costs of all this are $3.50 for a head gasket and about two hours labor—top price, maybe $20.) However,

Exhibit 5A-3

since most cars are phased out of service after five years, it has been estimated by the California Air Resources Board, that 85 to 95 percent of the cars on the road in 1976 will have been produced since 1971, and all these cars will operate on lead-free gasoline.

LEADED GASOLINE CONTRIBUTES SUBSTANTIALLY TO THE HIGH LEVEL OF ATMOSPHERIC LEAD AND CONSTITUTES AN EXTREMELY SERIOUS HEALTH HAZARD.

Lead is a toxic element which can produce liver, kidney and brain damage and deterioration of the central nervous system. Children are especially susceptible to lead poisoning; among them mental retardation and other signs of central nervous system involvement are common. The California State Air Resources Board Standard is 1.5 micrograms per cubic meter of air. Los Angeles has the highest concentration of lead in the air of all major American cities, 5.7 micrograms per cubic meter on the average. A concentration of lead in the air in L.A. County as high as 71.3 micrograms per cubic meter has been recorded during a peak traffic period. This is 47 times the California standard!

PESTICIDES

Opponents say we will have epidemic diseases and termites if we do not use the types of pesticides banned by Proposition 9. THIS IS NOT TRUE.

These persistent pesticides like DDT have only been in existence for about 30 years, yet the epidemics the opponents predict such as malaria or yellow fever have been unknown in California for many years prior to the introduction of these pesticides. However, should such an epidemic or other emergency occur, the legislature may, by four-fifths majority vote, authorize the use of such pesticides. Legislatures can and have acted quickly in emergencies, so this seems to be a reasonable precaution against such disaster.

We now know the devastating side effects of persistent chemical pesticides and herbicides on the reproductive systems of certain sea and bird life, and most scientists who have studied the problem agree that the dangers to man are such that banning of such pesticides is mandatory. Some of the herbicides being used in California have already been banned for use in Viet Nam by our military because they cause birth defects in children. The Environmental Protection Agency of the U.S. government has already recommended a complete ban on DDT and other persistent pesticides because they are not needed in the United States, and their dangers are well known.

The opposition claims we are banning the only known pesticide for termite control. THIS IS NOT SO. Diatumaceous earth is a safe and acceptable substitute and is widely used by exterminators today.

FLEXIBILITY

They say the law is inflexible and cannot be changed except by very difficult processes. THIS IS NOT TRUE.

The law can be made stricter at any time by the legislature or any pollution control agency which has that power today. If this law is not tough enough, we can make it tougher. However, we know how former pollution laws have been weakened through the influence of the big polluters. Therefore, the legislature is forbidden from weakening the law--from inserting loopholes which are the cause of so much pollution today.

In an emergency, the legislature can act as shown above in the case of pesticides, and it seems unlikely that any legislature would not respond to a genuine emergency. Other provisions can be changed at the next election either through the referendum or the initiative --the same processes we are using to pass it. And of course, we expect the polluters to challenge some provisions in the courts. We expect to win most of these challenges, but this is another method for adjusting or modifying the law.

PENALTIES AND INCENTIVES

The Clean Environment Act encourages a firm to clean up its pollution by a series of penalties and incentives. After a firm has been found to be violating pollution standards, it may be fined 0.4 percent of its gross sales for the previous year, each day it continues to pollute. For Standard Oil of California this would amount to approximately $18,000,000 per day. This type of penalty should get the polluters attention, unlike current penalties which may run $500 or $1,000 which are frequently assessed today.

However, our purpose is not to put Standard Oil or anyone else out of business. We want to clean up pollution. We believe no polluter will want to pay these fines and will therefore file a writ of compliance showing the steps he is taking to clean up his mess. As soon as he has done this, the fines will stop.

The polluter will then have a certain specified length of time to comply with the pollution laws. After he has complied, 75 percent of the fine he paid will be refunded. That should be a good incentive to comply quickly. The remaining 25 percent will be kept to pay for administering pollution laws, research into pollution problems, etc.

THE COST OF CLEANING UP AND MORE IMPORTANT--THE SAVINGS!

Since businesses and governments have no other money than what they receive from we the people as consumers and as taxpayers, we will ultimately bear the costs of cleanup. However, the National Wildlife Federation has estimated that the costs of cleaning up will be smaller than the costs we are now incurring from the pollution itself.

	Total for U.S.	Our share as Head of Family
Air & Water pollution damages	$28.9 billion	$481
Gross savings from cleanup (by 1976)	$22.2 billion	$370
Minus-cost of cleanup	$10.2 billion	$170
Net annual savings	$12.0 billion	$200

SOURCE: National Wildlife, Vol. 10, No. 2, Feb.-Mar., 1972, pp. 14-15.

With these facts, doesn't it make sense to vote for Proposition 9? Let's show the polluters they don't own California . . . we do! Let's clean up and make California a healthy and a beautiful place to raise our children.

VOTE YES FOR A CLEAN ENVIRONMENT. VOTE YES ON PROPOSITION 9.

Exhibit 5A-3 (cont.)

The following people
have endorsed
the Clean Environment Act
(Proposition 9):

The opponents of the Clean Environment Act (Proposition 9) plan to spend millions of dollars to discredit it.
Don't be fooled. Thousands of responsible Californians have already endorsed the Clean Environment Act as a sensible solution to a deadly problem.
For more information about the Clean Environment Act, contact:

People for the Clean Environment Act
3456 W. Olympic Blvd. Los Angeles, CA 90019 (213) 731-8321
Edwin A. Koupal, Jr., Executive Director Margaret Cheap, Treasurer

The following are against it:

OIL COMPANIES.
POWER COMPANIES.
BIG INDUSTRIAL POLLUTERS.
THE CHEMICAL INDUSTRY.
Etc.

Exhibit 5A–4

215

YOU CAN
GIVE OUR CHILDREN TOMORROW

Vote Yes on
Proposition 9
Tuesday, June 6, 1972

fact:
During smog alerts our children are kept off the playgrounds, while industry is allowed to continue emitting poisonous gases into our air.

Proposition 9 would close each source of industrial pollution exceeding permitted levels during a first stage smog alert.

This is only reasonable. Industry must be held accountable for its own pollution. The government provides tax incentives and low interest bonds for installation of pollution control equipment. Industry can well afford to clean itself up.

We must clean up too. Sulfur in diesel fuel means sulfuric acid in our lungs. Lead in our gasoline means lead in the air we breathe. Lead can produce liver, kidney, and brain damage and mental retardation in children.

We CAN restrict sulfur content in diesel fuel without causing disruptions in the trucking of goods and services. This fuel is currently available. It is a matter of industry's willingness to provide it for a larger market.

Unleaded gas is also available. By 1976 most cars will be able to run on unleaded gas; the remaining few will need only minor adjustments.

Everyone agrees that lead must be taken out of gasoline. Proposition 9 does it.

fact:
A nuclear accident from one nuclear power plant would release radiation equal to 100 Hiroshima-type atomic bombs.

Would you fly in an airplane that had never been tested? The emergency cooling systems of these nuclear power plants have NEVER BEEN TESTED. A mock up test done by the Atomic Energy Commission failed completely.

The risks are so great that insurance companies will not insure your home or your life in the event of a nuclear accident.

The nuclear power plants that NOW exist have already produced 100 million gallons of lethal radioactive waste. It will remain highly toxic for thousands of years. No SAFE place has been found YET to dispose of this waste.

Brownouts? Only if you believe the power companies, prices that that our power needs will double in 10 years. We don't. Remember, the power companies are in the business of creating a market for their service.

Proposition 9 calls for a five year ban on the construction of nuclear fission power plants, time to study SAFE means of meeting our power needs. Ralph Nader applauds this provision.

fact:
Many of the public officials we rely on to enforce our anti-pollution laws receive their paychecks from the same industrial polluters they are supposed to regulate.

Proposition 9 will make this illegal by providing conflict of interest clauses.

By including class action suits in its provisions, Proposition 9 finally gives citizens the right to protect themselves against environmental destruction. Concerned citizens have been trying for years to obtain this legal authority only because our government is reluctant to take its own agencies to court in matters of pollution.

Proposition 9 also protects people from dangerous, long lived pesticides and herbicides. It bans a select list that are known to cause birth defects, cancer, and even death in man. Safe alternate methods to control pests and weeds do exist. Chemicals that do not persist in nature are available. Also, biological pesticides are proving to be an even more direct and economical approach to the problem.

fact:
Smog costs the average American family an additional $268 a year: unnecessary doctor bills; extra car repairs, lost property values and higher food prices.

Why does every discussion about pollution always center on what it would cost industry to clean up, and not on what it costs every one of us to live in it?

It would actually cost us less to clean up NOW than to continue living with pollution.

Pollution control is a new industry creating many new jobs: designing, building, installing, and maintaining pollution control equipment.

Leonard Woodcock, president of UAW, predicted that "loss of jobs" would be nothing but a threat — a game plan used by industry to fight new pollution legislation. He argues forcefully that the working man's best interests could only be served by a total clean up of the environment. It is the working man who works in the filth and then goes home to the smoggiest part of the city where he raises his children. THESE CHILDREN DESERVE A BETTER LIFE. WE ARE ENTRUSTED WITH THEIR FUTURE. WE CAN'T LET THEM DOWN.

A partial list of the corporations that have contributed more than $1,000,000 to defeat Proposition 9, The Clean Environment Act. Original copy on file with the Secretary of State, Sacramento, California.

STANDARD OIL COMPANY OF CALIFORNIA	940,000.00
GENERAL MOTORS	25,000.00
FORD MOTOR COMPANY	20,000.00
AMERICAN CYANAMID	5,000.00
GULF OIL CORP	20,000.00
PACIFIC GAS & ELECTRIC	20,000.00
BRAVO OIL COMPANY	45,930.00
SOUTHERN CALIFORNIA EDISON COMPANY	25,000.00
KAISER INDUSTRIES	10,000.00
BANK OF AMERICA FOUNDATION	8,000.00
GENERAL ELECTRIC CORP	25,000.00
MONTROSE CHEMICAL CORP	10,000.00
E I DUPONT de NEMOURS & CO	25,000.00
STAUFFER CHEMICAL CO	25,000.00
CELANESE CORP	25,000.00
U.S BORAX & CHEMICAL CORP	10,000.00
AMOCO CHEMICALS	5,000.00
PACIFIC TELEPHONE	15,000.00
F M C CORPORATION	25,000.00
ETHYL CORPORATION	15,000.00
COMBUSTION ENGINEERING CO	5,000.00
BECHTEL CORPORATION	25,000.00
TEXACO INC	25,000.00
POWERINE OIL COMPANY	5,000.00
McGRAW EDISON COMPANY	5,000.00
WESTINGHOUSE ELECTRIC CORP	25,000.00
PACIFIC LIGHTING CORP	15,000.00
LOS ANGELES CLEARING HOUSE ASSOCIATION	25,000.00
ALLIS-CHALMERS	10,000.00
KERR McGEE CHEMICAL CORPORATION	10,000.00
MONSANTO COMPANY	12,000.00
ROHM & HAAS COMPANY	5,000.00
HERCULES INC	10,000.00
LESMAN BROS	10,000.00
BABCOCK & WILSON	15,000.00
U S STEEL CORP	10,000.00
FIRESTONE TIRE & RUBBER	250.00
B F GOODRICH COMPANY	2,500.00
GOODYEAR TIRE & RUBBER	8,545.00
KOPPERS CO INC FOREST PRODUCTS DIVISION	5,000.00
HEGGBLADE MARGULEAS TENNECO INC	10,000.00
CONSOLIDATED FREIGHTWAYS	5,000.00
P P G INDUSTRIES INC	10,000.00
THE ATCHISON TOPEKA SANTA FE RAILWAY SYSTEM	18,926.25
CALIFORNIA LAND TITLE ASSOCIATION	5,000.00
GENERAL TIRE & RUBBER COMPANY	2,250.00

The California Medical Association says:

"We are living in a state of chronic and increasing emergency due to pollution."

The problems grow worse while the legislators refuse to act and our pollution control boards refuse to effectively regulate industry.

And who suffers? We do!

The question is not whether we clean up our environment but when. The longer we wait the more difficult, the more expensive, and the more disruptive it's going to be. We must act now by voting yes on Proposition 9.

By tackling pollution today, it will be easier, cheaper, and much less chaotic.

The facts are frightening.

Cancer mortality rates are 25% higher in polluted areas than in areas of relatively clean air. Crop losses due to smog drive food prices up. Our very health, economic security, and well-being suffer. Yet big business would have us believe that we must not act in haste — that they too want to fight pollution but that this is not the time nor the way to do it. If we wait for them it will never be time.

The same vested interests who have for years been lobbying against environmental legislation in Sacramento are now pouring hundreds of thousands of dollars into a campaign against Proposition 9.

Isn't it sad that money can buy your vote?

Your vote is your voice! Stand up and be heard!

Some of the thousands of responsible Californians who endorse Proposition 9:

National Health Federation
Federation of American Scientists, Los Angeles Chapter
Los Angeles County Democratic Central Committee
California State Environmental Quality Study Council
Congressman Jerome B. Waldie
California Federation of Teachers, AFL-CIO
Virginia W. Taylor, San Diego Regional Central Committee
Friends of the Earth
Carol Burnett
Nanette Fabray
Burt Lancaster
Jack Lemmon
Eddie Albert
Walter Matthau
Carl Reiner
Robert Wise
U.S. Senator Mike Gravel
Protective Council of C.A. Senior Citizens
Congressman Augustus Hawkins
Bryan C. Crafts, Commissioner of the Cabrillo Marine Museum
Donald Freeman,
Michael Peters, M.D.,
Richard Ross, M.D.,
Alex Sweeten, Jr.,
Rabbi Albert M. Lewis, D.D.,
Fortney (Pete) Stark, Pres. Sec. Pacific State Bank
David Seiden, Pres. A.F.T.-AFL-CIO
Congressman Ronald V. Dellums

Limited funds have restricted us to one newspaper ad. If you would like further information on Proposition 9 please call the number below. **Help us spread the word** by circulating this ad to all your friends and neighbors. Additional funds will help us even now to buy radio and television spots. Enclosed is $_____

Name _____
Address _____
City _____ State _____ Zip _____

People for The Clean Environment Act
Margaret Cheap, Treasurer
3456 West Olympic Boulevard, Los Angeles, Calif 90019 731-8321

Exhibit 5A-5

216

On June 6th, pollution will be up for re-election.

While the politicians hem and haw, the people of California can cast a powerful vote against pollution on June 6th, by voting "yes" on the Clean Environment Act.

Passage of the Clean Environment Act will give California a group of tough, effective anti-pollution measures that the legislature can't water down and the environmental control agencies will have to enforce.

More than 500,000 Californians signed petitions to put the Clean Environment Act on the ballot, an unprecedented show of grass-roots strength. It's the first time in history that a grass-roots initiative has made a statewide ballot.

So if you get mad when the politicians you've elected won't vote against pollution, remember June 6th. That's the day we all go over their heads and vote pollution out of office.

Provisions of the Clean Environment Act

1. Phases out lead in gasoline
2. Authorizes shutting down of flagrant industrial polluters
3. Bans offshore oil drilling
4. Prohibits construction of new nuclear power plants for 5 years
5. Restricts manufacture, sale and use of DDT
6. Forbids conflict of interest by enforcement officials

For more information, contact People for the Clean Environment Act, 3456 W. Olympic Blvd., Los Angeles, CA 90019

Prepared in the interest of a clean environment by **Hall/Butler/Blatherwick, Inc.,** 3345 Wilshire Blvd., Los Angeles
Art Direction by Tom Kelly/Written by Al Maleson
Engraved by Mitchell & Herb Engraving Co.

Support the Clean Environment Act.

Exhibit 5A–6

Exhibit 5A-7. People's Lobby Television Commercial: "Candice Bergen"

Video
Frame

A, B, C	*Audio* This was a very special place to grow up. Animals, trees, clear view of the city.
D	Now the city is hardly ever in view and when it is, there's a cloud of smog around it.
E	Like most Californians I care about the effects of pollution on our lives. . . . Now we have an alternative . . . Prop. 9, The Clean Environment Act, will appear on the ballots on the June 6 election.

F	Dr. Irving F. Fengelsdorf (Ph.D. in Chemistry from University of Chicago) will answer some basic questions about Prop. 9.
G	The opposition to Prop. 9 says that the transportation system will cease to run and that 100,000 jobs will be lost because the Act proposes the banning of diesel fuel.
H	It is technically feasible to produce alternatives to diesel fuel. If pressed by law, the oil companies could do so. The courts will give the companies enough time.
J	The opposition claims that if Prop. 9 is passed and the use of lead-based gasoline is banned, most cars in California will be inoperable. Within four years 85% of all cars on the road will be able to operate on low lead gas.
K	Prop. 9 will ban the use of persistent pesticides such as DDT.

	At this time we find traces of DDT on every continent . . . on birds in the arctic. We don't know the effects yet, but laboratory tests on birds and animals show that DDT can cause cancer. There are alternatives, both chemical and non-chemical, to DDT.
M	The opposition states that the proposed 5-year moratorium on nuclear power plants will be counterproductive, forcing us to rely on our depleting supplies of conventional fuel.
	Join me and thousands of other Californians on June 6 in voting yes for Prop. 9.
O	More Jobs, Better Health, Stronger Economy. Yes on 9.

218

Exhibit 5A-8. People's Lobby Television Commercial: "Refinery"

Video
Frame

A

B

C

Paid for by PEOPLE FOR
THE CLEAN ENVIRONMENT ACT

Audio

Our pollution control laws aren't being enforced.

Politicians don't like to get tough with the big polluters because the big polluters finance their campaigns.

That's why 1/2 million California voters worked to put the Clean Environment Act on the ballot.

Take politics out of pollution. Vote for Prop. 9.

Exhibit 5A-9. People's Lobby Television Commercial: "Cartoon"

Video
Frame

Audio
Background music

220

Exhibit 5A-9 continued

D

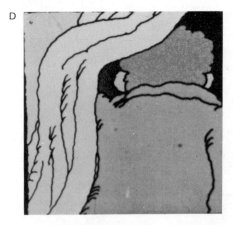

E

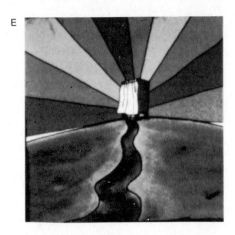

F

G

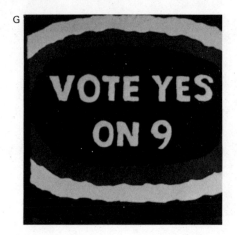

Appendix 5B

**The CAPI Media
Campaign**

TRANSPORTATION BREAKDOWN

One innocent-sounding section alone —limiting the content of sulfur in diesel fuel to 0.035 per cent—would virtually bring the economy of California to a halt.

Most trucks, trains, and transit buses operate on diesel fuel. Except for a very small amount of scarce, imported fuel, the sulfur content of diesel fuel available today is many times the amount allowable under Proposition No. 9.

It would take an undetermined number of years and enormous capital outlay to build refineries capable of producing such fuel in quantity.

This simply means that if Proposition No. 9 were enacted, the vast majority of trucks and trains that transport food and other basic necessities of life to all Californians would cease to run.

Diesel-powered transit buses would be retired from service, forcing a heavier reliance on private automobiles—thus increasing the pollution problem, instead of reducing it.

SEVERE UNEMPLOYMENT

Lost jobs in the transportation industries would number in the hundreds of thousands. The additional unemployment in industries and businesses idled because of a transportation breakdown would be staggering.

Responsible Conservationists

Urge

Vote NO

on

Proposition No. 9

Following is the official text of the

VOTERS ARGUMENT AGAINST PROPOSITION NO. 9

which will be distributed by the Secretary of State of California before the June 6 election.

Your job, your future, your ability to provide the basic necessities of life for your family, depend on the defeat of Proposition No. 9, the Pollution Initiative, at the June 6 election.

Proposition No. 9 is so extreme, so unworkable, so devastating in its adverse effects on the day-to-day living problems of every Californian, that its enactment would set back the cause of environmental improvement for years to come.

Exhibit 5B-1

PESTICIDE PARANOIA

Proposition No. 9 would ban a long list of pesticides used in the production of food, in the control of epidemic diseases and for the destruction of household pests. For some uses, including termite control, there are no known substitutes. For many uses, allowable substitutes are less effective, must be applied more often, are highly dangerous to handle, and are toxic to pets and birds and beneficial insects such as bees.

POOR AUTO PERFORMANCE

Proposition No. 9 phases out lead in gasoline in four years. Federal proposals would phase out lead, but over a longer period of time, making allowance for the driveability of cars presently in use. Under Proposition No. 9 many, possibly most car owners, would be stuck with cars that could not be driven effectively, if at all.

CLEAN POWER BANNED

For five years, Proposition No. 9 bans construction of nuclear power plants, the only major source of clean electric energy, thus forcing heavier reliance on generating plants powered by air-contaminating fossil fuels. Again, Proposition No. 9 would increase pollution, instead of reducing it.

In every area covered by the Initiative, increasingly strict anti-pollution regulations are being enforced by local, state and federal agencies. These regulations can be adjusted if proved unworkable or counter-productive.

Proposition No. 9's complex, arbitrary regulations would be frozen into law. For all practical purposes, even in the face of dire economic or epidemic emergency, none of its provisions could be changed except through time-consuming court challenges and the lengthy and cumbersome process necessary to bring such a change before the people for a vote.

Vote NO
on Proposition No. 9

Signed:

DR. J. E. McKEE, Professor of Environmental Engineering; Former Member, Advisory Committee on Reactor Safeguards, Atomic Energy Commission

MYRON W. DOORNBOS, President, Southern Council of Conservation Clubs

JOSEPH J. DIVINY, First Vice-President, International Brotherhood of Teamsters

CALIFORNIANS AGAINST
THE POLLUTION INITIATIVE

870 Market Street, San Francisco, CA 94102
1127 Wilshire Boulevard, Los Angeles, CA 90017

Co-Chairman:

DR. EMIL M. MRAK, Chancellor-Emeritus, University of California, Davis

Exhibit 5B-1 continued

225

Too many bugs in Prop. No. 9

VOTE NO ON NO. 9

CALIFORNIANS AGAINST
THE POLLUTION INITIATIVE

LOSING YOUR JOB WON'T SOLVE POLLUTION

Exhibit 5B–2

Losing your job won't solve Pollution!

Vote NO on No. 9

CALIFORNIANS AGAINST THE POLLUTION INITIATIVE

Exhibit 5B-3

Exhibit 5B-4. CAPI: Text of Television and Radio Commercials*

30-second TV

Video	Audio
People walking in lighted city street—then the lights go out (blackness, shadowy forms)	Announcer (voice over): Who wants darkened city streets at night?
Nuclear power plant by ocean—sparkling blue sky	Proposition 9 would cause severe power shortages in California by stopping construction of clean nonpolluting nuclear power plants for five years.
Woman scrubbing clothes with scrubboard in old-fashioned laundry tub	Who wants to go back to the scrubboard?
Family huddled around fireplace—candles for light	Or depend on the fireplace to heat their home?
Card: Vote NO on No. 9	Vote NO on Proposition 9.
	The preceding announcement sponsored by Californians Against the Pollution Initiative.

20-second TV, No. 1

Video	Audio
Beautiful blue sky Breadline—or unemployment line	Everybody is in favor of clean air—but losing your job won't solve the pollution problem.
Train coming to a halt (or derailed?) Truck stopped at a crossing signal	Proposition 9 would halt virtually all train and truck transportation of food and other products in California—throwing millions of people out of work.
Card: Vote NO on No. 9	Vote No on 9.
	The preceding announcement sponsored by Californians Against the Pollution Initiative.

60-second TV

Video (film or animation?)	Audio
Beautiful blue sky Breadline—or unemployment line	Announcer (voice over): Everybody is in favor of clean air but losing your job won't solve the pollution problem.
Train coming to a halt Truck stopped at a crossing signal	Proposition 9 would halt virtually all train and truck transportation of food and other products in California—throwing millions of people out of work.
Empty stocks in a supermarket	And you would be unable to provide the basic necessities of life for yourself and your family.
Lighted city at night—then blacked out	Electricity blackouts won't solve the problem either. Proposition 9 actually would *increase* pollution—not reduce it—by banning construction of *non-polluting* nuclear power plants for five years.

*Radio commercials were the audio portion of TV commercials.

228

Exhibit 5B–4 continued

Mosquitoes, termites, etc. (buzzing background sound)

Banning pesticides that protect your home from termites and protect *you* from epidemic diseases such as malaria won't solve the problem either.

Card: Vote NO on No. 9

Proposition 9 is *no way* to combat pollution. Vote No on 9.

The preceding announcement sponsored by Californians Against the Pollution Initiative

10-second TV spot

Video
Card: Vote NO on No. 9

Audio
Announcer (voice over): Losing your job won't solve the pollution problem. Vote NO on Proposition 9.

The preceding announcement sponsored by Californians Against the Pollution Initiative.

20-second TV spot, No. 2

Video
Mosquitoes, termites, etc. (buzzing background sound?)

Audio
Announcer (voice over): Who wants to bring back malaria?

Card: Vote NO on No. 9

Proposition 9 would ban pesticides that protect your food supplies, protect your home from termites and other pests, and protect *you* from epidemic diseases.

Vote No on 9—there are too many bugs in it!

The preceding announcement sponsored by Californians Against the Pollution Initiative.

Exhibit 5B–5

The Fraudulent Way To Combat Air Pollution

Air pollution is of vital concern to every man, woman and child in California.

Fortunately, a great deal is being done about it — by regulatory agencies at every level of government.

Every county in the state now has an Air Pollution Control Board, with powers to enforce standards for emissions of air contaminants, and to shut down plants that don't meet them.

Ten years ago, in Los Angeles County, 50 per cent of all air pollutants (other than from natural sources) came from industrial plants and businesses. Today, the Air Pollution Control Board has succeeded in reducing industrial air pollution to the point that such sources now contribute only about 10 per cent.

But the sponsors of Proposition No. 9, on the June 6 ballot, say that the Pollution Control Boards aren't tough enough. They want to make it much more difficult for industrial plants to stay in business.

For example, Proposition No. 9 would require that, whenever a smog alert is called, certain plants must shut down — regardless of whether or not the particular types of emissions from those plants are contributing to the smog problem.

But even if they succeeded in closing down **all** industrial plants **permanently** — with all the unemployment problems that would result — 90 per cent of the air pollution would remain — because **90 per cent** of the smog problem is caused by automobile exhausts.

Hopefully, increasingly restrictive California automobile emissions standards and Federal requirements for highly advanced smog control devices will substantially reduce smog in the next few years.

But the sponsors of Proposition No. 9 contend the problem is so serious that drastic steps must be taken **right now.** If so, why didn't they put up for voter approval a requirement that when a smog alert is called, all autos must be off the streets within two hours, with tough penalties for violators?

That would be the only way to effectively reduce smog, **right now.**

Proposition No. 9 is a fraud. It would cause widespread unemployment, but it wouldn't reduce air pollution, in any effective way.

Vote NO on Proposition No. 9

CALIFORNIANS AGAINST THE POLLUTION INITIATIVE

870 Market Street, San Francisco, CA 94102
1127 Wilshire Boulevard, Los Angeles, CA 90017

*MYRON W. DOORNBOS, President, Southern Council of Conservation Clubs
Co-Chairman*

Exhibit 5B-6

The Sacred Mosquitoes of California

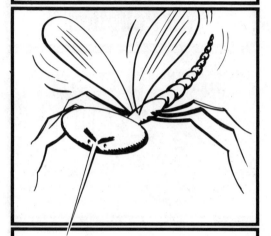

Who wants to bring back typhoid? Or malaria? Or encephalitis? Only people who love mosquitoes.

The sponsors of Proposition No. 9 on the June 6 ballot must love mosquitoes—also termites, cockroaches and silverfish. Because Proposition No. 9 makes illegal the use or possession of a long list of chemicals, including the only effective pesticides for controlling various pests.

They must hate bees, though. Because the substitute pesticides that could still be used, though far less effective for many purposes, are death on bees. They're also dangerous to humans and pets.

If Proposition No. 9 passed, you could be arrested for having on your premises a can of insect spray you'd purchased some time ago if it happened to contain one of a long list of suddenly illegal ingredients.

A university scientist could be arrested for experimenting with any of these banned chemicals in a laboratory research project.

What kind of sense does all this make?

Like most things about Proposition No. 9, it doesn't make any sense at all.

It doesn't make sense to risk the resurgence of epidemic diseases that have been kept in control for so many years that most of us have virtually forgotten they ever existed.

It doesn't make sense to risk the destruction of forests and agricultural crops.

It doesn't make sense to prohibit scientists from experimenting to develop new knowledge in the field of pest control.

It doesn't make sense to forbid the use of the only known effective means of protecting your house from termite infestation.

Proposition No. 9 is senseless—and very dangerous.

There's good in most religions, and harm in some. The protected, "sacred cows" of India have contributed to that country's abject poverty for centuries. It would be the height of folly to yield to the fanatics who, in their zeal for a new "religion," would inflict on all of us the "sacred mosquitoes" of California!

Vote NO on Proposition No. 9

There are too many bugs in it!

CALIFORNIANS AGAINST THE POLLUTION INITIATIVE

870 Market Street, San Francisco, CA 94102
1127 Wilshire Boulevard, Los Angeles, CA 90017

DR. EMIL M. MRAK, Chancellor-Emeritus, University of California, Davis
Co-Chairman

Exhibit 5B–7

Would you vote to Stop all Truck and Freight Train Transportation in California?

You certainly wouldn't if you happen to be one of the 1,000,000 Californians who work directly in the transportation industry! You'd lose your job within a few days after election.

And if you think about it for a minute or two, you realize that no matter what you do for a living, you'd be in serious trouble.

Businesses of all kinds would no longer be able to market their products.

Farm crops would rot in the fields and on the trees.

Unemployment would reach staggering proportions.

You wouldn't be able to provide yourself and your family with the basic necessities of life!

Nobody in his right mind would vote "yes" on such a stupid, vicious proposal. Yet that's what you're being asked to do when you go to the polls on June 6 to vote on Proposition No. 9 — the Pollution Initiative.

Down in the fine print, Proposition No. 9 contains an innocent-sounding provision limiting the content of sulfur in diesel fuel sold for use in internal combustion engines in Californa to .035 per cent.

The limit now in effect is .5 per cent — 14 times as much!

The very small amount of diesel fuel now available that would meet this ridiculous requirement is insufficient even to fill the needs of public transit buses, which run on the lowest sulfur content diesel now in production.

If Proposition No. 9 should pass, the next day the great majority of trucks and diesel-powered freight locomotives would have to stop running — because there would be no "legal" fuel available to operate them!

It would take an undetermined period of time — two years? — six years? — nobody knows for sure, before refineries could be adapted at enormous expense to produce diesel fuel in the quantity needed to meet our transportation needs.

Knowing the facts, nobody in his right mind would vote for Proposition No. 9.

LOSING YOUR JOB WON'T SOLVE POLLUTION!

And voting for Proposition No. 9 won't solve pollution. The Technical Advisory Committee of the Air Resources Board of California reports that even if the sulfur content of diesel fuel required by Proposition No. 9 could be achieved, it would reduce sulfur-dioxide emissions in Los Angeles County by only three-tenths of one percent! What a price you're being asked to pay to accomplish virtually nothing!

Vote NO on Proposition No. 9

CALIFORNIANS AGAINST THE POLLUTION INITIATIVE

870 Market Street, San Francisco, CA 94102
1127 Wilshire Boulevard, Los Angeles, CA 90017

MYRON W. DOORNBOS, President, Southern Council of Conservation Clubs Co-Chairman

Exhibit 5B-8

233

What Happens When You Have to Ration Electric Power?

For three weeks in February, electric power was rationed in England because of a shutdown of coal supplies to fuel generating plants.

The headlines tell the story:

A short period of electric power rationing almost wrecked England's economy.

Can you imagine the effect that **permanent** power rationing—with recurring brownouts and blackouts—would have on the people of California?

IT COULD HAPPEN HERE!

Proposition No. 9, on the June 6 ballot, would ban for five years construction of nuclear power plants, including those now being built.

If our normal power needs could be met at all, they would have to be met by increased reliance on fossil fuel burning steam generating plants, which emit pollutants into the air. Nuclear plants, by contrast, are a **clean** source of electric energy.

Thus, Proposition No. 9, which is promoted by its sponsors as an anti-pollution measure, would **increase** air pollution instead of reducing it. At the same time, it would force upon all Californians the insane risks involved in rationing electric power: widespread unemployment, darkened city streets, the loss of such labor-saving devices as electric stoves and washing machines.

DON'T BLACKOUT YOUR FUTURE!

Vote NO on Proposition No. 9

CALIFORNIANS AGAINST THE POLLUTION INITIATIVE

870 Market Street, San Francisco, CA 94102
1127 Wilshire Boulevard, Los Angeles, CA 90017

DR. EMIL M. MRAK, Chancellor-Emeritus, University of California, Davis
Co-Chairman

Exhibit 5B–9

Part III
Economic, Sociopolitical, and Legal Implications
of Advocacy Advertising

Introduction to Part III

What ails us most is not what we have done with America but what we have substituted for America. We suffer primarily not from our vices or our weaknesses, but from our illusions. We are haunted, not by reality, but by these images we have put in place of reality.

—Daniel J. Boorstin, The Image

The primary rationale for advocacy advertising on the part of corporations rests on the premise that they are being squeezed out of the public communication space by more vocal activists, that their viewpoint is not getting fair exposure. They too have a right to protect their interests, to present their understanding of an approach to a complex social issue in which they have a vital stake, and to refute the allegations of their critics.

To their opponents, the question of overwhelming importance is also access to the public communication space, which would be denied groups unable to match the financial resources of the large corporations. They contend that corporate advocacy advertising is propaganda aimed at brainwashing the public; that such advertising should be prohibited in the case of certain classes of companies and industries because they are regulated; that provision should be made for dissenting viewpoints to be presented to the public; and that society's interests would be better served if people were exposed to all the significant and divergent views on major issues of public policy.

My analysis in the preceding sections leads me to conclude that advocacy advertising, *as it is being currently practiced by major corporations and industry groups, with some notable exceptions, is of largely questionable value and doubtful effectiveness* on economic, sociopolitical, and ideological grounds. Notwithstanding, advocacy advertising can serve a vital function in broadening the area of public debate on issues that are socially important but have been hitherto confined to academic journals, legislative corridors, and committee rooms. With proper safeguards and self-restraints, advocacy advertising can promote greater public awareness of complex issues by making available to larger segments of the public increasing quantities of information of a substantive nature, presented in understandable form.

Even if one were to concede the arguments of the critics as to the one-sidedness of its presentation, advocacy advertising may succeed in elevating the level of open discussion by mobilizing critics to respond to the arguments of business in a manner that is less rhetorical and more factual. Thus advocacy advertising may succeed, despite itself, in fulfilling a public purpose and serving the public interest by encouraging and helping people to make intelligent choices among various options that affect their lives and the very fabric of society.

237

Similarly, it may also help business by making sure that its views are given a fair hearing, and once the social choices have been made, by enabling it to adapt to the new sociocultural environment in a rational manner and without doing irreparable harm to the society's income-producing institutions or the underlying values by which a nation distributes its resources, develops its goals, and plans for its future.

In seeking restraints on corporate behavior, critics place heavy emphasis on legal and regulatory mechanisms that are supposed to inflict financial penalties of varying degrees on the offending corporation. The rationale is that if the penalty for wrongdoing is greater than the alleged gains of the corporation, it will act as a deterrent. However, this is not necessarily the case. It is based on two assumptions about corporate behavior that in real life do not hold true, i.e., the corporation is always a rational (in the economic sense) decision maker and a profit maximizer.[1]

Nor can the law be used to coerce changes in behavior if there is a wide discrepancy between the requirements of the law and the accepted norms of social and peer group behavior. Laws primarily codify current social norms and expectations and seldom lead social change. There are three reasons why laws may lag behind social change and are inadequate as a deterrent or a preventive device to control behavior of individuals or corporations. One, social norms are dynamic in nature and change over time, whereas legal change, which is much more formal, is delayed and must await the enactment of a law or statute. Two, specific social values may contradict each other, whereas there is a presumption of consistency in the legal code. Three, the formal structure of the law confers a degree of social acceptance on the legal code that a social system may not be willing to accord certain activities during a transitional period, although it may tolerate such activities informally, and on a small scale.[2] Thus the coercive aspect of the law may provide a good deterrent for the most blatant sorts of illegal acts. However, these acts may not necessarily be those with the most adverse impact on society. As Christopher Stone comments:

Controlling corporations through law becomes not only . . . a misplaced faith on negative reinforcement . . . but it is also the worst sort of negative reinforcement, one administered almost randomly (or so it seems) by a non-respected source.[3]

The critics of advocacy advertising are primarily concerned with control and enforcement mechanisms in order to narrow the scope of this advertising and increase corporate public accountability in this and other areas. Their ideas can generally be classified into the categories of the tax deductibility argument, and the proof of accuracy or the ad substantiation argument. Businesspeople have argued strongly against any measures that might mean censorship of their message and tend to inhibit free speech and public debate. They opt for the open market test of public acceptance or rejection of their ideas. Both these approaches have certain inherent logic and are not necessarily on the opposite ends of the spectrum. They deserve careful analysis and evaluation.

The ideas set forth here are intended as a framework for discussing various types of strategies to be pursued rather than a specific program of action to be followed. Some of these proposals have already been made by other writers elsewhere and are included here for purposes of evaluation and comprehensiveness. They call for action from both business and other groups, including government, influential in the determination and making of public policy.

Notes

1. Christopher D. Stone, *Where the Law Ends: The Social Conflict of Corporate Behavior* (New York: Harper & Row, 1975), pp. 35-57.

2. S. Prakash Sethi, "Dimensions of Corporate Social Performance: An Analytical Framework for Measurement and Evaluation," *California Management Review*, spring 1975, pp. 58-64.

3. Stone, *Where the Law Ends*, p. 42.

6

The Tax Deductibility Argument

Too many people feel that the government is the handsome young prince and that its kiss of controls will awaken the sleeping beauty of our economy. Personally, I'd rather bite into the poisoned apple of inflation than feel the caress of a government.

> −E. Mendel de Windt,
> chairman of the board,
> Eaton Corporation[1]

Many critics of business have characterized most of the recent corporate institutional advertising, especially by large energy-related corporations, as political in nature, aimed at propagandizing and justifying business's self-interest, and influencing and manipulating public opinion in favor of business-supported legislation. They contend that such advertising should therefore be considered grassroots lobbying as defined by federal laws, court decisions, Internal Revenue Service (IRS) regulations, and Federal Power Commission (FPC) standards for tax and accounting treatment of various operating and nonoperating expenses of the companies it regulates.[2]

The Arguments for Nondeductibility

There is a long legal tradition in the United States that business expenses incurred in both direct and indirect lobbying are considered nondeductible. Prior to 1962, the Treasury Department gave a broad interpretation to what should be considered lobbying expenses. The Supreme Court has also held on various occasions that nondeductibility for tax purposes of promotional expenses related to grassroots lobbying is not a limitation on free speech prohibited by the First Amendment to the Constitution.[3] In justifying the rationale for nondeductibility of grassroots lobbying expenses, the Supreme Court held in the case of

---

Unless otherwise specifically stated, all direct quotes in this chapter pertain to personal interviews or written communications with the author.

241

Cammarano v. *U.S.* that there has been "a continued congressional concern with the use of large sums of money to finance the engineering of consent—to 'make' public opinion on matters of legislation—particularly where large economic interests are on one side of the controversy."[4]

The Revenue Act of 1962 brought about a significant change in the treatment of lobbying expenses under section 162(e). Subsection 162(e) (1) allowed deductions for "direct" lobbying, which is defined as direct appearances, or submission of statements and sending communications to committees or members of legislative bodies with respect to legislation or proposed legislation of direct interest to the taxpayer. Also deductible are dues paid to membership organizations, such as business leagues and labor unions, which are attributable to direct lobbying. At the same time, the law specifically prohibited deductions for grassroots lobbying. Section 162(e)(2)(B) states that expenses incurred "in connection with any attempt to influence the general public or segments thereof with respect to legislative matters, elections, or referendums" are not deductible as ordinary and necessary business expenses. The prohibition also applied to the pro rata dues paid to membership organizations engaged in such activities to any substantial degree.[5]

The current IRS regulations permit the deduction of institutional/goodwill advertising as a business expense provided it is "ordinary and necessary," is intended to "keep the taxpayer's name before the public," and is "related to the patronage the taxpayer might reasonably expect in the future." They specifically permit deductions for advertising expenditures that present views on economic, financial, social or other questions of a general nature, provided such advertising does not involve the type of "grassroots" lobbying prohibited under section 162(e).[6] However, as Lester G. Fant, an attorney with the tax law firm of Cohen & Uretz of Washington, D.C., stated in his testimony before the Senate subcommittee, "The general language that permits deductions for the cost of presenting views on economic, financial or social questions does not override the prohibition against deductions for grassroots lobbying."[7] The IRS regulation states that "expenditures for lobbying purposes, for the promotion or defeat of legislation for political campaigns, or for the carrying on of propaganda (including advertising) relating to any of the foregoing purposes are not deductible from gross income."[8]

Critics have argued that nondeductibility of expenses for grassroots lobbying—in which they include most of the advocacy advertising currently practiced by large corporations and industry associations—is necessary and desirable because it serves the purpose of an established public policy; it is intended to alleviate the inequality in tax treatment between business and nonbusiness interests when engaged in public debate over controversial issues with legislative import; and it makes the tax policy neutral in terms of encouraging or discouraging a certain type of activity.[9] However, as Cooper convincingly argues, the suggested rationale behind the three arguments is analytically weak and internally inconsistent.[10]

Analysis of Nondeductibility Arguments

The *public policy* agrument,[11] which has no basis in the law, has been narrowly applied by the courts in cases where expenditures stem from "activities which, if not clearly illegal, are shocking to the public conscience." Thus while the courts have disallowed payment of criminal fines and bribes, they have permitted deductions of legal expenses incurred in unsuccessfully defending against a criminal charge, thereby making illegal activity less expensive and frustrating public policy.[12] The Supreme Court in the case of *Commissioner* v. *Tellier* affirmed that public policy grounds for disallowing deductions should be invoked only in extremely limited circumstances, where the allowance of a deduction would "frustrate sharply defined national or state policies," and that the "policies frustrated must be evidenced by some *governmental* declaration of them."[13] As Cooper points out, the public policy grounds for disallowance are so weak that the IRS has routinely allowed deductions for treble damage payments by antitrust law violators.[14]

It should be apparent that lobbying itself is neither illegal nor contrary to public policy. The 1962 act legitimizes direct lobbying as a deductible business expense, a form perhaps subject to greater abuses than grassroots lobbying. Therefore, the rationale for disallowance must be sought elsewhere.

The *equilibrium* argument implies that an independent citizen is at a disadvantage compared to a businessperson if the expenses for grassroots lobbying in the latter's case are tax deductible while in the case of the independent citizen they are not. The equilibrium argument in support of nondeductibility was presented in the government's brief in *Cammarano* v. *U.S.*:

At the present time, under the prevailing interpretation of [162], any campaigns financed by industry to influence legislation cannot be charged to the Government by taking these expenses as a deduction. The financing is thus entirely out of pocket of the concerns involved. This is equally true as to any citizens' organizations which might be formed to conduct similar campaigns, since contributions to these campaigns would not qualify as charitable contributions and accordingly are not deductible. The same is true of labor organizations. Thus tax equilibrium exists. If the expenses of the business community were to become deductible, this equilibrium would be upset. While the business community could deduct their expenses, all others could not, *even with respect to the same* legislation.[15]

Cooper, however, considers this argument to be somewhat specious. If equilibrium is indeed intended between business and other competing interests, then deductions should not be allowed for a variety of other activities, such as litigation between the business firm and the individual consumer, or the polluting firm and the citizens' group, and proceedings before such regulatory agencies as the FTC, ICC, and FCC. Second, in allowing business a deduction for direct lobbying expenses while disallowing such deductions for citizens, Congress specifically considered and rejected the equilibrium argument. The deductibility of business expenditures is based upon a reasonable expectation of future earnings. In the case of the individual, the expenditures are incurred for some personal benefit or satisfaction. Since a business *will* pay taxes on future income, tax equilibrium is achieved by *allowing* deductibility.[16]

The equilibrium argument, however, cannot be lightly dismissed. Although the U.S. Congress may have specifically rejected the equilibrium argument in the case of direct lobbying expenses, it does not follow that it should be the case for grassroots lobbying expenses. The differential treatment of various expenses for different classes of taxpayers also implies that certain other expenses could be accorded similar treatment both for individuals and businesses. Moreover, the link between a large part of advocacy advertising expenditures and "a reasonable expectation of future earnings" is at best indirect and tangential. A similar argument can be made in the case of individual taxpayers. Grassroots lobbying activities may also result in legislative activities that would have a positive impact on an individual's income stream.

The tax neutrality argument suggests that government should refrain from encouraging or discouraging such activity through neutral tax provisions. However, in abstract terms, this neutrality would be nullified if all other types of business expenses that may reasonably be expected to generate future earnings are classed as deductible while one particular type, i.e., grassroots lobbying, is classed as nondeductible. *Thus, in case there is indeed a rationale for disallowing deduction, it may be found in disequilibrium, whereby a certain type of activity is consciously discouraged.* It is a course based perhaps on the fear of an aggregation of economic interests that so dominate the public communication space through paid advertising that it is made difficult, if not impossible, for proponents of opposing viewpoints with insufficient or inadequate financial resources to gain a reasonable amount of access to the media.[17] The disproportionate power and influence that a well-organized and financed campaign can exert are amply documented. An individual citizen or even a citizen's group is at a distinct disadvantage against the professional skills and finances of an organized business group. As Fant points out, the preparation and publication of advertisements and other uses of communications media are extremely expensive. A skillful media campaign is one of the most effective means of influencing the affairs of the state. The well-financed supporter of an idea has a built-in advantage in persuading the public to his point of view.[18]

The disequilibrium argument leads one perilously close to the restrictions on free speech that are constitutionally proscribed. A comprehensive analysis of this issue is beyond the scope of this book, but major elements of the problem are presented in Chapter 7, where I analyze the question of requiring proof of accuracy or substantiation of statements for issue-oriented and editorial-type advocacy advertisements. Existing court decisions make nondeductibility of institutional advertising related to grassroots lobbying legal, but the issue is far from settled and future court decisions or legislative action may change the situation.[19] For the present, the discussion is confined to an improvement in the enforcement climate of the existing laws and Treasury Department regulations.

Proposals for Reform by Critics

Critics have argued that one reason for confusion lies in the laxity of the IRS and FPC in the development and enforcement of regulations applicable to institutional advertising. To clarify the situation would require the Treasury Department to take a "strict line in requiring a showing of the relationship between advertising and selling goods."[20] Instead of presuming that goodwill advertising is "generally deductible," the IRS should presume to the contrary, with the burden of proof placed on the advertiser. All goodwill advertising should be treated as "covert lobbying unless it can be shown to have no substantial purpose other than (1) to promote the sale of a taxpayer's goods or services, or (2) to achieve some other ordinary and necessary business goal that properly supports deductions."[21] Various criteria have been suggested to determine if a particular ad is political in nature and involves grassroots lobbying. These incude the following:

1. A reference, explicit or implicit, to some proposal currently pending before a legislative body.
2. An absence of fair and balanced presentation.
3. Existence of real or potential conflict between business and nonbusiness interests on questions of public importance.
4. Likelihood that the subject discussed is suitable for legislative attention, regardless of whether action ultimately results.
5. An invitation to readers or listeners to express their views.
6. The nature of the activity addressed in the ad is such that the disparate financial and organizational resources of business will normally give business excessive power.
7. A person of average intelligence and experience would interpret the advertisement as an effort to gain support for the advertiser's position on some issue appropriate for legislative attention.[22]

In a more general vein, Lester Fant suggests three tests[23] that must be applied to determine whether an advertisement is grassroots lobbying and therefore nondeductible:

1. Content. The advertisement must concern "legislative matter," which is much broader in scope than "legislation or proposed legislation," and under some circumstances may include matters that are not the subject of pending legislation at the time a particular advertisement is run. The objective is to provide a

counterbalance for the superior organizational and financial strengths of the sponsoring business with respect to legislative matters. The need for this offset is as great when business is preparing the public for anticipated legislation as it is when such legislation is actually pending.

In the case of *Consumer Power Company* v. *United States,* the court considered ads published by private companies that related to publicly operated power companies. Some also attacked public power companies as "creeping socialism." Furthermore, although some ads exhorted readers to contact their congressman, others did not. There was no legislation pending at this time to which the ads were related. The court disallowed these expenditures on the grounds that they amounted to grassroots lobbying.[24]

2. Attempting to influence the general public. An advertisement that presents only one side of an issue would appear on its face to be an attempt to influence the general public. However, an advertisement relating to a legislative matter could fairly present all factors relevant to both sides of an issue and thereby serve a purely educational purpose.

3. Seeking financial gain at the expense of the general public. This test is applied to expenditures in connection with matters in which business and a segment of the public at-large conflict, and the advertisement promotes business's selfish interests. Such expenditures should be disallowed as ordinary and necessary expenses for tax purposes.

Problems with the Reform Proposals

The good intentions of the critics notwithstanding, the proposals outlined earlier are of doubtful value both on grounds of operational effectiveness and achievement of objectives. The proposals would impose a heavy burden on the IRS in terms of setting precise rules for determining deductibility that would be general enough to cover broad areas of advertisement content and yet specific enough to be operational. The IRS has had considerable difficulty in determining when to disallow deductions for business expenses in apparently simple cases such as payment of fines. To think that rules could be developed to cover an activity with a high degree of subjectivity of interpretation is to show a lack of understanding of the complexity of the problem and the nature of advertising. Consider, for example, the testimony of Lester Fant, a tax attorney, before Senator Hart's subcommittee. In elaborating on the three tests referred to earlier, he stated that the same ad could be classified as either deductible or nondeductible depending on the specific circumstances of the case, what preceded that particular ad, and the overall communication context within which the ad was presented. Furthermore, he concedes that, given the same set of rules, two experts could classify the same ad differently.

A related problem would be that of the heavy burden imposed on the courts to interpret these imprecise rules. At best, it would prohibit overt grassroots type of advocacy advertising from being deducted as ordinary business expenses. However, this is not the problem area. A major part of advocacy advertising falls in an in-between category in which the ads contain multiple messages, are subject to genuine differences of interpretation, and grassroots lobbying is at best covert. Some ads might become "political" after the fact if they generate public discussion and controversy and make the issue potentially a legislative matter.[a]

The complexity of determing which ads should be considered either totally or partially grassroots lobbying was well brought out in the testimony of various witnesses before Senator Hart's subcommittee. The subcommittee had sent 100 ads to various companies to ask how they would classify them: as the deductible type of institutional/goodwill advertising or as the nondeductible type of political or grassroots lobbying advertising. An analysis by Media Access Project concluded that almost all these ads should be considered political under the law and under Internal Revenue or Federal Power Commission regulations, since they pertained to pending or intended legislation or legislative matter and were therefore designed to manipulate public opinion to influence a legislative matter. But all the companies responding to the subcommittee's inquiries, with the sole exception of Mobil Oil, contended that on the basis of advice from their tax and legal experts, the ads were normal and necessary business expenses and therefore tax deductible or fell in the gray or uncertain area. Herbert Schmertz of Mobil Oil stated in his testimony that Mobil's institutional advertising was divided into groups: Group 1 consisted of ads of the so-called "Red Cross" variety urging viewers to watch Mobil-sponsored shows and programs on public (educational) television networks, support local opera and theater, and donate to other worthy causes. Group 2 dealt with fuel conservation and safe driving, noncontroversial ads about subjects on which the company felt it had some expertise, and whose issues were considered to be in the public interest. Group 3 dealt with issues of a broad socioeconomic nature, such as technology and conservation. Group 4 ads are in the nondeductible category.[25]

---

[a]Harold C. McKenzie of the Georgia Power Company cites one such example. In the Senate hearings, Harvey Shulman had contended that one of Georgia Power's ads explaining the need for rate increase was political because FCC, in 1973, had directed two Georgia stations to provide equal opportunity to opposing viewpoints. The complainant in this case was the Media Access Project, "whose spokesmen publicly acknowledge that the Project's primary goals are the political objectives of the ultimate replacement of capitalism with socialism." McKenzie concluded that while the company made every effort to present opposing viewpoints in its ad program, the Project took every opportunity to politicize the issue. According to McKenzie, "Ironically, the Media Access Project now points to the FCC case as evidence that the subject advertisements are political. In reality, any political connotations which the advertisements may have acquired has been the result of public statements of a political nature by Media Access Project's client in the FCC proceedings, Georgia Power Project. It is patently obvious that in the case of a group with political goals as broad as those of the Georgia Power Project virtually any informational message of substance could be politicized by publicly proclaiming that it is inconsistent with the political goals espoused by such group." Testimony of Harold C. McKenzie, senior vice-president, Georgia Power Company, in *Hearings*, pp. 156–157.

The question of where education ends and lobbying begins is not clear-cut. It is unlikely that any two readers of this book will arrive at a similar conclusion in classifying different advocacy advertisements. Nor is it possible to state clearly what the public interest is when different publics are on the opposite side of the issue or to suggest what to do when public and corporate interests merge. The courts have constantly widened the area of discretion within which corporate management can legally make tax-deductible charitable contributions to causes that benefit the whole society (and therefore all corporations) and within which their relevance to a particular donor is at best tangential and at worst nonexistent. Since business can legitimately argue that these ad programs are indeed in the public interest—no matter how nebulous and farfetched the relationship—one is hard put to deny their contention on a selective basis.

Second, business can argue that corporate survival is not exclusively dependent on the selling of products or services. Traditional public image advertising has been justified on the grounds that it builds goodwill for the company in the minds of present and potential consumers of the company's goods and services. However, since a change in the public perception of a corporation's activities could seriously impair its survival and profitability through increased political and governmental control, advocacy advertising can be legitimately considered a business expense.

Harold Johnson, senior vice-president of American Electric Power, gives his company's ad campaign a good deal of the credit for "persuading the White House, the EPA, and important senators and congressmen to postpone the enforcement of Clear Air Act standards from 1975 to 1985." Mr. Johnson believes that what happens to the economy and how government regulates business can and does affect corporate profits in a major way, and therefore impacts company operations and its survival. An ad campaign designed to correct serious wrongs is of major importance to a company's performance and consequently to the public it serves. Suppose that a relaxation of clean air standards on coal burning environmental standards on coal mining increases the supply of coal and reduces the price paid by the utility by $1 per ton. In 1974 alone, this would have resulted in a saving of $30 million to AEP's customers (see Chapter 4).

In defending Georgia Power's deduction of its institutional ads, Harold McKenzie asserted that dissemination, through advertising, of factual information indicating the nature of present and future financial problems affecting the company and its customers was responsible institutional advertising. It was certainly not "political propaganda [and] we would be guilty of dangerously misleading the public if we remained silent during this period and did not inform our customers of the true circumstances of their supplier of electric energy."[b]

---

[b]*Hearings*, p. 149. McKenzie states: "If the premise is accepted that the public has a right to information which affects them in a direct and meaningful way, the next question is whether it is appropriate to disseminate this information through the traditional advertising media? We have found that the use of our institutional and goodwill advertising is by far the

He also defended the paid advertisement as a more economical form of communicating to the public—customers and investors—and therefore cheaper for the company.

In defending his company's position before the subcommittee, Joseph Dowd of American Electric Power contended that Congress, by broadening the scope of the 1962 law, had indeed encouraged communication to the public of "views on economic, financial, social, or other subjects of a general nature," which was the intent of its ad program. Furthermore, all the cases cited dealt with the Internal Revenue Code of 1939 and Treasury Department regulations promulgated under the IRS code of 1954, both of which had been either overruled or liberalized by Congress in 1962. There are no court decisions under the 1962 law that are now applicable.

The imposition of twin conditions—outlined earlier—as suggested by the critics of corporate advocacy advertising will have the effect of tying down the issue in a bureaucratic and legal morass that might effectively discourage its use by corporations, thereby serving the interests of critics, if this is indeed their objective.[c] The affairs of modern large corporations are so inextricably linked with almost every aspect of our lives that it is hard to imagine that a corporation can indeed fund a worthwhile, and yet socially potent and therefore controversial, issue of public concern which does not affect, however remotely, some aspect of that corporation's activities. A corporation could therefore be accused of engaging in grassroots lobbying regardless of its motives.[d] Ironically, Shulman's analysis of the 100 ads sent by Senator Hart's subcommittee to various corporations makes the same point by showing that with very few exceptions, almost all the ads were classified by him as pertaining to some legislative matter.[26]

However, I do not believe that the corporate critics' primary aim is to inhibit all such advertising, because to do so would be self-defeating. Despite the countless millions of dollars of corporate resources allegedly spent by big business "to propagandize to the public on controversial matters" and charged off as operating expenses, thereby subsidizing them from the public coffers,[27] actual business spending on institutional/goodwill advertising is a very small amount when measured in terms of total advertising expenditures, sales revenues, or net

---

least expensive way for us to communicate. If we sent the individual item of information to each of our customers, the postage cost alone would be more than $100,000."

[c]This was the feeling expressed by Dowd of AEP at the hearings when he stated: "it has been our experience that those who oppose the deductibility of advertising costs or their chargeability above the line are generally also opposed to the substance of those ads." *Hearings*, p. 113. George Cooper does believe that it would not be difficult to formulate rigid rules which could clearly differentiate between political and nonpolitical types of goodwill/institutional advertising. See Cooper, "The Tax Treatment," pp. 851–854.

[d]Cooper disagrees: "Although there is a natural reluctance to risk discouraging public service activities by business, this result should not be too disturbing. Any company sincerely wishing to engage in public service activities should be able to find ample outlet for its wishes in activities which are not legislatively oriented" ("The Tax Treatment," p. 855).

profits. As previously noted, expenditures for institutional advertising by the ten largest corporate advertisers were $85.36 million in 1974. This represented .046 percent of sales and .67 percent of net income for these companies in 1974. Of the ten largest corporations in terms of institutional advertising, eight companies were among the 100 largest national advertisers in 1974. The corporate image advertising expenditures of these eight represented 18.3 percent of their total advertising in 1974.[28]

The next question has to do with what part of this image advertising constitutes grassroots lobbying and is therefore a nondeductible expense for tax purposes. Even if we were to take the midpoint between the claims of the industry spokesmen at the hearings that almost all the advertising expenditures questioned were deductible expenses and the allegations made by Media Access Project that almost none of these were deductible expenses, we are forced to the inescapable conclusion that the amount of money involved in the controversy from the business viewpoint is so small as not to materially affect the decision to undertake such advertising.

For example, McKenzie of Georgia Power stated in his testimony before the subcommittee hearings that his company spent less than one-third of one percent of its revenues in good faith efforts to communicate with customers, investors, and the general public, and he comments that "for a company in an industry as complex as the electric utility industry," such a small expenditure "simply can't be regarded as excessive or unreasonable under any criteria."[29] The reader may remember that advocacy advertising as defined in the first section of this book is much broader in scope and covers all forms of adversary advertising, regardless of to whom or what it is addressed. Thus such a definition would include the ads Shulman and other corporate critics would concede to be part of "ordinary and necessary" business expenses. One example of such a broader notion of advocacy advertising is that conducted by Microdot, Inc., whose company president, through paid newspaper advertisements, warned presidents of medium-sized corporations about the dangers of losing their independence through takeover raids by bigger corporations which may be less efficient and less profitable, and therefore interested in acquiring the assets of smaller, more profitable companies. Another example is that of the advertisements of the National Association of Motor Bus Owners in which the advertisers criticize Amtrak as a high-cost, heavily government-subsidized operation and contend that the need for intercity mass transit can be met far more efficiently and economically through independent bus companies (a specimen ad appears in Appendix 1A).

It should therefore be apparent that where business feels that its future prosperity or indeed survival may depend on ability to communicate its viewpoint and position to the public and to opinion leaders, it is not likely to be deterred by tax considerations. It should also be apparent that business would not like its credibility doubted or its motives suspected when its vital interests are at stake. This is the situation at present. Public opinion polls show a wide-

spread distrust of business on.the part of the general public that is being reinforced by almost daily disclosures of political payoffs or other wrongdoing by
corporations in the United States and abroad. Under these circumstances, it
would not be in the interest of business to create a controversy over the deductibility of advertising expenditures and thereby divert public attention from the
substantive issues being raised in the advertisements. Also bear in mind that
these ads appear in a generally hostile news and editorial environment and are
aimed primarily at informing and influencing opinion leaders, who are generally
well-educated, informed, and skeptical of self-justifying statements served up in
paid advertisements by parties with vested interests.

Businesspeople are quite aware of these handicaps. E.F. Loveland, vice-
president of Shell Oil, states: "It is indeed a sad state of affairs when business
finds it necessary to resort to advertising to clarify important issues affecting its
activities. *Advertising is one of the least effective ways of doing this particular
job*" (Emphasis added).[30] Other spokespeople have also bemoaned the problem
of insufficient exposure of the business position on various issues of public
policy vital to it and have defended the use of paid advertising as the only significant outlet available. They maintain that the public expects to be informed
about the corporation's view of various social problems and what companies are
doing to alleviate them.

John Crichton, president, American Association of Advertising Agencies, in
a letter dated July 16, 1974, to Senator Philip A. Hart, states:

In today's climate, institutional or corporate advertising has become an unavoid-
able way of life for more and more companies if they are to stay healthy and
grow, or sometimes even stay alive. As an indispensable ingredient of corporate
profitability, present and future, institutional advertising is plainly entitled to
treatment as an "ordinary and necessary" business expense which may be deducted from before-tax income.

A reputation for high quality products and services is no longer enough to
guarantee their acceptance in the marketplace. People have come to expect
companies to be good citizens in every sphere of corporate life. One recent study
found that 73% of the group surveyed believed that corporate management
should be committed both to earning a profit and to helping solve social problems. A company's failure to live up to the public's growing demands for social
responsibility may depress sales of its products and services, excellent though
they may be. A poor reputation for good citizenship may also adversely affect
employee morale and productivity, stockholder relations, the price of the company's stock, its ability to secure financing, and its success in recruiting talented
personnel, one of the most critical needs of companies of all sizes.

Silence by a company in the face of attacks upon its policies and practices
is interpreted as an admission of guilt. Corporate advertising provides one avenue
of self-defense, but it is a limited one.[31]

Loveland of Shell Oil states:

Comments printed in editorial columns and aired on daily news programs are far more effective. Lacking ready access to these high impact media, we chose to publish the advertisements in question simply because our critics had been eminently successful in using both the print and electronic media to present their views of our profits to the public. Our advertisements thus were essentially a defensive move designed only to properly balance the perspective on the subject.[32]

Similar views have been expressed by a great many other corporate executives including those from the companies that have advocacy media campaigns currently under way.

Thus it would appear that business has a stake in minimizing controversy over advocacy advertising and also in neutralizing adverse criticism about the financing of advertising programs. The fears of critics about the spending of millions of tax dollars in support of corporate propaganda are likely to be highly exaggerated and may be another form of opposition designed more to gain a tactical victory than correct a grievous wrong. As I have shown, the corporation will avoid taking deductions on advertisements that clearly fall in the category of grassroots lobbying. The critics would be frittering away their meager financial resources and energies by questioning deductibility for advertisements that fall in the gray area. They could perform a more important social function by pursuing strategies to increase their own access to media as well as that of other groups who represent alternative viewpoints, thereby enriching the quality of information available to the public on important issues.

Recommendations for Corporate Action

There is considerable merit in the approach used by Mobil Oil of classifying its institutional/goodwill advertising into deductible and nondeductible categories, and it should be followed by all corporations. This approach involves submitting all ads to an outside counsel for an opinion on deductibility. Moreover, the company has adopted a "conservative standard in determining deductibility under the statutes, regulations, and case law on the subject."[33] Presumably all corporations seek legal advice in determining whether a particular ad expenditure falls within the legal definition of "ordinary and necessary" business expenses. In this case, however, *the emphasis should be not on what ad expenses can be squeezed into the deductibility area, but on what expenses must stay out because they fall in the gray area and therefore may become controversial.* The benefit of the doubt should go against the corporation, because to do otherwise would be counterproductive.

To further improve credibility, the corporation should consider setting up an advisory panel consisting of the corporation's public affairs officer and three outside members, preferably a journalist, an informed citizen, and an educator. The role of this panel would be solely to render advice as to whether or not a particular ad deals with issues that may be construed in the minds of readers as falling within the definition of grassroots lobbying.

It is not inconceivable that these two recommendations could result in more advertisements being classified as nondeductible, thereby obligating companies to incur more expense than otherwise planned. This would, however, be a highly judicious use of funds. There does not seem to be much substance to the argument that such a course would discourage corporate spending in the public interest—an argument not dissimilar to the one advanced to support the deductibility of corporate charitable contributions. To the extent that a corporation wants to claim deductibility for ad expenses it considers in the public interest, it is not unreasonable to expect that these expenses be subjected to public scrutiny. But when business feels that it must inform the public about its notion of what is in the public interest, it should be willing to do so without any support from the federal treasury. If the subject matter of the ads is so vital to corporate survival, the maintenance of a free marketplace for ideas, and the sustenance of democratic institutions as corporate executives repeatedly inform us, then we must conclude that it should be worth their while to disseminate those ideas without any regard for tax consequences. If anything, this course of action should further support a corporation's posture as an institution imbued with public spirit. Furthermore, as Cooper points out, since nonbusiness individuals get no deductions for services performed outside the context of the charitable contribution structure, it is not reasonable to award business a more favored position:

This is not to suggest that business, especially the corporate giants, might not have a degree of public responsibility as a result of its vast power. But it is one thing to recognize this responsibility and quite another to say it is tax deductible. The fact that carrying out this responsibility would be a nonprofit making aspect of corporate activity might well be advanced as precisely the reason why the activity should not be deductible.[34]

Corporations should also seriously consider a suggestion made by Harvey Shulman of Media Access at the hearings—i.e., to label each institutional/goodwill ad as to whether it is treated by the company as deductible or nondeductible. For example, the ad might have a small notation at the bottom as "IRS/ deductible" or "FPC/≠ 930" to indicate that the company considers that ad to be nonpolitical in nature.[35] If the corporation has taken the necessary steps outlined earlier to assure itself of the deductible or nondeductible character of a given advertisement, it should not be unwilling to publicly admit or advertise such a determination for fear that it would prejudice its case before the public or diminish the strength of the arguments made in the advertisement. On the contrary, this action is likely to be viewed by unbiased readers as an indication of the corporation's openness and candidness, and contribute to the positive image of the ad content and the sponsoring corporation. For similar reasons, it would be futile and ill-advised for the corporations to engage in petty arguments, e.g., that they were being singled out for discriminatory treatment by the critics, that such a labeling requirement is unnecessary, or that it should not be accepted because it was suggested by a corporate critic.

Notes

1. E. Mandell de Windt, "Corporate Communications—Top Management Perspective," *Crosscurrents in Corporate Communications: Highlights of the 1975 Fortune Seminar* (New York, 1975), p. 13.

2. U.S. Senate, *Energy and Environmental Objectives, Hearings Before the Subcommittee on Environment of the Committee on Commerce*, Part 2 (Washington, D.C., 93rd Congress, 2nd Session, May 6 and July 18, 1974), pp. 39-67. [Hereinafter cited as *Hearings*.]

3. *Ibid.*, pp. 83-84. See also *Textile Mill Securities Corp.* v. *Commissioner*, 358 U.S. 498 (1959).

4. *Hearings*, p. 51.

5. George C. Cooper, "The Tax Treatment of Business Grassroots Lobbying: Defining and Attaining the Public Policy Objectives," *Columbia Law Review*, 68, 5 (May 1968), 803. See also Treasury Regulation 1. 162-20(c)(4) 1965; Internal Revenue Code of 1954, 162(e)(2).

6. *Hearings*, pp. 43-44. According to the IRS regulations: "A deduction will ordinarily be allowed for the cost of advertising which keeps the taxpayer's name before the public in connection with encouraging contributions to such organizations as the Red Cross, the purchase of U.S. Savings Bonds, or participating in similar causes. In like fashion, expenditures for advertising which present views on economic, financial, social, or other subjects of a general nature, but which does not involve any of the activities specified in paragraphs (b) or (c) of this section for which a deduction is not allowable, are deductible if they otherwise meet the requirements of the regulations under Section 162. Expenditures for lobbying purposes, for the promotion or defeat of legislation for political campaigns (including the support or opposition to any candidate for public office), or for the carrying on of propaganda (including advertising) relating to any of the foregoing purposes are not deductible from gross income. The cost of advertising to promote or defeat legislation or to influence the public with respect to the desirability or undesirability of proposed legislation may directly affect the taxpayer's business."

Expenditures for the promotion or defeat of legislation, in the words of IRS, "Include but shall not be limited to expenditures for the purpose of attempting to: (1) Influence members of a legislative body directly, or indirectly by urging or encouraging the public to contact such members for the purpose of proposing, supporting or opposing legislation; or (2) influence the public to approve or reject a measure in a referendum, initiative, vote on a constitutional amendment, or similar procedure."

7. *Hearings,* p. 83.

8. *Ibid.,* p. 43.

9. Shulman, in *Hearings,* pp. 45, 53-54; see also the statement by Lester G. Fant III in *Hearings,* p. 85, and *Cammarano* v. *U.S.* (1959).

10. Cooper, "The Tax Treatment," pp. 807-816.

11. G.D. Webster, "Deductibility of Lobbying and Related Expenses," *American Bar Association Journal,* 42 175 (1956); G.G. Tyler, "Disallowance of Deductions on Public Policy Grounds," *Tax Law Review,* 20 (1965), 665. Note "Deducting Business Expenses Designed to Influence Governmental Policy as 'Ordinary and Necessary': *Cammarano* v. *United States* and a Bit Beyond," *Yale Law Journal,* 69 (1960), 1017; and "Tax Treatment of Lobbying Expenses and Contributions," *Harvard Law Review,* 67 (1954), 1408.

12. *Commissioner of Internal Revenue* v. *Sullivan,* 356 U.S. 27 (1958); *Commissioner* v. *Heininger,* 320 U.S. 467 (1943).

13. *Commissioner* v. *Tellier,* 383 U.S. 687 (1966).

14. Cooper, "The Tax Treatment," pp. 807-808. See also David B. Weaver, "Taxes and Lobbying—The Issue Resolved," *George Washington Law Review,* 31 (1963), 938.

15. Brief for Respondent, at 12, 35-36 (emphasis in original), cited in Cooper, "The Tax Treatment," p. 810.

16. Cooper, "The Tax Treatment," pp. 810-812.

17. *Ibid.,* pp. 813-816. See also Dean E. Sharp, "Reflection on the Disallowance of Income Tax Deductions for Lobbying Expenditures," *Boston University Law Review,* 39 (1959), 365.

18. Fant in *Hearings,* p. 80. See also Cooper, "The Tax Treatment," pp. 813-816. For a discussion of the power of the corporation, see Phillip L. Blumberg, *The Mega Corporation in American Society* (Englewood Cliffs, N.J.: Prentice-Hall, 1975); Christopher Stone, *Where the Law Ends: The Social Control of Corporate Behavior* (New York: Harper & Row, 1975).

19. For a discussion of the inconsistency of the present deduction disallowance with traditions of free speech, see Cooper, "The Tax Treatment," pp. 830-841. The principal court cases dealing with the issue are *Valentine* v. *Chresetensen,* 316 U.S. 52 (1942); *United States* v. *CIO,* 335 U.S. 106 (1948); *Grosjean* v. *American Press Co.,* 297 U.S. 233 (1936); *Cammarano* v. *United States,* 358 U.S. 105 (1943). See also "Note, Freedom of Expression in a Commercial Context," *Harvard Law Review,* 78 (1965), 1191; "Corporate Political Spending and the First Amendment," *University of Pittsburgh Law Review,* 23 (1962), 847; and "Comment, Constitutional Law—Freedom of Speech and the Corporation, *Villanova Law Review,* 4 (1959), 377.

20. Cooper, "The Tax Treatment," p. 853. See also the testimony of Samuel Black, attorney, Tax Analysts and Advocates, Washington, D.C., in *Hearings,* pp. 136-143.

21. Cooper, "The Tax Treatment," pp. 850–856. See also *Southwestern Electric Power Co.* v. *United States,* 312 F. 2d 437 442 (ct. cl. 1963); *Addressograph-Multigraph Corp.*, 14 P-H TAX CT. MEM. 45,058 (1945).

22. Written statement (pp. 33–34) of Harvey J. Shulman, attorney, Media Access Project, Washington, D.C., before the U.S. Senate Subcommittee on Environment, May 6, 1974. See also Cooper, "The Tax Treatment," and Weaver, "Taxes and Lobbying."

23. *Hearings,* pp. 86–90.

24. *Consumer Power Company* v. *United States,* CA 427 F 2nd 78 (1970).

25. Written statement of Harvey Shulman submitted to the subcommittee. Statement not published as part of the *Hearings Report* but included in the subcommittee records. See testimony by industry executives, namely, Herbert Schmertz of Mobil Oil, Joseph Dowd of American Electric Power, E.F. Loveland of Shell Oil, and Harold C. McKenzie of Georgia Power Company in *Hearings,* pp. 100, 113, 128, 148–149, 156–157.

26. Written statement (exhibits B, D, E) of Harvey Shulman submitted to the Subcommittee *Hearings.* Statement not published as part of the *Hearings Report* but included in the subcommittee records.

27. Shulman, in *Hearings,* p. 44.

28. *Public Relations Journal,* November 1975, pp. 36–37. The corporations are American Telephone & Telegraph, Exxon, General Motors, Shell Oil, Texaco, Phillips Petroleum, General Electric, Mobil Oil, DuPont, and International Telephone & Telegraph.

Sales and net income figures are from "The Fortune Directory of 500 Largest Industrial Corporations." *Fortune,* May 1975, pp. 208ff, and "The Fortune Directory of 50 Largest Utilities," *ibid.,* July 1975, p. 126. The figure that corresponds to sales is designated as Operating Revenues for American Telephone & Telegraph.

"The Top 100 National Advertisers in 1974," *Advertising Age,* June 30, 1975, pp. 3, 56–57. The eight corporations and their rankings among the top 100 national advertisers are General Motors (2), American Telephone & Telegraph (19), International Telephone & Telegraph (37), Mobil Oil (39), General Electric (42), Exxon (73), DuPont (80), and Shell Oil (91).

The total advertising expenditures for the eight corporations in 1974 were $395.7 million.

29. *Hearings,* p. 148.

30. *Hearings,* p. 124.

31. *Ibid.,* p. 196.

32. *Ibid.,* p. 125.

33. *Ibid.,* p. 100.

34. Cooper, "The Tax Treatment," p. 855.

35. *Hearings,* p. 54.

7
Proof of Accuracy or Ad Substantiation
Is It Feasible or Desirable?

The great enemy of clear language is insincerity. When there is a gap between one's real and one's declared aims, one turns as it were instinctively to long words and exhausted idioms, like cuttlefish squirting out ink.

—George Orwell, "Politics and the English Language"

One of the major issues in the debate on advocacy advertising pertains to whether advertisers should be required to provide proof of accuracy as to the statements, and to substantiate the claims, made in their ad copy. For example, both American Electric Power and Mobil were charged in the media by their critics and other commentators for making statements in their ads that were self-serving half-truths and notable more for what they did not say than what they said. It was also contended that hypotheses and opinions were presented as facts although cause and effect relationships were not clearly established. The problem is not confined to advocacy advertising but is, in fact, endemic to all advertising. In the case of advocacy advertising, however, it is critical because of the nature of the issues addressed and the potential for a pervasive and cumulative effect on public opinion and public policy formation.

The issue has three interrelated aspects. The first has to do with whether or not a government agency has the authority, under existing statutes, to control or regulate such advertising. On the surface, it would appear to be a relatively uncomplicated problem. In arguing for tax deductibility for these advertising expenditures, corporations contended that advocacy advertising was primarily commercial speech, and that their expenditures were "ordinary and necessary" ones incurred in the normal course of business. If this contention is accepted, one could then argue that such advertising should be subject to all the relevant statutes against deception in advertising and ad substantiation regulations promulgated by the Federal Trade Commission (FTC).[1] The problem, however, is far from simple. It involves the constitutional question of freedom of speech. American Electric Power and Mobil Oil both claimed their ads to be

---

Unless otherwise specifically stated, all direct quotes in this chapter are from personal interviews or written communications with the author.

accurate but objected to their prior submission to a third party for certification of accuracy.

Next, there are the problems related to enforcement by the FTC or some other governmental agency, e.g., the adequacy of enforcement powers; the availability of financial resources and technical expertise necessary for carrying out an effective enforcement program; and the difficulty in operationally defining, on an a priori basis, what is "deception" and reasonable substantiation or proof of accuracy.

Last, we must also consider the inhibitive effect on the free dissemination of ideas that might be a consequence of imposing arbitrary constraints on the ad content in advocacy advertisements. As I shall demonstrate, it is well nigh impossible to develop reasonably objective measures of proof of accuracy for most advocacy advertising without making them so onerous as to be unimplementable, or ad hoc and therefore capricious. Nor do I believe that such measures are necessary if the objective is to promote public dissemination of opposite viewpoints and ideas. There are other and easier measures that could accomplish the task more effectively. There is also the danger that much will be lost—in terms of the exposition of alternative opinions and viewpoints that advocacy ads generate in the news media through news analysis and editorials.

Advocacy Advertising and Ad Substantiation

The contention that advocacy advertising is commercial speech and should be subject to the ad substantiation requirements of the Federal Trade Commission was expressly made by the Media Access Project in a petition filed before the Federal Trade Commission on behalf of six United States senators and congressmen on January 9, 1974.[2] The petitioners specifically sought (1) an extension of the Federal Trade Commission's advertising substantiation rules to all commercial advertising, (2) making available to the Federal Trade Commission and subsequently to public inspection all information relied upon by *certain* advertisers who made claims in specific advertising attached with the petitions, and (3) the requirement that environmental and energy-related claims in all commercial advertising by oil, utility, and electric appliance firms be substantiated.

To accomplish these objectives, the petition suggested that the provisions of the product advertising substantiation program of the Federal Trade Commision as promulgated in 36 Fed. Reg. 12058 (June 24, 1971, *amended* 36 Fed. Reg. 14680, August 7, 1971) be amended to apply to certain environment and energy-related advertisements and also to the commercial advertising of oil, utility, and electric appliance firms. The changes proposed were these (changes shown in italics):

Definition: Commercial advertisements are those advertisements sponsored directly or indirectly by corporations or other businesses organized primarily to sell goods or services for profit and which have, as their dominant theme, (1) the promotion of the advertiser's goods or services, (2) the promotion of the advertiser's operations, activities, or policies or (3) the giving of advice or information in connection with the use of the advertiser's products or services.

Substantiation Rule: Advertisers shall be required, on demand by the Commission, the owner of any medium which the advertiser proposes to use, or any other interested person to submit to the Commission with respect to any commercial advertisement such tests, studies or other data or information (including testimonials or endorsements) as they had in their possession prior to the time claims, statements or representations were made and which purport to substantiate any claims, statements or representations made in the advertisement regarding (1) the safety, performance, efficacy, quality or comparative price of the product or service advertised, (2) the operations, activities or policies of the advertiser or, (3) any advice or information given to persons in connection with the use of any product or service sold, leased or otherwise provided by the advertiser.

Prohibition: Any commercial advertisement which makes any affirmative misstatement, fails to disclose any material fact, or makes any unsubstantiated claim shall be deemed to be in violation of the prohibition in 15 U.S.C. 45 (a)(6) against "unfair methods of competition in commerce and unfair or deceptive acts or practices in commerce."

Exemption: Advertisements which (1) express, as their dominant theme, one side of a controversial issue of public importance and (2) contain the following explicit statement, prominently displayed: "This is a political advertisement intended to present this business' views on a controversial issue of public importance," shall not be subject to these rules.[3]

The petition charged that during the recent energy crisis, several energy-related industries were chided or formally charged by public officials "with unwise, unethical or illegal practices which have contributed to, or caused, energy shortages in order to increase their economic stranglehold on the energy industry and undermine the recent successes of the environmental movement."[4] It should be noted, however, that no formal proceedings were instituted against any of the companies so charged, and all the court suits were dismissed. In order to counteract these adverse pressures, the industry resorted to a massive advertising and lobbying campaign to create a favorable image of the companies and the industry, to press for the solution of environmental and energy problems through different use and consumption patterns of the products and services sold by the companies, and to advocate the enactment of industry/company-supported environmental and energy-related legislation. The petition cites numerous cases of alleged deception and misrepresentation in the ads of various companies[a] and indicates that the general approach in all the ad programs seems to have been to put the onus for solving the energy crisis on individuals and government agencies

---

[a]The companies whose ads were analyzed in the petition and characterized as containing falsehoods or half-truths included Bethlehem Steel, Potlatch Forests, St. Regis Paper, Shell Oil, Middle South Utilities System, Tenneco, Champion International, Amoco Oil, Mobil Oil, Exxon, Pacific Power and Light, Wheelabrator-Frye, General Electric, and The Southern Company. "Petition Before the Federal Trade Commission," pp. 5–22.

and to argue for further support of the ever-increasing financial needs of the industry so that exploration for and production of more fuel can be accomplished.

FTC's Authority to Act

The petition contended that unfair or deceptive advertising practices fall within the broad prohibitions of section 5 of the Federal Trade Commission Act [15 U.S.C. Sec. 45(a)(6)] wherein the commission is directed by Congress to prevent the use of unfair methods of competition and to protect consumers, manufacturers, and merchants from the deceptive acts or unfair methods of a dishonest competitor. To accomplish these ends, the commission is empowered to promulgate rules such as those proposed by the petitioners.[5] The FTC's advertising substantiation program, hitherto applied only to product claims, is applicable with greater force to claims and statements made in image or informational advertising because such advertising is capable of injury to consumers and competitors. Since the public currently holds the industry in low esteem, it would look askance at a company making environment-related claims if they could not be substantiated. Similarly, the public would be more willing to favor the honest company which is willing to substantiate its claims.[6]

Exempted Advertisements

The petitioners recognized that certain advertisements may have as their dominant theme the expression of a corporate viewpoint on controversial issues of public importance facing public officials. They proposed that such advertisements should be afforded First Amendment protection.[7] However, in order to express the intent of the advertiser and also inform potential readers, including purchasers, investors, and employees, such ads should be expressly labeled as follows:

This is a political advertisement included to present this advertiser's views on a controversial issue of public importance.[8]

Public Reporting and Disclosure

One of the purposes of FTC's product-related ad substantiation program and its public disclosure requirements was to assist consumers in making rational choices among competing products. The extension of this objective to image advertising would encourage "consumers, business people and *public interest groups* to aid the Commission, which has limited resources, in detecting violations of Section 5" [Emphasis added].[9]

Mobil's Response

In response to the petition, Mobil Oil filed a memorandum before the commission urging it to reject the petition on the grounds that it raises serious questions of First Amendment rights of freedom of speech and that as presently envisaged its application would be arbitrary and capricious. Mobil felt that it would be detrimental to the public interest to inhibit a fuller discussion of ideas regarding the energy crisis. A substantiation program would permit the Federal Trade Commission to question and challenge controversial views. The Constitution and a legion of decisions by the courts have made it clear that such an intrusion cannot be permitted because of its chilling effect on the free expression of ideas.[10] The freedom of speech argument is more generic in nature and will be dealt with in a subsequent section. The remainder of Mobil's arguments are briefly discussed here.

Mobil contended that traditional First Amendment doctrine precluded government restrictions on the exercise of free speech, except in the area of purely commercial speech. The company suggested that FTC's current ad substantiation rule was consistent with these principles in that it applied only to claims which related to some aspect of the product advertised. The petition's application "would obliterate this line on a sweeping basis by applying *a substantiation requirement to a category of claims including, inter alia, those whose dominant theme relates to the 'operations,' 'activities' or policies of the advertiser*" [Emphasis added].[11] The scope of such a ruling would be so broad that many forms of speech far removed from product solicitation might be covered: "For every potential untruthful claim which will be revealed or discouraged by such a rule, the expression of untold numbers of honestly held beliefs will be discouraged by the prospects of a substantiation requirement to be followed by a Section 5 proceeding where substantiation is deemed inadequate."[b] Mobil also contended that the application of ad substantiation rules to oil companies alone while excluding their critics would be one-sided and unfair:

Those who have publicly criticized the oil companies . . . have not been subjected to any requirement of substantiation. . . . [However], if Mobil wishes to defend its policies against the barrage of publicity leveled against it, the company must be prepared to substantiate each and every element of its defense. . . .[12]

The company objected as well to the provision in the petition whereby re-

---

[b]"Mobil's Memorandum Before the Federal Trade Commission," pp. 13–14. Mobil recognized the fact that petitioners did not seek substantiation for advertisements whose dominant theme concerned one side of a controversial issue of public importance. However, the company maintained that there was no clear line, where the energy crisis was concerned, between advertising which expresses a corporate viewpoint on controversial issues of importance facing public officials, on the one hand, and advertising which centered around the discussion of an oil company's operations or policies. Yet the petitions proposed a rule that would cover the latter, but not the former.

quirements of ad substantiation could be provoked by the commission's staff or "any interested person. This would in effect mean any person who disagreed with Mobil's policies or ideas could trigger regulatory action."[13] Thus it would appear that the corporate critics, regardless of the basis of their constituency or soundness of their criticism, could constantly harass a company by demanding substantiation while at the same time being completely free to make irresponsible claims. The solution, according to Mobil, was not to impose impediments to industry's exercise of free speech but to give Mobil and its critics greater access to the public for the expression of their various viewpoints. This would be in the best public interest.

FTC's Decision

On April 29, 1975, the Federal Trade Commission rendered its decision. It decided against taking any policy decision at that time and on the basis of that application. The commission stated that the constitutional test to be applied to any particular corporate image advertisement was whether the dominant appeal and likely effect of the advertisement was commercial, i.e., on the sale of goods and services. The FTC had ample authority to investigate any violations under sections 6, 9 and 10 of the Federal Trade Commission Act. However, corporate image advertising[14] involved substantial questions under the First Amendment where truth or falsity of a statement was not the sole test. The free speech guarantee required that government regulation allow breathing room for the expression of views on public issues. Under these circumstances, the commission believed it unnecessary to adopt a rule prohibiting advertisements that made affirmative misstatements, failed to disclose material facts, or made unsubstantiated claims.[15]

According to the FTC staff study, the commission had the responsibility to prevent deceptive and unfair practices with respect to corporate image advertising[16] and stated that "corporate image advertisements not protected by the First Amendment within the commission's jurisdiction which convey a deceptive or unfair image of the advertiser are cognizable under Section 5."[17] Although such advertising may not be selling directly any product or service of the corporation, it is placed for, and yields to the corporation directly or indirectly, economic benefit. The staff report contended that consumer interests were indeed affected by corporate image advertising and therefore the public interest would be served by encouraging full accountability by maintaining legal standards for corporate image claims, especially with respect to claims regarding corporate social responsibility. The staff statement then outlined some criteria by which it would determine at what point corporate image advertising moves from the economic domain, in which it is subject to regulation, to the First Amendment protected area of free speech. These criteria and their implications will be discussed in a later section, where we deal with the issues of the regulation and enforcement requirements of ad substantiation as applied to corporate image advertising.

Commercial Speech and the First Amendment

One of the major concerns with respect to requiring substantiation for corporate image advertising pertains to the First Amendment guarantees of free speech. This section is devoted to a brief discussion of the legal issues involved, analysis of various court decisions, and their application to the present study.

Despite a long string of court decisions, the fundamental question remains unsettled: to wit, whether commercial speech is an inferior form of speech and therefore should not enjoy the full protection of the First Amendment accorded free speech. One viewpoint is that the status of commercial speech as an inferior form of speech has been clearly established and the unsolved issues are those of definition, namely, when does pure speech become "primarily" or "secondarily" commerical speech? Should the sponsorship of the speech and the motives of the sponsor make any difference in determining whether or not a commercial speech is pure speech and therefore protected under the First Amendment guarantees? Or, should the content of the speech itself be the determining factor? It should be apparent that these definitions are not easily established, and therefore successive court decisions seem to have been made on an ad hoc basis, and appear to lack internal consistency or logic. For these and other similar reasons, the supporters of commercial speech argue that the perils to the guarantees of the First Amendment and its objectives of developing a free marketplace of ideas are so ominous in any attempts at fine tuning the definition of commercial speech that all commercial speech should be afforded the full protection of the First Amendment.[18]

The phenomenon of advocacy advertising has escalated the tension between the freedom of speech guaranteed by the First Amendment and the regulation of commercial advertising which is the FTC's obligation. In the evolution of the legal precedent a distinction has been made between commercial speech, which due to its ties to economic activity is regulated,[c] and political or pure speech, which enjoys the freedom guaranteed it by the First Amendment.[19]

Redish,[20] along with many other scholars, has criticized the cursory and inconsistent treatment meted out to commercial speech by the Supreme Court.

---

[c]Thomas Emerson, a leading scholar of the First Amendment, suggests that since commercial speech is associated with selling of goods and services, its status is necessarily linked with property rights rather than the First Amendment rights. He argues that "communications in connection with commercial transactions generally relate to a separate sector of social activity involving the system of property rights rather than free expression." *Toward a General Theory of the First Amendment* (1966), p. 105.

He traces the Court's negative approach toward commercial speech initially to the influence of the writings of Alexander Meiklejohn. Meiklejohn starts with the premise that the essence of political freedom is self-government, where the people are governors as well as the governed. Therefore, to protect the right of self-governance, it is important that we guard "those activities of thought and communication by which we 'govern.'"[21] Although this speech is accorded the absolute protection of the First Amendment, he draws a sharp distinction between it and "private speech," which should be protected under the due process clause of the Fifth Amendment. However, he makes it clear that such protection does not reach the absolute status held by political speech aimed at self-governance.

It remains unclear how one might go about determining different gradations of political speech and private speech. Nor can it be stated that *all* political speech assists in the self-governing function and no private speech performs such a function. In a world where increased complexity of economic affairs is becoming the dominant concern of political decision making, it would be difficult to separate those aspects of private speech that might be self-serving from those that might be informative for the people and thereby aid them in their self-governance function. As Emerson puts it, the premise behind the people's ability at self-government is that

The soundest and most rational judgment is arrived at by considering all facts and arguments which can be put forth in behalf of or against any proposition.... Hence an individual who seeks knowledge and truth must hear all sides of the question, especially as presented by those who feel strongly and argue militantly for a different view. . . . Conversely, suppression of information, discussion or the clash of opinion prevents one from reaching the most rational judgment, blocks the generation of new ideas, and tends to perpetuate error.[22]

The leading decision for the Supreme Court's distinction between commercial and noncommercial speech is that of *Valentine* v. *Chrestensen*,[23] in which a New York City municipal ordinance forbidding the distribution of commercial leaflets was held valid, thereby denying Mr. Chrestensen's right to distribute such leaflets although he had printed a political protest on the other side of the handbills. The Court held that the handbills were "purely commercial advertising" and that political protest was simply a ruse to escape from the application of the law.[d] Since then a string of court decisions has attempted to clarify

---

[d]The Supreme Court decision stated: "We need not indulge in nice appraisals based upon subtle distinctions in the present instance. It is enough for the present purpose that the stipulated facts justify the conclusion that the affixing of the protest against official conduct to the advertising of the circular was with the intent, and for the purpose, of evading the prohibition of the ordinance." 316 U.S. 55 (1942).

However, the dilemma of distinguishing between primary and secondary purposes was correctly anticipated early by Appeals Court Judge Clark, when in a dissenting opinion he sided with Chrestensen. The facts of the present case notwithstanding, Judge Clark felt that distinctions between protected and unprotected speech. The issue remains as unclear as ever, but based on these decisions, certain generalizations can be made as to the nature and degree of protection afforded commercial speech.

The Primary Purpose Test

The test of "primary purpose" established in *Valentine* v. *Chrestensen* was reaffirmed in subsequent cases. In one case, the source of the advertising was considered the determining factor and it was held that advertising on the back of religious handbills was protected.[24]

However, the mere fact that communication is paid advertising does not automatically preclude it from the protection of the First Amendment. In the case of *New York Times* v. *Sullivan*[25] false statements contained in a political advertisement placed in *The New York Times* were claimed as protected speech. The Court found that the profit motive was not sufficient to classify the advertisement as commercial speech, "That the *Times* was paid for publishing the advertisement is as immaterial in this connection as is the fact that newspapers and books are sold."[26] More important than the commercial nature of the communication, said the Court, was that the advertisement "communicated information, expressed opinion, recited grievances, protested claimed abuses and sought financial support on behalf of a movement whose existence and objectives are matters of the highest public interest and concern."[27]

The Economic Test

The mere presence of economic motive or interest in a message does not bar it from the First Amendment protection. In *Ginzburg* v. *United States,* the Court stated that "commercial activity, in itself, is not a justification for narrowing the protection of expression served by the First Amendment."[28] Examples of freedom of speech or expression, which is economic-related and yet protected speech, are those of picketing and labor presentations in connection with union-employer contests,[29] commercial distribution of motion pictures,[30] the distribution of religious handbills containing advertising to sell religious literature,[31] and commercial publishing.[32] Conversely, First Amendment rights are not violated by government regulation of false and misleading advertising where the risks to the public are often only minor economic risks.[33]

---

a mechanical and nonquantitative measure of comparison between commercial and noncommercial speech would be arbitrary, the only other alternative being looking into the motives of the distributor. However, he felt that such a "primary purpose" test would give a broad and potentially dangerous dimension to the police power of that state. Redish, "The First Amendment in the Marketplace," pp. 449–451. See also *Chrestensen* v. *Valentine*, 122 F. 2d 511, 515–516 (2d Cir. 1941).

The Matter of Public Importance Test

The mere fact that an advertisement does deal with matters of public importance does not render it a priori immune to regulation. In a 1973 case, *Pittsburgh Press Co.* v. *Pittsburgh Commission on Human Rights,*[34] the Supreme Court was offered an opportunity to clarify the distinction between protected and un-protected commercial speech. However, instead of abandoning the pure speech/commercial speech distinction, the Court simply reaffirmed the distinction without at the same time clarifying it. In the case, in which complaint was made against the distinction of help wanted advertising between male and female categories, such advertisements were considered by the Court "classic examples of commercial speech." The Court decided that such sex designations would not be allowed, and in allowing regulation of the material, gave new strength to the argument that purely commercial speech is not entitled to the protection of the First Amendment. The Court stated that although commercial advertising serves as a medium for exchange of information, it is not sufficient ground to abrogate the distinction between commercial and other speech.

In a different situation, the Supreme Court held that a ban on all cigarette advertising on television did not violate the First Amendment rights of the advertisers, despite the fact that cigarette advertising had earlier been held as stating one side of a controversial issue of public importance under the fairness doctrine. Nor was the fact that an allegedly defamatory statement was of "public or general concern" a sufficient cause to bar a defamation action.[35]

The "Good Faith" Test

In many cases, the courts have denied a communication First Amendment pro-tection where advertising claims were based on superstition or religious belief, either by sidestepping the religious issue by denying the existence of its rele-vance to the case or indicating that a fraud was committed because of the advertiser's lack of good faith.[36] Where pure speech is involved, however, value judgments as to its truth or attractiveness are not grounds for regulation. The Supreme Court has held that "the constitutional protection of the First Amend-ment does not turn upon the truth, popularity, or social utility of the ideas and beliefs which are offered."[37]

The Means of Delivery Test

In general, the Court has upheld prior nondiscriminatory restrictions on certain forms of delivery of a commercial message such as door-to-door canvassing, street distribution of handbills, and billboards. Also, restrictions have been held to be reasonable where the advertiser is using obscene language or excessive noise. However, the Court has not held similar restrictions to be valid where a particular form of communication may be "essential to the poorly financed cases of little people,"[38] although there was an expression of concern for the protection of broadcasts in the public interest by religious, social, or political groups.

The preceding discussion should make it clear that while denial of First Amendment protection to commercial speech may have been well established, the definition as to what is commercial speech is far from settled. Until there is a definitive agreement on this issue, the comment made by Justice Douglas in the 1959 *Cammarano* decision still seems appropriate: "The [Valentine] ruling was casual, almost offhand. And it has not survived reflection."[39]

In 1971, Justice Douglas asserted that subsequent Supreme Court decisions had eroded Valentine to the extent that a commercial *form* of publication did not negate the applicability of the First Amendment. Nor did he consider commercial *content* to be the controlling factor:

The language of the First Amendment does not except speech directed at private economic decision-making. Certainly, such speech could not be regarded as less important than political expression. When immersed in a free flow of commercial information, private sector decision-making is at least as effective an institution as are our various governments in furthering the social interest in obtaining the best general allocation of resources.[40]

It now appears that the Supreme Court may be getting ready once again to tackle the issue of defining the permissible constraints on purely commercial speech and the extent to which it is protected under the First Amendment guarantees of free speech. The Court recently voided portions of the New York State's fair campaign practices act—including portions that forbid a candidate to make racial attacks on another candidate or to misrepresent deliberately an opponent's qualification, contending that these restrictions "do not regulate only unprotected expression and are unconstitutionally overbroad and vague on their fact, but create 'substantial chill' and have significant likelihood of deterring protected First Amendment speech."[41] In another decision, the Court has held that provisions of the Federal Election Campaign Act that put limits on campaign expenditures by candidates for federal office or by other individuals to advocate election or defeat of candidates are void, "since those provisions place substantial and direct restrictions on the ability of candidates, citizens, and associations to engage in protected political expression, restrictions that the First Amendment cannot tolerate."[42] Thus the Court declared that spending money in politics is "speech" and protected by the First Amendment.

In the area of commercial speech, the Court voided a Virginia law that prohibited advertising of abortion services. In this case, the state of Virginia had tried to stop a local newspaper from publishing an ad for a New York abortion referral service.[43] As Justice Harry A. Blackmun put it:

To the extent that commercial activity is subject to regulation, the relationship of speech to that activity may be one factor, among others, to be considered in weighing the First Amendment interest against the government interest alleged. The relationship of speech to the marketplace of products or of services does not make it valueless in the marketplace of ideas.[44]

Thus the Court seems to have come closer to narrowing, if not completely removing, the limits on distinctions between "commercial" and "pure" speech.

In still another case with far-reaching impact on commercial speech, the Court held that commercial speech was not wholly outside the protection of the First and Fourteenth Amendments. Just because the advertiser's interest in a commercial speech was purely economic, it did not disqualify him from protection under the First and Fourteenth Amendments. Both the individual consumer and society in general may have strong interests in the free flow of commercial information.[45] In this case the Virginia Citizens Consumer Council and the state AFL–CIO challenged a regulation by the State Board of Pharmacy that prohibited any druggist from advertising prescription drug prices. The Consumers Council claimed that this ban violated the consumer's "right to know," while the state board argued that such regulations were intended to protect consumers from overpromotion to buy unnecessary drugs. The distinguishing feature of this case was that First Amendment protections of commercial speech were accorded not only to the speaker and the communication but to the recipient of the information, thereby extending the principle previously held in the case of pure speech.[46]

The Court voided the Virginia State Board of Pharmacy regulation which prohibited pharmacists from advertising the prices of prescription drugs. Writing for the majority, Justice Blackmun stated that there was *no* commercial speech that lacked all protection. That no line can ever be drawn between publicly "interesting" or "important" commercial advertising and the opposite kind. That free flow of commercial information, even an individual advertisement, may be of general public interest and may serve as an instrument to enlighten public decision making in a democracy—the intended purpose of the First Amendment. The Court held that some regulations on commercial speech, e.g., time, manner, and place restrictions, were still permissible "provided that they are justified without reference to the content of the regulated speech, that they leave open ample alternative channels of communication of the information."[47]

The FTC and the Enforcement of an Ad Substantiation Program

In the previous section it was noted that FTC had for the time being declined to institute action requiring substantiation of claims made in advocacy type advertisements. The FTC staff report had claimed that FTC indeed had the authority to proceed against corporate image advertisements which convey a deceptive or unfair image of the advertiser. However, the recent Supreme Court decisions indicate that such authority as applied to advocacy-type image advertisements is likely to be of doubtful validity.

The question, however, still remains as to what the impact of the FTC's potential enforcement requirements and procedures would be if some regulation of advocacy advertising is found to be constitutionally valid. Since image advertising is not currently subject to the FTC's substantiation requirement, we can draw some conclusions by considering the FTC's ad substantiation efforts in the area of product and service advertising.

Section 5 of the Federal Trade Commission Act of 1914, as amended, provides the basic mandate for FTC's activities and directs the Commission to prevent "unfair or deceptive acts or practices" as well as "unfair methods of competition."[48] Section 12 further provides that section 5 is violated whenever an advertisement is misleading in a material aspect. The objective of the program is to ensure that purchasers can be reasonably expected to compare the ad claims made by the advertisers and thus make informed choices in making product purchases. The advertisers are held to be in violation of the Federal Trade Commission Act if affirmative product performance claims are made without a reasonable and factual basis to substantiate them.[49]

Despite its potential for protecting the consumer through better information, the success of the ad substantiation program has lagged considerably behind its promise. One can therefore reasonably raise the question of the wisdom of the FTC or even some other government agency's involvement in regulating corporate advocacy advertising, with all that it entails. The program has had problems with product advertising, where definitional questions are supposedly less ambiguous, product claims more specific and therefore ascertainable, and public interest more clearly defined.

The Federal Trade Commission had expected that the ad substantiation program would (1) act as a deterrent to potential violators, (2) enable consumer and public interest groups actively to monitor the data on the public record and encourage them to alert the commission to any discrepancies between the ad claims and the substantiating documentation, and (3) strengthen competition in the marketplace by encouraging companies to challenge one another's ads on the basis of substantiation filed with the commission.[50]

The program, however, has bogged down in the masses of data furnished the commission by the corporations that have far outstripped the commission's ability to evaluate them both in terms of manpower resources and technical competence. Miles Kirkpatrick, then chairman of the Federal Trade Commission, stated in the Senate hearings that few members of the public used the opportunities offered them to study these materials, and where an effort was made, it was generally found that the supporting documents were too lengthy and too complicated to be comprehended by ordinary people. Nor did competitors come forward to challenge one another on the discrepancies in their respective ad claims. The only hopeful prognostication made by Kirkpatrick was that in view of the commission's substantiation program, advertisers were likely to be more careful about making performance claims in their ads.[51] The evidence on which such a hope is based is still largely conjectural, and it is doubtful whether it can indeed by generated.

The need for fairness in treatment, procedural delays, and the necessity of time-consuming evaluation of masses of technical data create an enormous time gap between the time of the initial request and final action. A time span of one to three years is not at all uncommon or considered unreasonable. Cases like those of Geritol and Carter's Pills took between 8 and 16 years to resolve.[52] The only publicly available systematic assessment of the FTC's ad substantiation was carried out by the GAO (Government Accounting Office) in 1972.[53] In a report to the Senate Commerce Committee, the GAO stated that the primary purpose of the ad substantiation program was to alert the public, the business community, and the commission to unsubstantiated advertisements.[54] For a variety of reasons, however, this mission was not fulfilled. The report concluded:

1. The FTC had only limited capabilities for evaluating technical data.
2. The nature of the program was such that other government agencies such as FDA could not rely upon it to serve their needs in the area of consumer protection. Most government agencies contracted by GAO expressed no interest in the data released by the FTC to the public.
3. An extremely small number of consumers made use of the FTC data. This may have been due to their technical nature, lack of analysis of summarization prior to release, or the fact that the data were outdated by the time they were released to the public.
4. Most consumer interest organizations contacted by the GAO stated that they were aware of the FTC's ad substantiation program but had no interest in making use of the data.

Richard Herzog, assistant director of the FTC's National Advertising Program, suggests that there has been a significant improvement in the ad substantiation program since the GAO report. Late in 1973, the commission instituted a complete and substantial revision of the ad substantiation program. One of the aspects of this revision was "to emphasize the law enforcement aspect of the ad substantiation program."[55] There were approximately 200 ad substantiation orders issued between 1971 and 1973. Of these only 8 or 10 percent resulted in cases. The number of ad substantiation orders since has been drastically reduced. As of January 1974, 30 ad substantiation orders have been issued, of which 9 have resulted in cases. Herzog also indicates that outside experts are now being increasingly used "in choosing the subjects of request, in the actual development of the technical questions to be directed to the advertiser, and in the evaluation of the materials preferred by the advertiser to substantiate the claim."

In a statement before the House Subcommittee on Commerce, Consumer and Monetary Affairs, FTC Chairman Calvin J. Collier stated that since January 1, 1975, the Division of National Advertising had received approximately 43,000 advertising-related citizen complaint letters. This compared with 8 national advertising-related public interest group petitions and between 10 and 15 national advertising-related complaints from competitors. However, in no instance did a citizen's complaint letter, a public interest petition, or complaint from a competitor result in the opening of an entirely new investigation into a matter that was not already a subject of interest to the staff. Collier also continued to hope as did his predecessor, Lewis Engman, that by making ad substantiation material available to consumers, it would aid them in evaluating for themselves the validity of advertisers' claims.[56]

While there has been a significant improvement in the execution of the program within the FTC, no data are publicly made available by FTC to evaluate its overall effectiveness or the quality and quantity of new information available to the public as a result of FTC's activities in the ad substantiation area. It is also not known how many consumers or public interest groups asked for ad substantiation data or made use of it. Such an evaluation is particularly important, since according to Herzog the commission's fundamental role is that of "the control of future conduct."

The unintended effect of the program has been an overemphasis on whether a given ad would pass the "legal" test, and not whether its claims are any more sound than before. Trappings often seem to obscure purposes. The need for elaborate documentation and the procedural delays with their associated costs in money and time may lead advertisers to resort to inane claims, thereby removing even more information content from the ad messages.

In an analysis of FTC's activities related to advertising regulation, Richard Posner showed that the commission's actions in the substantiation area were more likely to lead to a reduced flow of information and products to the consumer. The requirements for substantiation were so onerous that they were apt to discourage the advertising of claims that were costly to substantiate. The cost burden would fall more heavily on new products and new firms.[57] The commission hopes to correct this situation in the future as a result of the institution of the Policy Planning Protocols. The commission states that for a reasonable period of time following the introduction of a new feature or a new model, it will accept as a basis for the claims made for that product generally recognized scientific principles, provided the company immediately undertakes either scientific or engineering tests or user surveys that are capable of substantiating these claims.[58]

When it comes to developing standards for affirmative disclosure of aspects of products performance, Chairman Collier concedes that FTC has made very limited progress because of substantial technical difficulties in developing valid measures of performance or even the technical tests themselves.[59] If this is true for product-related advertising claims, one cannot help but be extremely cautious in suggesting that the commission launch similar actions in the case of image advertising in general and issue-oriented or advocacy advertising in particular.

Clearcut cases of misrepresentation or deception in advertising are identifiable, and few reputable corporations with nationally advertised brands are likely to resort to such practices intentionally where millions of dollars in sales and earnings are at stake and where the reputation of a given brand has been built over time. The problem lies in the major gray area where persuasion is subtle and the benefits alleged are essentially psychological. According to Posner's analysis

only a small fraction of the Federal Trade Commission's activities in the false-advertising area is consistent with a proper allocation of commission resources, considering the character of the false-advertising problem and the limitations of the commission's sanctions.[60]

The scope and enormity of the task that the commission has set for itself in the area of product and service advertising should be apparent and make the reasons for the comparative lack of effectiveness obvious. I am not, it must be emphasized, denying the need for FTC's police powers to monitor the deception in ads or to prosecute those who make fraudulent claims. Nor is there opposition to the ad substantiation program and its intentions among responsible industry organizations such as the Association of National Advertisers and the American Advertising Federation.[61] However, given the apparent limitations on the commission's ability to develop and manage an effective product advertising substantiation program, the wisdom of further expansion into advocacy advertising should be seriously questioned. In the latter case, the need for such a program is not clearly established, the scope of the commission's authority is vague, and the problems of enforcement appear insurmountable.

Analysis and Evaluation of FTC Staff Report and Other Proposals Requiring Substantiation for Corporate Image Advertising

Despite the problems encountered in interpreting and enforcing the substantiation requirement, the FTC staff report recommends that the commission proceed against unfair or deceptive corporate image advertising in situations where the dominant appeal and likely effect of the advertisement is commercial. Both American Electric Power and Mobil Oil have stated that their advocacy ads

are accurate and could be substantiated but have argued against such requirements on constitutional grounds.

However, since the issue is far from settled, an analysis of its implications is
in order. The FTC staff report suggests that in determining whether a corporate
image advertisement has a dominant commercial appeal and likely effect, the
following factors should be considered:

1. Whether the claims in the ad consist of claims relating to the sponsoring
   corporation's own activities as distinguished from assertions of fact, opinion,
   or views about general subjects or conditions
2. Whether elements typically found in the corporation's product advertisements—for example, logos, tag lines—are also present in the ad
3. Whether the corporation sells consumer products under a brand name identifiable or identical with that which appears in the ad
4. Whether the dominant purpose of the advertiser in disseminating the advertisement is economic
5. Whether persons viewing the ad are likely to perceive it as the expression of
   fact, views, or opinions with respect to a public issue
6. Whether the advertisement contains a reference to or depiction of any product or service in which the sponsor has a financial interest[62]

In a somewhat similar vein, Bird, Goldman, and Lawrence suggest the following criteria for determining whether a statement comes within the control
powers of the FTC:

1. The statement must have a tendency to deceive or be unfair to that segment
   of the public that receives it.
2. It must pertain to interstate acts.
3. The proportion of the population likely to be affected by the statement
   must be significant, i.e., the scope of control must be public concern rather
   than purely private interest.
4. The objectionable portion of the statement must not be trivial or insignifi-
   cant but must form the substance of the statement.[63]

Bird et al. suggest that we should discard those criteria which have been traditionally and historically used to distinguish between commercial speech and pure
speech. (See the section on commercial speech and the First Amendment.) They
contend that these criteria are either inadequate or unenforceable.[64] Instead,
they recommend a marketplace test as a guideline to FTC action. In order for
the advertisement to fall under FTC responsibility, they suggest that "the false,
deceptive, misleading, or unfair portion of the advertisement must have an
appreciable effect on the marketplace appeal of the advertiser's product or

service." The two requirements would be, first, "the questioned matter must pertain to the business of the advertiser . . . this requirement . . . recognizes the right of a company to argue public issues not directly related to its business." They suggest a further requirement, which must accompany the one above, that "the reasonable and natural consequences of using the deceptive or unfair material in the advertisement must be to influence the public or contribute *directly* [emphasis supplied] to the financial improvement of the advertisers position." This position is more lax toward advertisers than that taken by the FTC.[65]

Charles Ludlam[66] also argues for the Federal Trade Commission to assert jurisdiction because otherwise the vast majority of corporate image advertising will go unregulated. He feels that industry self-regulation has not worked and that other federal regulatory agencies like the FDA and SEC can play only a limited role. He also states that the alternative of using counteradvertising in broadcast media has been denied by the Court in *CBS* v. *Democratic National Committee,* and that the application of the "fairness doctrine" to image advertising is likely to be severely restricted where the issue treated is of a commercial nature. He also maintains that the FTC's role is primarily the regulation of economic relations, and therefore it would not be appropriate for the FTC to attempt to regulate image advertising by, for example, the Friends of the Earth, which has run ads against offshore drilling.

It would thus appear that the proponents of government regulation of corporate image advertising, especially as it relates to advocacy advertising, are simply begging the question rather than answering it. Their position presupposes the existence of substantial and widespread deception and unfair presentation of facts in corporate image advertising. This supposition in turn is based on the assumption that "deception" can indeed be precisely defined when applied to opinion or issue-oriented advertising messages, and further that such application to individual cases would not be so bogged down in procedural and judicial delays as to have a "chilling effect" on the free expression of ideas in the marketplace. The case for the regulation falls on all three grounds.

Deception and Unfair Practice as Applied to
Advocacy Advertising

In the context of product advertising, FTC considers deception on the basis not of what the advertiser did or said, but instead on how an advertisement was perceived by the receiver of the message. According to Richard Herzog of the Federal Trade Commission

The fact is that most of our advertising disputes within the last few years have concerned not the adequacy of substantiation but the meaning of the ad. . . . I strongly suspect that one of the reasons these problems [ad substantiation disputes with the industry] arise is because the technical people, when they are asked whether the ad is supported by the substantiation, are shown the ad rather than the various *meanings* that the ad has the capacity or tendency to convey to the consumer.[67]

Thus consumer perception becomes the ultimate standard in determining what claims are made in an ad. The emphasis is on the net impression left by an ad as distinct from the literal meaning of the words.

Limited space does not allow a discussion of the applicability of this approach as it pertains to product advertising. It has been criticized by many scholars, notably Nicosia,[68] and by business executives who question its validity on the grounds of psychological and communication theory, and on the enormous difficulty of converting the concept from an abstract notion to an operational definition. Distinguishing between persuasive and manipulative information is highly subjective and is rooted in differing values and goals. Moreover, information is a two-way process. The recipient does not necessarily perceive information in the manner it is intended but instead manipulates it for his own purposes, selectively choosing only those portions of information that fit his own frame of reference.

It would be highly inappropriate to determine the presence or absence of deception in advocacy advertising, especially as it relates to issues and opinions, based on the notion of the reader's perception of the meaning of the message. A simple example will make the point. Suppose a corporation is trying to persuade a significant segment of the population that it needs a higher profit to enable it to invest in better facilities which in the future would help keep prices stable or even lower them. Let's also accept for the sake of argument that this is an accurate statement as to the corporation's intentions and beliefs. Now suppose this group strongly believes, for whatever reasons, that this corporation, like all other corporations, has siphoned off profits for the shareholders, given poor service to consumers, and is now pleading poverty in order to get more profits. The group therefore believes that the company is lying. The company is trying to correct or change public perception and therefore in the initial stages the response to its message will be skeptical. Should we then concede that this message is deceptive, at least in reference to some readers? How would we go about requiring proof of accuracy? Moreover, as we have seen earlier, requiring substantiation in instances like this would amount to prior censorship and a restriction of free speech.

Supporters of regulation suggest that a large number of issue-oriented ads have themes which should be testable against scientific truths and acceptable standards or norms in various other disciplines. However, this is not necessarily so. The scientific fact may be no more than prevailing wisdom and to use it as a test of falsity may act to impede change and may simply be motivated by a desire to preserve the status quo. "If the boundaries of free speech were coextensive with the limits of permissible conduct, current habit would dictate current comment and the growth of ideas would be severely stunted."[69]

In its petition before the Federal Trade Commission, Media Access Project cites various examples of environment-related advocacy ads that are alleged to be deceptive. For example, it disputes the claims of Shell Oil that offshore drilling is safe, that Shell takes every reasonable precaution to keep waters clean around the platforms, and that fish yields are very high near its oil rigs. It asserts that these statements are untrue because cause and effect relationships assumed here simply do not exist. More fish may be due to a variety of factors; "even a junked car deposited on an ocean bottom will serve to attract fish who naturally seek protection from swift ocean currents or other forces." Similarly, the petition takes issue with a Champion International ad claiming its conservation and forest management plans have contributed toward stable lumber prices by noting that plywood prices had risen 56 percent during the last three years and furthermore that Champion International was seeking price increases for its lumber before the Cost of Living Council.[70] A close analysis would reveal these arguments to be somewhat specious. Although oil drilling platforms may not be the only cause of high fish yields, it cannot be said that they did not make any contribution. Plywood prices may have gone up 56 percent, but who is to say that they would not have gone even higher if it were not for sound forest management on the part of the lumber companies? There is another assumption in this approach which needs clarification, and that is that all advertisers are likely to err in the same direction and that the consumer is not likely to get different information from different sources. Business is not a homogeneous entity; different corporations advocate different positions on a given issue. Furthermore, people receive their information from a variety of sources with differing viewpoints and make their decisions based on their own perception of the value of various pieces of information and the credibility of the communicating medium.

As Justice Holmes noted in *Abrams* v. *United States,* there should be active encouragement for the dissemination of all points of view on matters of public concern without regard to accuracy and that by a sort of philosophical Darwinism, truth should come to be recognized and accepted:

When men have realized that time has upset many fighting faiths, they may come to believe even more than they believe the very foundations of their own conduct that the ultimate good desired is better reached by free trade in ideas - that the best test of truth is the power of the thought to get itself accepted in the competition of the market . . . That, at any rate, is the theory of our Constitution.[71]

On another dimension, consider, for example a series of recent ads run by U.S. Steel, Allied Chemical, American Electric Power, and Mobil Oil. In all these advertisements, the companies have argued variously that gas prices be deregulated and allowed to rise to the level of the market prices; that profits earned by American industry are not enough and that profits expressed as percentage of sales dollar are declining; and that a growth in energy supply is necessary to provide more jobs. One could dispute each one of these statements as being either half-truths or as stating opinions or theories as fact—for example, deregulation of gas prices may not help produce more gas if most of the available gas reserves are being exploited, and there is no guarantee that the extra profits generated by a gas company will necessarily be invested in further exploration for gas. The management may simply decide to invest these funds in other industries in order to diversify or earn higher returns on investment. In fact, this is what Mobil did; at the height of increasing fuel prices, it invested $500 million to acquire a controlling share of Marcor Corporation.[72]

The notion of earning per sales dollar may not be a true indication of profits because it does not take into account the different inventory turnover rates in different industries. Thus, a 2 percent return on the sales dollar in one industry may yield a higher return on investment than a 5 percent return on the sales dollar in another industry. Notwithstanding, a case can be made that in inflationary times, a ROI concept based on historical book value is misleading. Similarly, there is a historical trend showing a highly positive correlation between energy consumption and level of economic activity; as a matter of fact, the rate of energy production is universally used as an indication of economic growth. However, this does not necessarily imply that reverse will be true in the future or that alternative development paths that would need lower growth rates in energy production cannot be developed.

The point I wish to make is that just because the claims made in these advertisements are not likely to hold for all time and under all circumstances or are based on one set of hypotheses, they are not necessarily false or deceptive. It is fallacious to seek substantiation of these claims by suggesting that another set of hypotheses could also be used to explain a part of the relationship alleged in the ads or to demand that the statements be qualified because in the future another set of relationships may be more valid.

Finally, in his testimony before the U.S. Senate Subcommittee on the Environment, Harvey Shulman of Media Access Project bemoaned the fact that the post-1962 IRS rules broadened the scope of expenses related to lobbying that would be deductible as ordinary and necessary business expenses and treated as an above-the-line item. He called it "the exploitation of propaganda" and cited as an example "a heavy advertising offensive extolling the virtues of private enterprise and a laissez faire economic theory. . . ."[73] However, Mr. Shulman fails to state why extolling the virtues of the free enterprise system is considered exploitation propaganda. Nor does he state what type of substantiation would be needed to prove otherwise. One does not have to agree with the specific behavior of the sponsoring corporation to concur with the general philosophy of free enterprise in the capitalistic system. Furthermore, a strong belief in the free enterprise system is not likely to deter one from criticizing particular types of business behavior. On the contrary, it may spur criticism of such business practices as price fixing, anticompetitive behavior, and bribes and payoffs. It is not clear how one might go about substantiating such an argument, since we do not have any evidence of what the U.S. economy would be like under a different kind of social order. The best that can be done is to point to the record of other countries where economic arrangements are centrally directed, e.g., the USSR, or where a mixed pattern, albeit somewhat different than that of the U.S., of private and state ownership of productive facilities exists, e.g., the United Kingdom, France, and West Germany.

The purpose of this exercise is not to show that the free enterprise system is without faults, that the present system is truly and totally free enterprise, or that one fully agrees with all its premises. However, one cannot deny that cogent and sound arguments can be made as to its performance capabilities and that one can subscribe to the system without fully following its precepts. Nor is this a defense of the overly simplistic and often naive manner in which the arguments in support of the free enterprise system are made in most of the ad campaigns. But to dismiss the whole issue as "exploitation propaganda" implies an indifference to someone else's viewpoint, which is inappropriate when such fundamental questions as freedom of speech and expression are involved.

Perhaps an argument can be made that the information supplied was insufficient and therefore could lead to misconception. However, it would be well nigh impossible to set external standards for completeness of information where causal relationships may be highly complex and in many cases not completely understood. Should we therefore deny a person or a company the opportunity to take a particular course of action, with which others may disagree, but which has not been proved right or wrong? Moreover, all the counter assertions and explanations offered by the Media Access Project would deserve similar criticism if subjected to the same rigorous standards of substantiation it seeks for the advertisers.

Conclusions and Suggestions for Business Action

The present spate of demands for substantiation or proof of accuracy in the case of advocacy advertising are poorly conceived. Any potential harm in terms of reader deception is far outweighed by the benefits that accrue to society by maintaining an open marketplace for ideas and by encouraging vigorous debate on controversial issues. The locus of serving the public interest, therefore, must be found elsewhere than in imposing restrictions on dissemination of ideas. However, short of impinging on the First Amendment guarantees of free speech, there are many steps that can be taken with a view to improving the quality of debate and also increasing the number of issues discussed in the public communication space.

1. Paid advertising is not the only channel of communication and equal

access to the public communication space does not mean equal access to the same communication medium. As we have discussed in Chapter 3, those with nonbusiness viewpoints have a variety of other channels open to them to express their position, channels that may not be available with similar ease to business. Thus to the extent that opportunities for the airing of opposing viewpoints need to be brought about, it would be better if we were to afford opportunity to those who advocate those viewpoints rather than force business to publicize the adversary position. There is no way short of total censorship to force one group to air another group's viewpoint while it is explaining its own in a manner that would be satisfactory to the latter.

2. Most of the opinion or issue-oriented advocacy ads use editorial copy format. There is a potential for the reader to be misled and think of the ad as an editorial. This risk is further compounded when ads appear in editorial pages or close to editorial material. For example, Mobil's ad in *The New York Times* appears in the lower right-hand corner of the Op-Ed page. Although the ads are clearly identified with Mobil's name, the danger for confusion was recognized by no less a person than John Oakes, editorial page editor. He states:

These ads have no effect whatsoever on the editorial content of the Op-Ed page or of the editorial page. There's no question of these institutions—or anyone else—being able to "buy editorial space." But the kind of Op-Ed ads that Mobil, in particular, has been running for the last couple of years may give that illusion, simply because in a paid space they do present a distinctly "editorial" point of view.

I'd personally greatly prefer that that very special kind of "editorial-type" ad *not* be allowed on the Op-Ed page. I think it would be better—from the point of view of appearance alone—if we banned that kind of ad from Op-Ed, while of course allowing it to appear anywhere else in the paper.

To avoid any confusion in the minds of the readers and also make a clear distinction between the ad copy and the editorial, the news media should require the corporations to insert a statement at the bottom of their ad copy somewhat along the following lines:

IMPORTANT NOTICE: The contents of this advertisement are determined by the sponsor, who is solely responsible for their accuracy.

3. The news media should make every effort to ensure that the sponsor of the ad is clearly identified so that a reader is not misled as to the source of the opinion or the idea presented in the ad. This does not pose any problem where the sponsor is a corporation and is identified by name in the advertisement. However, when the originator of the ad falls in the elusive sponsor category described in Chapter 1, the problem of identity becomes important. For example, the reader is not likely to know who the real sponsors are when an advertisement or commercial is identified with such groups as Citizens for a Clean

Environment, Keep America Beautiful, People's Lobby, Californians Against Proposition 9, Center of Study of Responsive Law, and so on. These names are used to evoke positive responses in the minds of readers, responses the sponsors believe would not be likely to occur if their real identities were known to the reader. This is precisely the reason why the media should not allow it. Thus it behooves the newspaper or the magazine carrying this type of ad to indicate that, for example, Keep America Beautiful is a campaign sponsored by the brewing, glass container, metal, can, and paper industries; that the Center for the Study of Responsive Law is a group sponsored by Ralph Nader; that People's Lobby is comprised of a small number of individuals who are actively seeking to change laws in California in the direction they consider socially desirable; and that Californians Against the Pollution Initiative is a group sponsored primarily by the banking, construction, oil, utilities, and chemical industries in California to oppose People's Lobby and the referendum initiative sponsored by them.

This recommendation would apply to both the electronic and the print media. It is not an unreasonable requirement. Just as the broadcasters always precede a political message by saying "The following is a paid political advertisement," a similar caution in a printed political or advocacy ad would alert the reader as to the source of the message and should assist him in properly evaluating the contents. Furthermore, if corporations are confident of the accuracy of their ads, they should not be afraid of such a cautionary note.

It should be noted that Harvey Shulman of the Media Access Project made a similar suggestion in a petition filed with the FTC on behalf of six congressmen and senators. The label he proposed reads: "This is a political advertisement intended to present this advertiser's views on a controversial issue of public importance."[74] In my opinion this wording is both harsh and inappropriate. Not all the issues dealt with in advocacy ads are political—a term likely to have a pejorative connotation in this frame of reference. Moreover, whether or not an issue is controversial in the context of a specifically fixed time and event frame but may deal with an idea or an underlying social value that may not be limited to a short-run time constraint, e.g., a campaign to change or correct public perception on the role of profits in capital formation and economic growth. Such a campaign will be neither political nor controversial within the commonly understood meanings of these terms. And yet, there are honest differences of opinion between reasonable people as to the role played by profits in capital formation and economic growth and the nature of economic structure and industrial organization in a nation that may make their role more or less socially beneficial.

Although the news executives of the three television networks have contended (Chapter 3) that they do not all sell air time for issue-oriented ads, various conservationist groups disagree with this contention, stating that environment and energy-related institutional ads currently aired on the three networks are indeed editorial-type political ads and should be subject to the equal time requirements of the fairness doctrine. Although the issue has been currently resolved in favor of the networks, the debate is by no means over. To avoid any conceivable misunderstanding, the electronic media should seriously consider using an announcement along the lines suggested to precede broadcasts of institutional commercials that might be construed as offering an opinion or drawing a conclusion. This would be a better remedy than instituting still more rigorous standards for excluding corporate institutional commercials that might have the suggestion of an idea or an opinion.

Many news magazines identify editorial-type ad copy with the word "Advertisement" printed at the top of the page. The purpose is to avoid any identification between the advertisement and the magazine's own copy in the minds of the reader. However, this measure alone is inadequate, and it is not universally practiced. Therefore, a bold and clear-cut statement along the lines suggested would serve the interests of the reader and, at the same time, not encroach on the freedom of the advertiser to state his views without any inhibition or prior censorship.

4. The corporations, on their part, must observe the most stringent standards of accuracy and fair presentation. When the statement is of a controversial nature, it should be clearly *identified* as a personal viewpoint and not as a statement of fact.

5. Where a corporation presents specific data concerning its performance, compares its performance against those of other companies, or some external standard of adequacy, or uses someone else's statement for criticism or as a basis for support for its own statement, it should be willing to submit this data for public scrutiny in support of the statements made in the ad copy. Such a voluntary substantiation of factual information, where feasible and provided in comprehensible terms for the intelligent lay reader, would considerably improve the credibility of a corporation and the message it purports to convey.

Notes

1. 36 Federal Register 12058 (June 24, 1971), *amended* 36 Federal Register 14680 (August 7, 1971).

2. United States of America, Before the Federal Trade Commission, "Petition to the Federal Trade Commission (1) For Rules to Extend the Advertising Substantiation Campaign to All Advertising (2) To Request Substantiation for Certain Commercial Advertisements by Certain Advertisers (3) And to Commence Generally an Advertisement Substantiation Campaign in the Oil, Utility and Electric Appliance Industries in Regard to Environmental or Energy-Related Claims in Commercial Advertisements" (Washington, D.C.: Media Access Project, January 9, 1974). [Hereinafter referred to as the "Petition Before the Federal Trade Commission," January 9, 1974.]

The sponsoring corporations for the ads were Shell Oil, Mobil Oil, Tenneco, Middle South Utilities System, Champion International, Amoco Oil, Exxon, and Pacific Power and Light.

3. "Petition Before the Federal Trade Commission," pp. 2-3.

4. *Ibid.*, p. 4. See also "Moss Lays Shortage to Oil Firms," *Washington Post,* November 29, 1973, p. A-18; "Oilmen Defend Their Holdings in Other Fuels," *Washington Post,* December 7, 1973, p. A-9 (remarks of Senator Haskell); *Exxon Corp.* (1973 Transfer Binder) TRADE REG. REP. 20, 388 (F.T.C. 1973) (Complaint against eight oil companies); "Trust Suit Cites 20 Oil Companies," *The New York Times,* July 27, 1973, p. 39; "Florida Charges 'Gas' Conspiracy," *The New York Times,* July 10, 1973, p. 55; and "Environmental Gains Threatened by Crisis," *Washington Post,* December 11, 1973, p. A-1.

5. "Petition Before the Federal Trade Commission," pp. 24-25. See also *FTC* v. *Sperry & Hutchinson Co.,* 405 U.S. 233 (1972); *FTC* v. *National Petroleum Refiners' Association* (D.C. Cir. 1973), petition for cert. filed, 42 U.S.L.W.; *Giant Foods, Inc.* v. *FTC,* 322 F 2d 977, 981 note 9 (D.C. Cir. 1963), *dismissed,* 376 U.S. 967 (1964).

6. "Petition Before the Federal Trade Commission," pp. 26-27.

7. *Ibid.*, p. 23. See also *Valentine* v. *Chrestensen,* 316 U.S. 52 (1942); *Bread* v. *Alexandria,* 341 U.S. 622 (1951); *New York Times* v. *Sullivan,* 376 U.S. 255 (1964).

8. "Petition Before the Federal Trade Commission," pp. 23-24.

9. *Ibid.*, p. 26.

10. United States of America, Before the Federal Trade Commission, "Memorandum of Mobil Oil Corporation in Opposition to Petition to Extend the Advertising Substantiation Resolution of the Federal Trade Commission, Filed January 9, 1974" (Washington, D.C., April 4, 1974). [Hereinafter referred to as "Mobil's Memorandum Before the Federal Trade Commission."]

11. *Ibid.*, p. 13.

12. *Ibid.*, pp. 17-18.

13. *Ibid.*, p. 18.

14. The commission defined corporate image advertising as advertising "which describes the corporation itself, its activities or its policies, but does not explicitly describe any products or services sold by the corporation." Letter dated April 29, 1975, from the secretary of the Federal Trade Commission to Senators Thomas McIntyre, Frank E. Moss, and Birch Bayh, and Congressmen Les Aspin, Benjamin S. Rosenthal, and Andrew Young, transmitting the commision's decision on their application dated January 9, 1974, asking the commission to require substantiation for certain types of corporate image advertisements. The letter was accompanied by the "FTC Staff Statement of Proposed Policy Regarding Corporate Image Advertising." "Statement of Proposed Enforcement Policy by the Staff of the Federal Trade Commission Regarding

Corporate Image Advertising, December 4, 1974." [Hereinafter referred to as the "FTC Staff Statement of Proposed Policy Regarding Corporate Image Advertising."]

15. *Ibid.*, FTC's letter dated April 29, 1975, p. 3.

16. "FTC Staff Statement of Proposed Policy Regarding Corporate Image Advertising," p. 16.

17. *Ibid.*, p. 11.

18. For a comprehensive treatment of the topic, see "Development in the Law, Deceptive Advertising," *Harvard Law Review,* 80 (1967), 10004. For a discussion of the various facets of the First Amendment and its application to commercial speech, see Thomas I. Emerson, "Toward a General Theory of the First Amendment," *Yale Law Journal,* 72 (1963), 877, published in book form as *Toward a General Theory of the First Amendment* (New York: Vintage Books, 1966); Alexander Meiklejohn, "The First Amendment Is an Absolute," *Supreme Court Review,* 1965, p. 245; William J. Brennan, "The Supreme Court and the Meiklejohn Interpretation of the First Amendment," *Harvard Law Review,* 79 (1965), 1; "Community, Privacy, Defamation, and the First Amendment: The Implications of Time Inc. v. Hill," *Columbia Law Review,* 67 (1967), 926.

For a discussion and analysis of specific issues bearing on the two sides of the argument, see Charles E. Ludlam, "Abatement of Corporate Image Environmental Advertising," *Ecology Law Quarterly,* 4 (1974), 247; "Note: The Regulation of Corporate Image Advocacy Advertising," *Minnesota Law Review,* 59, 1 (November 1974), 189-222; Allen W. Bird, II, Thomas W. Goldman, and Keith D. Lawrence, "Corporate Image Advertising: A Discussion of the Factors That Distinguish Those Corporate Image Advertising Practices Protected Under the First Amendment from Those Subject to Control by the Federal Trade Commission," *Journal of Urban Law,* 4 (1974), 405; "Notes: Freedom of Expression in a Commercial Context," *Harvard Law Reveiw,* 78 (1965), 1191; Martin H. Redish, "The First Amendment in the Marketplace: Commercial Speech and the Value of Free Expression," *George Washington Law Review,* 39 (1970), 429; George C. Cooper, "The Tax Treatment of Business Grassroots Lobbying: Defining and Attaining the Public Policy Objectives," *Columbia Law Review,* 68 (1968), 801; *Fur Information and Fashion Council, Inc.* v. *E.F. Timme and Son, Inc.,* Brief for Association of National Advertisers, *Amicus Curiae,* Docket No. 73-2687 (2d Cir., April 1, 1974); "Corporate Freedom of Speech," *Suffolk University Law Review,* 7 (1973), 1117; "Petition Before the Federal Trade Commission"; "Mobil's Memorandum Before the Federal Trade Commission", "FTC Staff Statement of Proposed Policy Regarding Corporate Image Advertising."

19. *Valentine* v. *Chrestensen,* 316 U.S. 52 (1942).

20. Redish, "The First Amendment in the Marketplace."

21. Meiklejohn, "The First Amendment," p. 255, cited in Redish, "The First Amendment in the Marketplace," p. 435.

22. Emerson, *Toward a General Theory*, p. 7.

23. 316 U.S. 52 (1942).

24. *Jamison* v. *Texas*, 318 U.S. 413 (1943).

25. *New York Times* v. *Sullivan*, 376 U.S. 254 (1964).

26. *Ibid.*, p. 265.

27. The ad detailed alleged abuses to southern black students and solicited financial support for Martin Luther King. *Ibid.*, p. 266.

28. *Ginzburg* v. *United States*, 383 U.S. 463 (1966).

29. *Thornhill* v. *Alabama*, 310 U.S. 88 (1940); *Thomas* v. *Collins*, 323 U.S. 516 (1945); *NLRB* v. *American Tube Bending Co.*, 134 F 2d 993 (2nd Cir.) *cert. denied*, 320 U.S. 768 (1943). The Court has recently narrowed the scope of such protection by denying picketing rights within the bounds of a private shopping center.
See *Hudgens* v. *NLRB*, No. 74-773, 44 *U.S. Law Week* 428 (March 8, 1976).

30. Jeremiah D. Lambert, "Corporate Political Spending and Campaign Finance," *New York University Law Review*, 40 (1965), 1033.

31. *Jamison* v. *Texas*, 318 U.S. 413 (1943).

32. *Grosjean* v. *American Press Co.*, 297 U.S. 233 (1933); *New York Times* v. *Sullivan*, 376 U.S. 254, 265-66 (1964). Although the contents of a book may be protected speech, the advertisements for the book may still be regulated if it contains misleading information. This applies even to the title page of the book. Further, in the case of health books, it was held that although the ad may truthfully state the contents of the book, it may still be regulated if the assertions made therein do not meet "objective" medical standards. "Developments in the Law, Deceptive Advertising," pp. 1031-32, and the cases cited in notes therein.

33. Cooper, "Taxation of Grassroots Lobbying," p. 831. See also *Donaldson* v. *Read Magazine, Inc.*, 333 U.S. 178 (1948); *E.F. Drew & Co.* v. *FTC*, 235 F 2d 735 (2d Cir. 1956), *cert. denied*, 352 U.S. 969 (1957).

34. 413 U.S. 376, 388 (1973).

35. Ludlam, "Abatement of Corporate Image Environmental Advertising," pp. 268-279. See also *Capital Broadcasting* v. *Mitchell*, 333 F. Supp. 582 (D.D.C. 1971) (three-judge court), *aff'd mem.*, 405 U.S. 1000 (1972); *Banzhaf* v. *FCC*, 405 F 2d 1082 (D.C. Cir. 1968), *cert. denied*, 396 U.S. 842 (1969); *Gertz* v. *Robert Welch, Inc.*, 42 *U.S. Law Week* 5123 (1974).

36. "Developments in Law, Deceptive Advertising," pp. 1032-1033 and the cases cited in notes 32-35 therein.

37. *NAACP* v. *Button*, 371 U.S. 414 (1963).

38. *Ibid.*, pp. 1034-1036.

285

39. *Cammarano* v. *United States,* 358 U.S. 498 (1959), Justice Douglas concurring.

40. *Dun & Bradstreet Inc.* v. *Grove,* 404 U.S. 898 (1971) (dissenting opinion); *mem. denying cert.* to *Grove* v. *Dun & Bradstreet, Inc.,* 438 F 2d 433 (3rd Cir. 1971).

41. *Schwartz* v. *Vanasco,* 75-677, 44 *U.S. Law Week* 3390, January 13, 1976. See also Lesley Olsner, "High Court Voids New York Rules for Fair Campaign," *The New York Times,* January 13, 1976, p. 1.

42. *Buckley* v. *Valeo,* 75-436, 44 *U.S. Law Week* 4128, January 27, 1976. See also Lesley Olsner, "High Court Decided Campaign Spending Is Form of 'Speech,'" *The New York Times,* February 1, 1976, p. 1.

43. *Bigelow* v. *Virginia,* 95 S. Ct. 2222 (1975).

44. *Ibid.,* 16.

45. *Virginia State Board of Pharmacy* v. *Virginia Citizens Consumer Council, Inc.,* 74-895, 44 *U.S. Law Week* 4686, May 25, 1976.

46. *Lamont* v. *Post Master General,* 381 U.S. 301 (1965); *Kleindienst* v. *Mandel,* 408 U.S. 753, 762-763 (1972).

47. *Virginia State Board of Pharmacy* v. *Virginia Citizens Consumer Council, Inc.,* 74-895, 44 *U.S. Law Week* 4692 (1976).

48. 38 Stat. 717, as amended, 15 U.S.C. 41 (1970); 52 Stat. 111 (1938) [Wheeler-Lea Act].

49. "Notes, The FTC Ad Substantiation Program," *Georgetown Law Journal,* 61 (1973), 1427; "Developments in the Law, Deceptive Advertising," pp. 1063-1101; Ludlam, "Abatement of Corporate Image Advertising," p. 273; and "Petition Before the Federal Trade Commission."

50. Statement of Miles Kirkpatrick, chairman, Federal Trade Commission, before the *U.S. Senate Committee on Commerce, Hearings on S. 1461, Advertising 1972,* 92nd Congress, 2nd Session, Serial 92-70 (1972), pp. 23-24. [Hereinafter referred to as the "1972 Advertising Hearings."]

51. *Ibid.,* pp. 23-25. See also "The FTC Ad Substantiation Program," p. 1440; Harrison Wellford, "How Ralph Nader, Tricia Nixon, the ABA, and Jamie Whitten Helped Turn the FTC Around," *Washington Monthly,* October 1972, pp. 5, 10.

52. *Advertisement Substantiation Program, B-174702, Federal Trade Commission, Report to the Consumer Subcommittee, Committee on Commerce, U.S. Senate, by the Comptroller General of the United States Government Accounting Office (1972),* pp. 25-26. [Hereinafter referred to as the "GAO Report on Ad Substantiation Program".] "The Ad Substantiation Program," 1436-40; A.H. Travers, "Foreword," *Kansas Law Review,* 17 (1969), 551, 556-57; Tracy Weston, "Deceptive Advertising and the Federal Trade Commission: Decline of Caveat Emptor," *Federal Bar Journal,* 24 (1964), 548, 561.

53. "GAO Report on Ad Substantiation Program."

54. *Ibid.*, p. 5.

55. Calvin J. Collier, chairman, Federal Trade Commission, Statement before the Subcommittee on Commerce, Consumer and Monetary Affairs of the Committee on Government Operations, House of Representatives (June 24, 1976), p. 18.

56. *Ibid.*, pp. 3, 15.

57. Richard A. Posner, *Regulation of Advertising by the FTC* (Washington, D.C.: American Enterprise Institute for Public Policy Research, 1973).

58. Richard A. Herzog, "The Policy Planning Protocol for Deceptive and Unsubstantiated Claims: A Management and Legal Perspective." Remarks made before the 1976 Institute of Advanced Advertising Studies, American Association of Advertising Agencies, New York Council, Tarrytown, New York, June 24-27, 1976.

59. Collier, Statement before the Subcommittee on Commerce, Consumer and Monetary Affairs of the Committee on Government Operations, pp. 13-14.

60. Posner, *Regulation of Advertising by the FTC,* p. 31.

61. See the testimony of Peter W. Allport, president, Association of National Advertisers, and Mr. Howard Bell, president, American Advertising Federation, in the "1972 Advertising Hearings," pp. 252-263, 294-301.

62. "The FTC Statement Regarding Corporate Image Advertising," pp. 21-22.

63. Allen W. Bird II, Thomas W. Goldman, and Keith Lawrence, "Corporate Image Advertising: A Discussion of the Factors That Distinguish Those Corporate Image Advertising Practices Protected Under the First Amendment from Those Subject to Control by the Federal Trade Commission," *Journal of Urban Law,* 51 (1974), pp. 405, 415-16.

64. *Ibid.*, pp. 416-418.

65. *Ibid.*, pp. 418-420.

66. Ludlam, "Abatement of Corporate Image Environmental Advertising," p. 272. See also *CBS* v. *Democratic National Committee,* 412 U.S., 94 (1973); Friends of Earth advertisement, "Oil Companies Have Spent Millions Defending Offshore Drilling—for 50¢ You Can See What It Costs the Earth—And You," *The New Yorker,* August 12, 1972, p. 79.

67. Herzog, "The Policy Planning Protocol for Deceptive and Unsubstantiated Claims."

68. Francesco Nicosia, *Advertising Management and Society: A Business Point of View* (New York: McGraw-Hill, 1974).

69. "Developments in the Law, Deceptive Advertising," p. 1036.

70. "Petition Before the Federal Trade Commission," pp. 7-10.

71. *Ibid.*, fn 18. *Abrams* v. *United States,* 250 U.S. 616, 630 (1919) (Holmes dissenting).

72. "Mobil Oil to Pay Over $800 Million to Buy Marcor," *The Wall Street Journal,* August 7, 1974, p. 3.

73. Written statement of Harvey J. Shulman, attorney, Media Access Project, Washington, D.C., before the U.S. Senate, *Energy and Environmental Objectives, Hearings Before the Subcommittee on Environment of the Committee on Commerce* (Washington, D.C., 93rd Congress, 2nd Session, May 6 and July 18, 1974), p. 41.

74. "Petition Before the Federal Trade Commission," p. 24.

8

Media Access for Opposing Viewpoints A Framework for Cooperation Among Business, Opposing Groups, and the News Media

The great enemy of communication, then is the illusion of it. We have talked enought but we have not listened. And by not listening we have failed to concede the immense complexity of our society—and thus the great gap between ourselves and those with whom we seek understanding.

—William Whyte, Is Anybody Listening?

No system of free expression can be totally protected from abuses and excesses except by total prohibition, which is self-defeating. It is a democratic imperative that we foster the widest possible exhange of ideas and expression of viewpoints. Under a fairly designed set of procedures and rules to ensure adequate media access for different groups without regard to their financial resources, advocacy advertising could become an invaluable tool for developing a well-informed body politic.

There is some apprehension in the minds of social critics that unrestrained use of advocacy advertising would clog the public channels of communication with one-sided messages which would not necessarily add anything to the public's information base. Thus William Sheehan, president of ABC News, while stating his opposition to allowing advocacy commercials on the electronic media, observes that it would add "lots of voices but would not contribute very much to the thought processes."

Ir is not inconceivable that encouragement of public debate on controversial issues will generate wasted effort and also distorted information and one-sided presentation of ideas. The value of this debate, however, should not be measured by the extent of nuisance caused by it. The constitutional notion of free speech is based on the assumption that the "widest possible dissemination of information from diverse and antagonistic sources is essential to the welfare of the public."[1] Nevertheless, the questions raised by the two sides are quite significant and could become critical in the foreseeable future with the expansion in advocacy advertising in general, and with one or more corporate campaigns becoming

---

Unless otherwise specifically stated, all quotes in this chapter are from personal interviews or written communications with the author.

particularly controversial. Our concern, therefore, is to ask what should be done to foster a free and unrestrained exchange of ideas in the public communication space. Another objective might be to protect certain segments of society from receiving distorted information that might adversely influence their views on major issues of public policy.

Three important issues deserve careful analysis if we are to develop a modus vivendi for accommodating different group interests and viewpoints, and at the same time fulfill the broader public purpose, i.e., to encourage and maintain maximum feasible flow of unrestrained information from a variety of sources to enable the public to make informed and intelligent decisions.

1. What are the prospects that corporate advocacy advertising will so overwhelm the media as to make it difficult, if not impossible, for opposing viewpoints to receive public expression? If this situation comes to pass, will it so distort the available information to the public that it will adversely affect the social decision-making process?

2. What are the avenues of correction that might be used if a significant number of advocacy campaigns are found to contain information that is highly tilted in one direction and might create misleading impressions in the minds of the public? I am assuming that this advertising would be outside the FTC's substantiation requirements applicable to certain types of corporate image advertisements (see Chapter 7).

3. What are the alternative ways by which the nonbusiness viewpoints can be assured a fair hearing in the marketplace for ideas? As I shall discuss later in this section, I believe it would be necessary and indeed highly desirable to provide media access for certain types of unconventional viewpoints.

Corporate Advocacy Advertising—Can It Overwhelm the Public Communication Space?

Most of the businesspeople interviewed believed it was highly unlikely that paid advertising by corporations would ever dominate the public communication space. Their reasons advanced can be summarized as follows:

1. In the foreseeable future, business is seen as fighting an uphill battle to *correct* the imbalance against business that currently exists in the information available to the public. Peter Allport, president, Association of National Advertisers, states, "I haven't seen any instance where the business community has been able to brainwash or propagandize. It is a long way from dominating the communication processes of the country."

Moreover, business is not a monolithical entity and does not speak in unison nor is it likely to do so in the future. The interests of oil industry may run counter to the interests of the lumber industry or mass transportation. Even within a given industry, the interests of the larger and dominant members may be at odds with those of the smaller members. One example of intra-industry conflict can be seen in the recent controversy in New York State between savings and loan institutions and commercial banks, where the former are advocating the passage of legislation permitting savings banks to provide check cashing privileges to their depositors free of charge while the commercial banks are opposed to the passage of this legislation. Needless to say, both groups purport to indicate that the action advocated by their particular group is in the public interest. (For an illustration of the advertisements in this campaign, see Appendix 1A.).

2. Even if a substantial number of the country's largest corporations were to spend all their institutional advertising budgets on advocacy-type campaigns, it would still not be sufficient to squeeze out the opposing viewpoints, because (a) There is not enough money in the corporate coffers to buy that much media space. (b) It would become incredibly boring and people would stop buying newspapers and magazines. This would be self-defeating. (c) There are specific magazines and newspapers geared to meet the information needs of certain types of readers. These magazines and newspapers are not likely to accept advertisements they believe might alienate their readership. (d) One can always start a new newspaper or magazine where there is a large group of readers whose needs for a particular type of information are currently not being fulfilled. (e) The broadcast media are currently unavailable to business for paid commercials on controversial issues and one source that business cannot dominate even if it wanted to do so.

3. Another set of arguments has to do with the news environment of the medium in which paid editorial advertisements are run. The news environment, it is contended, is generally quite hostile to business, thereby reducing the credibility of the advertisements—a problem not encountered by those groups whose viewpoints are supported in the editorials or who receive favorable coverage.

One can indeed find evidence to show that various news media have been critical of specific aspects of particular advocacy campaigns even when they have been supportive of the corporation's right to engage in advocacy advertising. This is true of both business-oriented and general major newspapers and magazines. Furthermore, as John E. Mandable, vice-president, marketing and advertising sales, *Newsweek*, points out, the attitude of the reader toward advertising is an important restraining factor when an issue is discussed in a paid ad. The reader knows who paid for it and will look upon the message as a partisan point of view on the part of those who are running the ads. On the other hand, he is more likely to turn toward the editorial and news pages in the same magazine for a balanced and analytical coverage of the issue.

Lewis Young, editor-in-chief of *Business Week,* observes that the potential effectiveness of a message is reduced when it is presented as an advertisement:

"One of the most difficult things that the advertisers have to do is to prove the value of advertising when they are selling products. Justifying that advertising when they are selling ideas is going to be much tougher. I don't think people will throw money around just doing that." Garth Hite of the *Atlantic Monthly* expresses a somewhat similar view. "Our readers are intelligent and mature," he says; "we assume that when they see advertising in the *Atlantic*, they will know that it is paid space." Professor George Lodge of the Harvard Business School believes that Mobil's campaign is a waste of money and likely to be counterproductive: "It is naive on the part of Mobil to think that readers will believe a paid advertisement by an oil company self-righteously proclaiming its virtues and hurtling blame on those who dare to differ with them."

This explanation ignores or understates two important factors. One, the effect of advertising builds over time. Thus although individual ads in themselves may not be very persuasive, their cumulative effect can be considerable. Through constant repetition over a long period of time, a corporation should be able to build a positive attitude in the minds of readers toward its message, regardless of the inherent accuracy or objectivity of the message or its information content. The second factor has to do with the combined effect of the advertising campaigns run by several corporations emphasizing a similar theme. Thus while business may not be a monolithic entity, a large number of companies are using common themes in advocacy campaigns dealing with pollution, consumerism, government regulation, economic growth, the energy crisis, and the virtues of the free enterprise system. These campaigns invariably have similar copy messages, common adversaries, and suggest similar pro business solutions. Thus corporate advocacy campaigns, taken individually, may not be influential in forming favorable public opinion, but their combined effect is likely to be considerable and cannot be ignored.

Thus even if a group were able to counteract the information presented in a specific advocacy advertisement through a paid advertisement of its own, or if a newspaper were to carry a story or editorial correcting any false impression created by a particular ad, they are in no position to do so continuously and match the efforts of the corporation for the entire duration of the time when such an advocacy campaign is being run. The former would be unable to follow this course because of financial contraints; the latter would be deterred by the demands of covering other types of news. A newspaper or magazine simply could not let its news coverage be determined by the type of advocacy advertising carried in its pages. The corporation thus has a distinct advantage over other groups in conveying its message to the readers.

The preceding discussion leads me to conclude that there are indeed reasonable grounds for concern that advocacy advertising campaigns, when pursued by a significantly large number of corporations, over a period of time, can overwhelm the information mix available to the public and thereby squeeze out or sharply reduce the expression of alternative viewpoints on important issues af-

fecting society. It is therefore legitimate to discuss whether any avenues currently exist or can be made available to society in case there is a need to develop
means for correcting information distortions created by corporate advocacy
campaigns or to provide media access for alternative viewpoints. These two
issues are discussed in detail in the subsequent sections.

Avenues for Correction If Advocacy Campaigns Are Found To Be Highly Distorted

The undesirability of deploying regulatory mechanisms to require advertisers
to substantiate statements and claims made in their advocacy advertisements
was discussed in Chapter 7. The whole premise of advocacy advertising is based
on providing information that shows the sponsor in a favorable light. However,
there is also an underlying assumption that the information will improve the
quality of public debate. To the extent that exaggeration and public deception
can take place, a variety of corrective mechanisms are currently available which
are noncoercive and voluntary in nature. These range from the pressure of
market forces to the self-regulation by the industry. They are briefly summarized here:

Market Pressure. An argument can be made that market pressure provides an
excellent mechanism for self-restraint and correction and that no further efforts
are necessary. Herbert Schmertz of Mobil Oil expresses the sentiment of most
businesspeople when he says that in putting out its views, a company generates
one of two types of reaction: it is proved wrong and loses credibility and is
worse off than before, or it increases the spectrum of information. A company
launching an advocacy campaign becomes the target of social critics and thereby
invites public scrutiny. Therefore, it is logical that it would go to great lengths
to ensure the accuracy of its position and of the supporting facts.

Availability of Other Viewpoints. Another argument against the need for any
corrective mechanism is that while the market forces take care of extremely
exaggerated and one-sided claims or statements, the nature of advocacy advertising is such that any additional corrective devices are unnecessary. No one
source of information can be totally objective. Even if the information is self-
serving from the industry's point of view, it is nonetheless information.
According to to Rober Lubar, *Fortune*'s managing editor, at *Fortune* they try
to be honest, but they cannot be totally objective. "There aren't always two
sides to a question. There is always the danger of the public being misinformed.
The way the public is protected is to have absolute freedom of others to answer." Rober M. Bleiberg, editor of *Barron's*, goes one step further. He says it
is not impossible for corporate advertising to be misleading. As an example, he

considers the American Trucking Association's current antideregulation campaign to be misleading. However, he would not try to prevent it. He comments:

By definition these people are trying to get their viewpoint across. They have no further responsibility. I, as a newspaperman, have a responsibility to get all sides of the issue. I don't just accept one viewpoint whether it comes from the corporation involved in an anti-government campaign, or from the government in an anti-corporation campaign. It is remarkable that one should assume that the information we get from the government is unbiased and the information we get from the corporation is necessarily slanted. My own experience has been the other way around.

Public Censure. Another variation of the market pressure argument is that of public censure of corporations that tend to mislead the people. By being overly aggressive in their advocacy campaigns and fighting all their critics indiscriminately, such corporations invite public attention to the dispute. And overreaction tends to confirm, in the minds of the readers, that the corporation may indeed have something to hide. Garth Hite, publisher of *Atlantic* magazine, provides one example. In its March 1976 issue, the *Atlantic* published an article entitled, "Ripoff at the Supermarket." Safeway, the largest supermarket chain in the country, reacted by pulling the magazine out of its supermarkets. "Safeway wasn't even mentioned in the article. By throwing us out of their stores they allied themselves with the focus of the article." Consequently, the story was picked up by the three television networks, independent radio and television stations across the country, *The New York Times,* and *Time* magazine, among others. "It's a classic example of corporate stupidity and overreaction. We're delighted. We're selling a lot of magazines."

I agree with the essential merit of these arguments. However, in themselves they cannot remedy the situation. They assume that the reader has both the technical means and the necessary time to understand and question the accuracy or substantiveness of many of the complex arguments made by the sponsors in such important areas as government regulation; adequate levels of profits (how many people even know or comprehend the complexities involved in defining profits or how to evaluate and compare performance of different firms and industries, and the relevance of such expressions as profits as a percent of sales dollar); pollution controls; and conservation; the relationship between unemployment, inflation, and level of prices prevailing in specific industries; and when an industry is concentrated and likely to be monopolistic in character.

Nor can we depend on the news media to do the job. It should be pointed out that one of the reasons offered by business institutions for advocacy advertising is to correct the alleged inaccuracies and inadequacies in the coverage of complex issues by the news media. We cannot now turn around and claim that the same journalists who could not originally understand the complex issues are now more able to grasp the logic of the claims made in advocacy ads and explain them to their readers. It is also unrealistic to assume that the news media can and should shoulder the entire burden of providing a counterbalance to advocacy ad campaigns, especially when they become more prevalent and conducted by a large number of companies. As I stated in the chapter on business and the news media (Chapter 3), this would have the effect of putting the news media in a position where their agenda was largely being determined by the advertisers. By carefully selecting the types of items they cover in their advocacy campaigns, advertisers can confine the debate within narrower limits and thereby divert attention from broader issues of more fundamental character. In the case study of the Clean Environment Act Initiative (Chapter 5), People's Lobby attributed a large part of its defeat to the fact that it got sucked into a debate and devoted all its resources to refuting the charges and allegations made by the opposition, with the result that little time and energy were left to present its case. Such a strategy may be highly desirable from business's viewpoint, but in the long run it will neither silence the corporate critics nor reduce the pressure for further "reform" (read control and regulation by government) of the rules of the game within which business operates.

The suggestion that excessive advocacy advertising will become so boring as to drive readers away also does not hold. Product and brand advertising is a case in point. Even here there is not enough evidence to indicate at what level saturation is achieved and negative returns set in. Advertising expenditures in the United States continue to rise every year and now exceed $24 billion a year. And yet there is no end in sight. Nor has it generated the kind of counterresponse that the logic of "market pressure" arguments would indicate. On the other hand, we have come to depend on seller-supplied information as the primary source of data on which to base our purchase decisions. The fact that we get similarly superficial and one-sided product information from a multitude of producers is irrelevant and does not improve the quality of our decisions. There is every reason to believe that a similar process will take place in advocacy advertising and that public interest will be poorly served unless some means are found to enrich the information base in the public domain from a variety of sources and not let it be dominated by a single source or few sources.

Two-sided Presentation of Arguments

Some critics of corporate advocacy advertising have suggested that a good corrective device would be to require corporations to present both sides of the argument in their advocacy ads.[2] However, I do not believe this to be either a feasible or a desirable alternative, for there are invariably more than two sides to most controversial issues. Thus a corporation would be hard pressed to select among the many sides or to determine the relative importance that should be accorded to the positions of various groups. The space constraints of an advertisement make it impossible to give adequate treatment to all but a couple of viewpoints. On a more important level, it is unrealistic to assume that a corporation could give equal space or satisfactory treatment to a viewpoint that it believes to be erroneous or misplaced. In this I agree with the position taken by Herbert Schmertz of Mobil Oil, who believes that such an approach would dilute the quality of debate.

The experience of the Carbonated Beverage Manufacturers Association is illustrative in this respect. They ran an ad in the *Reader's Digest* Special Environment Issue in September 1971. The ad purported to present both the pro and con arguments for using nonreturnable cans, with a conclusion that showed the social gains from using cans outweighed the costs (Appendix, Exhibit 8A-1). The campaign came under severe criticism from consumer and environmental groups, who accused the can industry of misrepresenting their position and understating the severity of the problem. One executive familiar with the issue stated that the campaign generated so much negative reaction that the can industry ended up spending a couple of million dollars to undo the damage.

Self-regulation by Industry

Self-regulation by industry is another approach by which individual members can be persuaded to maintain certain standards of objectivity and fairness in their advertisements. Self-regulation is designed to serve two objectives: the protection of consumers from deceptive messages, and the protection of one advertiser from the unfair competitive practices of another.[3]

No self-regulating mechanism currently exists whereby complaints relative to corporate advocacy advertisement from the public can be handled. Moreover, based on our experience with industry efforts at self-regulation in advertising and other activities, it is doubtful whether such a course would be productive and worth pursuing. The inhibition of antitrust laws and the difficulty in getting competitors to agree on an industry standard has hindered the setting up and enforcement of industrywide self-regulation. Industry codes are not stringent enough, and when violations by member firms are apparent, enforcement has often been weak or nonexistent. It is important to note that because of antitrust legislation, there is no mandatory adherence to standards that might be promulgated by any of the self-regulation organizations. The effect of self-regulation is further diluted because member firms are reluctant to use either moral suasion or public censure on other firms that do not abide by the standards. Public pressure, an important compliance tool, is thus not used.

National Advertising Review Board

The National Advertising Review Board (NARB) is the primary agency with responsibility for administering voluntary standards developed by the advertising industry. NARB is sponsored by the National Advertising Review Council, Inc. (NARC), which was formed by four organizations: American Advertising Federation (AAF), American Association of Advertising Agencies (AAAA), Association of National Advertisers (ANA) and Council of Better Business Bureaus (CBBB). The directors of NARC provide advice and counsel on standards for self-regulation which NARB administers. NARB was created in May 1971 as an appeals board or review level for the self-regulatory decisions made by the National Advertising Decision (NAD) of the National Association of Broadcasters (NAB). NAD receives a complaint from any source, or initiates inquiries on its own if it feels advertising is deceptive. The advertiser is contacted and asked for substantiation. If the substantiation is adequate, the case is closed. If it is not, the advertiser is asked to modify or eliminate the offending advertisement. If NAD cannot find a satisfactory settlement, the issue can be appealed to the NARB by either the complainant or the advertiser. The NARB, consisting of 50 members (30 from the advertisers, 10 from ad agencies, and 10 from the public interest) can then convene a five-member panel to review the case. The panel may refer a case to the FTC if it too finds the ad deceptive and the advertiser unwilling to change it. By June 30, 1975, the NAD had heard 879 complaints. Three hundred ads (or 34%) were substantiated and continued to run. Eleven ads (or 1%) have been referred to the NARB. The remainder are pending or were administratively closed.[4] The NARB has never taken a case to the FTC. It has no legal authority to enforce its judgments.

In June 1974, the National Association of Broadcasters announced a new code aimed at reducing abuses in children's advertising. The code called for, among other things, a reduction in commercial time from the 1971 level of 16 minutes per hour to 14 minues in the late afternoons on Monday through Friday, and under 10 minutes in the Saturday and Sunday morning time devoted primarily to children's programming, by December 31, 1975.[5]

Despite the fact that the FCC hailed this new code in its Children's Television Report and Policy Statement,[6] Donald McGannon, president of Westinghouse, which is responsible for Group W Broadcasting, was openly critical of the NAB and industry efforts at self-regulation. He had removed Group W from participation in the TV code in 1969 and from the NAD in protest against a code he feels is too week. During hearings on children's television advertising conducted by the House Commerce Subcommittee on Communications, he stated: "Self-regulation has not worked effectively in the area of children's programming and the Code of the NAB still does not go far enough."[7] A study conducted in December 1975 by Earle F. Barcus of Boston University showed that television stations around the country were regularly squeezing more commercial time in children's programming than the maximum permissible under the NAB code.[8]

As of 1974, the NAD/NARB review function has been largely confined to consumer advertising. In regard to energy-related image ads by corporations, the NARB was approached early in 1974 by Senator Thomas J. McIntyre (D, New Hampshire) with a request to establish a panel to develop a policy on energy-related ads. Edwin D. Etherington, chairman of NARB, rejected the request, stating that NARB was not established to provide a "censorship program or a blanket prohibition against advertising by type or source."[9] However, while defending the advertisers' "right and obligation to make their views known," he suggested that advertisers should scrupulously avoid adding to the public's confusion through their image advertisements or increasing apparent public distrust of business by tying energy-related ads to companies' economic interests. He laid down three broad standards for the companies to follow in environmental and energy-related image advertising:

1. The advertiser should clearly identify his personal interest in the public policy position advocated in the ad.
2. In case reference is made to any research data, the source of such information should be provided in the copy.
3. In advocating a public policy position, the advertiser should be factual and also avoid being accusatory or inflammatory.

Alternative Ways for Airing Viewpoints Different from Those of Business

I believe there is a clear need for encouraging greater exposure of other viewpoints, not necessarily antibusiness, on issues of public importance. It is imperative that the debate on the issues be sharp and positions clear. The best way to handle it is to let the spokesperson of a particular viewpoint present it in a manner he or she considers most advantageous. There are a variety of ways by which one can endeavor to change the behavior of the corporations. Where it is the intent of the society to proscribe a certain type of behavior, e.g., illegal price fixing, monopoly, collusion, the law can be used to develop an effective deterrent. The market forces also can be relied upon to carry a large part of the burden. But let us not be blind to the fact that there are circumstances when these traditional restraints become inadequate. We need alternative approaches to improve the quality of public decision making aimed at determining the level of acceptable behavior for corporations and other social institutions. Some of these mechanisms are internal to the corporation and deal with the behavior of individual managers and the company decision-making process. These will be discussed in the next chapter. In this section, I shall devote my attention to various measures that can be used to improve the flow of ideas from a variety of sources into the public communication space.

There is a significant body of opinion among businesspeople and media people that there is no need for providing alternative ways for airing viewpoints different from those of business on the ground that these viewpoints are already overrepresented or that existing mechanisms are sufficient to provide adequate exposure to all relevant viewpoints. Some of the arguments of businesspeople against the news media that were presented in Chapter 3 are relevant here and need not be repeated. I will devote my attention to only those arguments advanced by business and media people that relate to opposing groups.

The point most often made by businesspeople is that groups opposing business's position, e.g., consumer and environmental groups, have no problem getting substantial coverage in the press through news stories. "We've been unable to get coverage, but they have not," says Mr. Schmertz of Mobil Oil. "Without our ads there is a very substantial imbalance in favor of the viewpoint of environmental and consumer groups. Our ads go a small way to redressing that imbalance." Oddly enough, businesspeople also equate the ability of a group to raise funds with its legitimacy to speak for or against a certain viewpoint. As we have seen in Chapter 5, Clem Whitaker, Jr., president of Whitaker & Baxter, the public relations firm that managed the successful industry-supported campaign against the Clean Environment Initiative, Proposition 9, claimed that the opposition's lack of funds was indicative of the fact that it was not supported by the people. Herbert Schmertz of Mobil Oil makes the same point. But he goes a step further and uses a similar argument to rationalize Mobil's expenditures on advocacy advertising:

Their [the opposition groups] ability to raise money to support a point of view is also an indication of whether they have a constituency to support them. Otherwise they are just self-appointed keepers of the public morals and don't have the right to have a wide forum. We have a wide constituency. We have 200,000 shareholders who support us. We submit ourselves to an election every year. Have they ever submitted themselves to any election? With any constituency? Our 200,000 shareholders have invested money. If they are dissatisfied they can sell their shares and this company will go out of business. They have domonstrated a support for what this company is doing in a variety of ways.

Some media people also do not feel that alternative viewpoints need any help in being brought before the public. Lewis Young, editor-in-chief of *Business Week*, says that advocacy advertising gets criticized by people who do not agree with it and do not like to see that view in print. Robert Lubar, managing editor of *Fortune*, says:

I don't, at the moment, feel sorry for these groups. I think they are very powerful. Somehow or the other they are able to sway quite a lot of public opinion and they deserve the right to have a chance to do that. I don't think of them as being outmatched. They have a way of wielding a kind of power which at the moment is very impressive. If you can get expert opinion to say something, even if it really is not that well informed, the public is very much more swayed than if you pay a lot of money to advertise your viewpoint.

The news industry spokespeople also contend that environmental and other groups have easy access to the news columns and that their viewpoint is covered adequately.

As with all the other arguments of business groups discussed in the preceeding sections, most of the contentions made here are partially true as to the undesirability of providing additional avenues for expressing alternative viewpoints. However, they do not go far enough. Let us take these arguments one at a time:

1. The inability of the journalist to cover the business viewpoint intelligently and comprehensively could apply with equal logic to the viewpoints of environmentalists, consumerists, and those who seek greater government control of corporate behavior to increase business's public accountability.

2. If the public has greater confidence in expert opinion, what is there to prevent corporations from having experts support their viewpoint? Furthermore, to the extent that there is substantial merit to the position taken by business on controversial issues of public policy, there should be experts available to speak out publicly in support of that position and get media coverage.

3. It is a spurious argument to suggest that since a group cannot raise money, therefore it does not have a constituency. It is not the constituencies of people but the constituencies of ideas that are at stake. If the expression of an idea were to depend solely on the number of people that currently support it, new and controversial ideas would never see the light of day. How do we know how many people would support an idea until they have had a chance to be exposed to it and evaluate it in terms of its relevance to their physical and sociopolitical environment?

4. It is also egregious for corporate managements to claim that, unlike the opposing groups, they have a constituency in their shareholders who support them in a variety of ways. Legal and business scholars such as Melvin A. Eisenberg, Phillip I. Blumberg, Christopher Stone, and Myles L. Mace, have shown— and legal literature is replete with research and analytical studies that effectively demonstrate—that stockholders by and large exercise little control on the management which directs the affairs of the company through its control of proxy machinery.[10] Furthermore, the board of directors in most corporations

is largely composed of either corporate officers or outside directors whose appointment to the board is at the pleasure of the executive officer, who are dependent on management for their information, and who are therefore sympathetic to the top management and generally concur with its decisions. Only rarely and under extreme circumstances have the outside directors taken measures to counter management's decisions or instigate management changes at the top. In general, these actions have come in response to disclosures of gross violations of law or mismanagement on the part of the corporation's officers, and under pressure from some regulatory agency such as the Securities and Exchange Commission.[11]

If corporate managements were so interested in finding out the feelings of their stockholders, they would not display such resistance to entertaining stockholders' proposals requiring the companies to disclose information concerning activities in such areas as pollution control, minority hiring, investments in South Africa, or management involvement in bribes and payoffs abroad. Available evidence indicates that managements have fought against disclosing such information and that such proposals have had little success.[12] Moreover, in claiming the support of shareholders, corporate managements do not employ the same standards of democratic consent as they use for the opposing groups. For example, it would be interesting to see what type of support management would receive if it were to ask stockholders for specific permission to spend funds for non-tax-exempt advocacy advertising, where they are made aware of the views of those who oppose such expenditures or the positions expressed in the advertising, and also where only those shareholders actually responding are counted.

A Plan for Providing Greater Exposure for Diverse Viewpoints on Important Public Issues

Advertising Space for Alternative Viewpoints

The best approach to supplement the current efforts of the news media in providing exposure to alternative and yet potentially socially desirable viewpoints is through developing some mechanism by which advertising space is made available to deserving groups who are otherwise unable to afford such exposure. This approach has a certain similarity to counteradvertising applied to the broadcast media under the fairness doctrine where the Federal Communications Commission requires broadcasters to seek out and present both sides of a controversial public issue. (See Chapter 3, Appendix 3A for a more complete discussion of the fairness doctrine and its applicability to commercial messages).[13] The FCC policy statement on counteradvertising excludes product commercials from the counterad requirements but considers editorial advertising to be within the purview of the fairness doctrine. As I have noted in Chapter 3, the application of the fairness doctrine to the broadcast media has had the effect of removing all advertising dealing with controversial issues from radio and television.

In my approach, the emphasis would not be on "counter" but on "positive" alternatives. Thus ads would not be aimed at responding to specific issues in a certain ad or an ad campaign but would be designed to provide a particular kind of information to the public on important issues where such information is not available. Thus environment-related ads would concern themselves with showing the advantages of conservation as they pertain to the quality of life. They may also demonstrate that conservation need not cause loss of employment. Appendix Exhibits 8A-2 through 8A-6 provide examples of ads that come somewhat close to meeting these criteria.

Although these ads have been sponsored by conservation and other public interest groups, they do not attack a specific company or a corporate program. In this sense they are different from those presented in Chapter 5, where People's Lobby ads were directed against an industry-supported group, Californians Against the Pollution Initiative (CAPI), and were aimed at securing voter approval of Proposition 9. Exhibit 8A-2 is an ad that encourages people to report the polluting companies under the Water Refuse Act of 1899. Exhibits 8A-3 ("Should We Also Flood the Sistine Chapel So That Tourists Can Get Nearer the Ceiling?") deal with the competing claims of conservation, preservation of national monuments, and tourism and economic interests. Exhibit 8A-4 deals with culture and detente with the Soviet Union. Exhibit 8A-5 is an informative ad about food stamps and who is eligible for them, and Exhibit 8A-6 discusses the plight of American Indians. Unfortunately, I was unable to find examples of non-business-sponsored advocacy ads that dealt with the issues of the working of the economic system and the role of economic institutions and met the criteria outlined above.

I would like to suggest two ways in which this objective can be accomplished. The first one deals with broadening the scope of public service advertising to include other issues and sponsors that are currently covered. The second one proposes direct action by business and the news media to encourage public expression of diverse viewpoints on controversial social issues. I belive that the two approaches outlined here would encourage greater innovation and experimentation in the ad campaigns on the part of different groups. Furthermore, under those approaches, it should be feasible for the broadcast media to participate in the program. I must also emphasize that the nature of the program is totally voluntary and depends for its success on persuading all concerned that pursuing such a course would serve the public interest better without necessarily hurting their self-interest.

Broadening the Scope of Public Service Advertisements

Almost all news media, print and electronic, provide free ad space or air time for public service ads. They are used to encourage public participation in such activities as the Red Cross, United Crusade, the Boy Scouts, and to publicize noncontroversial issues such as fire prevention, aid to education, and the free enterprise system. A majority of these campaigns are developed by the Advertising Council, a private nonprofit group sponsored and supported by advertisers, advertising agencies, and the media. The Ad Council runs these campaigns in cooperation with the print and electronic media. Most of the magazines and newspapers and television stations interviewed by this author indicated that they used the Ad Council as the primary source for their public service ads; some like *Business Week* and *Fortune,* used this source exclusively.

An analysis of the Ad Council campaigns shows that its concept of important public issues is narrowly based and deals primarily with well-established traditional charities and social causes. Thus emerging issues of vital public concern are seldom included. The late Howard Gossage, a well-known adman, once stated that the Ad Council was willing to advocate causes, "but only those that would be thought of as controversial by people who are *for* cancer or against safe driving."[14]

It should be apparent that because of its membership, the Ad Council would have a certain pro business bias, and despite its claim of nonpartisanship, it is not likely to promote issues that might be looked upon unfavorably by important segments of business. The Ad Council's recent campaign to "enhance public understanding of the American Economic System"[15] has, for example, drawn fire from public interest groups such as the People's Bicentennial Commission, a Washington-based public interest group, which charged that the campaign was a propaganda effort for big business, gave a distorted and one-sided view of the free enterprise system, and was advocacy by omission. The Ad Council maintains that the ads in the American Enterprise System campaign are intended to educate and not to advocate a position. The People's Bicentennial Commission disagrees and has vowed to take legal action under the fairness doctrine against those broadcasting stations that run the Ad Council's commercials but refuse to run commercials prepared by the People's Bicentennial Commission.[16]

There is no reason why the scope of public service advertising should not be broadened to cover a greater diversity of issues and viewpoints. Notwithstanding the nonpartisan nature of the Ad Council, it should not be the only source of determining which causes and issues deserve public support. Other groups should be brought in to present other approaches and viewpoints. I believe such an action would be a constructive one and would improve the quality of public discussion and increase the diversity of issues covered. Before I outline a program for how it might be accomplished, I should point out that my interviews with members of the news media revealed a great reluctance on their part toward changing or enlarging the scope of their public service ad programs. Their reasons fall into the following two categories: (1) If the news media started giving free space to different groups, there would be no end to the number of requests. Lewis Young of *Business Week* says that if free advertising space is made available, "you'll be amazed by the number of people coming out of the woodwork who feel that they have an issue and are eligible." There would never be enough money to satisfy all requests. (2) The media will have to select among competing groups to determine who are qualified to receive funds. Rober Lubar of *Fortune* feels it would be a never-ending process.

These two points are interrelated. But to concede them would be begging the question. By limiting the donation of space to a particular group like the Ad Council, the news media are indeed making decisions as to who is entitled to this space. John E. Mandable of *Newsweek* concedes as much by saying that the Ad Council is not likely to choose any viewpoint that would run counter to that of some major advertisers. When asked whether he would consider providing free ad space to other groups that are not approved by the Ad Council, Mandable stated, "I would certainly consider it but I don't think that unless they had an endorsement from some other source, they would have a high priority." He was unable to state what other kind of endorsement would be acceptable to him.

Further, it was shown by Nat Hentoff (see Chapter 3) that different newspapers used quite subjective and arbitrary criteria in rejecting an advertisement by the Citizens Council of America that quoted Abraham Lincoln to the effect that he believed in the separation of races and advocated superior and inferior positions between the white and black races. Any alternative that attempts to reduce this arbitrariness merits consideration.

Establishment of a Public Service Advertising Space Allocation Committee

I propose that every newspaper, newsmagazine, radio, and television station should consider the establishment of a committee with the *advisory* role of recommending the allocation of ad space to different public interest and public service groups. This committee should be comprised of two exectuvies of the news medium and should also include three outstanding citizens with diverse outlooks and social perspectives. It is important that the outside members are not identified with and do not represent a special interest group but instead bring a breadth of vision to the deliberative process.

A large part of free ad space still should be allocated to traditional charitable causes, but steps should be taken to allow new groups and ideas a place for expressing their viewpoints. The space should not be given to those groups who are capable of raising funds to pay for advertisements, nor should it be allocated to advocacy groups that do not have tax-exempt status. Such a group represents a specific constituency and should be obliged to pay for the public expression of its viewpoint, or seek alternative ways to do so. The news media should publicly disclose its disbursement of free air time and ad space for general information to make people aware of its activities in this area. This would be in keeping with the notion of greater accountability, the public's right to know, and the news media's obligation to inform the public.

This is a modest proposal. The advisory character of the committee ensures that a news medium's prerogative to accept or reject specific ads would not be impinged upon. On the other hand, it would improve the quality of the allocation process and would be in the public interest.

Direct Efforts by Business and the News Media to Encourage Public Expression of Alternative Viewpoints: A National Council for Public Information

Business has most to lose from public misinformation and therefore should take every possible step to improve the quality of public information and debate. This would lead to better public understanding of complex issues affecting business and society and would therefore improve the process of public policy formulation. To accomplish this purpose, I propose the establishment of a National Council for Public Information (NCPI). Ths council will receive its major financial support from business corporations and trade groups. In addition, it will receive contributions of ad space and commercial air time from the news media. The news media contributions will represent a part of what the various media allocate to public service advertising and commercial announcements. The rationale for the business and the media participation in NCPI, and the broad outline of its organizational structure and modus operandi, are discussed below.

Business Participation

It is suggested that corporations should allocate funds equal to, say, between 25 to 50 percent of the amount spent by them on advocacy advertising to be used for purchasing advertising space for public expression of those viewpoints which, though important, would not receive exposure because of lack of funds. I should state that my interviews with corporate executives indicate that with some notable exceptions, companies are reluctant to venture in this direction. David Finn of Ruder & Finn, a public relations firm, recommends that companies should be willing to pay 100 percent of the cost of buying space in serious publications for examining different viewpoints on complex public issues where nobody knows what the right answers are. Two corporate executives who preferred to remain anonymous indicated that they would consider recommending to their companies an allocation of a reasonable amount of funds for such a program provided it is supported by other corporations representing a broad spectrum of business and industry, and provided that steps are taken to ensure that the disbursement of funds does not fall under the control of elements that represent extreme viewpoints and are antibusiness by conviction.

A policy of supporting the public expression of alternative viewpoints is *not* contrary to the corporation's self-interest. Instead, it should help in the development of a company's planning process, and also contribute to its public credibility. It could go a long way in reducing the legitimacy gap between societal expectations and corporate performance, the need for which was discussed in Chapter 2. David Finn of Ruder & Finn provides one rationale for corporate support by saying:

It would be very wise to show that a corporation is listening to what the other fellow is saying. If the company pays for time to let the other fellow make his best presentation, the president of the company will certainly read what appears in his space. And he will listen. He will overcome a lot of half-information that comes in newspaper articles or from his advisors who may be telling him what they think he wants to hear. Serious critics are also frustrated because their viewpoints do not come through. If a corporation really means what it says and wants to do what is best for the society—I believe that's what most corporate executives really do mean—this would be one way to accomplish this.

A company's advocacy advertising is aimed at telling the public about its position on major public policy issues in which the company has a vital stake. However, to improve its credibility, the company contributes to the purchase of commercial time and space to give public expression to other experts who offer solutions different from those supported by the company.

Media Participation

I believe that it would be appropriate for the broadcast media to participate in such a program. The media participation could be around 25 percent of the ad space allocated by them to public advertising. The implications for participation by the media in this program can be briefly summarized as follows:

1. It would broaden the scope of viewpoints represented in public service advertising.

2. It would indicate a willingness on the part of the news media, especially the electronic media, to experiment with new formats. The electronic media

have been criticized by both business and nonbusiness groups for their unwillingness to explore different alternatives in their public affairs programming and discussion of socially important issues.

3. There is no danger that participation in this program would in any way adversely affect the responsibility of the media in determining their news and editorial agenda. The media would have the sole discretion of accepting or rejecting an advertisement. Since the ads and commercials are received through NCPI, they are one step removed from the corporate sponsor. So there is no direct response to a controversial ad. It was noted in Chapter 3 that the broadcasters feared that by controlling the type of message in their advocacy ads, a corporation would be able to control the type of response and thereby determine the direction of public debate. The approach outlined here overcomes this objection. The news media in general, and the electronic media in particular, *need accept only those ad messages that would add to the medium's own coverage of an issue.*

In terms of the electronic media, this should apply not only to allocation of free time, but also the sale of air time for discussion of those issues that are being covered in their regular public affairs programming. The objective is to *complement* and not *replace* a radio or a television station's, or a network's, efforts in the discussion of a public issue. A station or the network does not have to air a commercial on a given issue if it feels that the station's own coverage has been adequate. The problems of the fairness doctrine are minimized because the emphasis in the selection of ad messages will not be so much on opposing a specific course of action but on the discussion of alternative approaches to complex social issues. The NCPI selection process for ad campaigns is designed to achieve this end.

Organization of NCPI

The NCPI should be directed by a board of directors composed of eminent persons, including corporate executives, with a national record of public service. In order for the program to be successful

1. The board members must be independent and collectively competent in evaluating the credentials of parties seeking air time or space under the program.

2. The test of independence for the board members, the credentials of the parties, and the types of proposals to be funded should be a conservative one. Although the board should be willing to accept novel ideas, the mere radical nature of an idea would not qualify it for funding. In other words, the burden of proof must be on the party seeking variation in currently accepted practices and existing solutions to certain social problems. This should protect the program from being charged with partisanship and also prevent groups representing extreme positions from gaining access to media for personal glorification.

3. The criteria for determing the eligibility of groups and proposals for funding by NCPI would be similar to those outlined in the previous section where I discussed the establishment of a Public Service Advertising Space Allocation Committee; i.e., the space should not be allocated to those groups capable of raising funds to pay for advertising. Further, advocacy groups who do not have tax-exempt status would be ineligible.

NCPI's program and group selection process will operate much like those of the National Science Foundation. Public interest groups will make proposals to NCPI for funding. NCPI's board, with the assistance of outside advisors, will select the proposals for support. The emphasis here would be on the discussion of general ideas rather than opposition to specific corporate actions or government decisions. For example, a proposal to discuss specific alternatives to the Alaska pipeline would be ineligible. But a proposal to discuss the ecological nature of Alaska and different ways by which its economy can be developed while preserving its environment should be acceptable. Clearly, such a discussion could not ignore the pipeline issue, but it would be part of a general understanding of the relationship between environment and economic growth and the alternative ways by which the two could be combined. The line between counteradvertising against a special program and advocacy of alternative approaches to social problems is not always easily defined. However, I am confident that given reasonable discretion and mutual trust among the parties concerned, viable programs can be developed.

Once the proposals have been selected for funding, NCPI can invite advertising agencies to submit campaign ideas and budgets that would translate these proposals into reality. NCPI will appoint ad hoc committees comprised of representatives from various groups, academic scholars, and communications and technical experts to evaluate these ideas for their feasibility and appropriateness. The final approval will rest with the NCPI board.

This approach would also overcome another problem currently faced by many public interest groups; i.e., the reluctance of established public relations and advertising agencies to undertake assignments from these groups. John O'Toole of Foote Cone & Belding says that ad agencies may turn down such accounts because the amount of billings involved is likely to be quite small. And yet by accepting them an agency may drive out other commercial accounts with substantial billings even when there is no direct conflict of interest.

Lest I give the impression that NCPI is a top-heavy bureaucratic organization, let me state that I envisage the number of campaigns approved each year by NCPI to be no more than ten. Therefore, the amount of work involved in the selection and approval process should be manageable. Moreover, the structure of NCPI as outlined here is not rigid, but is offered as a basis for further discussion and refinement.

Notes

1. *Associated Press* v. *United States,* 326 U.S. 1, 20 (1945). Cited in George L. Cooper, "The Tax Treatment of Business Grassroots Lobbying: Defining and Attaining the Public Policy Objectives," *Columbia Law Review,* 68 (May 1968), 80.

2. U.S. Senate, *Energy and Environmental Objectives, Hearings Before the Subcommittee on Environment of the Committee on Commerce,* Part 2 (Washington, D.C., 93rd Congress, 2nd Session, May 6 and July 18, 1974).

3. A.B. Stridsberg, *Effective Advertising Self-Regulation* (International Advertising Association, Inc., 1974). For a discussion of self-regulation efforts in different industries, see "Developments in the Law—Deceptive Advertising," *Harvard Law Review,* 80 (1967), 1005, 1143-1151.

4. Roland Campbell, Statement before the Senate Subcommittee on Communications of the Senate Committee on Commerce, *Hearings on the Fairness Doctrine* (Washington, D.C., 94th Congress, 1st Session, April 30, 1975), p. 175.

5. "ACT Says Stations Aren't Living Up to Rules on Ads in Children's TV: Stations Say Group Is Way Off-Base," *Broadcasting,* December 22, 1975, pp. 28-29.

6. Federal Communications Commission, "Children's Television Report and Policy Statement," October 31, 1974, FCC 74-1174.

7. Donald McGannon, Statement before the Senate Subcommittee on Communications of the Senate Committee on Commerce, *Hearings on the Fairness Doctrine*, p. 175.

8. "ACT Says Stations Aren't Living Up to Rules," pp. 28-29.

9. "NARB Chairman Defends Rights of 'Image' Ads," *Editor & Publisher,* March 16, 1974, p. 19.

10. See S. Prakash Sethi, *The Unstable Ground: Corporate Social Policy in a Dynamic Society* (Los Angeles: Melville, 1974), pp. 107-167; Phillip I. Blumberg, "The Politicization of the Corporation," *The Business Lawyer,* July 1971, p. 1551; Melvin A. Eisenberg, "The Local Roles of Shareholders and Management in Modern Corporate Decision-Making," *California Law Review,* January 1961, p. 1; Melvin A. Eisenberg, "Access to the Corporate Proxy Machinery," *Harvard Law Review,* 83 (May 1970), 1489; Melvin A. Eisenberg, "Legal Models of Management Structure in the Modern Corporation: Officers, Directors, and Accountants," *California Law Review,* 63 (March 1975), 375; J. A. C. Heatherington, "Fact and Legal Theory: Shareholders, Managers, and Corporate Social Responsibility," *Stanford Law Review,* January 1969, p. 109; Myles L. Mace, *Directors: Myth and Reality* (Boston: Division of Research, Graduate School of Business Administration, Harvard University, 1971); Ralph Nader and Mark Green (eds.), *Corporate Power in America* (New York: Grossman, 1973); and Christopher D. Stone, *Where the Law Ends* (New York: Harper & Row, 1975).

11. See the case of "Northrop Corporation, Los Angeles," in S. Prakash Sethi, *Up Against the Corporate Wall,* 3/e (Englewood Cliffs, N.J.: Prentice-Hall, 1977), in press; *"Herald Co.* v. *Seawell*: A New Corporate Social Responsibility?" *University of Pennsylvania Law Review,* 121 (May 1975), 1157; and Joseph H. Flom and Peter A. Atkins, "The Expanding Scope of SEC Disclosure Laws," *Harvard Business Review,* July–August 1974, p. 109.

12. See Phillip I. Blumberg, "Reflections on Proposals for Corporate Reform Through Change in the Composition of the Board of Directors: Special Interest or Public Directors," in S. Prakash Sethi (ed.), *The Unstable Ground: Corporate Social Policy in a Dynamic Society* (Los Angeles: Melville, 1974), p. 112; and James Hoy, "Socal's Dissent Shareholders Mobilize," *Business and Society Review,* winter 1975–76, p. 42.

13. Tom A. Collins, "Counter-Advertising in the Broadcast Media: Bringing the Administrative Process to Bear Upon a Theoretical Imperative," *William and Mary Law Review,* 15 (1974), 799; Paul D. Scanlon, "The FTC, the FCC, and the 'Counter ad' Controversy: An Invitation to 'Let's You and Him Fight?'" *Antitrust Law and Economics Review,* 5 (fall 1971), 43.

14. Quoted in Jerry Mander, "EcoPornography: One Year and Nearly a Million Dollars Later Advertising Owns Ecology," *Communication Arts: Environment,* 14, 2 (1972), 54.

15. Written Statement of Robert F. Keim, president, Advertising Council, Inc., before a subcommittee of the Committee on Government Operations, *Oversight Hearing on Commerce Department Payment to the National Advertising Council for Promotion of the Free Enterprise System* (Washington, D.C. 94th Congress, 1st Session, July 30, 1975), p. 25.

16. Philip H. Dougherty, "Economic Drive Spurs Conflict," *The New York Times,* April 22, 1976, p. 57.

Appendix 8

Specimen Ads

WHAT THE CAN PEOPLE ARE DOING

Frankly answering the question:

Cans, Bad Guys or Good Guys?

A can is a nice thing when you want a soda or a beer. But it doesn't do much for a landscape or a highway. We know that very well because we make cans. So here's the story. Both sides.

Cans are bad guys. Cans are all over the streets and highways. Cans cause litter.

Cans are good guys. Out of all the litter on the streets and highways, over 83% isn't cans.

Still, somebody has to do something. So we've been working with people who are developing a machine that can actually pick the litter off the roads. We call it the octopus.

Cans are bad guys. Returnables were better. Return to returnables.

Cans are good guys. The can is one of the safest, cleanest, cheapest containers ever invented. If we return to returnables, prices may go up. Because the system is set up for non-returnables, and it will cost money and jobs to change it. Besides, people don't return returnables.

Cans are bad guys. You use them once and throw them away. They can't be recycled.

Cans are good guys. We've already set up recycling centers for used cans. (Steel and aluminum. Beer and soda and food.) More are coming. This costs us money, but it doesn't cost you anything. You bring us the cans and we'll recycle them.

We know it would be easier and better if all you had to do was throw your cans in a garbage pail. So we're supporting the development of automated machines that magnetically separate cans from the rest of the garbage. It's already happening in many cities and it will soon be happening in others. We hope that eventually every can in every city will be recycled.

*The Can People: American Can Co., Continental Can Co., National Can Corp., The Heekin Can Co.

Exhibit 8A-1

REWARD · REWARD

EVERY WATER POLLUTER IN THIS COUNTRY HAS A PRICE ON HIS HEAD!!

BUT THE LAW THAT PROVIDES FOR REWARD HAS GONE ALMOST UNNOTICED.

· THE WATER REFUSE ACT of 1899 ·

made it unlawful "to throw, discharge, or deposit any refuse matter of any kind or description whatever into any navigable water of the United States." The only exception is when a permit to pollute is obtained from the Army Corps of Engineers.

$500⁰⁰ TO 2500⁰⁰ A DAY!

The law makes every individual and corporate polluter subject to a fine of 500 to 2,500 dollars for each day of the violation.

And whoever catches the polluter can get half the fine as a reward.

There are over 40,000 industrial polluting plants in this country operating outside the law.

If you want to know how to catch them write for The Bounty Hunters' Guide on Water Pollution, The Project on Clean Water, Natural Resources Defense Council, 36 West 44th Street, New York, N.Y. 10036.

The best way to fight water pollution is to make your own waves.

Prepared by the Stern Concern

Exhibit 8A-2

313

SHOULD WE ALSO FLOOD THE SISTINE CHAPEL SO TOURISTS CAN GET NEARER THE CEILING?

EARTH began four billion years ago and Man two million. The Age of Technology, on the other hand, is hardly a hundred years old, and on our time chart we have been generous to give it even the little line we have.

It seems to us hasty, therefore, during this blip of time, for Man to think of directing his fascinating new tools toward altering irrevocably the forces which made him. Nonetheless, in these few brief years among four billion, wilderness has all but disappeared. And now these:

1) There is a bill in Congress to "improve" Grand Canyon. Two dams will back up artificial lakes into 148 miles of canyon gorge. This will benefit tourists in power boats, it is argued, who will enjoy viewing the canyon wall more closely. (See headline). Submerged underneath the tourists will be part of the most revealing single page of earth's history. The lakes will be as deep as 600 feet (deeper for example, than all but a handful of New York buildings are high) but in a century, silting will have replaced the water with that much mud, wall to wall.

There is no part of the wild Colorado River, the Grand Canyon's sculptor, that will not be maimed.

Tourist recreation, as a reason for the dams, is in fact an afterthought. The Bureau of Reclamation, which backs them, prefers to call the dams "cash registers." They are expected to make money by sale of commercial power.

They will not provide anyone with water.

2) In Northern California, four lumber companies are about to complete logging the private virgin redwood forests, an operation which to give you an idea of its size, has taken fifty years.

Soon, where nature's tallest living things have stood silently since the age of the dinosaurs, the extent of the cutting will make creation of a redwood national park absurd.

The companies have said tourists want only enough roadside trees for the snapping of photos. They offer to spare trees for this purpose, and not much more. The result will remind you of the places on your face you missed while you were shaving.

3) And up the Hudson, there are plans for a power complex — a plant, transmission lines, and a reservoir on top of Storm King Mountain — destroying one of the last wild and high and beautiful spots near New York City.

4) A proposal to flood a region in Alaska as large as Lake Erie would eliminate at once the breeding grounds of more wildlife than conservationists have preserved in history.

5) In San Francisco, real estate developers are day by day filling a bay that made the city famous, putting tract

houses over the fill; and now there's a new idea — still more fill, enough for an air cargo terminal as big as Manhattan.

There exists today a mentality which can conceive such destruction, giving commerce as ample reason. For 74 years, the 40,000 member Sierra Club has opposed that mentality. But now, when even Grand Canyon can be threatened, we are at a critical moment in time.

This generation will decide if something untrammelled and free remains, as testimony we had love for those who follow.

We have been taking ads, therefore, asking people to write their Congressmen and Senators; Secretary of the Interior Stewart Udall; The President; and to send us funds to continue the battle. Thousands *have* written, but meanwhile, the Grand Canyon legislation has advanced out of committee and is near a House vote. More letters are needed and more money, to help fight a mentality that may decide Man no longer needs nature.*

| AGE OF TECHNOLOGY |
| FIRST MAN — 2 MILLION YRS. AGO |
| FIRST ELEPHANTS — 60 MILLION YRS. AGO |
| FIRST REDWOODS — 130 MILLION YRS. AGO |
| FIRST MAMMALS — 180 MILLION YRS. AGO |
| FIRST DINOSAURS — 180 MILLION YRS. AGO |
| FIRST TREES — 250 MILLION YRS. AGO |
| FIRST REPTILES — 275 MILLION YRS. AGO |
| FIRST FISHES — 400 MILLION YRS. AGO |
| GRAND CANYON — 550 MILLION YRS. AGO |
| FIRST CORALS — 575 MILLION YRS. AGO |
| FIRST SPONGES — 650 MILLION YRS. AGO |
| BIRTH OF THE EARTH — 4 BILLION YRS. AGO |

David Brower, Executive Director
Sierra Club
Mills Tower, San Francisco

☐ Please send me more details on how I may help.

☐ Here is a donation of $_____ to continue your effort to keep the public informed.

☐ Send me "Time and the River Flowing," famous four color book which tells the complete story of Grand Canyon, and why T. Roosevelt said, "leave it as it is." ($25.00)

☐ Send me "The Last Redwoods" which tells the complete story of the opportunity as well as the destruction in the redwoods. ($17.50)

☐ I would like to be a member of the Sierra Club. Enclosed is $14.00 for entrance and first year's dues.

Name_____

Address_____

City_____ State_____ Zip_____

---

*The previous ads, urging that readers exercise a constitutional right of petition, to save Grand Canyon, produced an unprecedented reaction by the Internal Revenue Service threatening our tax deductible status. IRS says the ads may be a "substantial" effort to "influence legislation." Undefined, these terms leave organizations like ours at the mercy of administrative whim. (The question has not been raised with any organizations that favor Grand Canyon dams.) So we cannot now promise that contributions you send us are deductible—pending results of what may be a long legal battle.

The Sierra Club, founded in 1892 by John Muir, is nonprofit, supported by people who, like Thoreau, believe "In wildness is the preservation of the world." The club's program is nationwide, includes wilderness trips, books and films — as well as such efforts as this to protect the remnant of wilderness in the Americas. There are now twenty chapters, branch offices in New York (Biltmore Hotel), Washington (Dupont Circle Building), Los Angeles (Auditorium Building), Albuquerque, Seattle, and main office in San Francisco.

Exhibit 8A-3

314

שלום

Welcome to the Bolshoi Ballet

But That's About All

The Bolshoi Ballet is welcome. Cultural exchange is welcome. Detente. Peace among nations. All are welcome.

However, we find it hard to reconcile the beauty of the ballet with the repression of culture and freedom. Both are products of the U.S.S.R.

Soviet Jews are denied the right to emigrate freely; to practice their religion; to study their culture and ancestral language. In recent months their situation has worsened: emigration drastically curtailed, telephone communications cut, mail blocked. Many Jews have been summarily arrested. Some are given harsh sentences after closed trials.

The issue of human rights transcends borders.

International agreements on emigration transcend any country's internal policies.

WE PROTEST. We protest the abuse of Jews in the U.S.S.R. who are persecuted, imprisoned, deprived of their jobs and kept under secret police surveillance because they want to emigrate to Israel. Send this ad as a protest, or write your own protest to the Soviet Minister of Culture, c/o Embassy of the U.S.S.R., 1125 16th Street, N.W., Washington, D.C. 20036.

Meanwhile, welcome to the Bolshoi Ballet.

COMMISSION ON SOVIET JEWRY
of the Community Relations Committee
Jewish Federation-Council of Greater Los Angeles

Prepared in the public interest by The Maxwell Arnold Agency, San Francisco.

Exhibit 8A–4

315

$5

WRH
STA

Food Stamps mean more food for people with a small income.
If you are eligible it's your legal right to buy food stamps at a discount or get them free.

WHO GETS FOOD STAMPS?
Food stamps are for people who support a big family on a small income. Or for elderly people who earn little and live on Social Security. Or for anybody with a small income who is eligible. Depending on your income, the government sells you food stamps at a big discount or gives them to you free.

AS GOOD AS MONEY.
Food stamps are like money. You use them to buy food as if they were cash. They stretch your food dollars and let you feed your family better. With food stamps you can get twice as much food for your family without spending any more money.

GOOD AT MOST
GROCERY STORES.
Almost all food stores take food stamps for food purchases. It's a good deal for the store because it increases total business when you use food stamps to buy extra food.

YOU HAVE A LEGAL RIGHT
TO FOOD STAMPS.
Your legal right to food stamps is protected by Federal Law. In addition, you have a legal right to get food stamps as soon as you move to a new area. And you have a legal right to a quick decision on your application for food stamps.

FIND OUT IF YOUR FAMILY
IS ELIGIBLE NOW.
You do not have to be unemployed or on welfare to be eligible for food stamps. However, you should check with your local welfare office to find out whether you are eligible, where to go and what to do. In some areas, the local welfare office even gives out or sells the stamps. If you run into any problems, write:

FOOD STAMPS
ROOM 301
1424 16th STREET N.W.
WASHINGTON, D.C. 20036

Don't cheat your family out of better meals for less money. Remember: $5 can get you $10 with food stamps.

An advertisement for you by PUBLIC COMMUNICATION, INC., 2005 L Street N.W., Washington, D.C. 20036
Prepared in cooperation with the National Welfare Rights Organization, Washington, D.C.

Exhibit 8A–5

316

Maybe I should have been a lawyer

WHEN I WAS A KID in high school I might have tried to get myself to law school. Except in those days it seemed impossible, for a Mexican American.

As a matter of fact, right now out of 50,000 law school students in this country, there are only 400 with Spanish surnames. High school kids in the Mexican American minority can't see themselves through the seven years it takes to get a law degree.

And yet a law degree is the single most important thing a young Mexican American can have today —to help his neighbors, his community, his fellow-citizens in our Mexican American culture, to help them fulfill themselves as equal and valuable members of the American democratic society.

A lawyer in the Mexican American community means just about everything in helping my fellow Mexican Americans to learn, grow and flourish, and receive the full protection and benefits of American law and justice.

Whether you realize it or not, let me say that for a long time the Mexican Americans in this country haven't exactly had a fair shake in business, jobs, schools and civil rights. Not by a long shot. And it harms our whole country.

The Mexican American Legal Defense and Educational Fund has a great program to send Mexican American students through law school. It does it with money it raises itself, and with money that law schools and foundations provide to match.

So I am asking you to help. Don't get me wrong. There's nothing I like better than being a first-string quarterback. But now I can also see what it means to be a first-string lawyer.

Jim Plunkett

Exhibit 8A-6

Can Advocacy Advertising Be Made More Effective? Some Guidelines for Business

To dispel the ghosts which populate the world of our making will not give us the power to conquer the real enemies of the real world or to remake the real world. But it may help us discover that we cannot make the world in our image. It will liberate us and sharpen our vision. It will clear away the fog so we can face the world we share with all mankind.

—Daniel Boorstin, The Image

Advocacy advertising can become a cutting edge in further opening the process of public information. It can contribute to improved understanding on the part of the public of what can be reasonably expected of business in fulfilling a society's expectations. But it calls for great care on the part of business institutions in the use of this important instrument. It also requires a gradual change in the behavior of business institutions, where current methods of operation and standards of performance fall short of the expectations of large segments of society. None of this, however, will come to pass if considerable restraint is not exercised by business in the use of advocacy advertising. Devoid of a desire for change and a substantive effort in this direction on the part of business institutions, advocacy advertising will become just another in the continuing efforts of business to defend today's reality and status quo with yesterday's ideology and raison d'être. In the event large corporations are content to pursue a course primarily of partisan propaganda in their public communications, the consequences could affect every aspect of our society. It will not reduce the scope of conflict, but enlarge it. It will not contribute to the quality and diversity of public information, but worsen it. By escalating the level of noise, it will increase public antagonism which will express itself through greater government restrictions on the conduct of business than are necessary or desirable. Business will have no one to blame but itself and just as predictably will buy more ad space to bemoan the fact of public ignorance, media hostility, and political opportunism. Robert Lubar of *Fortune* warns: "They [the businessmen] tend to create trouble for themselves in stirring up antagonism instead of trying to placate it. Both sides

---

Unless otherwise specifically stated, all direct quotes in this chapter are from personal interviews or written communications with the author.

319

have a lot to learn and the public will benefit if they both do." Nor will it serve the society's purpose if critics class all advocacy advertising as undesirable and against the public interest. In a climate of mutual distrust and name calling, the critics cannot claim to represent any larger public interest than their own, or to be interested in hearing viewpoints that are not variations of their own.

A number of suggestions for corporate action have been made in previous chapters where I dealt with the tax deductibility, ad substantiation, and co-operation with the news media, and need not be repeated here. In this chapter I shall devote my attention to specific actions that corporations should take in terms of their communications programs, and also in terms of initiating changes in corporate behavior and performance where such changes are called for.

Advocacy Advertising, FTC, FCC, IRS, and the First Amendment

A corporation must have a clear understanding of whether it wants to treat advocacy advertising as commercial speech or protected speech. The two approaches have different consequences for corporations and public policy. Any attempt by a corporation or business in general to "have it both ways" will lead to greater public skepticism of corporate motives than currently exists and will defeat the purpose of advocacy advertising by enmeshing it in unnecessary controversy.

Although in the previous chapters the roles of FTC, FCC, and IRS were separately considered, there is a definite relationship among the Federal Trade Commission's determination of whether or not an advertisement is commercial or protected speech, the IRS determination of whether advertising expenses are related to the patronage the taxpayer might reasonably expect in the future or to grassroots lobbying, and the Federal Communications Commission's determination of whether an ad does or does not raise a controversial issue of public importance. The relationship among these determinations is even more important than the results of each determination.

The relationship among them arises from the fact that the "grassroots lobbying" and "controversial issues" standards are—as is the FTC standard—based on the First Amendment. That is, the First Amendment would bar the FTC from regulating the truth or falsity of an ad when the ad is a form of grassroots lobbying or raises a controversial issue of public importance. Similarly, if the ad is commercial speech regulatable by the FTC, the ad will also give rise to patronage and not raise a controversial issue. Therefore, if a corporation takes a business expense deduction, it is inappropriate for it to argue that the FTC cannot regulate. Conversely, if the advertiser can take no deduction, the FTC may not regulate. In the case of broadcast media, however, the FCC must still rule on the application of the fairness doctrine whether or not a corporation has taken a deduction.

No coordination currently exists among the determinations of the three agencies despite the overlapping of considerations. The ideal situation would be to develop clear guidelines for business on the consequences of running different kinds of ads. The businessperson will than have the choice, for example, of regulation and deduction, or no regulation and no deduction. However, as I have noted in earlier chapters, such guidelines would be extremely difficult to develop. Although some further clarification is possible and is desirable, any attempt to develop detailed specifications to satisfy all foreseeable situations would become too rigid and thus counterproductive.

Development of a Corporate Program For External Communications

In order to develop a successful external communication program with its many constituent publics, the corporation must (1) perceive correctly the nature, extent, and source of social pressures that confront it. It must make a substantial improvement in its ability to scan and monitor changes in the environment that might lead in the future to demands for new or greater corporate involvement in social problems; and (2) strengthen internal organizational structures and decision-making processes to develop relevant and effective response patterns to external social pressures and problems.

As presently constituted, the public relations department performs a "window out" service for the corporation. That is, it communicates to the world an image the corporation has of itself. The typical public relations officer is not an expert in the company's primary activities and has not had any line responsibility or experience. He or she seldom plays a significant role in making major corporate decisions and only a minor role in making those decisions that are to be carried out by the department. Robert Dilenschneider, a senior vice-president with Hill & Knowlton, one of the nation's largest public relations firms, says, "It may sound harsh, but in most companies public relations people do not deal with the top. If you can't deal with top-level people and command their respect, then there is no way you are going to change their minds about advertising or anything else." Thus the public relations officer's effectiveness in relating corporate needs to societal pressures and expectations is severely limited. More often than not, he or she is reduced to the role of corporate apologist. Just as often, he or she is ignored by corporate critics who insist on talking to top management because they recognize that decisions relating to corporate social responses are made by top management and only communicated by public relations departments.

The first change in the activities of public relations department should be in the area of information dissemination. The role should be enlarged from "window out" to include "window in." That is, instead of merely telling the world what the corporation would like the world to hear about itself, the public relations officer should also tell corporate management what the rest of the world thinks of it and why. Many of the decisions concerning corporate policies and social conflicts are not integrated into the mainstream of corporate activities. A corporation's communication network is not programmed to receive the information that would alert it to problems in the social arena. On the contrary, the communication network is more likely to filter out such information as being extraneous to the decision at hand and therefore irrelevant. A public relations officer can use his knowledge to sensitize management to changes in the external environment and what they mean for the corporation. In other words, he or she should become an instrument of environmental scanning and analysis for the corporation.

The new role of the public relations officer would be incomplete if it were to be confined only to information gathering and improvement of the communication process. The next step is to make sure that information relating to social concerns becomes part of the inputs that go into corporate decision making. Without being facetious, I suggest that *the title of vice-president of public relations be changed to that of vice-president of corporate integrity.* In this new capacity, this executive will be charged with the responsibility for seeing that management carefully evaluates the possible broader implications, both positive and negative, of all major corporate decisions *before* they are implemented. This approach is not unlike the environmental impact statements that government agencies are required to make prior to embarking on major projects of social importance. By forcing line managers to think through the larger social, political, and economic effects that their decisions might entail, this vice-president would be acting as the corporate conscience or the society's ombudsman.

Advocacy Advertising and Corporate External Communication Programs

Advocacy advertising should be an integral part of the total corporation communication program, which in turn must bear a close relationship to the activities of the corporation, the role it projects for itself in the society, and the expectations of the society for corporate performance. Too often advocacy advertising is confined to what the corporation wants the world to hear rather than what the world wants the corporation to talk about. The program should involve both paid and unpaid communication. It should be a continuous program built around the long-range objectives of the firm. Robert Dilenschneider of Hill & Knowlton contends that few companies have established total communication programs. "Companies don't realize they have to start today to get them where they want to be in 1985."

Improving Public Credibility of Advocacy Campaigns

The adversary nature of advocacy advertising makes it imperative that corporations strive to make their message credible to an otherwise skeptical and even hostile audience. One element of such credibility would be clear identification of the message with the sponsoring corporation, and the willingness of the corporation openly to state the nature and purpose of such advertising. Various measures of how this might be accomplished were discussed in Chapters 6 and 7, where I dealt with the tax deductibility and substantiation issues as related to advocacy advertising.

Mere identification of the corporation with the ad message is not enough. For reasons previously discussed (Chapter 7), I do not believe it to be feasible or socially desirable that corporations be required to submit to some externally imposed criteria for accuracy or truth of the statements made in their advocacy ads. However, this does not absolve the corporation from the need of assuring its readers that the statements made in the ads are indeed true and accurate. One approach to accomplish this would be for the corporation to appoint a committee of three or four outside persons, e.g., academicians and prominent citizens, with expertise in the subject matter to be discussed in the ads. The committee members will render opinions on each ad as to the accuracy and fairness of the position stated therein. This opinion would be advisory in character. Given the stature of the committee members, an endorsement by them would go a long way toward improving the public credibility of the corporation and the viewpoint it supports. Although such a course may not satisfy all corporate critics, it would at least put the corporate message on equal footing with those of its critics in the eyes of the public.

Treatment of the Message Content

Corporations must exercise a great degree of self-restraint in developing the content and style of their ad messages. Advocacy ads are likely to be subjected to more intense scrutiny and analysis by corporate critics. The targeted primary audiences of these campaigns, namely, the opinion leaders, are better informed than the average citizen and are less likely to be swayed by glib statements or empty clichés. David Finn of Ruder & Finn warns that when a company buys space to tell its story, it naturally turns to advertising specialists. The risk is that the statement becomes too slick and simplistic and therefore not credible. A company may feel that its message is being told the way it wants it to be. The reader, however, may feel it is much less believable.

It is imperative that a corporation presenting its views in the advocacy format maintain a high standard of integrity in the treatment of the subject matter or it will end up in escalating the level of partisan squabbling. Irony, if it is to be effective, should lightly etch a phrase, and not drip from each word. A stance of pure opposition—opposition as an end in itself, rather than some larger positive social commitment—is self-defeating and likely to be short-lived.

Mr. Schmertz of Mobil Oil appreciates this concern when he says that his company has made a fundamental decision to make a significant intellectual commitment to the subject matter in its ad campaign rather than giving it a superficial treatment: "We probably lose readers. But in the long haul unless you are prepared to put yourself on the line both intellectually and philosophically, you will never gain long-term leadership and recognition of substance." With few exceptions, Mobil's advocacy ad campaign has received high marks for content quality from the corporate executives I have interviewed. Editors of the various news media, including some of those that have been the subject of Mobil's criticism, consider Mobil's ads to be generally accurate and a good treatment of the subject matter. But the campaign has not escaped criticism. Mobil has many critics in the oil industry who believe that Mobil writers are talking only to themselves and their friends in these advertisements. These commentators contend that the people who are really critical of the industry, and whose understanding and favorable opinion is important to the industry, are being turned off.

General versus Specific Issues

One important aspect of advocacy campaign has to do with whether or not a company has articulated a program that provides a unifying standard for corporate policies and actions. This is the program with which the company must identify itself. It follows that advocacy campaigns by individual corporations that plead for business as a whole are not likely to be successful because a company cannot control the activities of other members of the business community. When contradictions occur between the real world and what the corporation has presented, the result will be an inevitable loss of credibility. Advocacy advertising is most effective when it attacks an isolated issue on which a corporation has been misunderstood or its position inaccurately reported. The company is then in a strong position to defend its viewpoint, offer independent expert opinion, and substantiate its claims.

Ironically, while Mobil has been praised for the overall tone of its advertising, it has been criticized for distortion of facts and statements when it attacked its adversaries on a specific issue or statement of fact (Chapter 3). In analyzing the Mobil campaign, a *Wall Street Journal* story noted that many critics believed big companies (especially oil companies) deserved their bad reputations, and that big ad budgets such as Mobil's would tell the public more clearly and convince it more persuasively of the harmful social impact of some of their activities than statements by critics of big business.[1] William Small of CBS News considers the Mobil ads "extremely clever," which makes him suspicious "because this is an ecopolitical position taken by a large corporation. I don't look upon them preparing and putting in ads for altruistic reasons. I don't think I will often find a Mobil ad that is critical of the oil industry."

The preceding discussion indicates it is quite doubtful whether a patently one-sided appeal that ignores the rationale of the opposing viewpoints or ridicules it is likely to be very effective. It may even be counterproductive and may defeat the very purpose it was designed to accomplish (see also Chapter 4).

Broadening the Scope of Expression by Corporate Executives

Businesspeople have been criticized, and with ample justification, for their unwillingness to meet with the news media as well as other social groups and give their views on controversial social issues (see also Chapter 3). Occasionally, when interaction does take place, the picture that generally emerges is that of the top executive, flanked by the corporate counsel and a public relations officer, giving bland and evasive responses to questions.

Some corporate executives perceive this problem primarily as one of technique and have resorted to seminars on "how to interview effectively" or "how to appear on TV." Important though it may be, technique cannot substitute for substantive dialogue between a chief executive officer and representatives of the news media or other groups. One does not expect a professional, polished performance from a chief executive officer so much as the thoughtful articulation of opinions and a willingness to state a position.

Frederick W. West, Jr., president of Bethlehem Steel, suggests that executives become more accessible to reporters. He also suggests that businesses sponsor educational seminars to train reporters in specialized fields that they have to cover as part of their business news assignments.[2] Similar opinions were given by Marshall Loeb of *Time* when he said that the chief executive officer should encourage other members of management to speak publicly through all possible forums about their views even though they may be somewhat different from those held by him: "He should make clear that there is no 'party line' or company line to which the employees need adhere. They should *not* be expected or obliged to say certain things. Managements should trust that their employees are intelligent, alert people who can and do make sound judgments. Businessmen should present disparate points of view rather than *the* corporate point of view."

Such a decentralized approach to public communication carries with it a risk that conflicting opinions might emerge on a given issue from within the corporation. However, it would also show the corporation in more realistic terms and make it concede errors of judgment when they occur. The company would not be forced to defend every action, no matter how trivial, in terms of corporate survival, management prerogatives, or defense of the free enterprise system.

More Effective Use of In-House Communication Organs

Corporations have been increasingly using annual reports, employee magazines, and special reports to publicize their activities in such areas as pollution control, minority hiring, quality of life, and consumerism. Some companies have even gone further and used these communication vehicles to criticize Congress, regulatory agencies, and other groups whose activities they consider to be inimical to the corporate as well as the public interest.[3] The messages are perhaps intended to reinforce the views of those who believe in the company's position, and to change the opinion of those readers who have not yet made up their minds. However, the impact on the latter group will be impaired if the corporation conveys an image of publishing partisan propaganda aimed at a captive audience and carried in a medium whose contents it controls.

One approach to remedy the situation would be for the corporation to publish simultaneously, and in the same medium, an evaluation of its actions and viewpoints by an outsider. One example of such an effort is that of Atlantic Richfield Company, Los Angeles (ARCO). In 1975, it published a special report on the social programs of activities in which ARCO had been involved. In the same report the company published a critique of its activities, as well as their public depiction, by Milton Moscowitz, a well-known San Francisco-based journalist of business affairs and a critic in the area of corporate social responsibility.

Another approach would be for the corporations to invite responsible spokespeople of opposing viewpoints to present their views in corporate house organs where views of the management on controversial issues of public importance are also presented. This would improve a corporation's standing in the eyes of the readers by demonstrating the company's willingness to let the readers choose from alternative viewpoints. Herbert Schmertz of Mobil Oil does not agree with this approach. He contends that corporate critics have already had much more public access for expressing their viewpoints than has business:

They [critics] put out newsletters—do they give us space in their newsletters? They shouldn't—that would dilute the debate. It is imperative that the debate be sharp, the positions clear, and the source identified. It would be impossible to have a wide ranging and robust debate if we took space in their media or they in ours. It tends to co-opt each other.

This statement begs the question rather than answers it. It is no clear how presenting divergent viewpoints would either dilute the quality of debate or coopt the spokespeople. It is in the interest of the corporation to improve its credibility with the public at large and it should pursue those strategies which fulfill the objective regardless of what the critics do. What the corporations need are bold, innovative approaches that raise their public stature rather than short-run considerations that sink them in narrow partisan quagmire. It is hard for the corporation to claim a higher public purpose when its strategies and tactics are no different from those of groups whose motives it questions.

Speaking Out Against Wrongdoers

The cause of business is poorly served when corporate spokespeople concentrate their fire on corporate critics but refuse to speak out against businesspeople and business practices that are illegal or that are considered socially irresponsible. By refusing to take a public position against corporate wrongdoers they invite criticism against all businesses and convey the image of business as a monolithic entity.

Businesspeople are quick to take up cudgels against any group whose performance is found wanting and are not hesitant about criticizing radical groups, government bureaucrats, consumerists, environmentalists, and the news media. And yet, when it comes to cleaning their own houses or keeping them in order, their voices are strangely muted. For example, Donald S. MacNaughton, chairman of the Prudential Insurance Company of America, exhorts the news media "to assume the responsibility for establishing sound minimum performance standards for all the practitioners of your profession." He goes on to suggest that "it shouldn't be possible, as it is today, for anyone to enter the reportorial or editorial field without having acquired the necessary credentials by way of a sound training program. Nor, for another example, should the press discourse on any subject, particularly complex ones, except through members with an expertise on the subject."[4]

And yet few businesspeople have assumed the responsibility of advocating a code of conduct for their own peer group or of having peer group pressure brought to bear upon those who have been found to have engaged in socially irresponsible behavior. There have been some efforts in this direction, following Watergate and the disclosure of widespread illegal payoffs by large corporations. However, most commentators concede that the efforts are not likely to succeed in the foreseeable future in changing or improving corporate behavior.[5]

Most professional associations have procedures to take action against those members who violate professional standards. Even the AFL–CIO saw fit to expel teamsters and longshoremen when they "violated minimum standards of corporate democracy." But, as Arthur Schlesinger, Jr., points out, in the past sixteen years not one businessman has ever been censured or barred from any business organization for wrongdoing that both the government and the corporation admitted existed. "Apparently there are, at least in the eyes of business associations, no minimum standards of corporate decency." According to Schlesinger:

If business leaders expect the reverence they seem to think is their divine right, they must deal with their own Augean stables. For the whole system is involved in a crisis of legitimacy. Nor can they hope to circumvent this crisis by public relations, institutional advertising, programs in "economic education." . . No amount of Madison Avenue magic is going to persuade the American people that American business is different from what it is.[6]

Congruence Between Internal Activities and Public Posture

No amount of advocacy advertising is likely to yield better public understanding of business's role in society and agreement with the social policies and programs supported by business if there is a large gap between the image business wishes to promote and what business does. Public images are formed not only by the type of awareness that is created through corporate advertising but also through the multitude of transactions that a person has with a corporation in terms of products, services, and news about individual companies and business in general. A corporation's messages constitute a very small input in an individual's cognition of his relevant world. Unless corporate activities are congruent with the public image it wishes to promote, there will be a spate of other images about the corporation, carried through alternative communication forms, that will be incongruent with the image the corporation intended to develop through its institutional advertising program. Advocacy advertising can play a healthy role only if a company is making other efforts to bring its performance in line with public expectations.

There must be a recognition on the part of business that some of the criticism leveled against it is legitimate and that efforts should be made to remedy the situations within business that are creating the problems. Otherwise, business cannot escape externally imposed constraints on its activities. In the words of Arthur Schlesinger, "The only answer lies in performance. . . . For if business cannot clean its house, the government will clean the house of business." Or as Mayo J. Thompson, who was named by the Direct Selling Association in 1976 as "Champion of Free Enterprise," remarks: "So long as there are those who will not listen to the small voice of conscience within, then the policemen must stand ready on the outside."[7]

From Defensive Negativism to Positive Activism

In an earlier chapter I suggested that one of the main purposes of corporate advocacy advertising was to seek social validation or legitimacy for its actions. This quest for legitimacy by the corporation is crucial to its survival and growth. Given that both corporations and their critics seek to narrow the gap between corporate performance and social expectations, the concept of legitimacy can be viewed as a three-stage phenomenon—i.e., *social obligation, social responsibility, or social responsiveness.*[8] Legitimization involves not only the type of corporate activity, but the *process* of internal decision making, the perception and manipulation of the external environment—physical, social, and political—to make it more receptive to corporate activities, and the nature of accountability. Each of the three stages of the legitimacy concept employs a different approach to the decision-making process, the strategy for perception and manipulation of the environment, and the notion of accountability.

Social obligation implies that a corporation is fulfilling its social contract so long as there is a market demand for its goods and services, and it is not violating any laws. However, by themselves, these criteria are not sufficient. Market performance may reflect only short-term concerns, while the accounting system may ignore certain vital costs that could be relevant in the long run. Similarly, legal criteria largely reflect the minimum acceptable standards that are invariably behind changing social expectations. Thus, *traditional economic and legal criteria are necessary but not sufficient conditions of corporate legitimacy.*

The second stage of the legitimacy concept is characterized by *social responsibility.* It does not require a radical departure from the usual nature of corporate activities or the normal pattern of corporate behavior. It is simply taking steps ahead of time—before the new social expectations are codified into legal requirements. By adapting before it is legally forced to, a corporation can be more flexible in its response pattern and achieve greater congruity with social norms. Legitimacy is therefore achieved at a lower social and institutional cost. *The criteria for social responsibility imply bringing corporate behavior up to a level where it is in congruence with the currently prevailing social norms, values, and expectations for its performance.* It is important to note that while the concept of social obligation is *proscriptive* in nature, that of social responsibility is *prescriptive* in nature.

The third stage in the adaptive behavior is termed *social responsiveness.* The implication of this position is not to determine how a corporation should respond to extant social pressures, but to decide what its long-run role in a dynamic system should be. At this stage, the corporation must anticipate the changes that are likely to take place in the system in the future. These changes may be a result of the corporation's current activities, or they may be due to the emergence of social problems in which corporations must play an important role. Corporations must therefore initiate policies and programs that minimize the adverse side effects of their present and future activities. They must also develop capabilities that prepare them to accept the challenges that the system may, at a future date, come to consider appropriate for corporations to tackle. The important distinction to note here is that *while social responsibility activities are prescriptive in nature, activities related to social responsiveness are anticipatory and proactive in nature.*

A study of current corporate advocacy advertising campaigns, annual reports, public relations materials, press releases, and speeches by executives indicates that, with a few exceptions, most corporations prefer to defend their normal activities primarily on the basis of criteria which fall within the definition of *social obligation*. Almost all the public-interest-related activities undertaken by corporations, however, fall in the category of *social responsibility*. This is also the main arena of business-society conflicts. It is important to note that when operating under the concept of social responsibility, corporations do not consider these activities an integral part of their operations, i.e., producing and marketing goods and services. Instead, these activities are considered an added burden which the corporation has undertaken out of a sense of social conscience and good citizenship. The implicit attitude of noblesse oblige leads to the mistaken notion that decisions in this area are *discretionary*. The corporation believes it is not obliged to follow any external dictates as to the amount and manner in which corporate resources for social projects are expended. Consequently, it is often ill prepared for the negative backlash that follows seemingly appropriate charitable acts.

The consequences are not hard to foresee. Not only have corporations not enjoyed public accolades for their actions, they have been unable either to mollify their critics or improve their public image. The critics have argued that these corporate activities are generally cosmetic in character—too little and too late—and are motivated more by corporate self-interest than by a concern for the public good. Another criticism of their activities has been that they rarely change corporate behavior in its main function of producing goods and services, which is precisely the area where a corporation's influence in society and its capacity to do good or to inflict harm is infinitely greater.

I would therefore like to submit that while corporations today largely employ a social obligation concept of legitimacy, they must evolve toward an attitude of social responsiveness. This is necessary if they are to survive in the face of escalating social demands and maintain themselves as viable institutions in a pluralistic society serving a freely and openly determined public purpose.

Managers as Philosophers

An important step in the movement of the corporation from the social obligation state to that of social responsiveness requires that corporate managers must look at their role in a broader social context. In a highly complex and interdependent society, no institution can determine its role without regard to the purposes and expectations of other institutions in the society. Thus, corporate managers must develop a cohesive social philosophy if they are to understand the need for looking at whole systems, and detect social values, concepts, and relations before they are hardened into rigid positions.[9]

Such a posture involves dissenting from traditionally held and "safe" positions supported by a majority of business leaders. It also involves willingness to chart a new and bolder course for the company and even the society. Admittedly, many of the positions taken by the manager under these circumstances would be unpopular both within and without the business world. But they would display a courage of convictions, thereby forcing the society to take notice, and challenging the corporate critics to formulate substantive alternatives rather than merely criticize the status quo.

Philosopher-managers, however, are not easily found in the higher echelons of corporate managements. Rober Bleiberg of *Barron's* believes that people who reach the top in corporations are not necessarily advocates. "They think like politicians and bureaucrats, operating in that milieu. One can count on fingers of a couple of hands the number of corporations run by entrepreneurs today. The bigger the corporation, the bluer the chip, the less likely it will be run by anything other than an organization man who has reached the pinacle by his ability to fit in. He is not a person to take up cudgels."

In a similar vein, Robert Dilenschneider of Hill & Knowlton states that corporations are run by people who have been with their companies for a long time. They are generally operations people.

By the nature of their work, they become inbred with a narrow concept of their role in society. They may be experts in their corporate function, but by virtue of the discipline they're trained in, they can't be as perceptive on the broader social purpose and the role of the corporation therein. These managers can become so involved in their companies that they don't look beyond the narrow confines of their immediate jobs to see the larger social element.

Difficult though it may be, it is not impossible to visualize a philosopher-manager. In trying to achieve broader social perspective, the manager does not have to give up a pragmatic outlook and an action-oriented reasoning process. Nor is it accurate to state that a broader social perspective is achieved only at the corporation's expense. The two are inseparable and interdependent. To concede that corporate interests are at variance with those of the society would be to admit that corporate critics are indeed right in their assumptions about corporate motives. Or worse, it would be an indication, on the part of the manager, of a misguided view of the role of business in society. The manager may need only a willingness to try to relate himself and his activities to society in a broader context than economics, and an open-minded attitude about the social and political phenomena he sees around himself.

Epilogue

This book was written with a twofold purpose: to understand and analyze the role of advocacy advertising as a strategy of corporate response to social pressure for change in corporate behavior, and to consider its implications in the development of public policy in a pluralistic society. I do not contend that the ideas and approaches outlined here will either completely resolve the questions raised in relation to advocacy advertising or eliminate conflict between business and other social institutions. However, to the extent that they generate serious discussion and dialogue among fair-minded people, this book will have served a useful purpose.

Notes

1. Michael J. Connor, "Mobil's Advocacy Ads Lead a Growing Trend, Draw Praise, Criticism," *The Wall Street Journal*, May 14, 1975, p. 1. See also Gerald Astor, "The Gospel According to Mobil," *MORE*, April 1976, pp. 12-15.
2. Deirdre Carmody, "Reporters Chided on Business News." *The New York Times*, May 5, 1976, p. 38.
3. "Corporate Soapboxes: Companies Use Annual Reports To Make a Point," *The Wall Street Journal*, April 1, 1976, p. 1.
4. Donald S. MacNaughton, "The Businessman v. the Journalist," *The New York Times*, Sunday, March 7, 1976, sec. 3, p. 3.
5. Terry P. Brown, "Profit-Minded Chief at Bendix Tries to Set a Businessmen's Code." *The Wall Street Journal*, November 18, 1975, p. 1.
6. Arthur Schlesinger, Jr., "Government, Business, and Morality," *The Wall Street Journal*, June 1, 1976, p. 16.
7. *Ibid.*, p. 16.
8. For a detailed discussion of these criteria of legitimacy, see S. Prakash Sethi, "Dimensions of Corporate Social Performance: An Analytical Framework for Measurement and Evaluation," *California Management Review*, spring 1975, pp. 58-64.

9. The concept of philosopher-manager was elaborated upon in an earlier article by Dow Votaw and S. Prakash Sethi, "Do We Need a New Corporate Response to a Changing Social Environment," in Dow Votaw and S. Prakash Sethi (eds.), *The Corporate Dilemma: Traditional Values Versus Contemporary Problems* (Englewood Cliffs, N.J.: Prentice-Hall, 1973), pp. 170–191.

Bibliography

Articles, Books, Monographs

"ACT Says Stations Aren't Living Up To Rules on Ads in Children's TV; Stations Say Group Is Way Off-Base," *Broadcasting,* December 22, 1975, pp. 28-29.

Advertisement Substantiation Program B-174702, FTC Report to the Consumer Subcommittee, Committee on Commerce, U.S. Senate, by the Comptroller General of the U.S. Government Accounting Office, 1972, pp. 25-26.

Advertising Council, Inc., *The American Economic System . . . And Your Part in It* (New York, 1976).

Annual Report, American Electric Power Company, 1974.

Allport, Peter, president, Association of National Advertisers, Testimony before the U.S. Senate Committee on Commerce, Hearings on S. *1461, Advertising* (Washington, D.C., 92nd Congress, 2nd Session, Serial 92-70, 1972), p. 254.

Armstrong, R.W., "Why Management Won't Talk," *Public Relations Journal,* November 1970, p. 6.

Astor, Gerald, "The Gospel According to Mobil," *More,* 6, 4 (April 1976), 12-15.

Banks, Louis, "Media Responsibility for Economic Literacy." Speech given at Annual John Hancock Awards for Excellence in Business and Financial Journalism, "A Bicentennial Examination of the Free Market System," John Hancock Mutual Life Insurance Co., Boston, October 28, 1975.

Barnet, Sylvan M., Jr., A Global Look at Advocacy Advertising," *Public Relations Journal,* November 1975, pp. 17-21.

"The Birch Advertisement," *The New York Times,* December 20, 1963, editorial.

Bird, Allen W. II, Thomas W. Goldman, and Keith D. Lawrence, "Corporate Image Advertising: A Discussion of the Factors That Distinguish Those Corporate Image Advertising Practices Protected Under the First Amendment from Those Subject to Control by the Federal Trade Commission," *Journal of Urban Law,* 4 (1974), 405.

Blair, Etcyl H. (Director, health and environmental research, Dow Chemicals, U.S.A.), "Wherein It Is Argued That Regulators Are Threatening and Inhibiting Science," *The New York Times,* January 17, 1976, p. 25.

Bluhdorn, Charles G. (chairman, Gulf & Western Industries, Inc.), "'Uncle Santa,'" *The New York Times,* December 5, 1975, p. 39.

Blumberg, Phillip I., *The Mega-corporation in American Society* (Englewood Cliffs, N.J.: Prentice-Hall, 1975).

335

Blumberg, Phillip I., "The Politicization of the Corporation," *The Business Lawyer,* July 1971, p. 1551.

Blumberg, Phillip I., "Reflections on Proposals for Corporate Reform Through Change in the Composition of the Board of Directors: Special Interest or Public Directors," in S. Prakash Sethi (ed), *The Unstable Ground: Corporate Social Policy in a Dynamic Society* (Los Angeles: Melville Publishing, 1974), p. 112.

Blundell, William E., "Phillips Petroleum to Turn Over Control to Outside Directors in Settlement Suit," *The Wall Street Journal,* February 19, 1976, p. 7.

Boorstin, Daniel, *The Image* (New York: Atheneum, 1962).

Brennan, William J., "The Supreme Court and the Meiklejohn Interpretation of the First Amendment," *Harvard Law Review,* 79 (1965), p. 1.

Brown, Terry P., "Profit Minded Chief at Bendix Tries to Set A Businessmen's Code," *The Wall Street Journal,* November 18, 1975, p. 1.

Campbell, Roland, statement before the Senate Subcommittee on Communications of the Senate Committee on Commerce, *Hearings on the Fairness Doctrine* (Washington, D.C., 94th Congress, 1st Section, April 30, 1975), P. 175.

Carmody, Deirdre, "Reporters Chided on Business News," *The New York Times,* May 5, 1976, p. 38.

Carroll, Jerry, "People's Lobby—A Thorn for Politicians," *San Francisco Chronicle,* April 7, 1975, p. 9.

Cary, Frank (chairman of IBM), "Multinational Corporations as Development Partners," *The New York Times,* November 8, 1975, p. 27.

"CBS Lists Record Profits, Rejects an In-House Critic," *The New York Times,* April 22, 1976, p. 49.

"Chamber to Study Opinion of Business," *The Washington Star,* July 28, 1975.

"The Chinese Protest," *The New York Times,* May 17, 1973, editorial.

"Cigarettes and Advertisng," *The New York Times,* August 29, 1969, editorial.

Clotfelter, James, and B. Guy Peters, "Mass Media and the Military: Selected Readings of Fairness," *Journalism Quarterly,* 51 (summer 1974), 332-334.

Cohen, Reuben, "The Measurement of Corporate Images," in John W. Riley (ed), *The Corporation and Its Publics* (New York: Wiley, 1963), pp. 48-63, 64-76.

Colitt, Leslie R., "The Mask of Objectivity," *Nation,* June 17, 1968, p. 789.

Collins, Tom A., "Counter Advertising in the Broadcast Media: Bringing the Administrative Process to Bear Upon a Theoretical Imperative," *William and Mary Law Review,* 15 (1974), 799.

"Comment, Constitutional Law—Freedom of Speech and the Corporation," *Villanova Law Review,* 4 (1959), p. 377.

Communications Act of 1934, Ch. 652, S 315 (a) 48 Stat 1088 (1934).

"Community, Privacy, Defamation, and the First Amendment: The Implications of *Time Inc.* v. *Hill," Columbia Law Review,* 67 (1967), 926.

Connor, Michael J., "Mobil's Advocacy Ads Lead a Growing Trend, Draw Praise, Criticism," *The Wall Street Journal,* May 14, 1975, p. 1.

"Consolidated Electric Utility Hearing Examiner's Report and Recommendations" Before the Ohio Environmental Protection Agency in the Matter of Consolidated Electric Utility Cases. Case No. 73-A-P-120 *et al.* Columbus, Ohio, September 6, 1974.

Cooper, George C., "The Tax Treatment of Business Grassroots Lobbying: Defining and Attaining the Public Policy Objectives," *Columbia Law Review,* 68 (1968), 801.

Cooper, Ron, "How Arizona Utility Ran into Big Trouble over Costs and Rates," *The Wall Street Journal,* April 7, 1976, p. 1.

Corn, Ira G., Jr. (CED for the Michigan General Corporation, a conglomerate), "Problem: $1 Sold Is (X) Earned," *The New York Times,* February 7, 1976, p. 21.

"Corporate Freedom of Speech," *Suffolk University Law Review,* 7 (1973), 1117.

"Corporate Political Spending and the First Amendment," *University of Pittsburgh Law Review,* 23 (1962), 847.

"Corporate Soapboxes: Companies Use Annual Reports To Make a Point," *The Wall Street Journal,* April 1, 1976, p. 1.

Council on Economic Priorities, *Corporate Advertising and the Environment, Economic Priorities Report, September-October 1971,* 2, 3 (New York, October 1971), 28.

Crosscurrents in Corporate Communications: Highlights of the 1975 Fortune Corporate Communications Seminar, Fortune (New York, 1975).

Darling, Harry L., "How Companies Are Using Corporate Advertising," *Public Relations Journal,* November 1975, p. 27.

Deakin, James, *The Lobbyist* (Washington, D.C.: Public Affairs Press, 1966).

"Deducting Business Expenses Designed to Influence Governmental Policy as 'Ordinary and Necessary': *Cammarano* v. *United States* and a Bit Beyond," *Yale Law Journal,* 69 (1960), 1017.

"Developments in the Law, Deceptive Advertising," *Harvard Law Review,* 80 (1967), 1004, 1032-1033, 1063-1101.

deWindt, Ed Mandell, "Corporate Communications—Top Management Perspective," *Crosscurrents in Corporate Communications: Highlights of the 1975 Fortune Seminar* (New York, 1975).

"Discretion Urged in Press Power," *The New York Times,* May 4, 1976, p. 14.

"Donald C. Cook of American Electric Power," *Nation's Business,* September 1974, pp. 46–48.

"Donald Cook Takes on the Environmentalists," *Business Week,* October 26, 1974, p. 70.

Donovan, John B., "Mass Communication and the Adversary Establishment," *Intellect,* May–June 1975, p. 256.

Dougherty, Philip H., "Campaign on Economy Weighed," *The New York Times,* July 22, 1975.

Dougherty, Philip H., "Two Views of the Economic System," *The New York Times,* March 15, 1976, p. 50.

Dougherty, Philip H., "Economic Drive Spurs Conflict," *The New York Times,* April 22, 1976, p. 57.

Eisenberg, Melvin A., "Access to the Corporate Proxy Machinery," *Harvard Law Review,* 83 (May 1970), 1489.

Eisenberg, Melvin A., "Legal Models of Management Structure in the Modern Corporation: Officers, Directors, and Accountants," *California Law Review,* 63, 2 (March 1975), 375.

Eisenberg, Melvin A., "The Local Roles of Shareholders and Management in Modern Corporate Decision-Making," *California Law Review,* January 1961, p. 1.

"The Embattled Businessman," *Newsweek,* February 16, 1976, p. 58.

Emerson, Thomas, "Toward a General Theory of the First Amendment," *Yale Law Journal,* 72 (1963), 877.

Emerson, Thomas, *Toward a General Theory of the First Amendment* (New York: Vintage Books, 1966).

"Environmental Gains Threatened by Crisis," *Washington Post,* December 11, 1973, p. A–1.

"The Excesses of Proposition 9," *San Francisco Examiner,* March 19, 1972, p. 2–B.

Federal Communications Commission, "Children's Television Report and Policy Statement," October 31, 1974, FCC 74–1174.

Federal Communications Commission, *Fairness Doctrine and Public Interest Standards,* 39 Fed. Reg. 26372, 26380, 26381, (1974).

Federal Communications Commission, *The Report on Editorializing by Broadcast Licenses,* 13 FCC 1246, 1249 (1949).

Federal Trade Commission, "Statement of Proposed Enforcement Policy by the Staff of the Federal Trade Commission Regarding Corporate Image Advertising," December 4, 1974.

Federal Trade Commission, *Hearings on Modern Advertising Practices,* Docket 216–17–1 (1971).

Flanagan, George A., *Modern Institutional Advertising* (New York: McGraw-Hill, 1967).

Flom, Joseph H., and Peter A. Atkins, "The Expanding Scope of SEC Disclosure Laws," *Harvard Business Review,* July-August 1974, p. 109.

"Florida Charges 'Gas' Conspiracy," *The New York Times,* July 10, 1973, p. 55.

"The Fortune Directory of 50 Largest Utilities," *Fortune,* June 1975.

"The Fortune Directory of 500 Largest Industrial Corporations," *Fortune,* May 1975.

"The Freedom of Advertising," *The New York Times,* December 28, 1961, editorial.

"Freedom to Advertise," *The New York Times,* June 16, 1972, editorial.

"Fur Christmas," *The New York Times,* December 14, 1967, editorial.

Gallese, Liz Roman, "Boston's Sharon King Becomes Local TV Star by Knocking Products," *The Wall Street Journal,* October 20, 1975, p. 1.

Gerald, J. Edward, *The Social Responsibility of the Press* (Minneapolis: The University of Minnesota Press, 1963).

Graham, Gene S., "History in the (Deliberate) Making: A Challenge to Modern Journalism," *Nieman Reports,* September 1966, p. 3.

Graham, Gene S., "The Responsibility of the Doubly Damned," *Quill,* February 1968, p. 8.

Griffith, Thomas, "Must Business Fight the Press," *Fortune,* June 1974, p. 202.

Gwyn, Robert J., "Opinion Advertising and the Free Market of Ideas," *Public Opinion Quarterly,* summer 1970, pp. 246-255.

Hall, Gladwin, "Power Plant in Kansas 'Scrubs' Pollutants from Dirty Coal," *The New York Times,* September 8, 1975, p. 21.

Harris, Richard, *A Sacred Trust* (New York: New American Library, 1966).

Heatherington, J.A.C., "Fact and Legal Theory: Shareholders, Managers, and Corporate Social Responsibility," *Stanford Law Review,* January 1969, p. 109.

Hentoff, Nat, "Would You Run This Ad? A Survey of Publishers," *Business and Society Review,* summer 1975, p. 8.

"*Herald Co.* v. *Seawell*: A New Corporate Social Responsibility?" *University of Pennsylvania Law Review,* 121 (May 1975), 1157.

Hewens, Frank, and Fred Poppe, "New Imperatives for an Old Device," *Public Relations Journal,* November 1972, p. 10.

Hieronymus, William S., Jr., "Restoring Faith—Worried About Image, Business Makes Effort to Sell Itself to Public," *The Wall Street Journal,* June 12, 1973.

Hobbying, Enno, "Business Must Explain Itself," *Business and Society Review,* fall 1972, p. 85.

"How Good Is Economic Education?", *Fortune,* July 1951, pp. 84-86ff.

Hoy, James, "Socal's Dissent Shareholders Mobilize," *Business and Society Review,* winter 1975-76, p. 42.

Hunt, H. Keith, "Effects on Corrective Advertising," *Journal of Advertising Research,* 13 (October 1973), 15-24.

"Industry Feature: Corporate Advertising," *Madison Avenue Magazine,* January 1976, pp. 33-34.

Jacobs, Sanford L., "Firm's Ad Campaign 'Isn't Very Bright' Arab Holder Asserts," *The Wall Street Journal,* April 25, 1975, p. 18.

Jensen, Michael C., "Many U.S. Executives Reported in Favor of Overseas Bribes," *The New York Times,* February 13, 1976, pp. 45-49.

Johnson, Nicholas, and Tracy A. Westen, "A Twentieth Century Soapbox: The Right to Purchase Radio and Television Time," *Virginia Law Review,* 57 (1971), 547.

"Jugular Journalism" *Newsweek,* May 10, 1976. p. 79.

Kahl Associates, *Policy Analysis of the California Pollution Initiative* (Washington, D.C., February 1972).

Kary, Ramond E., "Scrubbers: Are they the Answer—Or the Problem?" Speech before the National Governors' Conference, Annapolis, Maryland, November 17-19, 1975.

Kirkpatrick, Miles (chairman, FTC) Statement before U.S. Senate Committee on Commerce, *Hearing on S. 1461, Advertising 1972,* (Washington, D.C., 92nd Congress, 2nd Session, Serial 92-70, 1972, pp. 23-24.

Kristol, Irving, "On 'Economic Education,'" *The Wall Street Journal,* February 18, 1976, p. 20.

Kristol, Irving, "When Virtue Loses All Her Loveliness—Some Reflections on Capitalism and the Free Society," *The Public Interest,* fall 1970, p. 4.

Lambert, Jeremiah O., "Corporate Political Spending and Campaign Finance," *New York University Law Review,* 1965, p. 1033.

Large, Arlen J., "Big Oil Beseiged—Congressional Outlook for the Breakup Plan: Wait Till Next Year," *The Wall Street Journal,* February 11, 1976, p. 1.

Leger, Richard R., "Sweeping 'Clean Environment' Referendum, California Looks Too Close to Call Now, " *The Wall Street Journal,* June 1, 1972, p. 25.

Lilliston, Lynn, "One Man's Family in Pollution War," *The Los Angeles Times,* July 30, 1971, p. 4.

"Lincoln's Hopes for the Negro: In His Own Words," *The New York Times,* February 16, 1972, advertisement.

Lodge, George C., *The New American Ideology* (New York: Knopf, 1975).

Loescher, Michael, "EPA Restudies Air Pollution Data in 14 States," *The Tampa Tribune,* March 4, 1976.

Ludlam, Charles E., "Abatement of Corporate Image Environmental Advertising," *Ecology Law Quarterly,* 4 (1974), 247-278.

Mace, Myles L., *Directors: Myth and Reality* (Boston: Division of Research, Graduate School of Business Administration, Harvard University, 1971).

MacNaughton, Donald S., "The Businessman Versus the Journalist" *The New York Times,* March 7, 1976, sec. 3, p. 14.

Maeder, Gary Williams, "Right of Access to the Broadcast Media for Paid Political Advertising—A Plea to Congress," *UCLA Law Review,* 28 (1974), 259.

Mander, Jerry, "EcoPornography," *Communication Arts: Environment,* 14, 2 (1972), 45.

Marcus, Stanley (chairman, Neiman-Marcus, Dallas), "The Business Landscape," *The New York Times,* December 15, 1975, p. 30.

Martineau, Pierre, "The Corporate Personality," in Lee H. Bristol, Jr. (ed), *Developing the Corporate Image: A Management's Guide to Public Relations* (New York: Scribner's, 1960), pp. 3-13.

McDowell, Edwin, "The Big Battle Over Scrubbers," *The Wall Street Journal,* February 7, 1975, p. 10.

McDowell, Edwin, "Donald Cook and Those Funny Ads," *The Wall Street Journal,* February 10, 1975, p. 20.

McGannon, Donald, Statement before the Senate Subcommittee on Communications of the Senate Committee on Commerce, *Hearings on the Fairness Doctrine* (Washington, D.C., 94th Congress 1st Section, April 30, 1975), p. 175.

McGinnis, Joe, *The Selling of the President* (New York: Trident Press, 1969).

Meiklejohn, Alexander, "The First Amendment Is an Absolute," *Supreme Court Review,* 1965, p. 245.

"Mobil Oil to Pay Over $800 Million to Buy Marcor," *The Wall Street Journal,* August 7, 1974, p. 3.

Moore, John C., "Notes: Advertising and Recent Developments in the Fairness Doctrine," *Washington and Lee Law Review,* (1972), 87.

"Moss Lays Shortage to Oil Firms," *Washington Post,* November 29, 1973, p. A-18.

Nader, Ralph, and Mark Green (eds.), *Corporate Power in America* (New York: Grossman, 1973).

"NARB Chairman Defends Rights of 'Image' Ads," *Editor and Publisher,* March 16, 1974, p. 19.

National Association of Manufacturers, *The Public Image of Business in a Time of Changing Values, A Discussion Paper* (New York: National Association of Manufacturers, June 1973).

Neckritz, Alan F., and Lawrence B. Ordower, "Ecological Pornography and The Mass Media," *Ecology Law Quarterly,* 1 (1974), 374.

"The New Concerns About the Press," *Fortune,* April 1975, p. 121, 130.

"News," California Labor Federation, AFL-CIO, March 9, 1972, p. 1.

Nicosia, Francesco M., *Advertising, Management, and Society: A Business Point of View* (New York: McGraw-Hill, 1974).

"1970-71 Expenditures for Corporate and Association Advertising," *Public Relations Journal,* November 1972, p. 26.

"1971-72 Expenditures for Corporate and Association Advertising," *Public Relations Journal,* November 1973, p. 30.

Norman, Adler, "The Sounds of Executive Silence," *Harvard Business Review,* July-August 1971, p. 100.

"Notes: Freedom of Expression in a Commercial Context," *Harvard Law Review,* 78 (1965), 1191.

"Notes: The FTC Ad Substantiation Program," *The Georgetown Law Journal,* 61 (1973), 1427.

Oakes, John B., "Confidence in the Press," *The New York Times,* May 5, 1976, p. 37.

O'Connor, Neal W., and N.W. Ayer, "Advertising," speech before Syracuse Press Club, *The New York Times,* November 24, 1975, p. 57.

"Oil Companies Have Spent Millions Defending Offshore Drilling for 50¢ You Can See What It Costs the Earth—And You," Friends of the Earth advertisement *The New Yorker,* August 12, 1972, p. 79.

"Oil Industry Group Plans Big Campaign to Block Legislation to Split Up Firms," *The Wall Street Journal,* November 11, 1975, p. 21.

"Oil Meets the Press: The Image Has Been Smeared and the Companies Are Largely To Be Blamed," *Dun's,* April 1974, p. 62.

"Oilmen Defend Their Holdings in Other Fuels," *Washington Post,* December 7, 1973, p. A-9 (remarks of Senator Haskell).

Olsner, Lesley, "High Court Decided Campaign Spending Is Form of Speech," *The New York Times,* February 1, 1976, p. 1.

Olsner, Lesley, "High Court Voids New York Rules for Fair Campaign," *The New York Times,* January 13, 1976, p. 1.

O'Toole, John E., "Advocacy Advertising—Act II," *Crosscurrents in Corporate Communications: Highlights of the 1975 Fortune Corporate Communications Seminar, No. 4* (New York, 1975).

O'Toole, John E., "Advocacy Advertising Shows the Flag," *Public Relations Journal,* November 1975, pp. 14-15.

"People in Business: Executives vs. the Newsmen," *The New York Times,* October 22, 1975, p. 59.

People's Lobby, *Economics of a Clean Environment* (Los Angeles: People's Lobby Press, 1971).

343

People's Lobby, *Pro and Con, 1971.*

People's Lobby, *Proposition 9 The Political Reform Act: A Fact for California, A Proposal for America* (Los Angeles, 1974).

Posner, Richard, *Regulation of Advertising by the FTC* (Washington, D.C.: American Enterprise Institute for Public Policy Research, 1973).

Powell, Lewis F., Jr., "Attack on American Free Enterprise System, Confidential Memorandum, August 23, 1971," *Washington Record Supplement.*

"The Price Tage on Institutional Advertising in 1974," *Public Relations Journal,* November 1975, pp. 36-37.

Redish, Martin H., "The First Amendment in the Market Place: Commercial Speech and the Value of Free Expression," *George Washington Law Review,* 39 (1970), 429.

"The Regulation of Corporate Image Advertising," *Minnesota Law Review,* 59,1 (November 1974), 189-222.

Report of the National Commission on Civil Disorders (New York: Dutton, 1968).

"Riding Out the Storm at Channel 13 with Jay Iselin," *The New York Times,* November 9, 1975, sec 2, p. 1.

Ristow, William, "The Old Coalition," *San Francisco Bay Guardian,* April 27, 1972.

Rockefeller, Nelson A., "Toward Energy Independence," *The New York Times,* February 24, 1976, p. 35.

Rood, W.B., "EPA Study—The Findings Got Distorted," *The Los Angeles Times,* February 29, 1976.

Rood, W.B., "Scientist Denies Bias in Records," *The Los Angeles Times,* April 4, 1976.

Scanlon, Paul D., "The FTC, The FCC, and the 'Counter Ad' Controversy: An Invitation to 'Let's You and Him Fight?'" *Antitrust Law and Economic Review,* 5, 43 (fall 1971), 43.

Schellhardt, Timothy D., "More Regulation by Government Gets 56% Backing in Poll," *The Wall Street Journal,* May 14, 1975, p. 16.

Schlesinger, Arthur, Jr., "Government, Business and Morality," *The Wall Street Journal,* June 1, 1976, p. 16.

"A Sense of Advocacy in Advertising," *Saturday Review,* June 15, 1974, p. 50.

Sethi, S. Prakash, "Business and the Consumer: Whither Goes the Confrontation?" *California Management Review,* winter 1974, p. 82.

Sethi, S. Prakash, "Dimensions of Corporate Social Performance: An Analytical Framework for Measurement and Evaluation," *California Management Review,* spring 1975, pp. 58-64.

Sethi S. Prakash, *Images and Products: Marketing, Institutional Advertising, and Public Interest* (Santa Barbara, Calif.: Wiley/Hamilton, (in press).

Sethi, S. Prakash, *The Unstable Ground: Corporate Social Policy in a Dynamic Society* (Los Angeles, Melville, 1974), pp. 107-167.

Sethi, S. Prakash, *Up Against the Corporate Wall: Modern Corporations and Social Issues of the Seventies,* 3rd ed. (Englewood Cliffs, N.J.: Prentice-Hall, 1977).

Sharp, Dean E., "Reflections on the Disallowance of Income Tax Deductions for Lobbying Expenditures," *Boston University Law Review,* 39 (1959), 365.

Shulman, Harvey J., written statement, *Energy and Environmental Objectives Hearings Before the Subcommittee on Environment of the Committee on Commerce* (Washington, D.C., 93rd Congress, 2nd Session, May 6 and July 18, 1974).

Simmons, Steven J., "Commercial Advertising and the Fairness Doctrine: The New FCC Policy in Perspective," *Columbia Law Review,* 75 (1975), 1087.

Snyder, Jean, "Even Though Own Readers Are Victims, Papers Ignore FTC Complaint Against A&P," *Media and Consumer,* December 1972, p. 13.

Spencer, William (president, of First National City Bank), "Never Say Die," *The New York Times,* December 24, 1975, p. 21.

Stevens, John D., and William E. Porter, *The Rest of the Elephant: Perspectives on the Mass Media* (Englewood Cliffs, N.J.: Prentice-Hall, 1973).

Stone, Christopher, *Where the Law Ends: The Social Control of Corporate Behavior* (New York: Harper & Row, 1975).

Stridsberg, A.B., *Effective Advertising Self-Regulation* (International Advertising Association, Inc., 1974).

Talarzyk, W. Wayne, *Contemporary Cases in Marketing* (Hinsdale, Ill.: Dryden Press, 1974).

Tanner, James C., "Big Oil Beseiged—Breakup Could Bring a Gasoline Price Rise and Less Competition," *The Wall Street Journal,* February 12, 1976, p. 1.

"Tax Treatment of Lobbying Expenses and Contributions," *Harvard Law Review* 67 (1954), 1408.

"The Top 100 National Advertisers of 1974," *Advertising Age,* June 30, 1975.

Travers, A.H., "Foreword," *Kansas Law Review,* 17 (1969).

"Trust Suit Cites 20 Oil Companies," *The New York Times*, July 27, 1973, p. 39.

"TV's Credibility Gap," *Newsweek,* January 6, 1969, pp. 42–43.

Tyler, G.G., "Disallowance of Deductions on Public Policy Grounds," *Tax Law Review,* 20 (1965), 665.

United States of America, Before the Federal Trade Commission, "Petition to the Federal Trade Commission (1) For Rules to Extend the Advertising Substantiation Campaign to All Advertising (2) To Request Substantiation for Certain Commercial Advertisements by Certain Advertisers (3) And to Commence Generally an Advertisement Substantiation Campaign in the Oil, Utility and Electric Appliance Industries in Regard to Environmental or Energy-Related Claims in Commercial Advertisements" (Washington, D.C.: Media Access Project, January 9, 1974).

United States of America, Before The Federal Trade Commission, "Memorandum of Mobil Oil Corporation in Opposition to Petition to Extend the Advertising Substantiation Resolution of the Federal Trade Commission, Filed January 9, 1974" (Washington, D.C., April 4, 1974).

U.S. Congress, *Hearings Before the Subcommittee on Heath and the Environment, Committee on Interstate and Foreign Commerce, and the Subcommittee on Environment and the Atmosphere, Committee on Science and Technology* (Washington, D.C., April 9, 1976).

U.S. Congress, *Oversight Hearings on Commerce Department Payment to the National Advertising Council for Promotion of the Free Enterprise System. Hearings Before the Commerce, Consumer and Monetary Affairs Subcommittee of the Committee on Government Operations* (Washington, D.C., 94th Congress. 1st Session, July 30, 1975). p. 1.

U.S. Environmental Protection Agency, "Environmental News," September 1974.

U.S. Environmental Protection Agency, *Flue Gas Desulfurization: Installations and Operations* (Washington, D.C., September 1974).

U.S. Environmental Protection Agency, *National Public Hearings on Power Plant Compliance with Sulfur Oxide Air Pollution Regulations, Report of the Hearing Panel* (Washington, D.C., January 1974).

U.S. Senate, *Energy and Environmental Objectives Hearings Before the Subcommittee on Environment of the Committee on Commerce,* Part 2 (Washington, D.C., 93rd Congress, 2nd Session, May 6 and July 18, 1974), pp. 41, 73.

U.S. Senate, Committee on Commerce, *Hearings on S. 1461, Advertising 1972* (Washington, D.C., 92nd Congress, 2nd Session, Serial 92-70, 1972).

"A Utility Defends a Scrubbing Plant," *Business Week,* August 31, 1974, p. 80.

Votaw, Dow, and S. Prakash Sethi (eds.), *The Corporate Dilemma: Traditional Values versus Contemporary Problems* (Englewood Cliffs, N.J.: Prentice-Hall, 1973).

Ways, Max, "Business Needs To Do a Better Job of Explaining Itself," *Fortune,* September 1972, p. 85.

Weaver, David B., "Taxes and Lobbying–The Issue Resolved," *The George Washington Law Review,* 31 (1963), 938.

Weaver, Paul H., "The New Journalism and the Old–Thoughts After Watergate," *The Public Interest,* spring 1974, p. 67.

Webster, G.D., "Deductibility of Lobbying and Related Expenses," *American Bar Association Journal,* 42 (1956), 1975.

Wechsler, James A., in *Bulletin of the American Society of Newspaper Editors,* February 1, 1957, p. 5, quoted from J. Edward Gerald, *The Social Responsibility of the Press* (Minneapolis: The University of Minnesota Press, 1963).

Weiss, E.B., "Management: Don't Kid the Public With Those Noble Anti-pollution Ads," *Advertising Age,* November 3, 1970, p. 80.

Wellford, Harrison, "How Ralph Nader, Tricia Nixon, the ABA, and Jamie Whitten Helped Turn the FTC Around," *Washington Monthly,* October 1972, pp. 5, 10.

Wells, Alan (ed.), *Mass Media and Society* (Palo Alto, Calif.: National Press Books, 1972).

Weston, Tracy, "Deceptive Advertising and the Federal Trade Commission: Decline of Caveat Emptor, *Federal Bar Journal,* 24 (1964), 548, 561.

Whyte, William, *Is Anybody Listening?* (New York: Simon and Schuster, 1962).

Wriston, Walter B. (chairman, First National City Bank), "On Classified Loans," *The New York Times,* January 30, 1975, p. 29.

Yeager, Kurt E., "Stacks vs. Scrubbers," Research Progress Report F–F–3 Electric Power Research Institute, July 1975.

Legal Citations

Abrams v. *United States,* 250 U.S. 616, 630 (1919).

Addressograph-Multigraph Corp., 14, P-H Tax CT MEM. $45,058 (1945).

Associated Press v. *United States,* 326 U.S. 1, 20 (1945).

Banzhaf v. *FCC,* 405 F. 2d 1082, 1101-02 (D.C. Cir. 1968) *cert. denied.*

Bigelow v. *Virginia,* 95 S.CT. 2222 (1975).

Bread v. *Alexandria,* 341 U.S. 622 (1951).

Buckley v. *Valeo,* 75-436, 44 *U.S. Law Week* 4128, January 27, 1976.

Cammarano v. *United States,* 358 U.S. 498 (1959).

"Cammarano v. *United States* and a Bit Beyond," *Yale Law Journal,* 69 (1960), 1017.

Capital Broadcasting v. *Mitchell,* 333 F. Supp. 582 (D.D.C. 1971) (3-Judge Court), *aff'd. mem.,* 405 U.S. 1000 (1972).

Columbia Broadcasting Sys. Inv. v. *Democratic National Committee* (CBS), 412 U.S. (1973).

Commissioner of Internal Revenue v. *Sullivan,* 356 U.S. 27 (1958).

Commissioner v. *Tellier,* 383 U.S. 687 (1966).

Commonwealth of Pennsylvania v. *Pennsylvania Power Company* in the Court of Common Pleas of Lawrence County, PA No. 2 of 1972, April 19, 1973, p. 7.

Consumer Power Co. v. *United States,* CA 427 F 2nd 78 (1970).

Donaldson v. *Read Magazine,* 333 U.S. 178 (1948).

Dun & Bradstreet Inc. v. *Grove,* 404 U.S. 898 (1971) 438 F 2d 433 (3rd Cir. 1971).

E. F. Drew & Co. v. *FTC,* 235 F 2d 735 (2nd Cir. 1956), *cert. denied,* 352 U.S. 969 (1957).

Exxon Corp (1973 Transfer Binder), Trade Reg. Rep. 20 388 (F.T.C. 1973).

Firestone Tire and Rubber Co., 81 FTC 398, 472 (1973), commission order upheld, 481 F. 2d 246 (6th Cir. 1973), *cert. denied,* 414 U.S. 1112 (1973).

Friends of the Earth v. *FCC,* 449 F 2d 1164.

Fur Information and Fashion Council, Inc. et al. v. *E. F. Timme & Sons, Inc.,* Brief for Association of National Advertisers, Inc., *Amicus Curiae.* In the U.S. Court of Appeals for the Second Circuit, Docket No. 73-2687.

FTC v. *National Petroleum Refiners' Association* (D.C., Cir. 1963), petition for cert. filed, 42 *U.S. Law Week.*

FTC v. *Sperry & Hutchinson Co.,* 405 U.S. 233 (1972).

Gertz v. *Robert Welch, Inc.,* 42 *U.S. Law Week* 5123 (1974).

Giant Foods, Inc. v. *FTC,* 322 F 2nd 977, 981 note 9 (D.C., Cir. 1963), *dismissed,* 376 U.S. 967 (1964).

Ginzburg v. *United States,* 383 U.S. 463 (1966).

Grosjean v. *American Press Co.,* 297 U.S. 233 (1933).

Hudgens v. *NLRB,* 74-773, 44 *U.S. Law Week* 428, March 8, 1976.

Jamison v. *Texas,* 318 U.S. 413 (1943).

Kleindienst v. *Mandel,* 408 U.S. 753, 762-763 (1972).

Lamont v. *Postmaster General,* 381 U.S. 301 (1965).

NAACP v. *Button,* 371 U.S. 414 (1963).

Neckritz v. *FCC,* 502 F 2nd 411 (D.C. Cir. 1974).

New York Times v. *Sullivan,* 376 U.S. 255 (1964).

NLRB v. *American Tube Bending Co.,* 134 F 2d 993 (2nd Cir.) *cert. denied,* 320 U.S. 768 (1943).

People's Lobby v. *Reinecke,* Los Angeles Superior Court, Decision No. WEC 25264, 1972.

Pittsburgh Press Co. v. *Pittsburgh Commission on Human Rights,* 413 U.S. 376 (1973).

Schwartz v. *Vanesco,* 75-677, 44 *U.S. Law Week* 3390, January 13, 1976.

Southwestern Electric Power Co. v. *United States,* 312 F 2d 437 442 *cert. denied,* 1963.

Textile Mills Corp. v. *Commissioner,* 314 U.S. 326 (1941).

Thomas v. *Collins,* 323 U.S. 516 (1945).

Thornhill v. *Alabama,* 310 U.S. 88 (1940).

United States v. *CIO,* 335 U.S. 106 (1948).

Valentine v. *Chrestensen,* 316 U.S. 52 (1942).

Virginia State Board of Pharmacy v. *Virginia Citizens Consumer Council, Inc.,* 74-845, 44 *U.S. Law Week* 4686 (May 25, 1976).

Wilderness Society (ESSO), 30 FCC 2nd 643 (1971), *reconsideration denied,* 31 FCC 2nd 643 (1971), *reconsideration denied,* 32 FCC 2nd 714 (1971).

Index

Index

351

Public Service Advertising Space Allocation
Committee, 304–305
Pulp and paper industry, 96–97

Radio, and Clean Environment Act
coverage, 201
Rall, David P., 134
Raub, Benjamin D., 88, 93, 94
Reader's Digest, institutional advertising of,
66
Reagan, Ronald, 182
Redish, Martin H., 263
Reform, proposals for, 245–252
Reinecke, Ed, 96, 198
Responsibility, social, 329–330
Responsiveness, social, 329
*Retail Store Employees Union, Local 880,
R.C.I.A. v. FCC,* 106
Rittenband, Lawrence J., 183
Romo, Hifinio, 185
Rosenthal, Benjamin S., 62
Ruder & Finn, 81

Sampson, Anthony, 85
Savings Bank Associations of New York
State, advertising of, 23, 50
Sawhill, John, 126
Schlesinger, Arthur, Jr., 328
Schmertz, Herbert, 75, 87, 89, 94, 98, 247,
293, 296, 299, 324, 326
Seib, Charles, 101
Self-improvement, in news media, 100–101
Senate, subcommittee of, 16, 131, 247, 251
Sheehan, William, 87, 88, 94, 289
Sherwin, Raymond, 198
Shulman, Harvey, 131, 249, 250, 253, 277,
280
Sierra Club, 189, 198; advertisement of,
314; and Proposition 9, 185
Sludge, 129
Small, William, 88, 89, 94
Smith/Greenland Co., 65
Social change, 238
Social pressure, 332. *See also* Public
Special-interest media, 77. *See also*
Media
Speech, commercial, 263–268. *See also*
Commercials
Sponsor, interest of, 10; types of, 12–13
Stark, Fortney H., 184–185

Steffens, Lincoln, 80
Stern Concern, advertisement of, 313
Stone, Christopher, 238, 300
Stridsberg, Albert, 16
Sulfur oxides, health effects of, 134
Supreme Court, 91–92. *See also specific
cases*

Technology, gas desulfurization, 128
Television, bias of, 87; and Clean Environ-
ment Act coverage, 201; networks, 88;
nonprofit public, 96–97. *See also* Broad-
cast media
Tennessee Valley Authority, 116
Textile Mills Corporation, 14
Thompson, Mayo J., 328
TRACC RECORD, 17, 53–55
Train, Russell E., 127, 134
Trotta, Liz, 93

Unfair practice, and advocacy advertising,
274–278. *See also* Fairness doctrine
United States Steel, advertising of, 23
Utilities, AEP, 115–179; electric, 9–10

Valentine v. Chrestensen, 264, 265
Viewpoints, opposing, 289–310

Wanvig, James L., 186
Warner, Raleigh, Jr., 75, 92
Warner & Swasey Co., 15; advertising of,
23, 51, 52
Washington Post, The, and AEP campaign,
133
Watergate hearings, 68
Wechsler, James A., 75, 76
Weiss, E.B., 66
Wells Fargo, 14
West, Frederick W., Jr., 75, 325
Whitaker, Clem Jr., 299
Whitaker & Baxter, 191–197; ad campaign
of, 64; advertising of, 202. *See also*
People's Lobby, Inc.
Whyte, William H., 59, 60
Wriston, Walter B., 69
Wrongdoers, speaking out against, 327–328

Young, Lewis H., 81, 291, 299, 304

Zuckert, Donald M., 65

About the Author

S. Prakash Sethi received the M.B.A. and Ph.D. from Columbia University and a graduate degree from Delhi School of Economics, Delhi University, India. Dr. Sethi is Professor of Business Administration at the University of California at Berkeley, where he teaches in the areas of political, social, and legal environments of business and international business. He has published extensively in such journals as *Business and Society Review/Innovation, Business Week, Journal of Marketing Research,* and *Annals of the American Academy of Political and Social Science.* Dr. Sethi is author of numerous books and is a consultant to many international corporations in the United States and Europe.